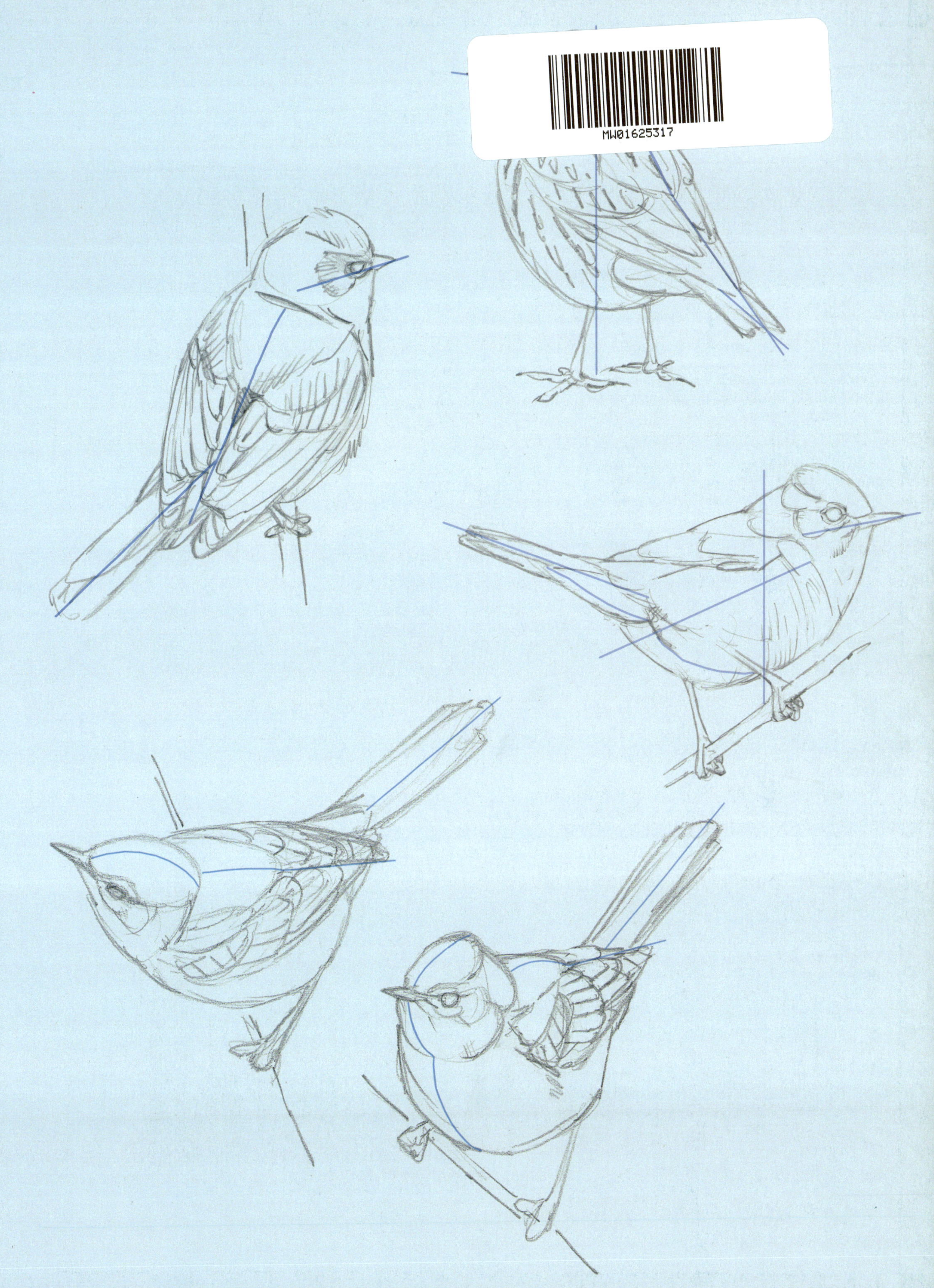

Sketching & Illustrating Birds

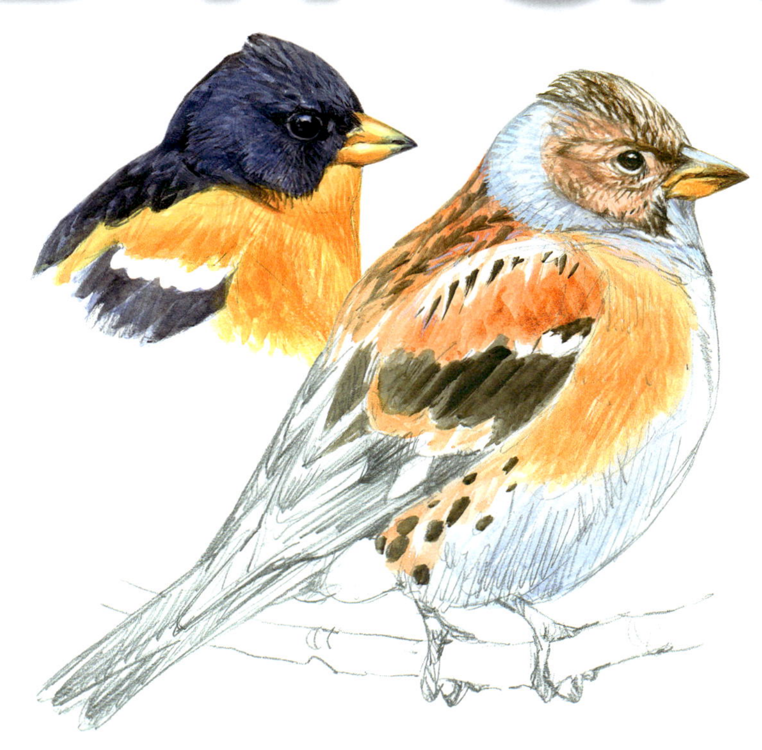

BARRON'S

SKETCHING AND ILLUSTRATING BIRDS

First edition for the United States, its territories and dependencies, and Canada published in 2015 by Barron's Educational Series, Inc.

English translation by
Michael Brunelle and Beatriz Cortabarria

Original Spanish title: *Dibujo de Aves*

Published by ParramónPaidotribo, S.L., Badalona, Spain

All inquiries should be addressed to:
Barron's Educational Series, Inc.
250 Wireless Boulevard
Hauppauge, NY 11788
www.barronseduc.com

ISBN: 978-0-7641-6791-1

Library of Congress Control No.: 2014952493

Editorial Director: María Fernanda Canal
Editing: UBEdició
Text: Juan Varela Simó
Typographical Correction: Roser Pérez
Graphic Design: Josep Gausch
Illustrations: Juan Varela Simó
Photographs: Nos I Soto
Layout: Estudi Guasch, S.L.
Production: Sagrafic S.L.

Printed in China
9 8 7 6 5 4 3 2 1

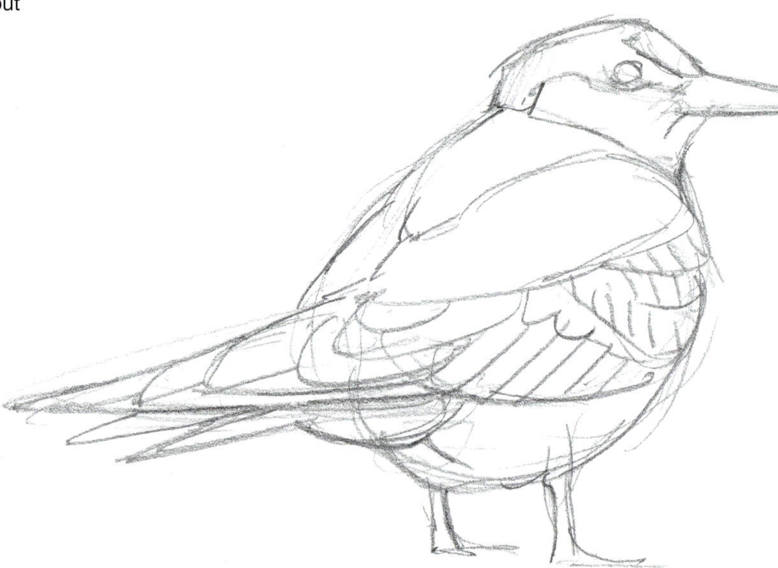

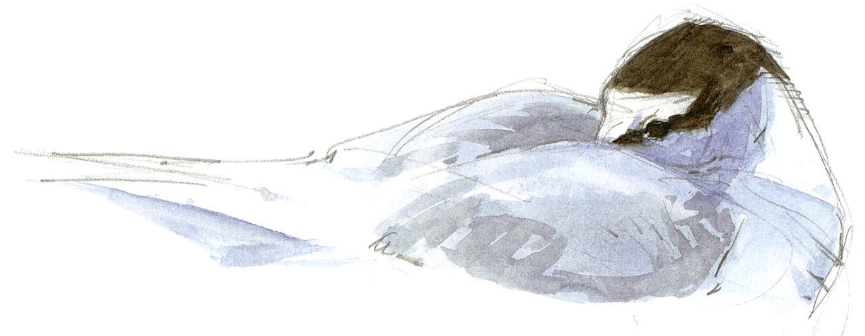

Sketching & Illustrating Birds

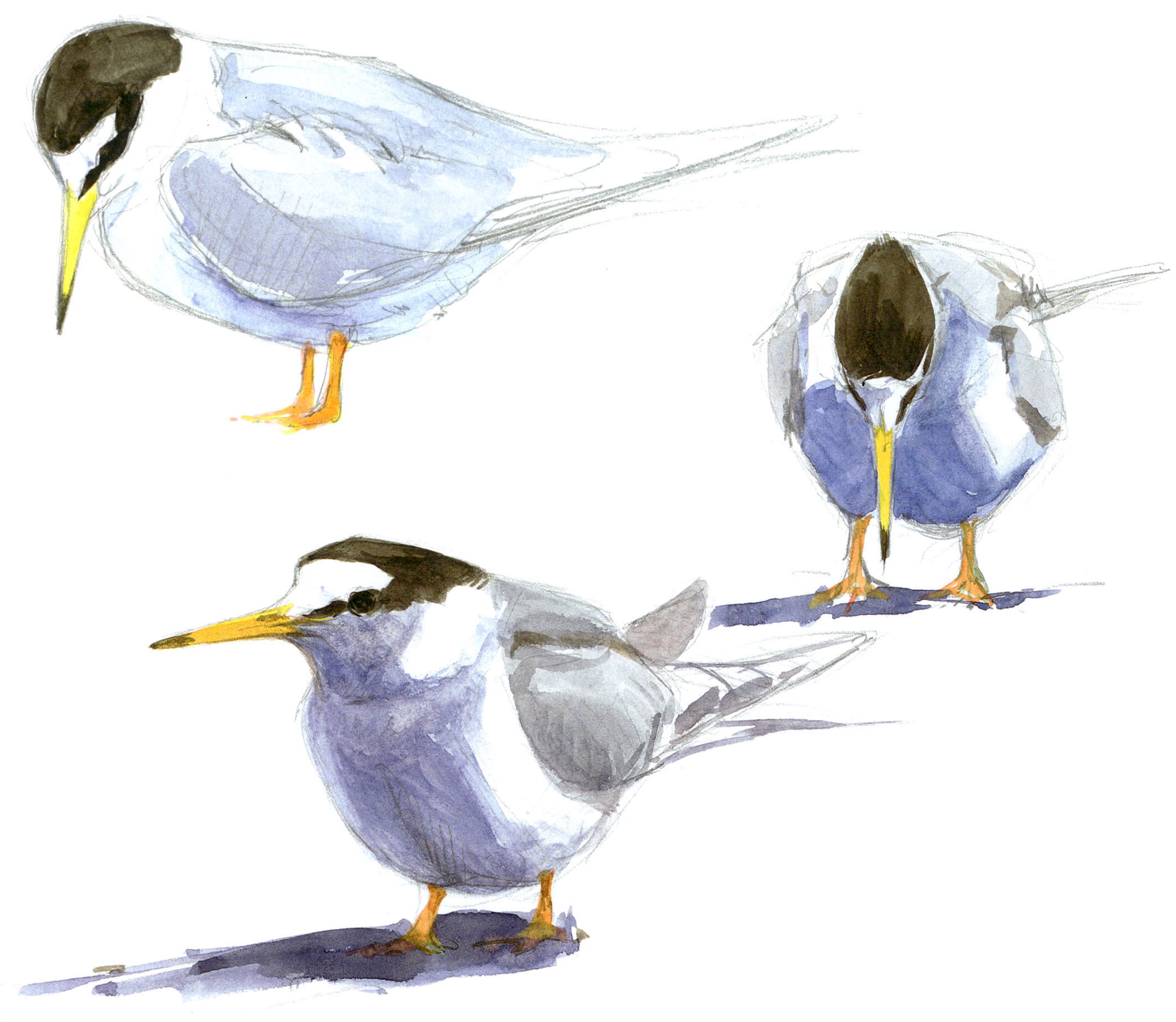

Contents

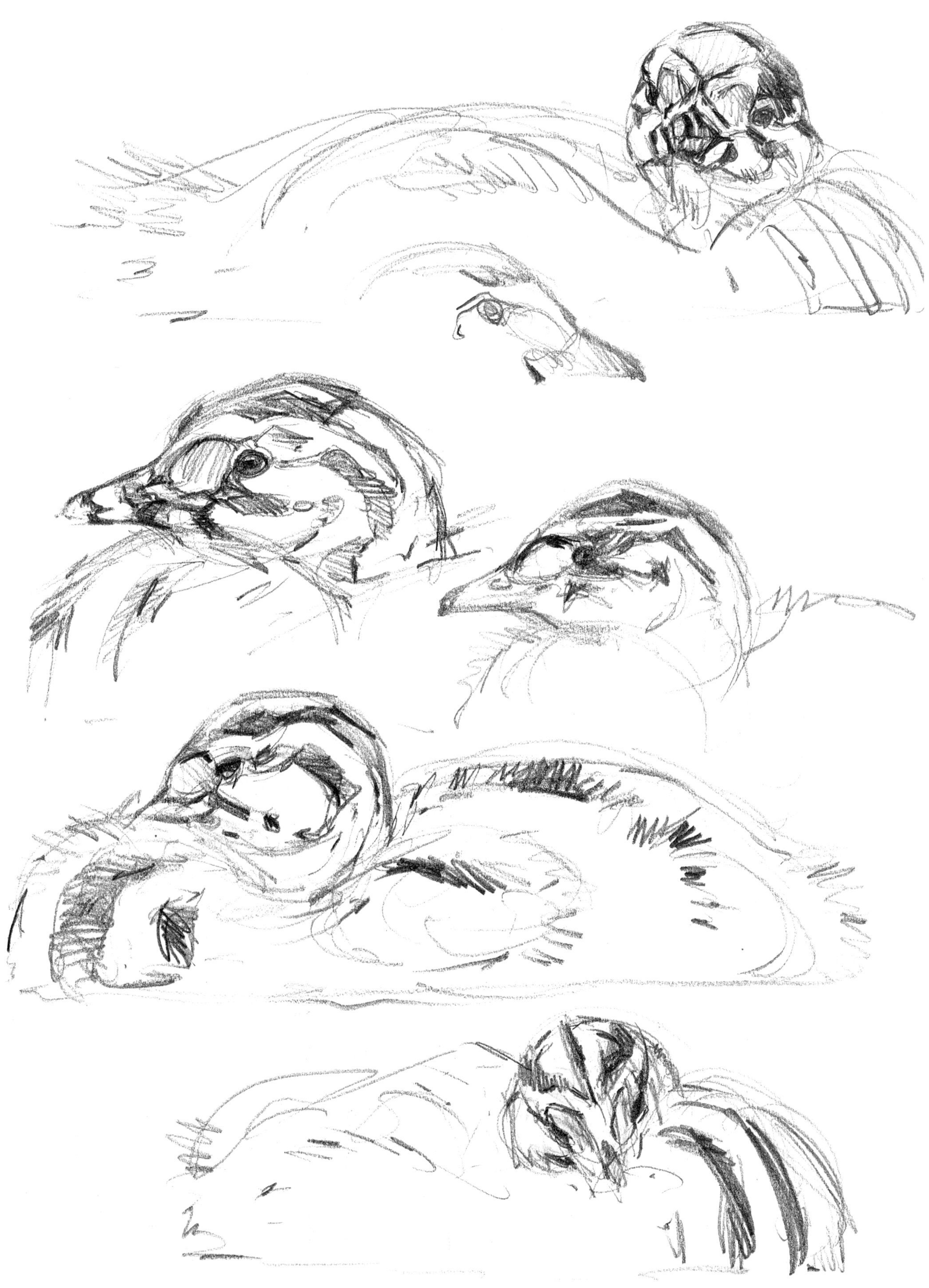

Introduction

To learn to draw, you must first learn to look, and there is evidence that humans have been looking at birds since time immemorial, and not only as a source of food.

Birds have been depicted in art almost since the beginning of humanity, when a person picked up a piece of charcoal and began to draw on the wall of the cave where he or she was living. But is was during the 16th century, with the development of the natural sciences, when we began observing birds more closely and no longer as religious or mythological symbols. The scientific expeditions to Africa and the New World required the presence of artists to illustrate the discoveries and to provide the detailed botanical and zoological descriptions. Beginning in the 19th century, lithography made it easier to add more delicate lines and colors than in etchings and engravings, and it was less expensive to reproduce images in books. Finally, the explosion of photography at the end of the 19th century allowed painters of the natural world to pursue the creation of paintings that were more than simple illustrations. Painters of birds have notably amplified their objectives through the centuries. Nowadays, in addition to their educational mission, they fulfill a decorative and artistic function in styles that range from photorealism to expressionism, and even bordering on abstraction.

The world of birds should be approached from two sides: one being an apprenticeship in different media and artistic techniques and the other being scientific knowledge of avian anatomy and habits. The combining of these two perspectives will create the best conditions for the wildlife artist. There is another factor that is important to take into account: the need to enter into the natural world that birds inhabit. It is there that artists will obtain ideas to work on later in the studio and will understand the anatomy and habits of birds. The goal of this book is to provide you with the basic tools of both perspectives and to teach you to look at birds instead of resigning yourself to being a mere copyist of photographs of animals that you have never seen in nature.

The innumerable species of birds offer the possibility of creating works of great richness and variety; that this is so can be seen in the work of thousands of amateurs and professionals dedicated to the subject, the different galleries and museums that exhibit and collect their work, and the prestigious associations that exist around the world.

Juan Varela

Juan Varela has a degree in biology from the Universidad Complutense de Madrid, and he is a world-famous artist. He has taken part in scientific research projects, balancing them with the creation of his own artwork. As an illustrator, he has contributed scientific paintings to several encyclopedias, books, and magazines; and, as an author, he has published 21 books, among them a manual for learning how to become a painter of nature subjects.

His work has been exhibited in galleries and museums in Europe, the United States, and Israel, and, on many occasions, has been selected a part of prestigious exhibitions like Birds in Art *in the Woodson Museum in Wausau, Wisconsin, and* The Natural Eye *in the Mall Galleries in London.*

He has given classes and conferences about art and nature, and is a member of the Artists For Nature Foundation and Artists For Conservation, one of whose goals is the conservation of the natural environment through art.

His work is based on observations from nature, and he has traveled to such diverse places as Alaska, Ecuador, Scandinavia, and Tanzania, where he created works that earned him the prize that is awarded annually by the Ministerio de Agricultura, Alimentación y Medio Ambiente de España (Ministry of Agriculture, Food, and Environment of Spain).

Female common merganser drawn on-site at Lake Michigan in the United States.

Materials and Their Use

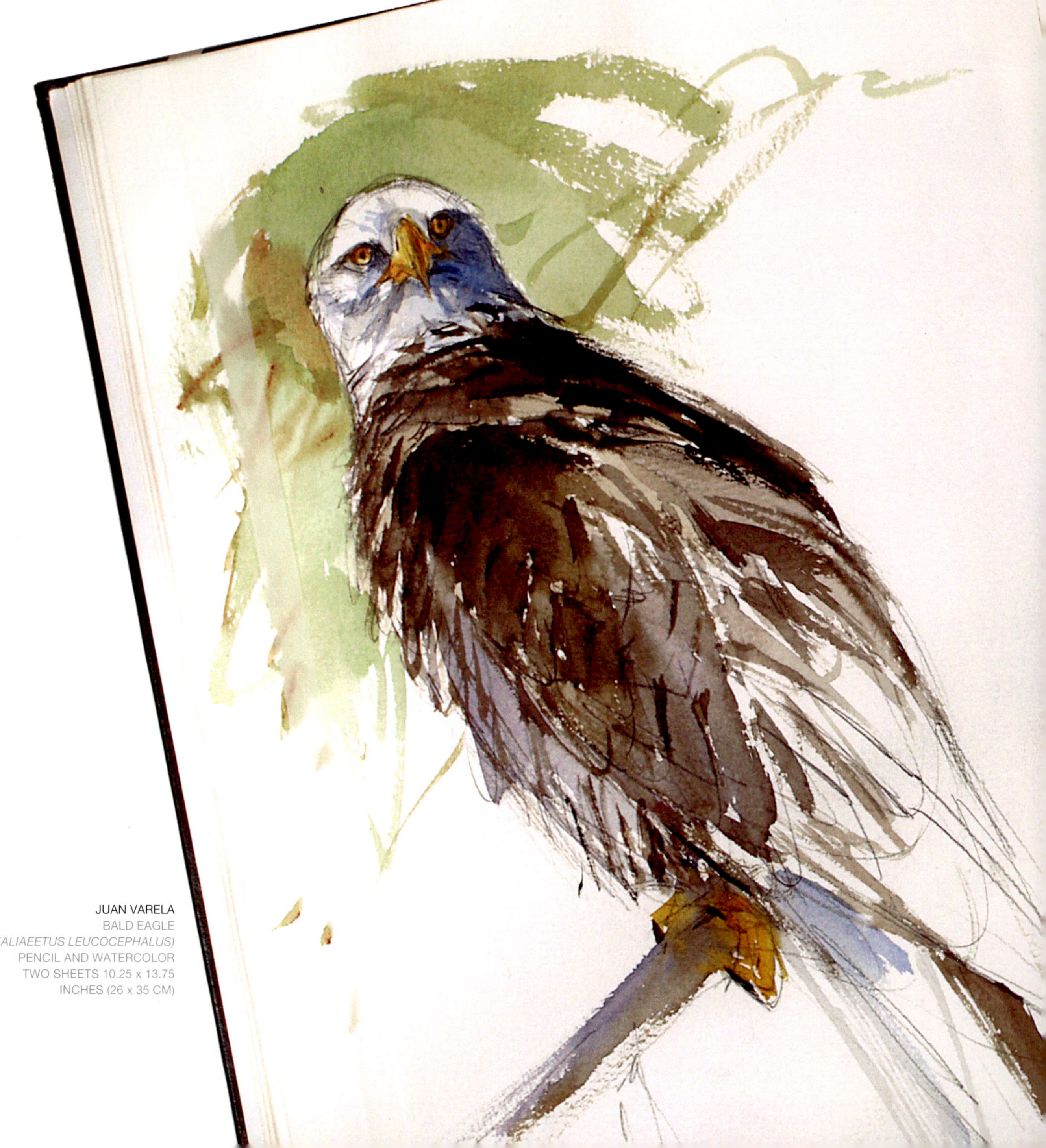

JUAN VARELA
BALD EAGLE
(HALIAEETUS LEUCOCEPHALUS)
PENCIL AND WATERCOLOR
TWO SHEETS 10.25 x 13.75
INCHES (26 x 35 CM)

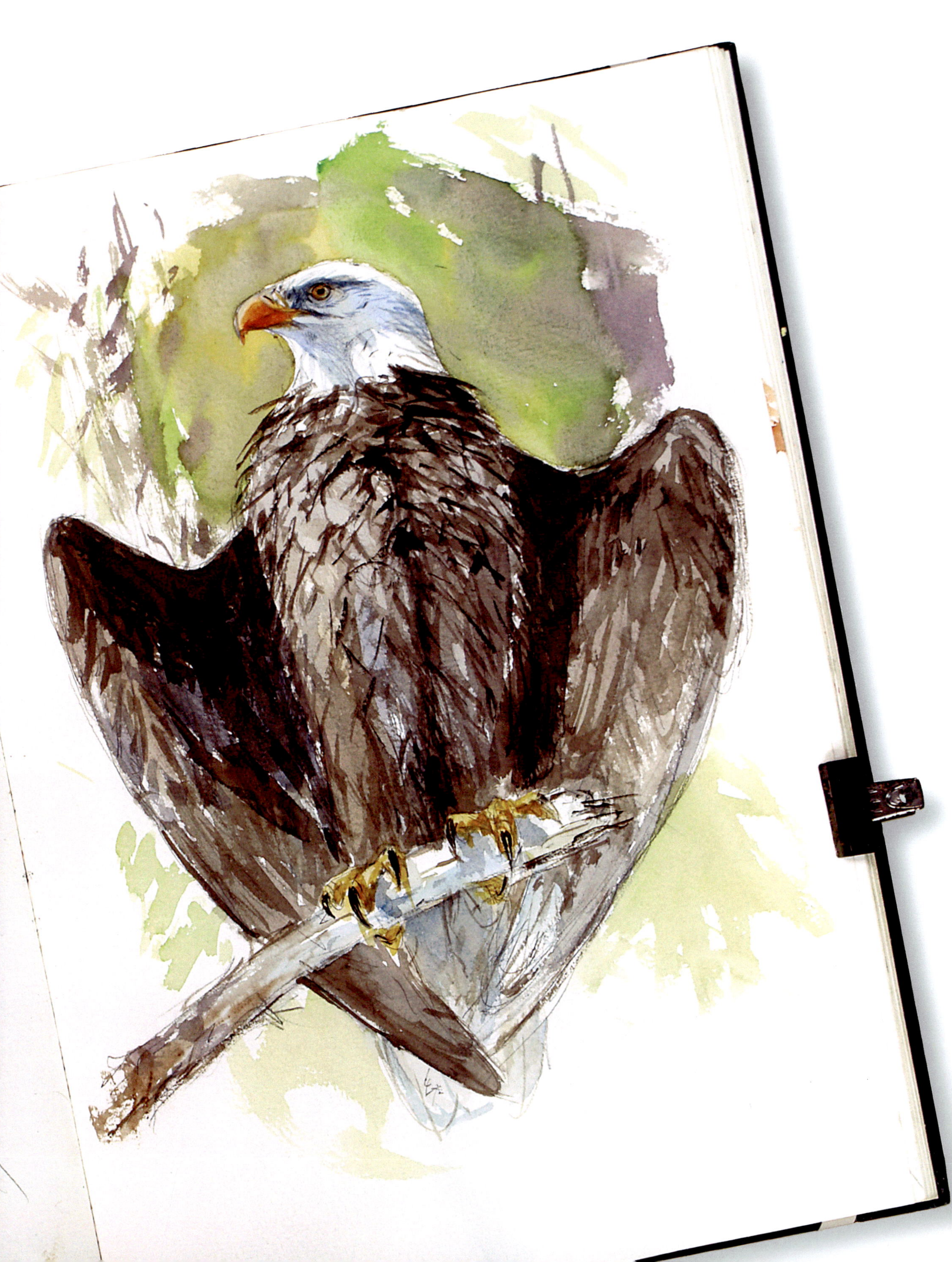

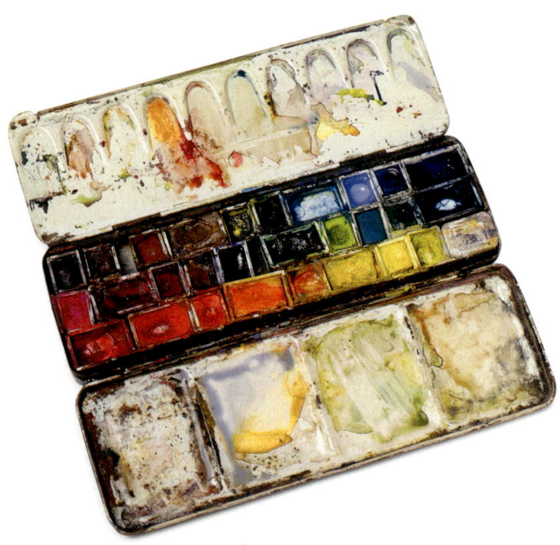

Notes and Initial Sketches

Tools and Media

The tools and materials used by an artist who specializes in birds are not very different from those used by any other art professional.

The brushes, pencils, pigments, and supports that are typical in drawing and painting are also used in this specialty.

The main difference is that the painter of birds usually goes outside and works from nature quite often, and this requires him or her to use equipment that is light, easy to transport, and, above all, very versatile.

But painters of birds also frequently work as illustrators. Some commissions require very detailed paintings, and this means using materials that allow more precision, whether in the field or in the studio.

In the following pages, we will show you all these tools and materials and indicate which ones are most useful in each case.

JUAN VARELA
STUDY OF A MERLIN *(FALCO COLUMBARIUS)*
PENCILS AND WATERCOLOR, 10.5 x 14.5 INCHES (27 x 37 CM)

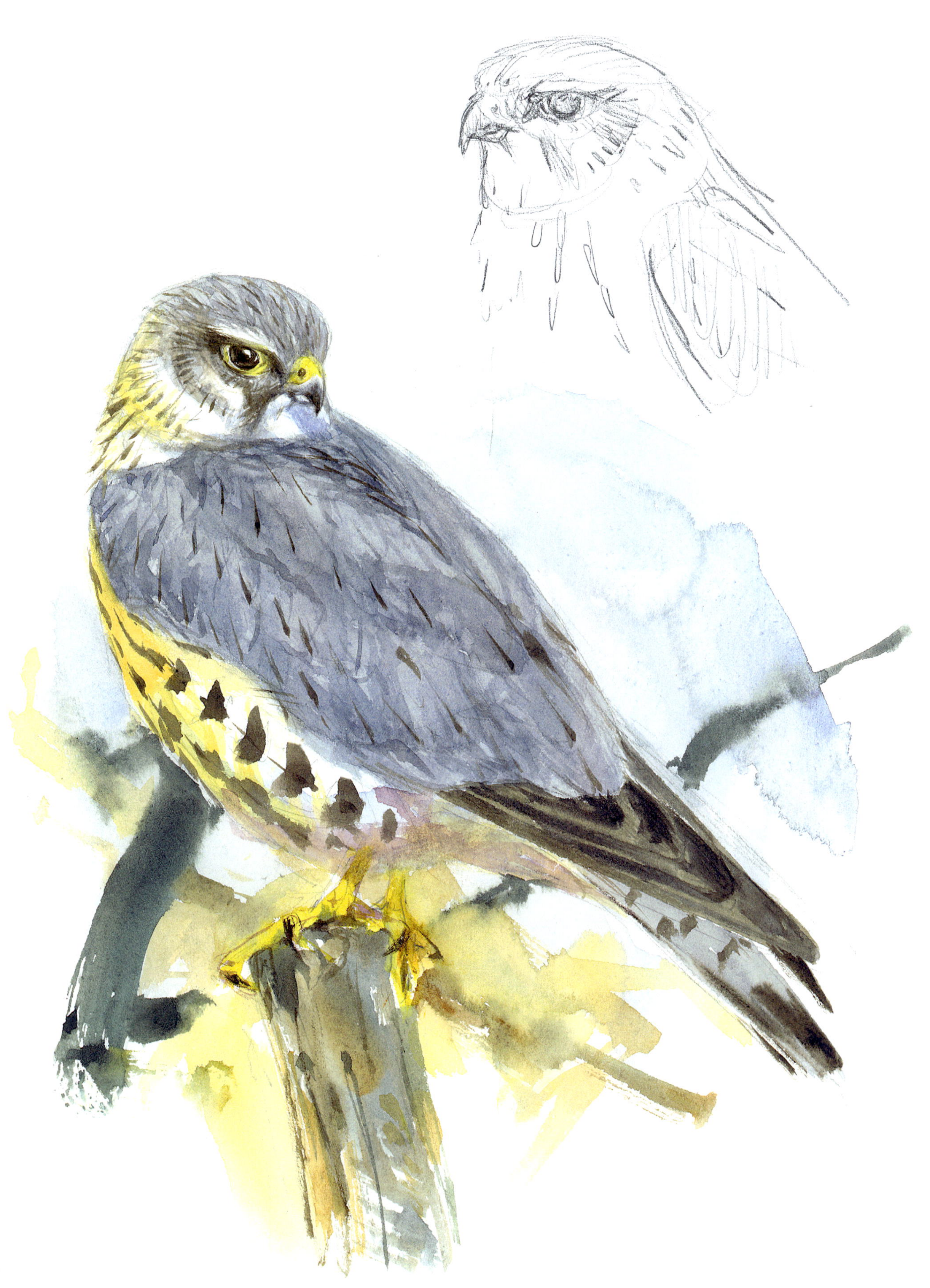

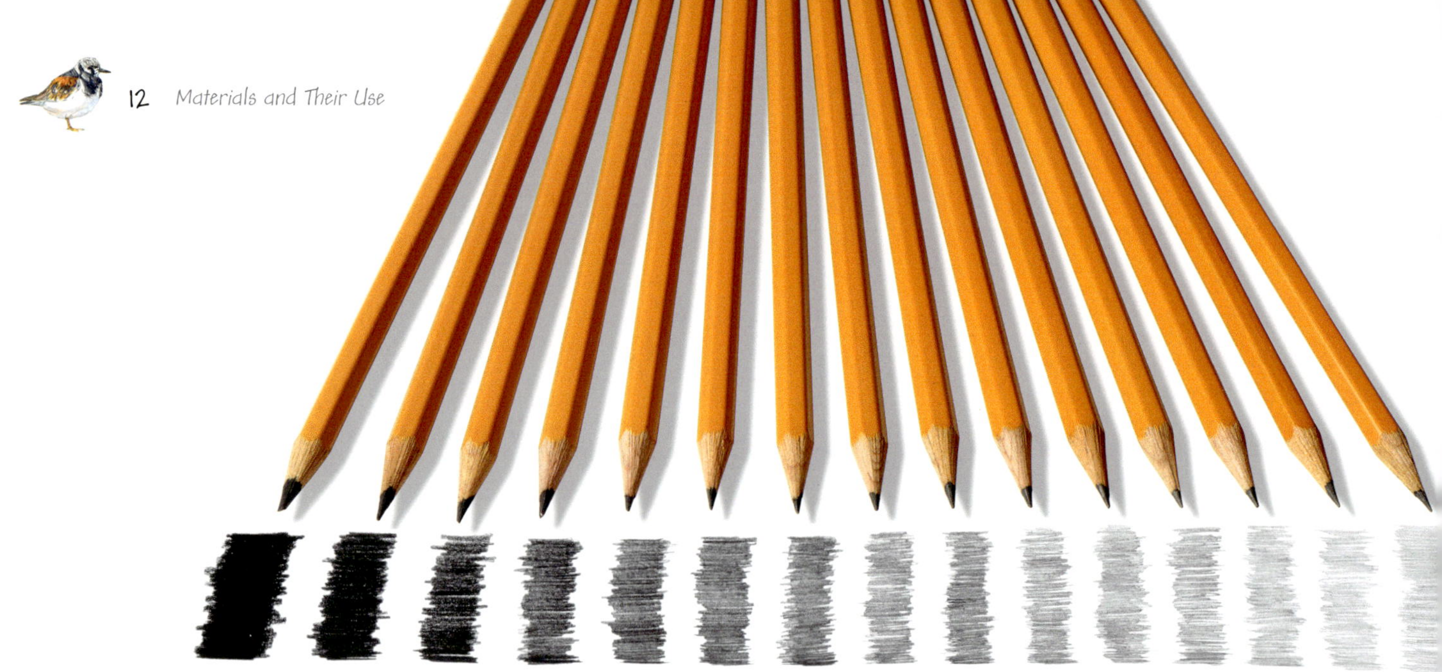

Since their invention, graphite pencils have been the most widely used medium for preparing preparatory sketches. They allow you to quickly and precisely draw outlines and suggest volume, shadows, and tonal variations.

Pencils of All Kinds

Without a doubt, the pencil is the most intuitive and versatile drawing instrument in existence. It allows you to quickly and precisely draw outlines and shade, and to adjust monochromatic tones or apply notes of color. In addition, it is an economical medium, easy to carry and clean, and it is sold in a wide range of colors and hardness.

GRAPHITE PENCILS

Graphite pencils are made of a mixture of graphite powder and finely ground clay in varying proportions, which gives them different hardness and a great variety of tones. Most manufacturers indicate the density using a combination of letters and numbers printed directly on the pencil.

The pencils with hard leads are indicated with the letter H (for *hardness*), and the soft lead pencils are printed with the letter B (for *blackness*). Both groups also carry numbers that run from 1 through 9. There is a pencil of intermediate hardness, which is designated with the letters HB.

Generally, artists prefer the smoothness and modulation of the soft leads.

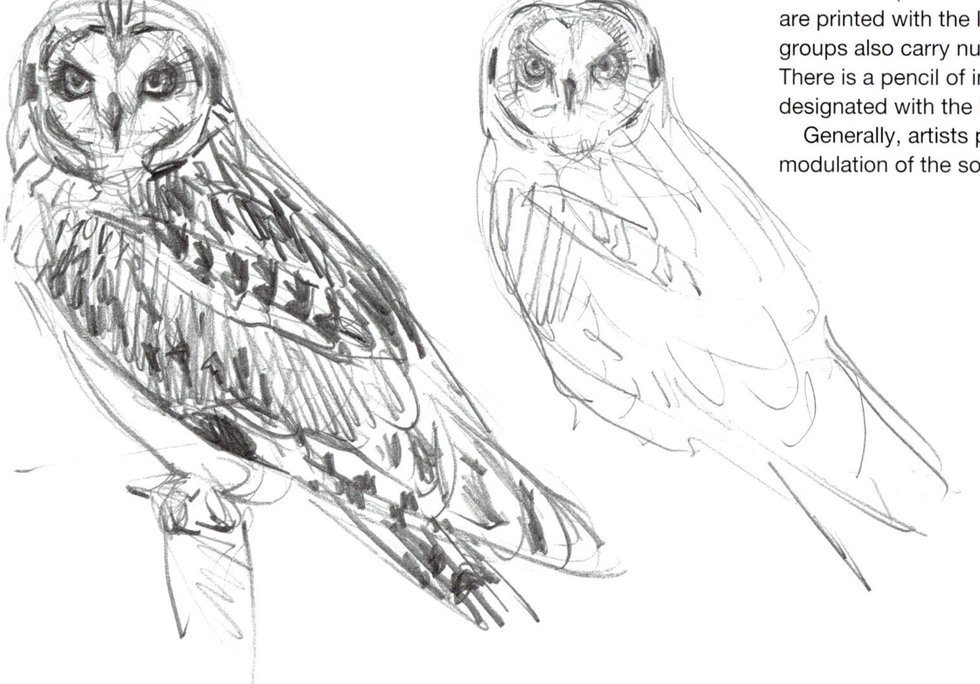

A simple pencil sketch can supply a lot of useful information for later work that is done in the studio.

Many artists feel it is more comfortable to carry one or two lead holders and a small case with graphite and color leads when they go outdoors to paint or draw. In the middle of working in the field, it is quicker to press a button to get a new point than to look for the sharpener and then use it to sharpen a wood pencil.

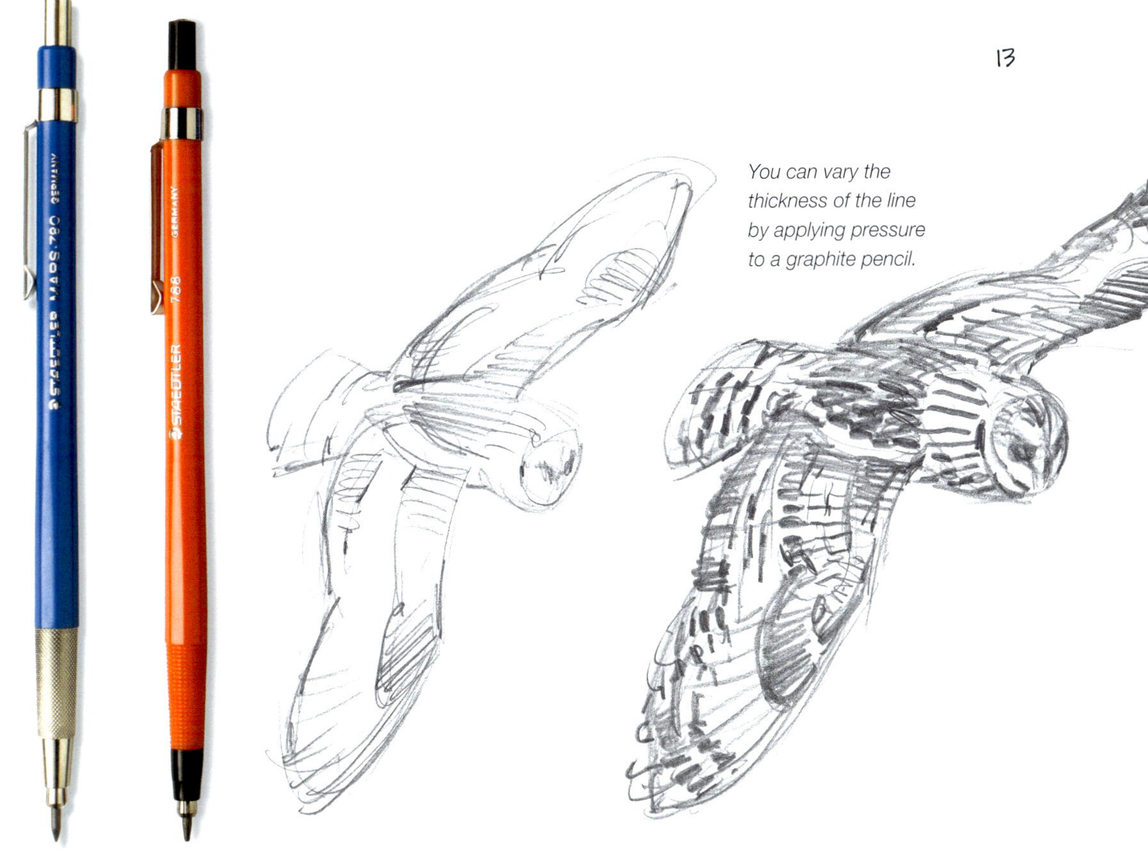

You can vary the thickness of the line by applying pressure to a graphite pencil.

LEAD HOLDERS

Lead holders eliminate the need to carry a pencil sharpener, and actually most of them contain a small pointer in the cap. There are different models, and they are made for different lead sizes, from 0.5 to 9 mm. The most useful for painters who specialize in birds are those from 2 to 5 mm and, occasionally, the 7 mm size. There are also leads made in different colors that fit the holders, so that the size and amount of the drawing equipment is quite small; 6 or 8 leads in basic colors, a few more of graphite, and a lead holder will allow you a wide range of possibilities.

It is not necessary to have an enormous selection of colors for making notes and sketches outdoors, because superimposing the colors will suggest different tones. Color pencils can be dryer and harder, or softer and more oily or waxy. The latter are less resistant to pressure, but they create more intense colors.

COLOR PENCILS

Color pencils are made of wax, pigments, and other components that create a very wide range of colors. They are not considered to be an appropriate medium for working in large formats, but they are great for making sketches and for inclusion in mixed media work. Nearly all manufacturers include water-soluble colors in their catalogues. These allow you to dilute the lines with water and blend them on the paper. Obviously, they do not have the same properties as watercolors, but they can be useful in small formats and for adding hints of color to sketches. There are also water-soluble graphite pencils of different hardness.

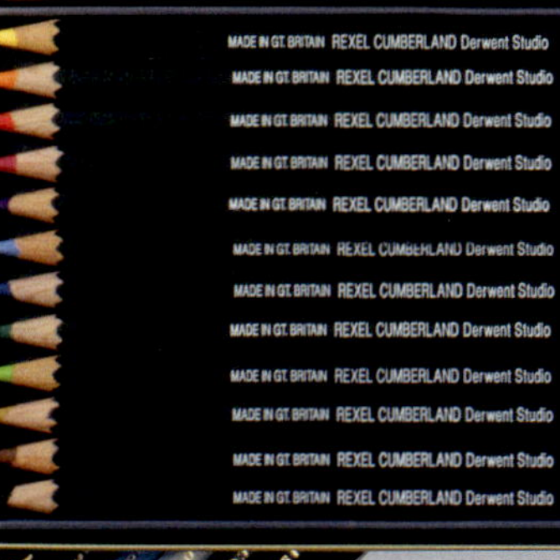

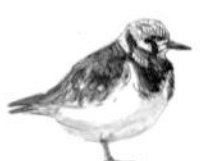

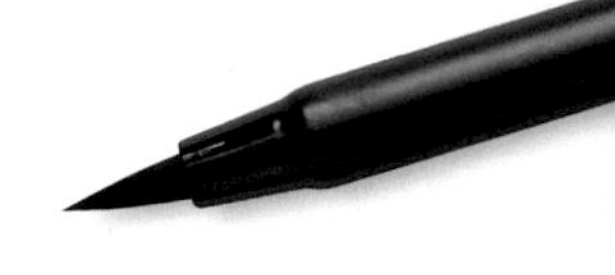

Drawing with ink is very challenging because it is difficult to correct mistakes. When you are making notes outdoors or making preparatory sketches, this is not a great problem, because the studies are for your own use. If the illustration is destined to be published in some other medium, then clean lines are more important. For this, you can make use of an initial sketch in pencil that serves as a guide.

Drawing with ink is a very valuable form of practice for learning to make a sure line and overcoming the fear of making mistakes

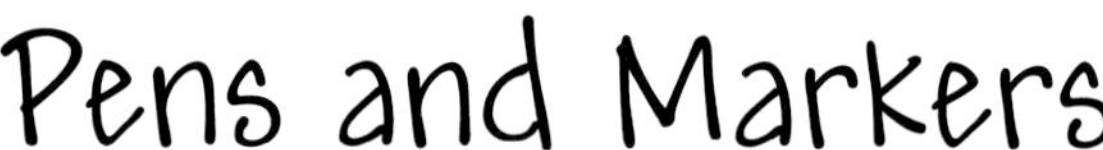

Pens and Markers

INKS

The most commonly used inks in drawing are water-soluble, whether temporarily (until they dry on the paper, like India ink) or always (meaning they can be diluted with a wet brush).

India ink is made from the carbon of burnt wood or bone mixed with shellac and water. In color inks, the carbon is replaced by pigments. They are generally not used for illustrations of birds, but are common to calligraphy and design work.

Water-soluble inks are used in fountain pens, so they will not clog. Markers usually have ink with an alcohol base, which evaporates quickly and is indelible when it is dry.

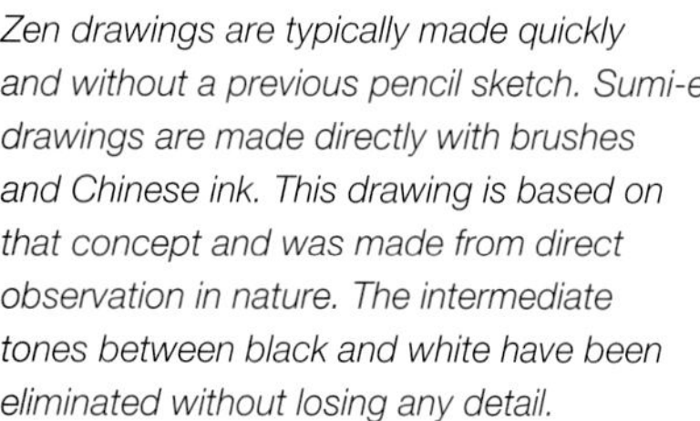

Zen drawings are typically made quickly and without a previous pencil sketch. Sumi-e drawings are made directly with brushes and Chinese ink. This drawing is based on that concept and was made from direct observation in nature. The intermediate tones between black and white have been eliminated without losing any detail.

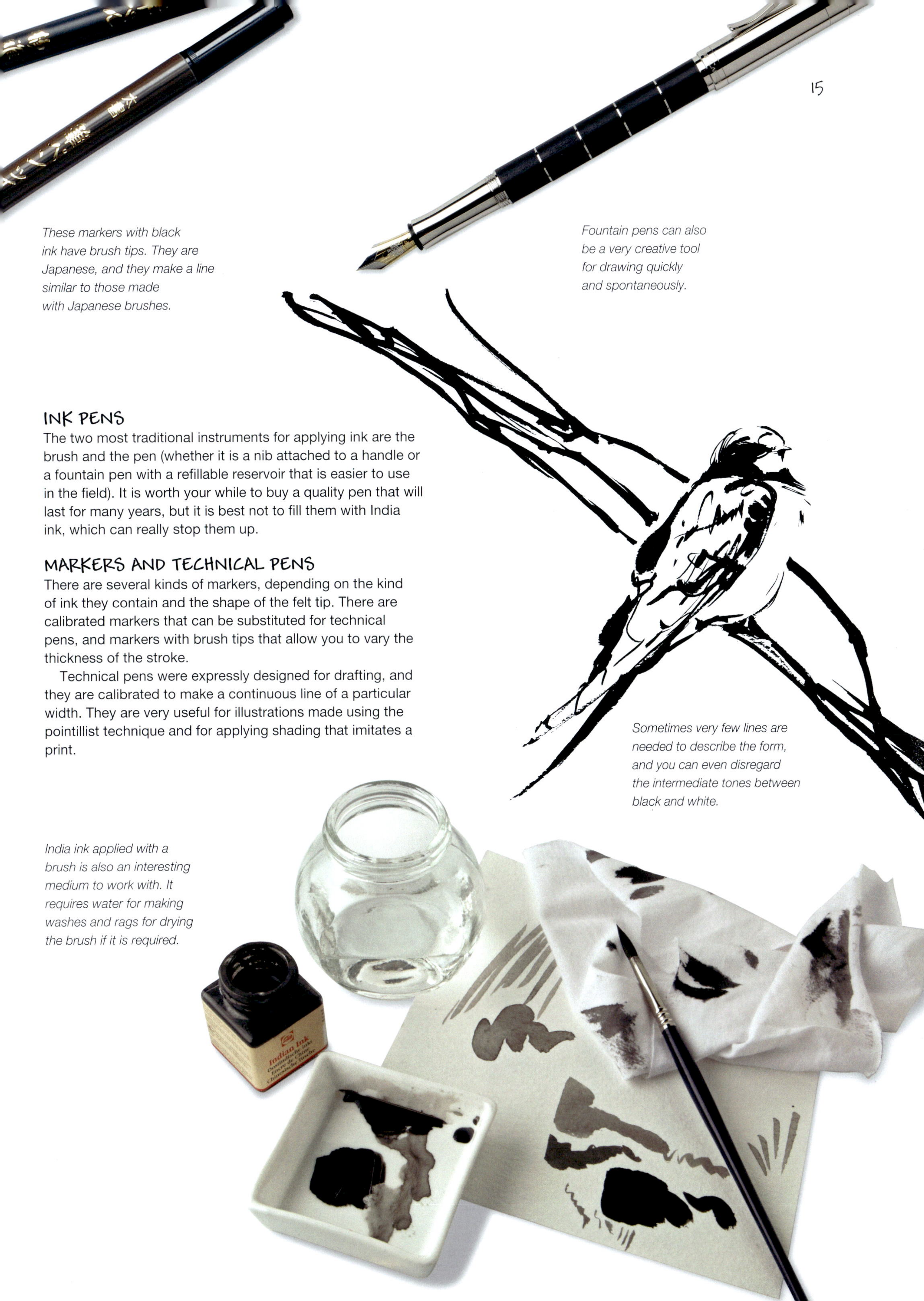

These markers with black ink have brush tips. They are Japanese, and they make a line similar to those made with Japanese brushes.

Fountain pens can also be a very creative tool for drawing quickly and spontaneously.

INK PENS

The two most traditional instruments for applying ink are the brush and the pen (whether it is a nib attached to a handle or a fountain pen with a refillable reservoir that is easier to use in the field). It is worth your while to buy a quality pen that will last for many years, but it is best not to fill them with India ink, which can really stop them up.

MARKERS AND TECHNICAL PENS

There are several kinds of markers, depending on the kind of ink they contain and the shape of the felt tip. There are calibrated markers that can be substituted for technical pens, and markers with brush tips that allow you to vary the thickness of the stroke.

Technical pens were expressly designed for drafting, and they are calibrated to make a continuous line of a particular width. They are very useful for illustrations made using the pointillist technique and for applying shading that imitates a print.

Sometimes very few lines are needed to describe the form, and you can even disregard the intermediate tones between black and white.

India ink applied with a brush is also an interesting medium to work with. It requires water for making washes and rags for drying the brush if it is required.

Brushes and Washes

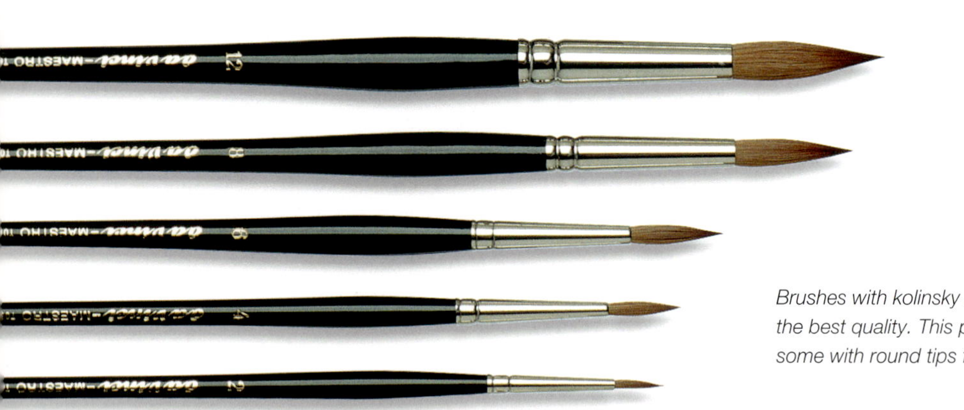

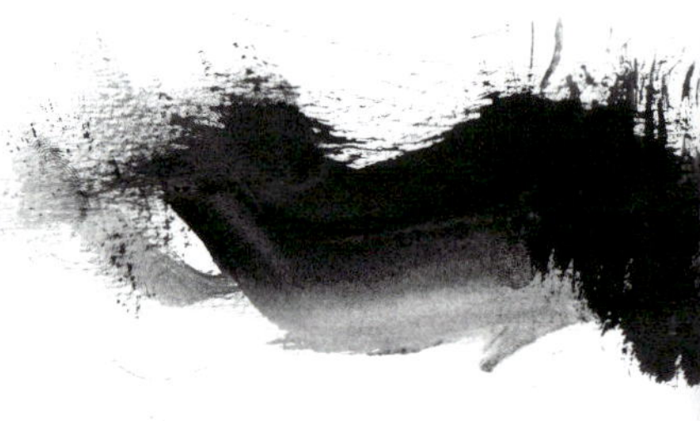

Brushes with kolinsky sable hair are the best quality. This photo shows some with round tips for watercolor.

Some sketches from nature and preparatory drawings are made in tonal ranges only—that is, without using any paint or different inks. The typical wash is a mixture of ink with different amounts of water that create the tonal values of the subject. It can be painted over a drawing in pencil, India ink, or even charcoal, which, when dissolved in water, will create different tones of gray. It must be applied with a brush on a paper that is heavy enough that it will not buckle when it is wet.

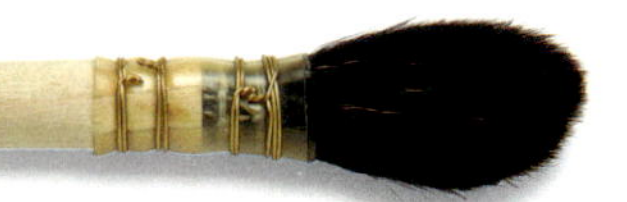

This squirrel hair brush is excellent for making washes, because it will hold a large amount of water.

SELECTING BRUSHES

There are different kinds of brushes that are manufactured for different uses. Brushes for oils and acrylics are usually made of hog or synthetic bristles, while brushes for watercolors and gouache can be made of sable or squirrel hair, or also synthetic. The first synthetic brushes that were commercialized were of poor quality; however, nowadays, they match the natural brushes in their flexibility and ability to hold paint quite well, and they are more economical. Brushes for oils usually have a long handle because working on large formats requires you to maintain a certain distance. Illustrating sometimes requires that you work more closely to the paper; therefore, watercolor brushes generally have shorter handles.

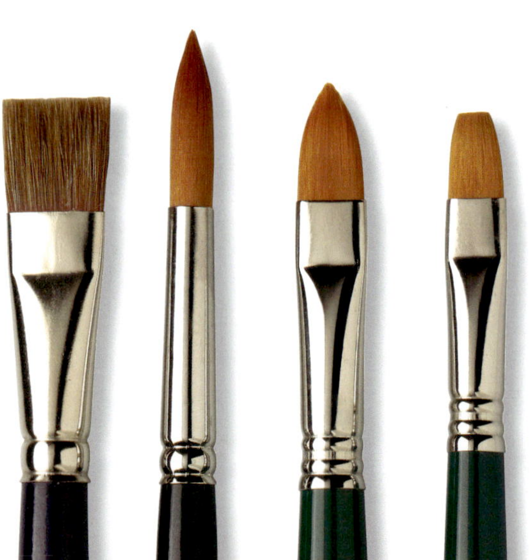

These are the most common shapes of the tips of paintbrushes: square, round, filbert, and bright.

The preference for their use is very personal, and depends on the type of line you wish to create; however, square brushes are ideal for spreading paint.

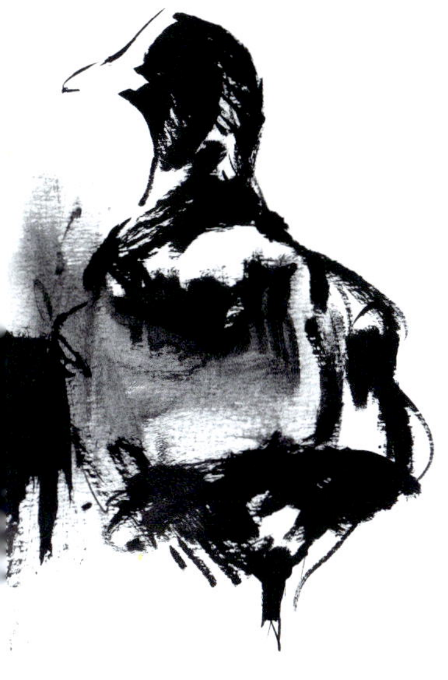

India ink and brush. Adding water to the ink while it is still wet will create tonal values. You can later draw new lines over the wash after it has dried.

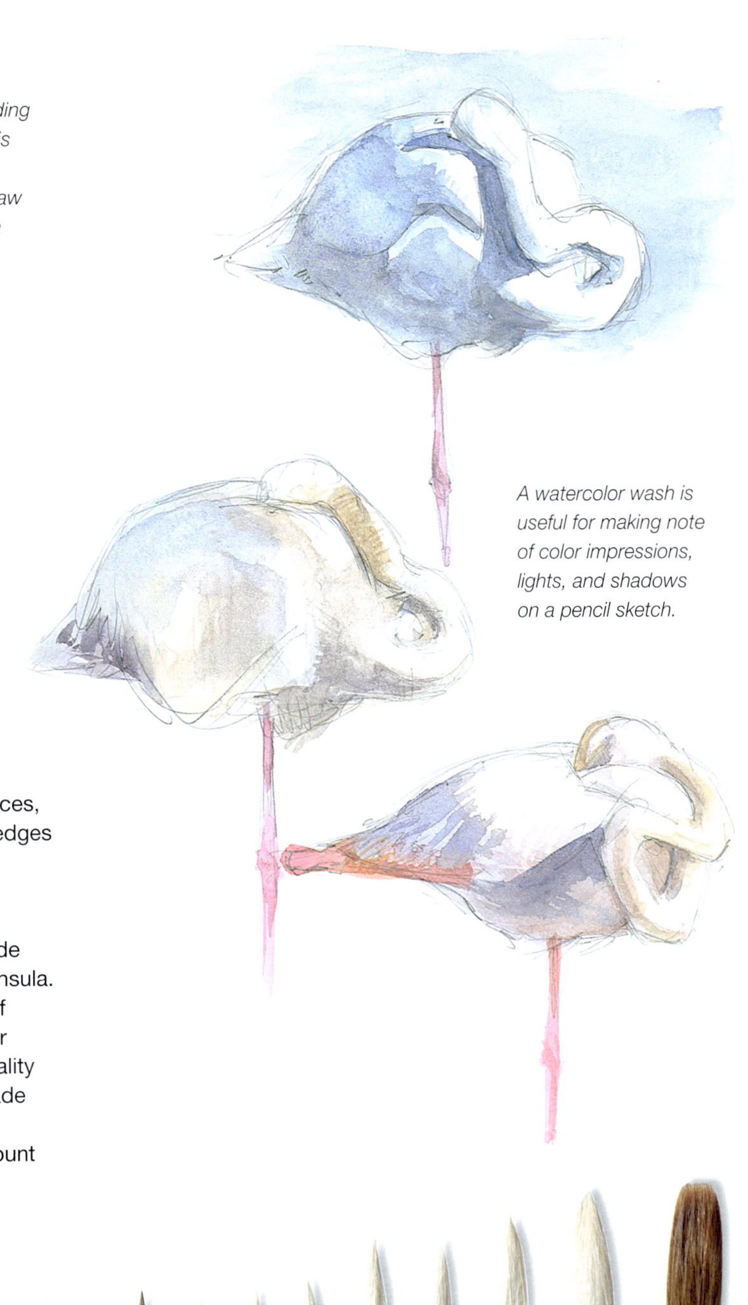

A watercolor wash is useful for making note of color impressions, lights, and shadows on a pencil sketch.

SIZES AND SHAPES

High-quality brushes are made by hand by very experienced artisans. Round ones are somewhat fat in the middle, but end in a very fine point, and can be used to draw lines and details, or for applying paint to a large surface. There is a very wide range of sizes that runs from 0 up to 20 or higher, depending on the manufacturer.

Flat brushes are used for applying paint to large surfaces, but you can also paint lines of different widths with the edges and corners.

TYPES OF BRUSHES

The most expensive and highest-quality brushes are made using Kolinsky sable, which comes from the Taymir peninsula. In reality, Kolinsky sables are not sables, but a species of mink that the local natives hunt for food and clothing. For painting details, the ideal brushes are sable and high-quality synthetic. Wide brushes and Japanese hake brushes made with goat hair are excellent for painting large surfaces. Squirrel brushes have very fine hair and hold a large amount of paint, and are very useful for making washes.

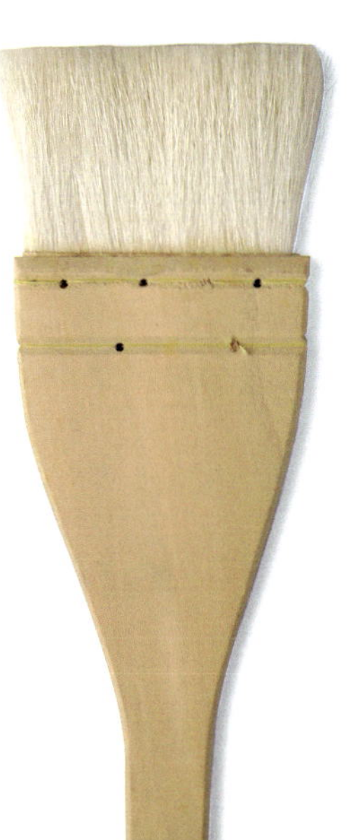

A hake brush made with goat hair for use in watercolor painting for spreading paint on large surfaces.

Japanese brushes can be very useful for the quality of lines that they make.

Watercolors and Gouache

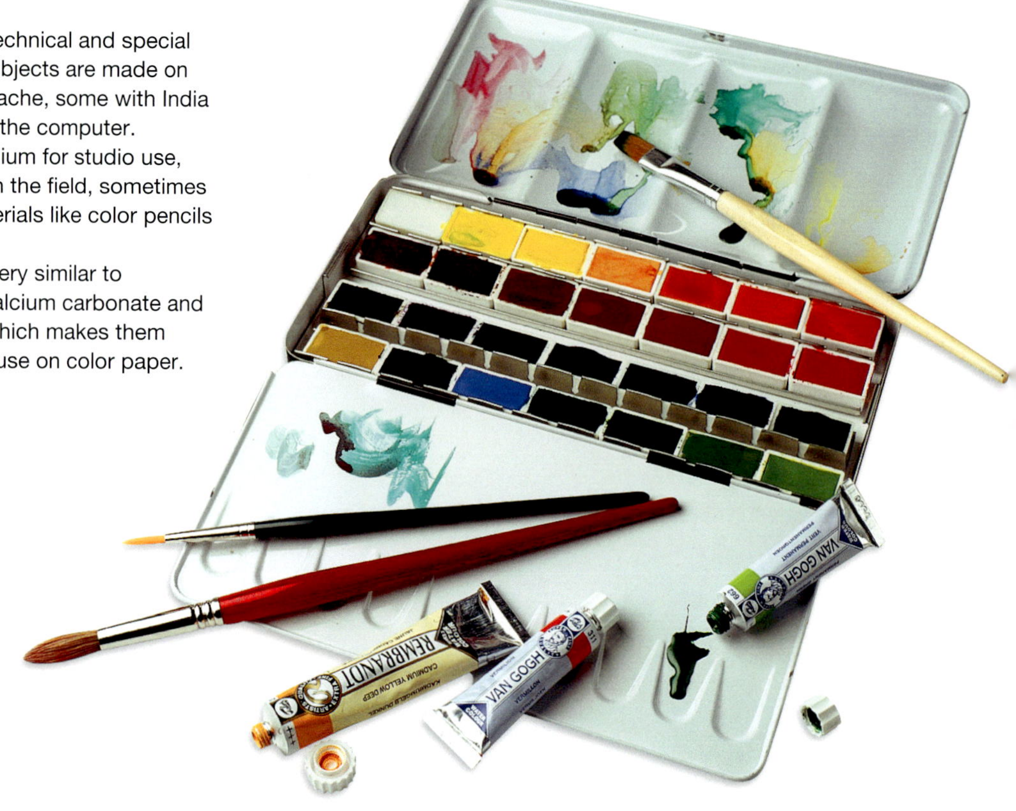

Most illustrations for today's technical and special interest books about nature subjects are made on paper using watercolor or gouache, some with India ink, and a growing number on the computer.

Watercolor is not just a medium for studio use, and most bird painters use it in the field, sometimes in combination with other materials like color pencils or wax crayons.

Gouache and tempera are very similar to watercolor, but they contain calcium carbonate and a denser charge of pigment, which makes them more opaque and suitable for use on color paper.

It is best to buy a few colors that are of high quality. Boxes with many colors are quite expensive and include colors that sometimes are not used. Large cakes are easier to handle and have a bigger surface.

WATERCOLOR FORMATS

Liquid watercolors are actually not watercolors, but mixtures of water with dyes instead of pigments; they tend to fade in sunlight and penetrate too deeply into the paper.

True watercolors come in cakes or in tubes. The composition of both forms is very similar, but the tubes are usually more practical in the studio for coloring large surfaces.

The most important consideration in this medium is the quality and the proportion of pigment in the mixture. The watercolors sold in the "artist" category are the most expensive, but they spread better and the colors are brighter.

Paint is combined with pencil lines when making quick studies in the field.

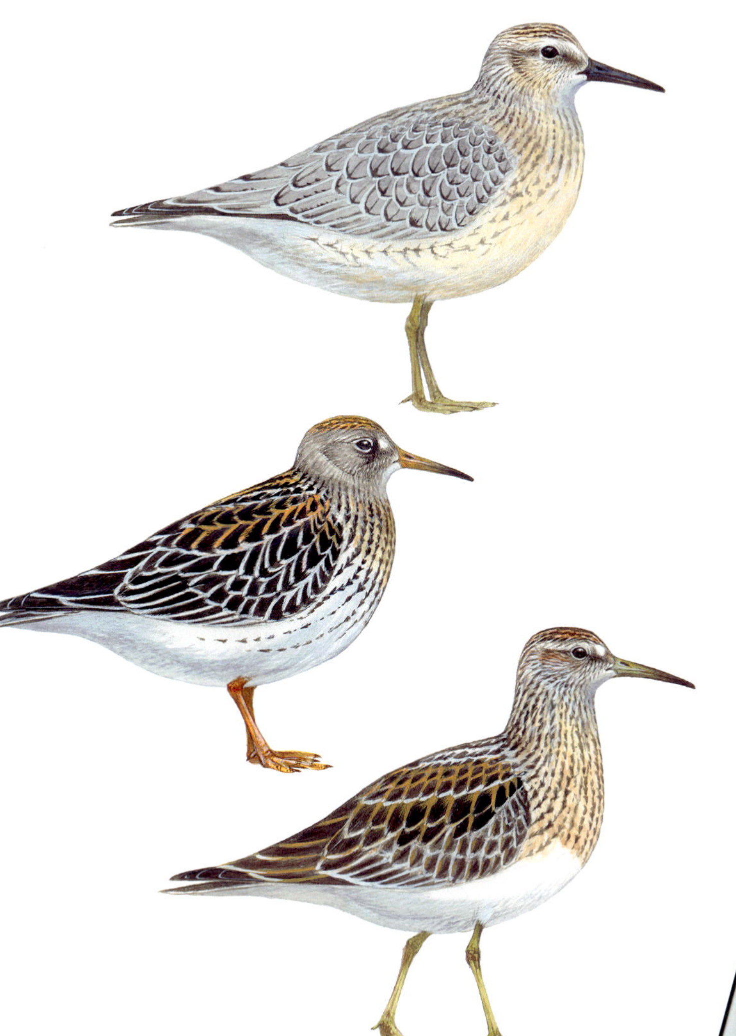

CHOOSING COLORS

The commercial names of colors vary by manufacturer and also by their composition. Nowadays, ingredients that are damaging to health are rarely used, like lead, which was commonly used as a pigment in the past. However, some names persist. One example of this is viridian green, which was manufactured with arsenic.

To begin with, it is best to stick to about 8 to 10 basic colors and increase the range from there if you consider it necessary.

Profile views of different dunlins. This illustration is used as a guide for identifying birds in the field. In this type of work, the details are very important, and you must make use of a combination of watercolor and gouache to outline the edges of the feathers and exactly capture the colors.

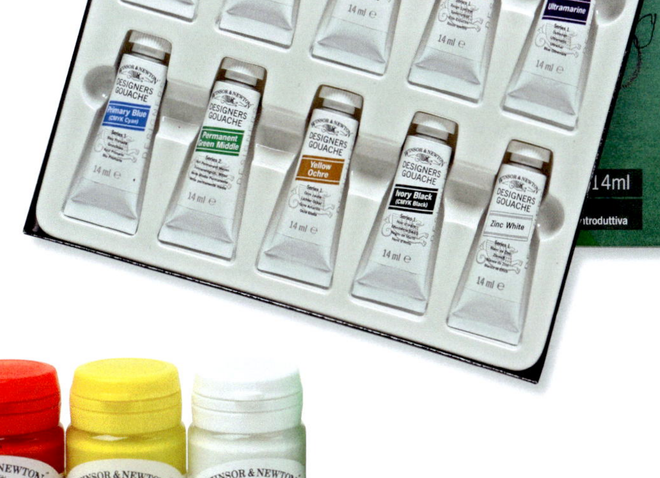

Gouache is often used in combination with watercolor to highlight the light areas against dark backgrounds or when working on color paper. Zinc white can be mixed with watercolors to create a finish similar to that of gouache, although it will never be as opaque.

Papers and Sketchbooks

In this photo are three types of surface texture seen full size. From top to bottom: fine grain, medium, and heavy. Watercolor papers have the appropriate texture on only one side, and the watermark will help you identify it.

The support that you work on is as important as your drawing tools. Paper is the best medium for sketching outdoors and preparatory drawings; it is also best for much of the work done in the studio. The roughness of its surface is a factor that will determine the amount of detail that will be in the work.

Works that will be reproduced by photomechanical means must follow certain norms or they will cause the process to be more costly. Industrial drum scanners cannot use large size paper or rigid supports. In these cases, works must be photographed. However, this increases the cost and complicates the entire process, so it is best to consult with the client before doing the work.

SKETCHBOOKS

For the artist, it is usually easier to use sketchbooks than loose sheets, because the paper is fixed, has a rigid support that is helpful when working in the field, and the drawings are kept in the order that they are made. Sketchbooks are commonly used for outdoor work, and they are available with a spiral binding or sewn to the binding like a book. The spiral allows you to turn the page all the way to the back to then work on the next sheet, but the pages rub together more and the pencil lines tend to smudge. Book binding allows you to draw on two pages at once without a gap between them.

Special sketchbooks for watercolors can have loose sheets or they can be glued on all four sides so they will not buckle when they are wet.

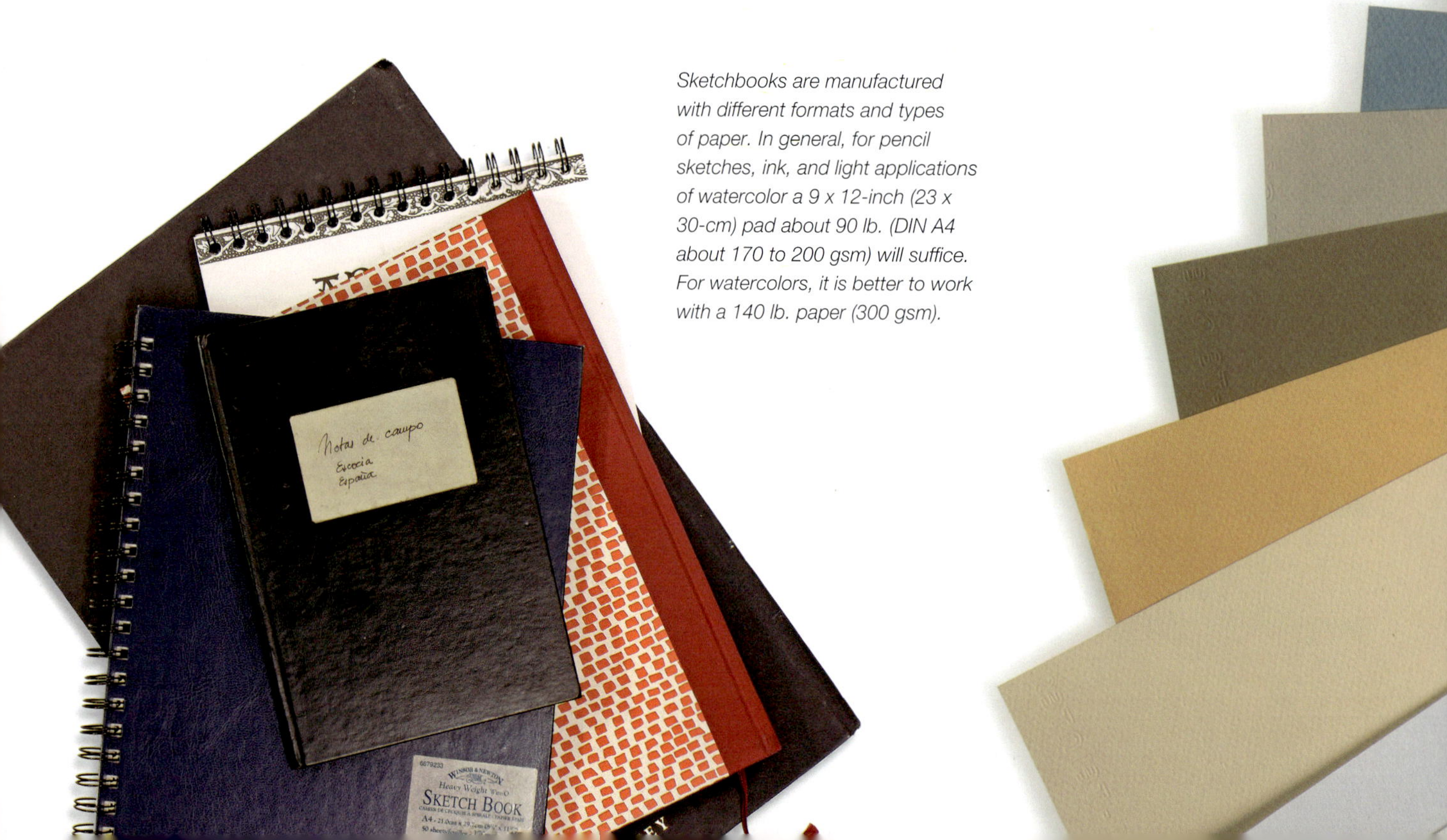

Sketchbooks are manufactured with different formats and types of paper. In general, for pencil sketches, ink, and light applications of watercolor a 9 x 12-inch (23 x 30-cm) pad about 90 lb. (DIN A4 about 170 to 200 gsm) will suffice. For watercolors, it is better to work with a 140 lb. paper (300 gsm).

THICKNESS, TEXTURE, AND COLOR

Color papers require opaque media like gouache or pastels to make light colors; those with a rough surface are ideal for creating textures by applying the colors with brushes that are slightly dry or with soft pencils. Artists with some pride should consider the paper as an important part of the creative process and not as a mere support. The weight of the paper is based on a ream of 500 sheets (the metric weight is based on grams per square meter). This number will give you an idea about the thickness of the paper, and at the same time its resistance to dampness.

The surface of the paper can be of three types: heavy texture, medium texture, and vellum. The second two are preferable for detailed work and for sketching in the field. The best drawing papers are made solely of cotton fibers, the rest have varying amounts of cellulose. If you want to create artwork that will last for a long time, you will have to use an acid-free paper. Otherwise, the paper will be destroyed by the acid after a few years.

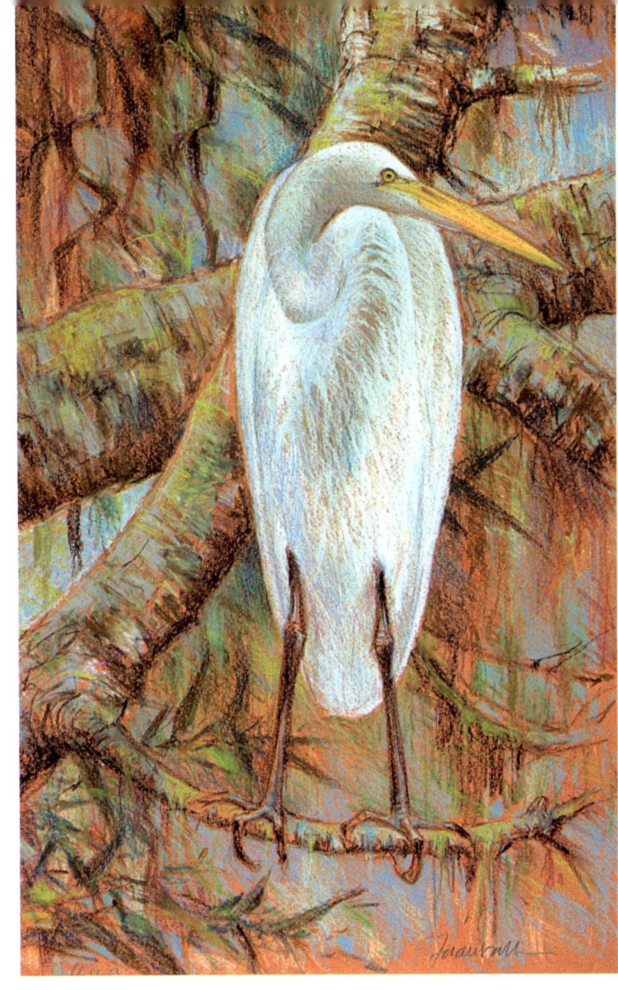

Color paper requires the use of opaque media like gouache and pastels, as shown in this example.

Here is a selection of papers that can be used for drawing birds. Heavy watercolor paper (A) and fine grain or smooth (B), Cartridge paper for drawing and ink (C), and a variety of color Canson papers for chalk and pastel (D).

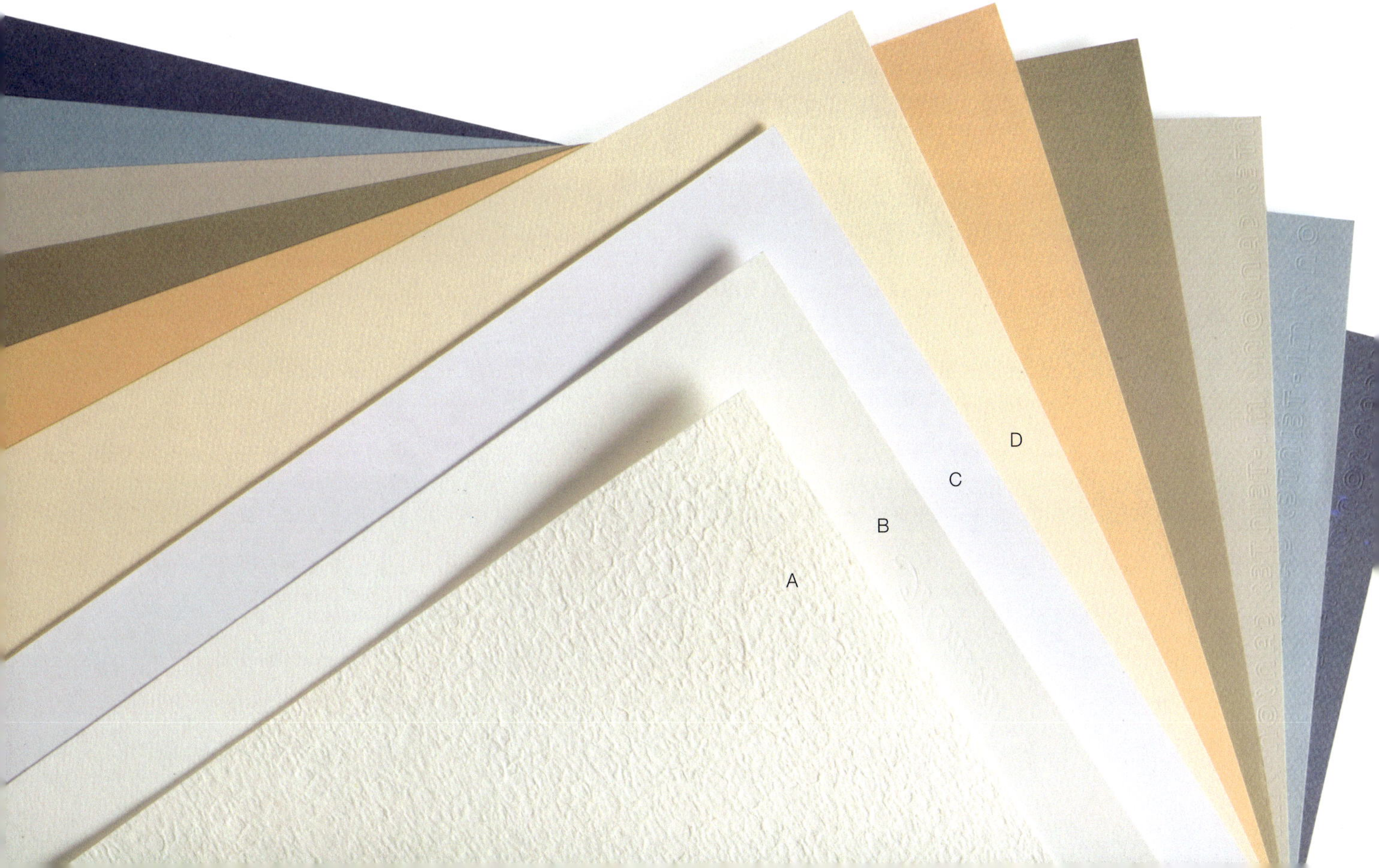

D

C

B

A

Media for the Studio

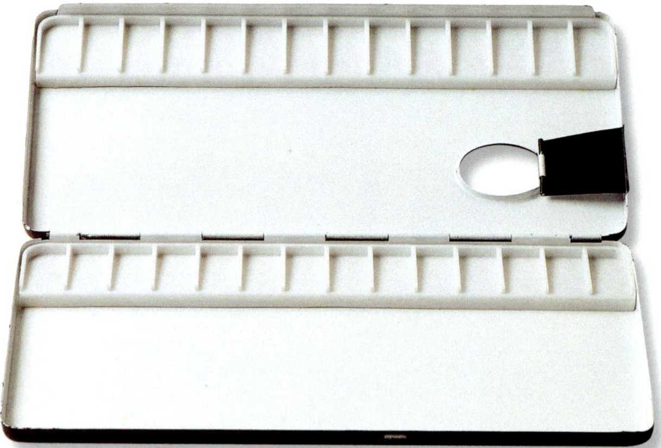

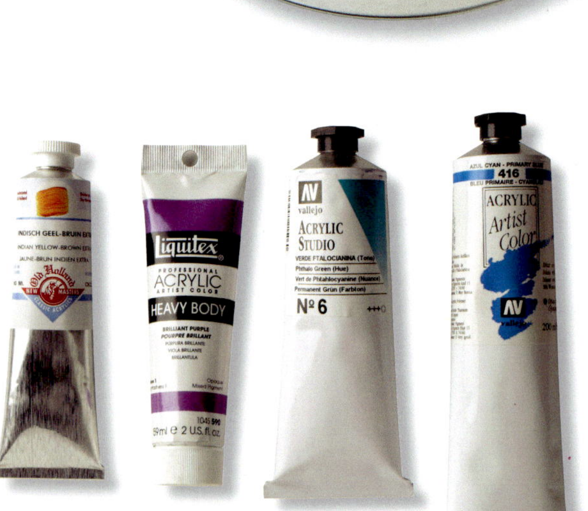

Tubes of acrylic paint and metal palettes, which are useful for working outdoors with water-base media.

When work is carried out in the studio, you will have some of the more complex materials at hand, like oil and acrylic paints. The latter can also be simple to use in the field, because it can be diluted with water and it dries quickly. In addition, the support does not require any special preparation, unless you are using canvas. Oils, on the other hand, except in the case of the modern water-base oils, do require a solvent and also a prepared support, because the oils will damage paper and canvas over time if they are not coated with a primer. For these reasons, and also because of their long drying time, oils are best used in the studio and are not commonly used for illustrations.

ACRYLIC VERSUS WATERCOLOR

Diluted acrylic paint looks similar to watercolor paint, but the difference is that, after it has dried, acrylic paint cannot be altered. This can be an inconvenience or an advantage, because you can create transparent layers of glazing similar to those used by other artists in other eras with oils and egg tempera, but in a shorter amount of time and with less difficulty. Like gouache, acrylic paint works well for making simple shapes with uniform and opaque layers.

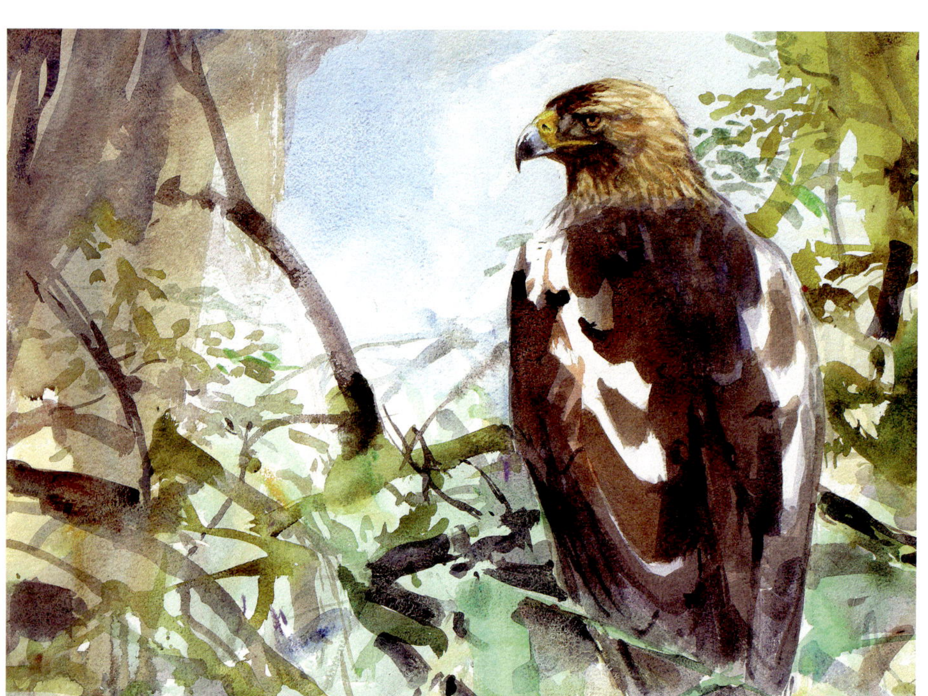

This painting was done with acrylics that were quite diluted on handmade paper. The paper was first prepared with a coat of gesso to make it less absorbent. Spanish Imperial Eagle, 20 x 28 inches (50 x 70 cm).

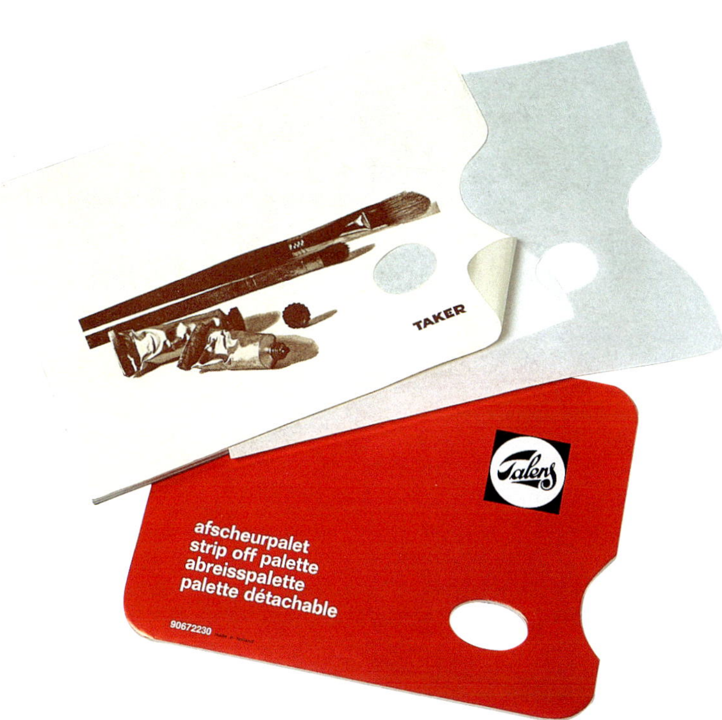

These are tubes of oils, in the traditional, water-base, and alkyd varieties, along with some pads of disposable palettes.

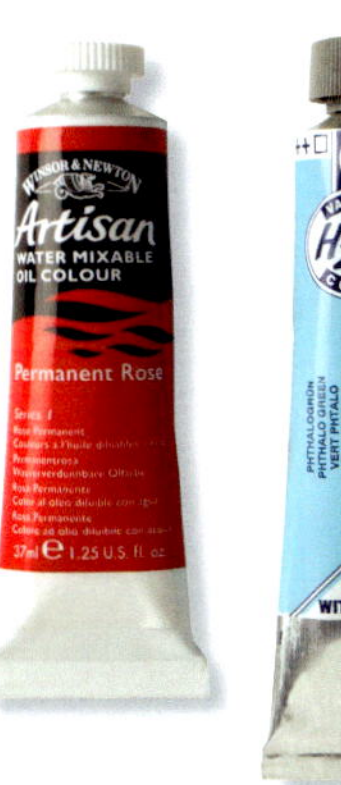

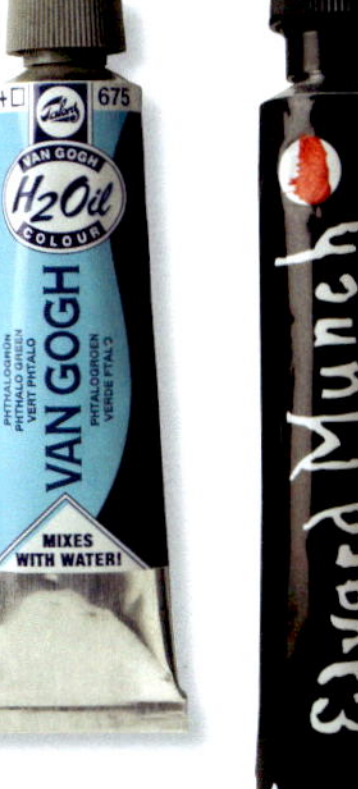

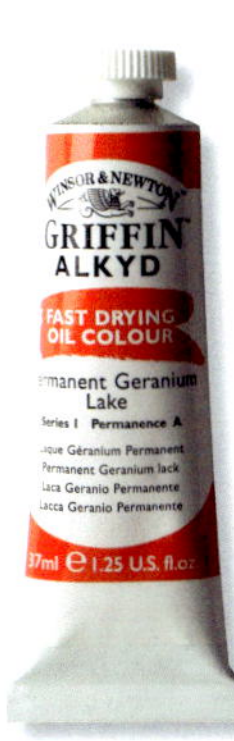

OILS, ALKYDS, AND WATER-BASE OILS

There are some traditional oil-base mediums that can be especially useful for artists that suffer from allergies to the solvents associated with oils or that do not want to wait a long time for oils to dry.

Alkyd paint, for example, contains organic solvents that do not irritate the skin, and it also dries very quickly, in barely two days. Water-base oils dry more slowly, but they can be diluted with just water. On the downside, the alkyd oils do not have as much body as conventional oils.

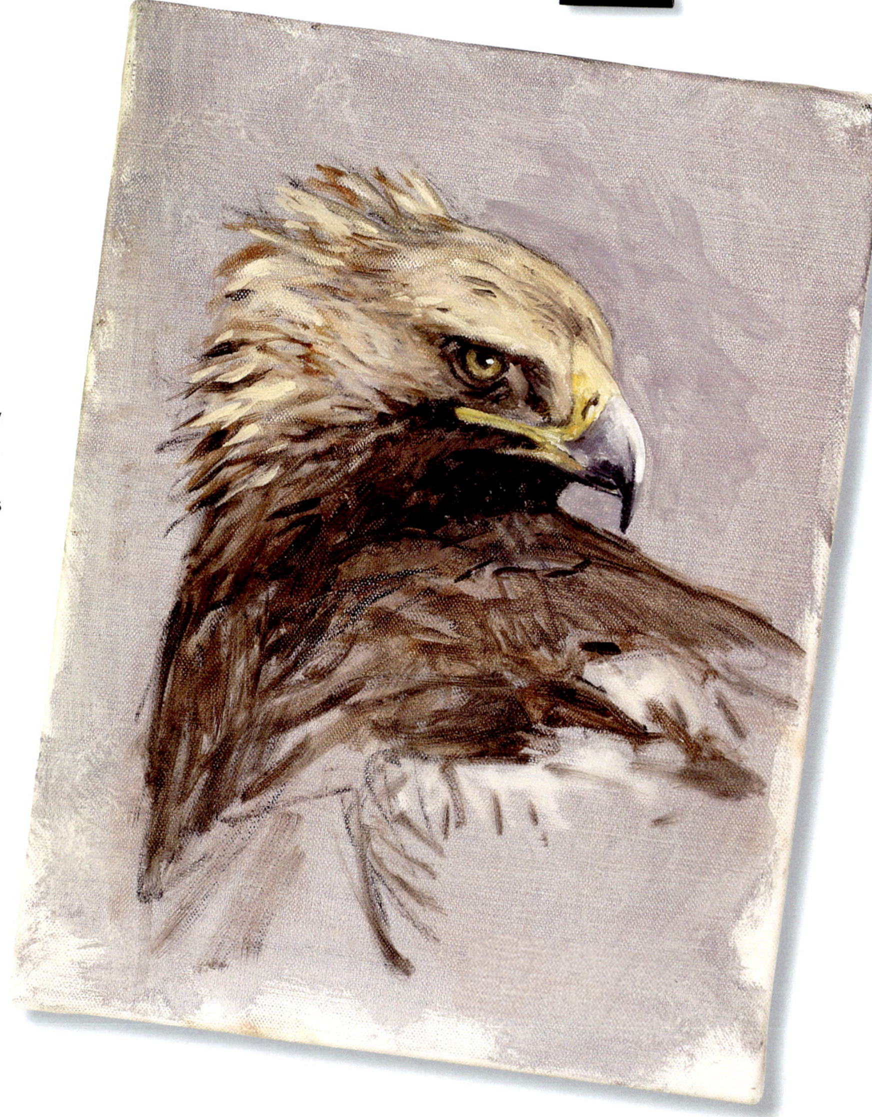

Study of a Spanish imperial eagle in oil.

Learning About Birds

JUAN VARELA
BAR-TAILED GODWIT IN WINTER
WATERCOLOR, 10.5 x 14.5 INCHES (27 x 37 CM)

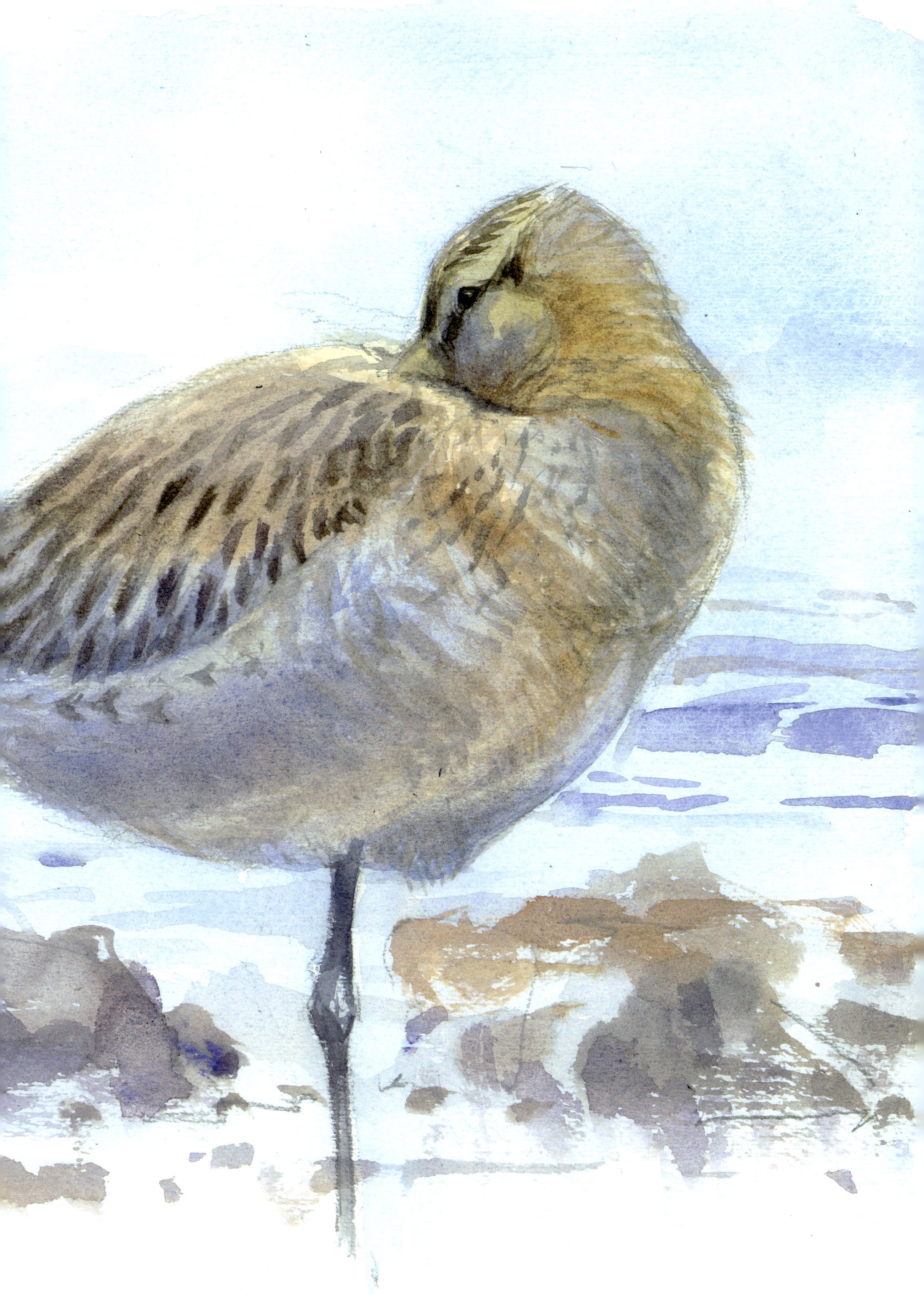

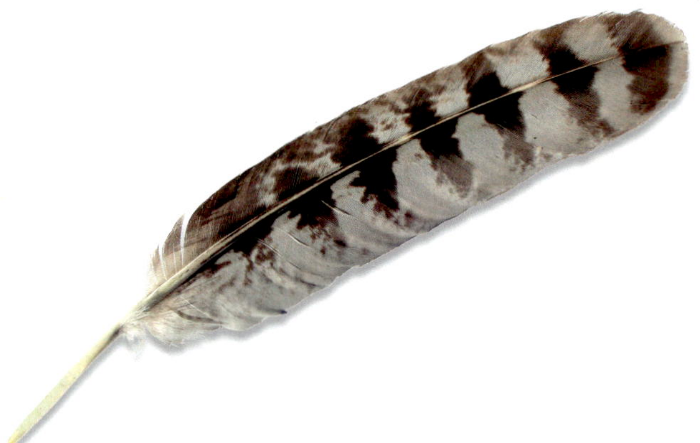

Anatomy for Artists
From Outside In

It is not easy to understand the form and movement of an animal if you do not first know its anatomy and habits very well. In the case of birds, the outside form is determined by the feathers, which modify its shape based on external factors like the wind and cold. Without this basic information, it will be very difficult to create an illustration that reflects the outer aspects of a bird and its movements in a convincing manner.

JUAN VARELA
BLUETHROAT (*LUSCINIA SVECICA*)
WATERCOLOR, 9 x 12.5 INCHES (23 x 32 CM)

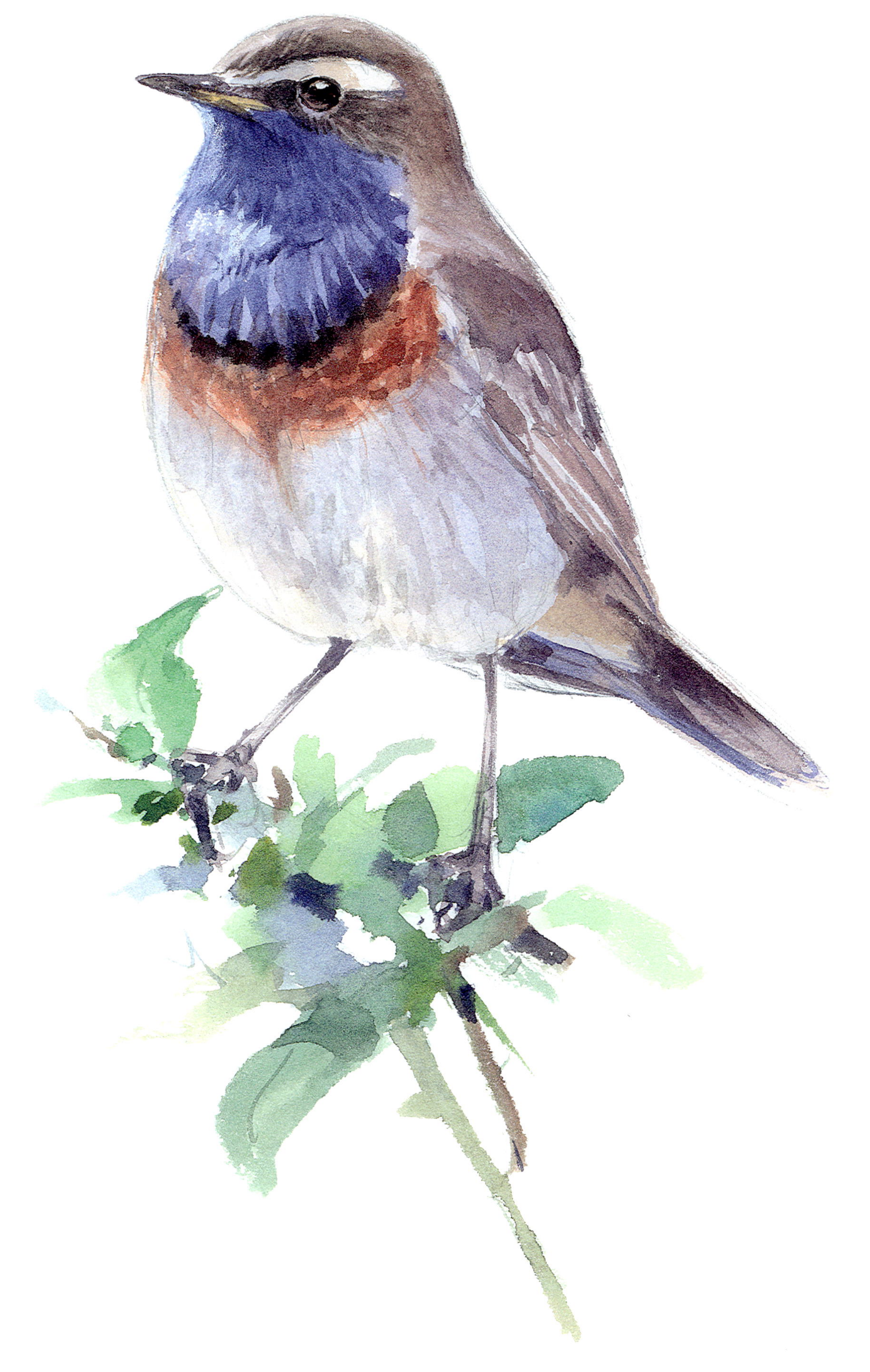

Basic Structure

In biology, as in medicine, every part of a living being has a very specific name. The nomenclature is used internationally and allows any reader of a technical or informational treatise to immediately understand what part of the body the author is referring to rather than depending on translations that might be erroneous. Some of these names come from Latin or have Latin roots, because this was the universal language of science until the middle of the 19th century. Knowing a large number of technical terms will be a great help to the artist who is looking for references and descriptions in biology books that do not have illustrations. Among birds, the groups of feathers also have very specific names, because it is necessary to identify them to explain processes like molting and for describing the extension and location of colors.

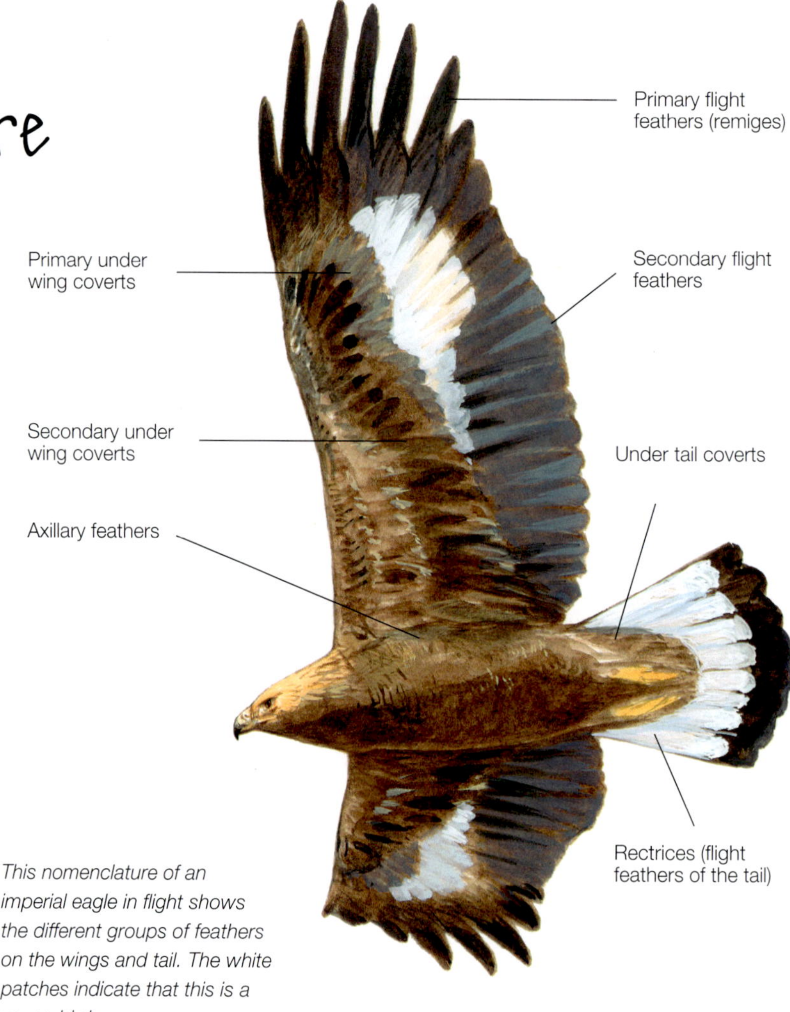

This nomenclature of an imperial eagle in flight shows the different groups of feathers on the wings and tail. The white patches indicate that this is a young bird.

Here is nomenclature for a perching bird. This yellow-rumped warbler lives on the American continent and is used as an example to show the names assigned to the different parts of a bird's body.

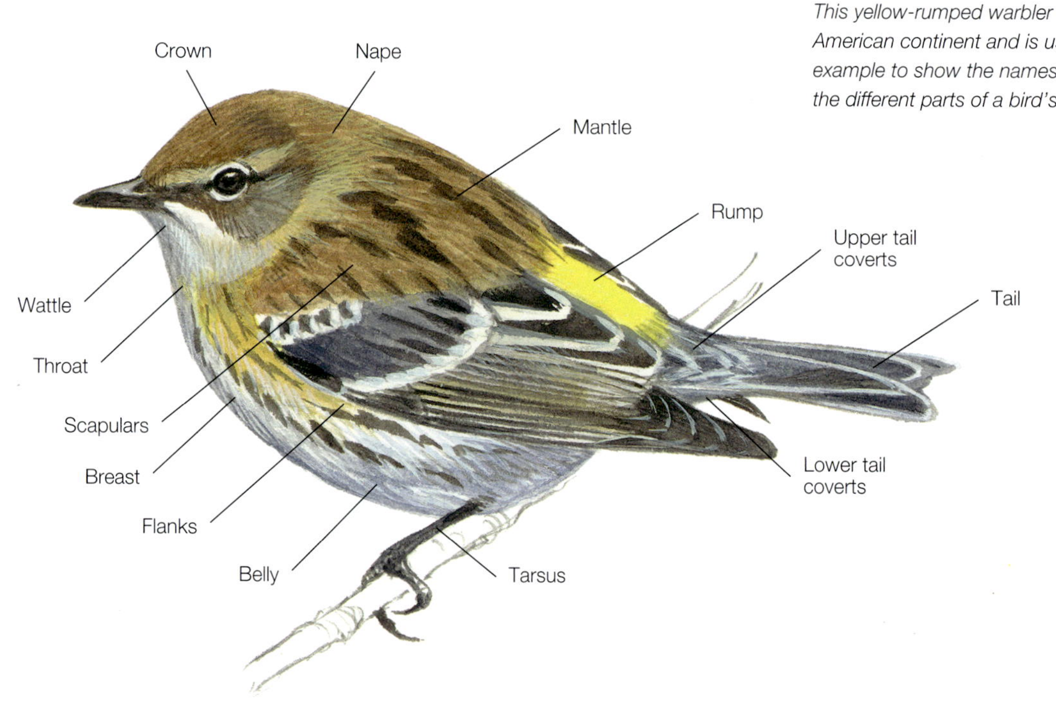

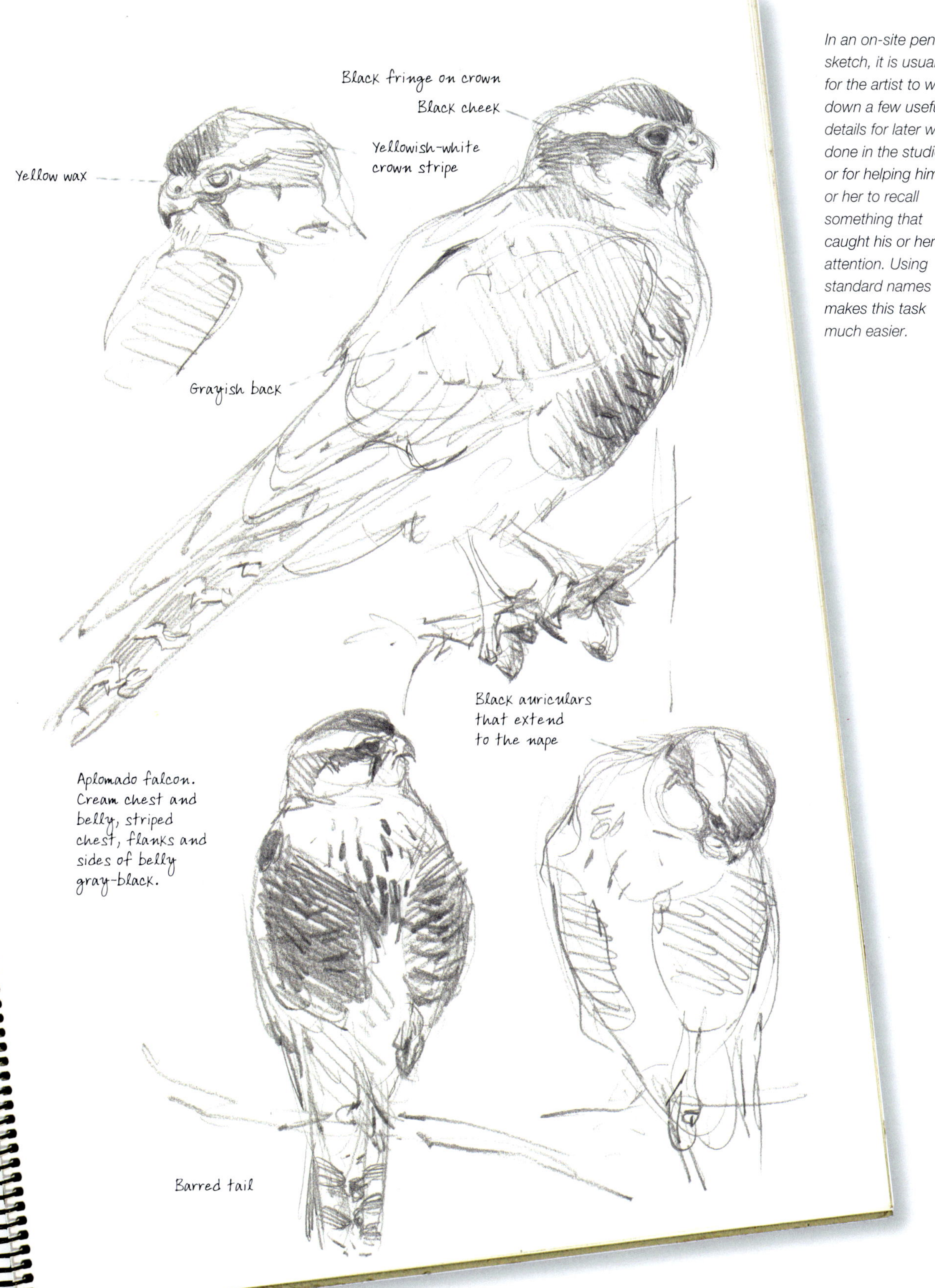

In an on-site pencil sketch, it is usual for the artist to write down a few useful details for later work done in the studio, or for helping him or her to recall something that caught his or her attention. Using standard names makes this task much easier.

Birds descend from the dinosaurs, and they began to diversify as species and disperse across the entire planet more than 150 million years ago. Nowadays, there are more than 10,000 species belonging to more than 230 families adapted to very different ecosystems, from the most torrid deserts to the Antarctic ice. It would be impossible to describe all of the known families in this book, or even the main ones. Still, we will make an effort to offer a very general classification of some species belonging to the most common families.

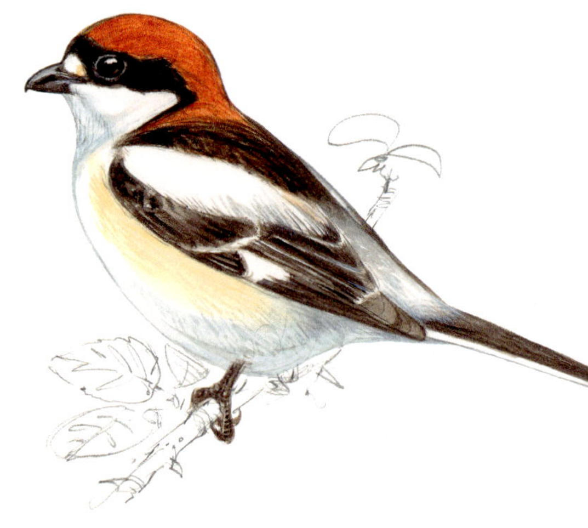

Different Groups, Different Proportions

The common shrike, an example of a small bird.

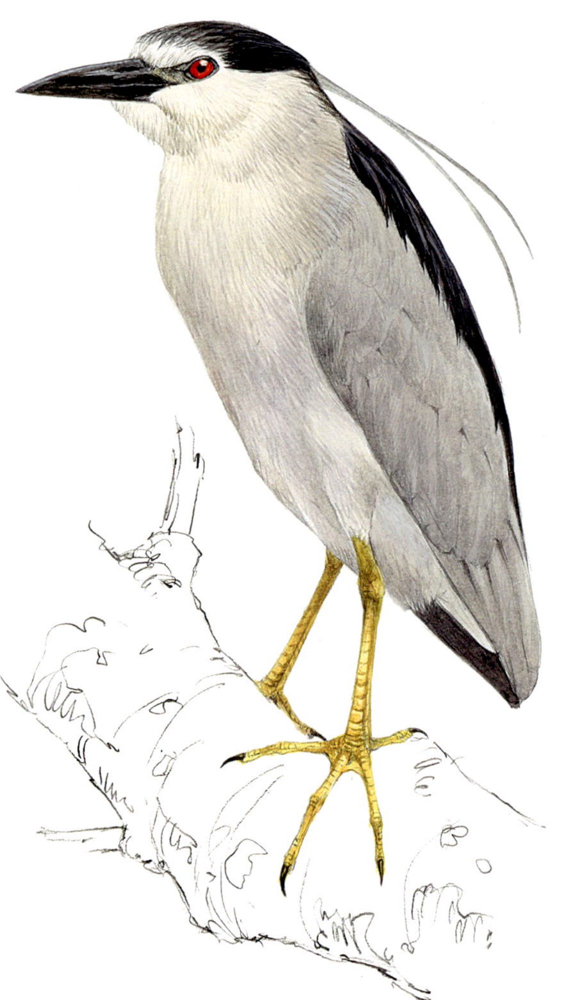

A heron.

THE SMALLEST ONES

The Passeriformes (or passerines), with about 5,700 species, includes most of the small- and medium-size birds, like sparrows, swallows, and crows, as well as hundreds of tropical species with bright coloring. They usually construct very elaborate nests, and many of them have melodic songs.

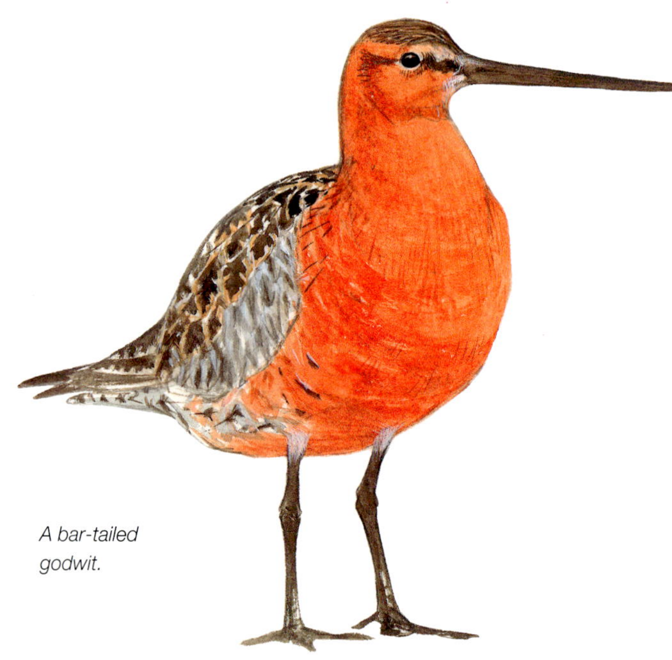

A bar-tailed godwit.

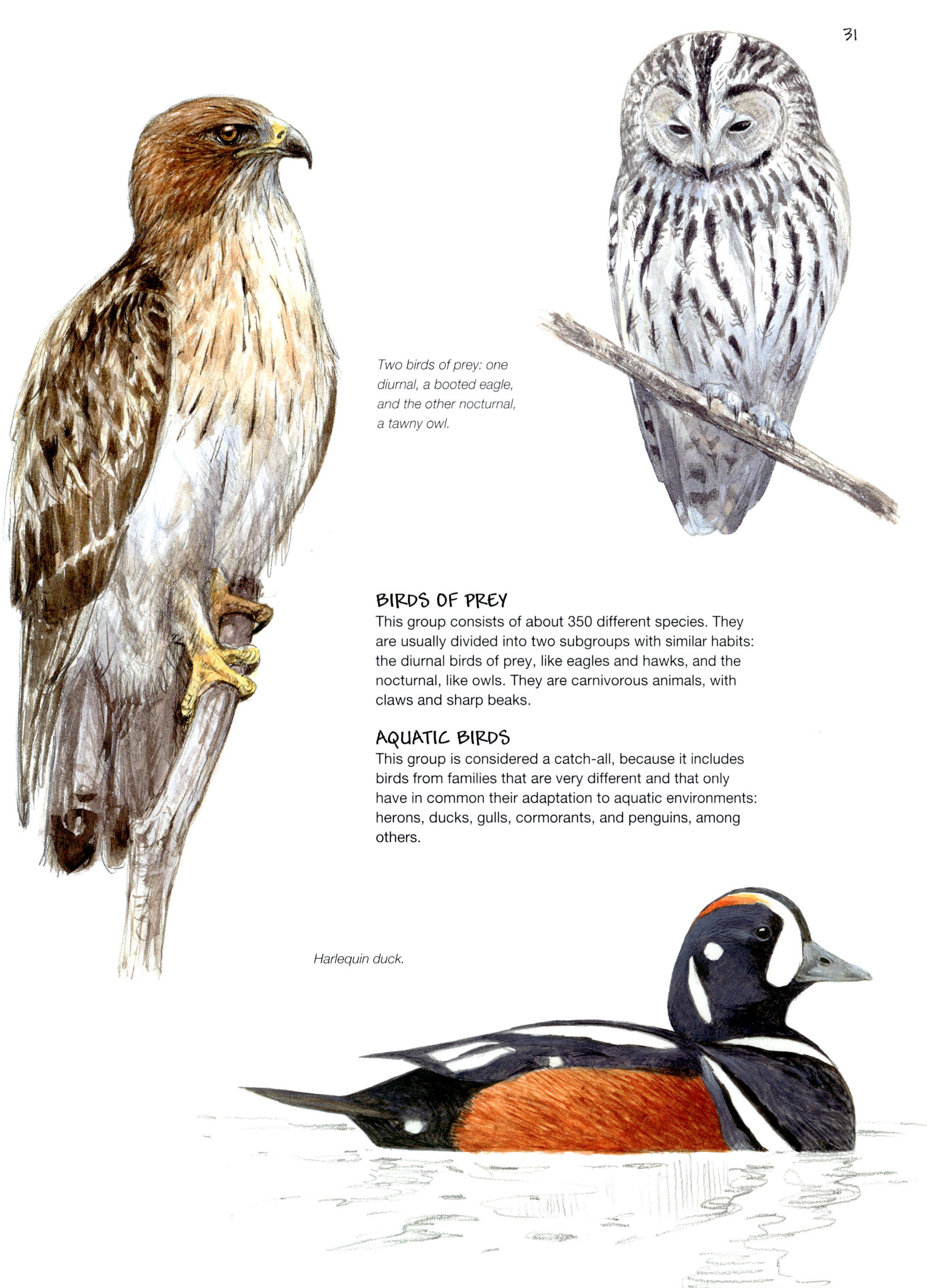

Two birds of prey: one diurnal, a booted eagle, and the other nocturnal, a tawny owl.

BIRDS OF PREY

This group consists of about 350 different species. They are usually divided into two subgroups with similar habits: the diurnal birds of prey, like eagles and hawks, and the nocturnal, like owls. They are carnivorous animals, with claws and sharp beaks.

AQUATIC BIRDS

This group is considered a catch-all, because it includes birds from families that are very different and that only have in common their adaptation to aquatic environments: herons, ducks, gulls, cormorants, and penguins, among others.

Harlequin duck.

Understanding the movements and attitudes of birds is not easy without an idea, even a minimal one, of how they are "constructed." Despite the tremendous variety of forms that nature has created, all birds share a similar internal structure—for example, extremely light bones, fused vertebrae in the back, toothless jaws in the shape of beaks, and upper limbs adapted to flight. Only a few species, among them ostriches and penguins, have lost the ability to fly.

Inside the Bird

THE SKELETON

The bones of birds are extraordinarily light and strong, their interiors made up of a network of fine bony strips similar to those that form the girders of a steel bridge. In flying birds, one of the most striking elements is the sternum in the shape of a keel that anchors the muscles of the breast. All the vertebrae from the base of the neck to the coccyx are fused to support the beating of the wings.

The small bones that form the wing are the same as those of the human arm, but those of the hand have fused, so you can only see three fingers.

The legs also match the pattern of all vertebrates, but the part that you usually see is the portion that, in a human, would correspond to the foot, the tarsus and the fingers, and the tibia. The thigh, the femur, is usually not visible.

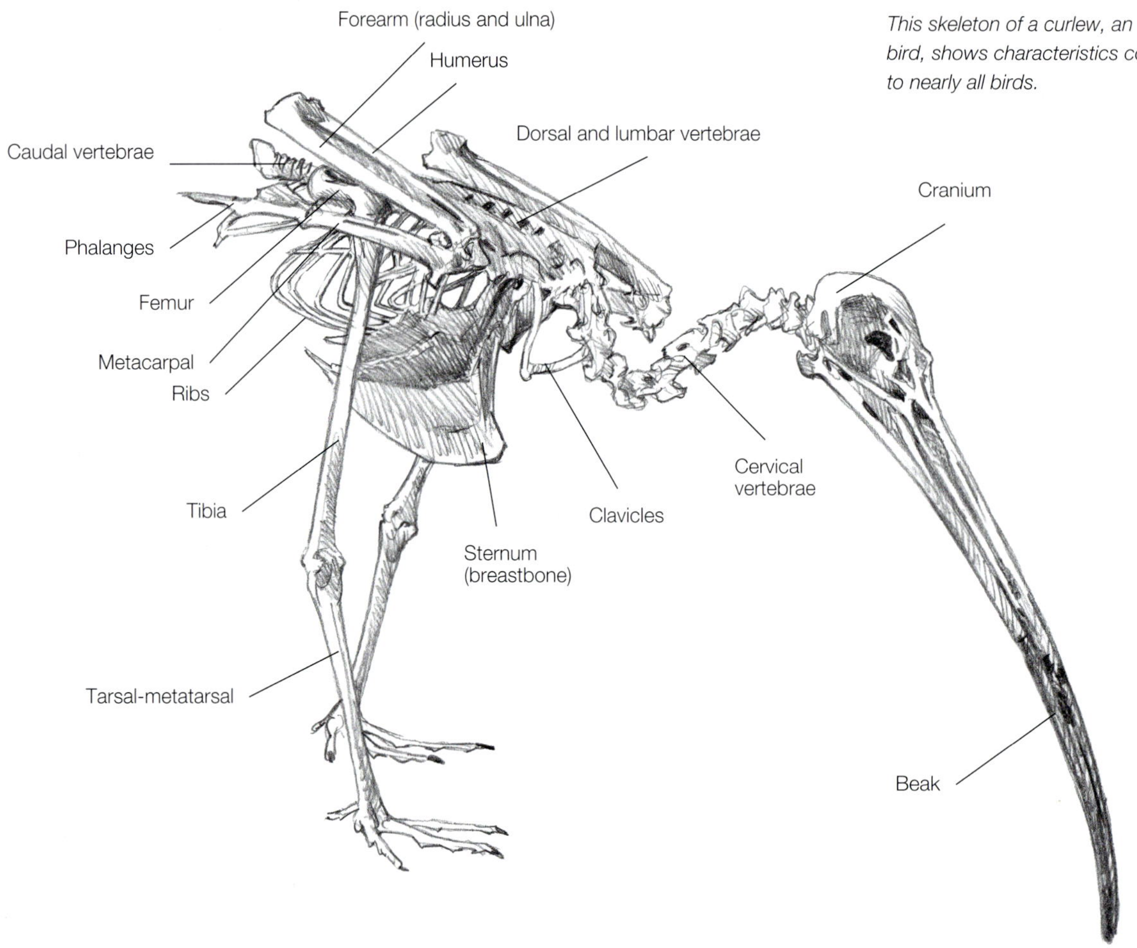

This skeleton of a curlew, an aquatic bird, shows characteristics common to nearly all birds.

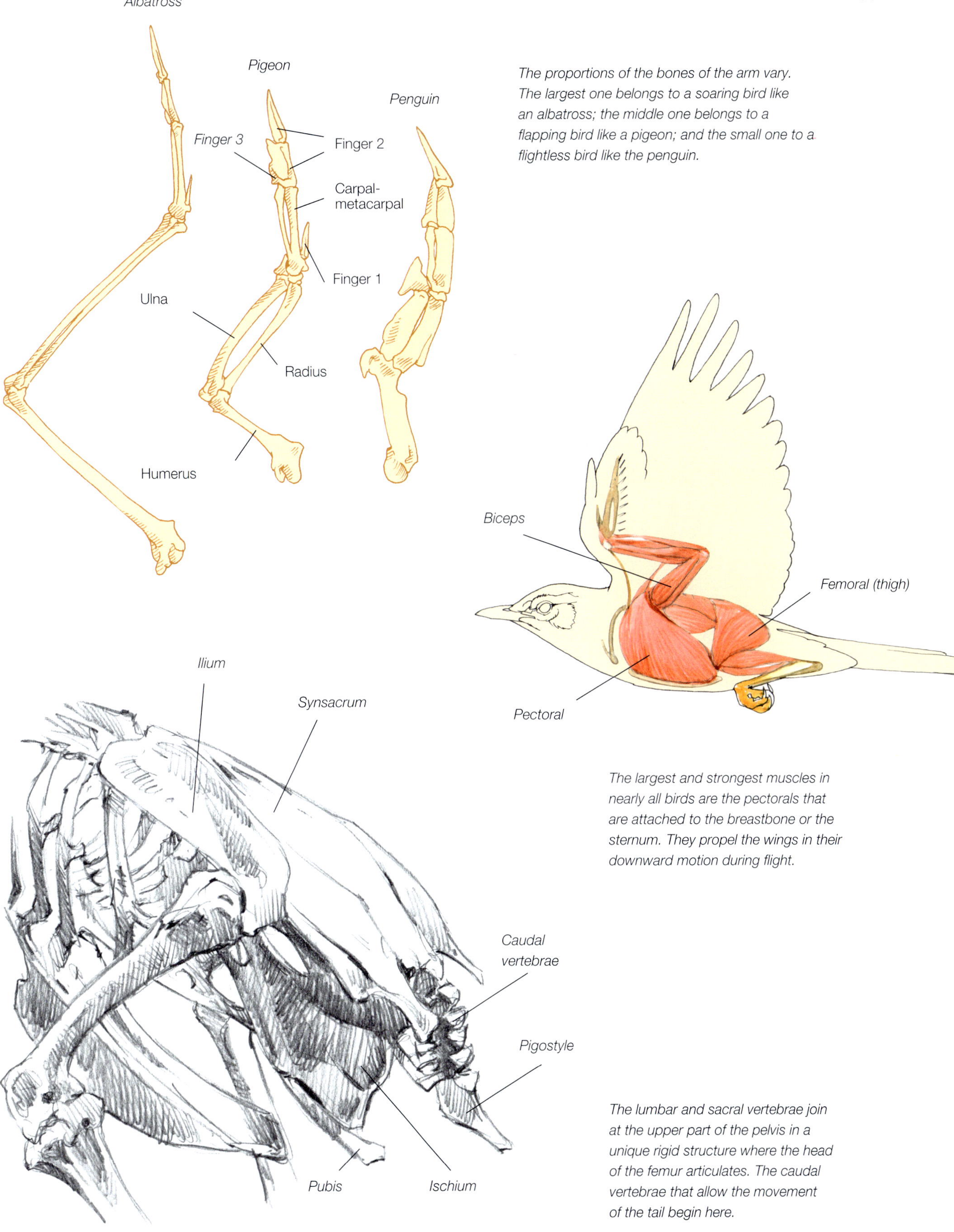

The proportions of the bones of the arm vary. The largest one belongs to a soaring bird like an albatross; the middle one belongs to a flapping bird like a pigeon; and the small one to a flightless bird like the penguin.

The largest and strongest muscles in nearly all birds are the pectorals that are attached to the breastbone or the sternum. They propel the wings in their downward motion during flight.

The lumbar and sacral vertebrae join at the upper part of the pelvis in a unique rigid structure where the head of the femur articulates. The caudal vertebrae that allow the movement of the tail begin here.

The Cranium

The cranium of a bird has quite a simple form that is reminiscent of its ancestors, the dinosaurs. All birds have a keratinized layer of epidermis known as the rhamphotheca that covers the maxillaries and gives the beak its shape and color. This layer, however, is more fragile than the bone; so, when we find the cranium of a bird in the wild, it frequently is not complete because the rhamphotheca will have disappeared. In some birds, like the toucans and hornbills, this structure is much larger than the cranium itself. Cassowaries, Australian flightless birds, have a bony protuberance on their skulls that looks like a wide horn, which is unique among birds. The rhamphotheca can have a pair of orifices that connect the nasal cavities. In many marine birds, these orifices are at the end of a pair of tubes located on top of the beak.

THE SENSES

Based on the size of the ocular cavity, we can deduce that birds greatly depend on their sense of sight, and apart from a few exceptions, little or very little on their sense of smell. Hearing is the second sense in order of importance, although many nocturnal birds rely more on it than on sight. Some aquatic birds have a sensitive organ on the tip of the beak that helps them find animals buried in the mud.

The size of a bird's brain in relation to its body is comparable to that of a monkey. In addition, many studies demonstrate that birds possess a high level of intelligence.

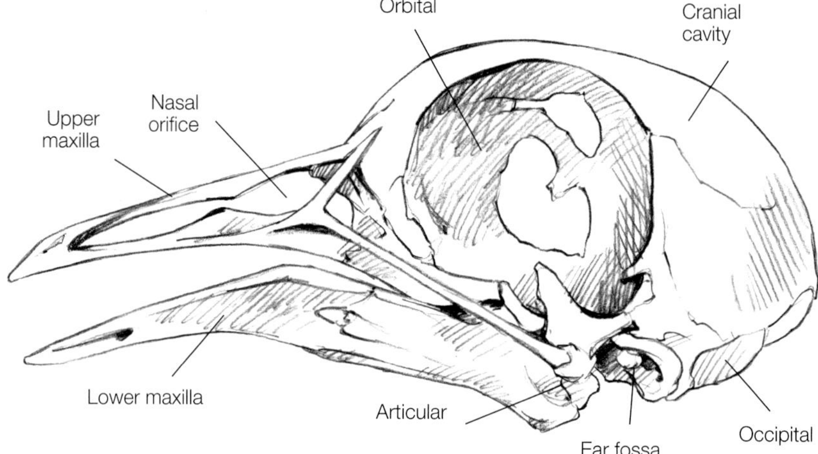

This sketch of the cranium of a dove shows its various bones and their names.

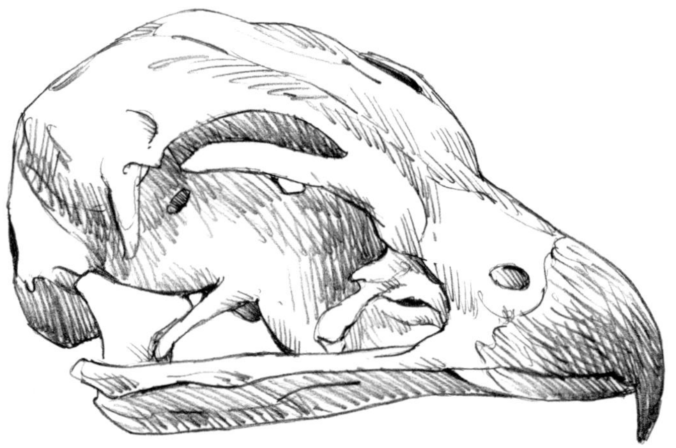

This is the skull of a peregrine falcon. In diurnal birds of prey, you can see the relative size of the strong sharp beak, which is used to catch large animals and tear them into pieces, either to eat or to feed chicks.

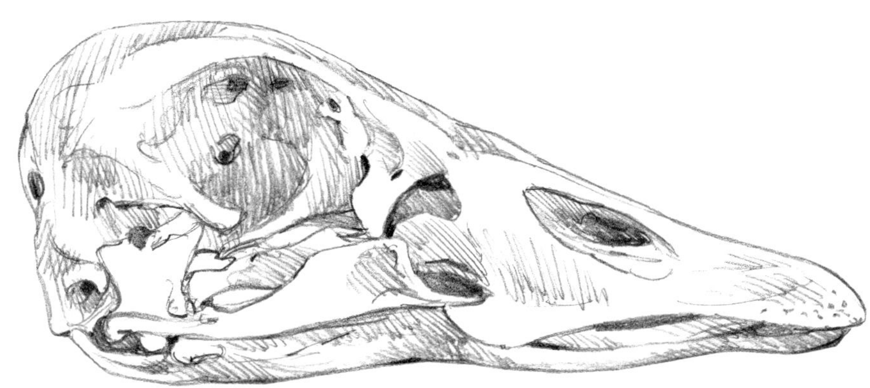

Goose. Ducks and geese usually feed on vegetation, grazing on the banks or diving in lakes and rivers.

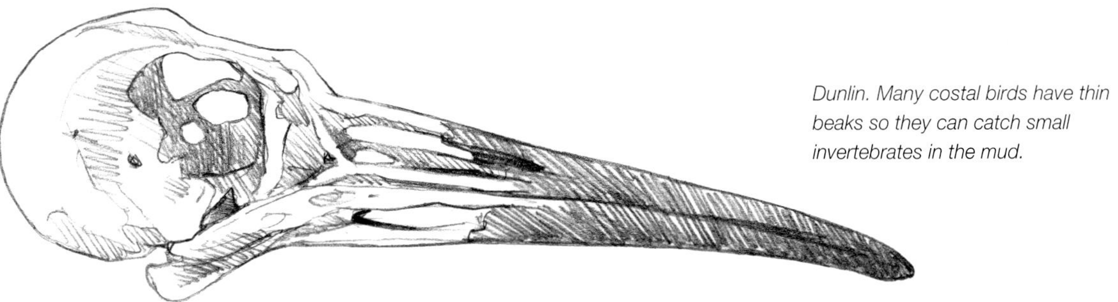

Dunlin. Many costal birds have thin beaks so they can catch small invertebrates in the mud.

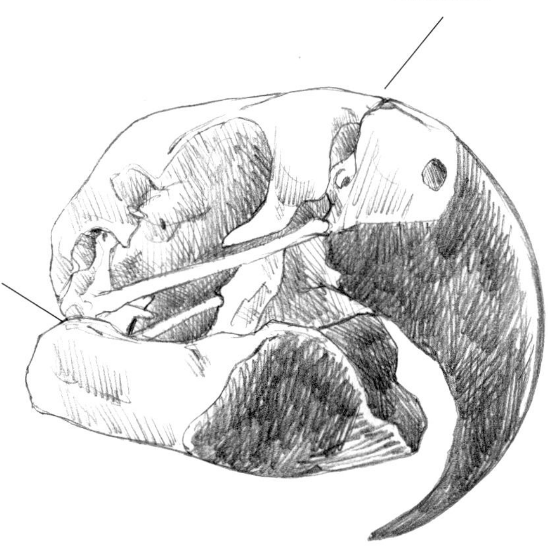

Articulation of the jaw of a guacamayo (Ara sp.). Most species of birds can only articulate their lower jaws. Parrots and a few other species, on the other hand, can raise their upper maxilla, because it is separate from the rest of the skull.

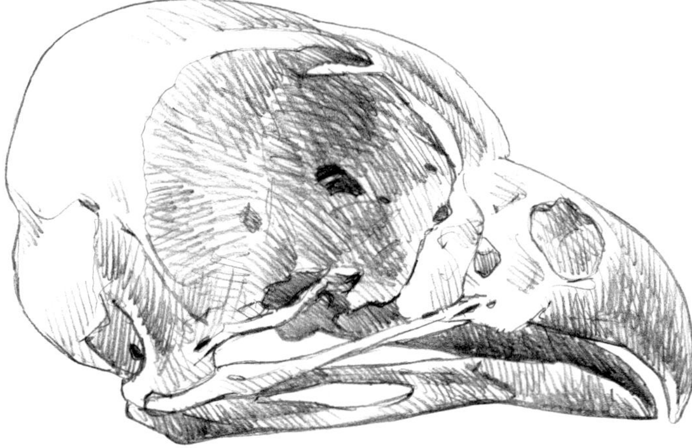

The cranium of this owl shows the large size of its occipital cavity. The beak is short, but it is wide, because an owl swallows many of its small prey whole.

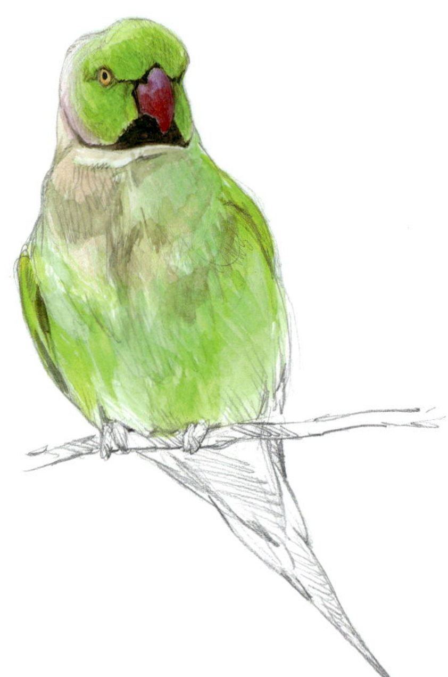

Feathers and Colors
To Protect and Communicate

Nearly the entire body of a bird is covered with feathers, structures that appeared in some species of dinosaurs, like the famous velociraptors that you see in the movies. Some feathers are of small or medium size and serve to keep birds' bodies warm, insulate them from humidity, and give them an aerodynamic shape that helps them fly. These are the contour feathers and the down feathers that are hidden beneath them. Other feathers are stiffer, and they create the planes of the wings and the tail. Finally, other feathers have an ornamental function, for attracting a mate for reproduction. Feathers show the typical colors of each species, which varies with the age and sex of the individual.

JUAN VARELA
TWO EUROPEAN BEE-EATERS (*MEROPS APIASTER*)
WATERCOLOR

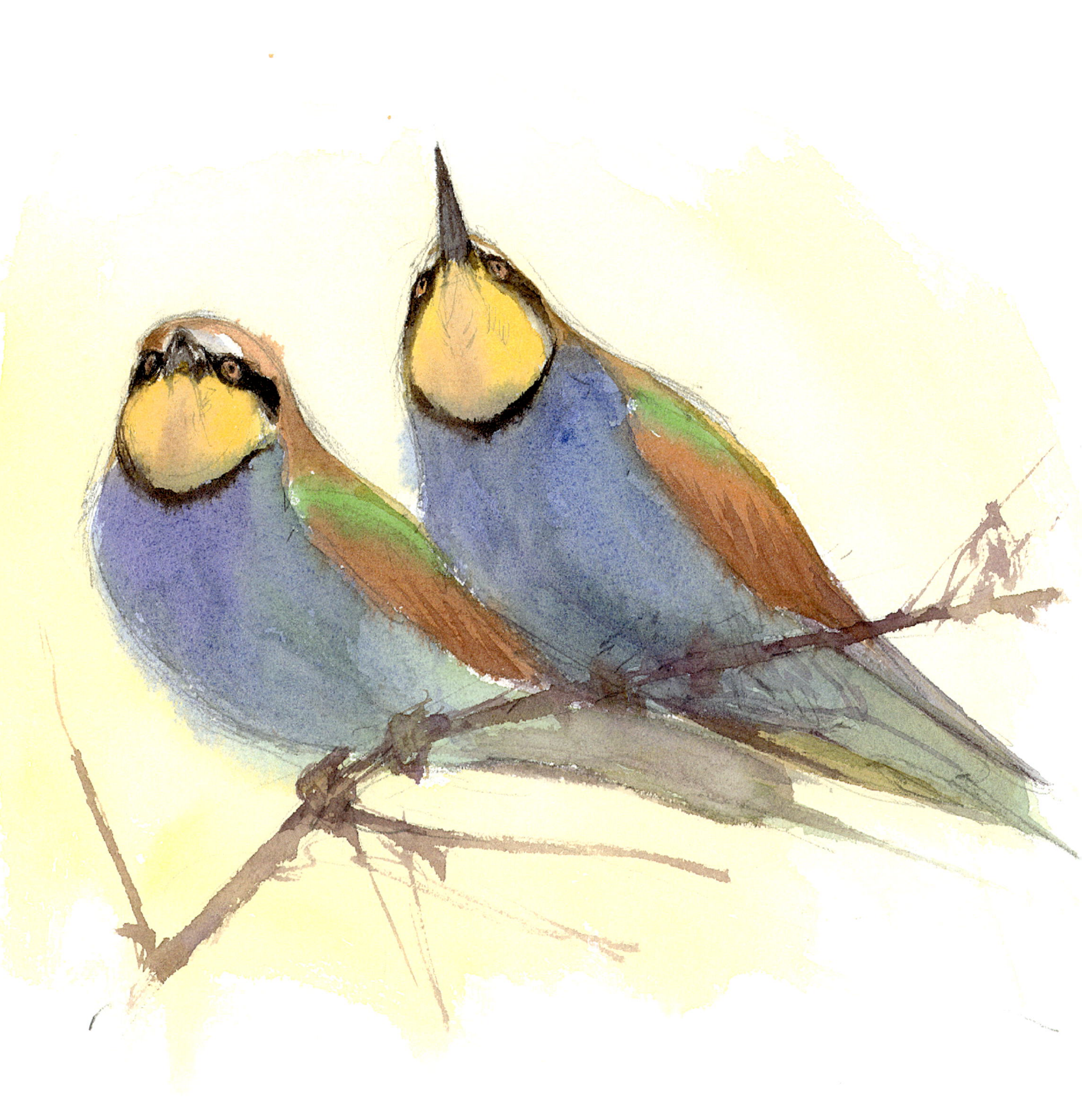

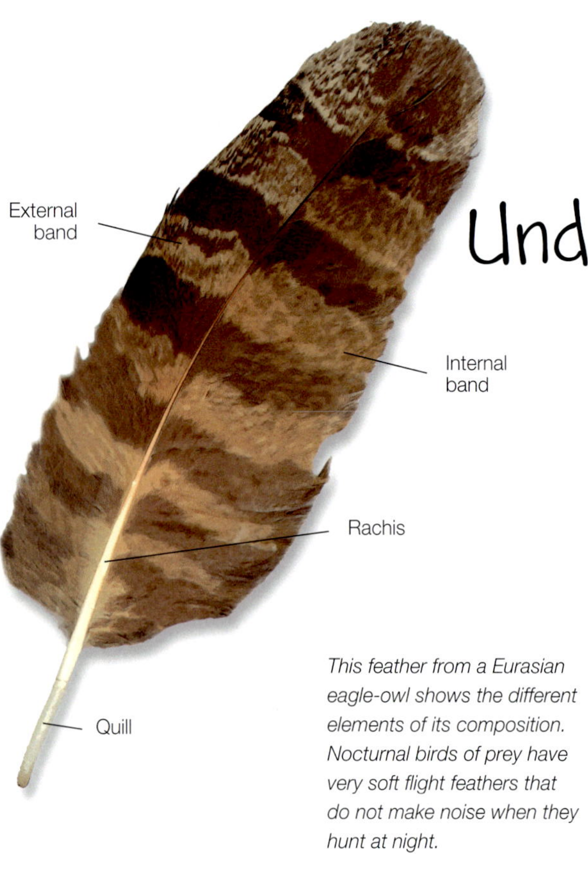

Understanding the Plumage

This feather from a Eurasian eagle-owl shows the different elements of its composition. Nocturnal birds of prey have very soft flight feathers that do not make noise when they hunt at night.

CHANGE OF COSTUME

Although feathers are similar to human hair in origin, they are not structures of continuous growth; therefore, once they reach a certain size, they stop growing. With chafing, they suffer considerable damage, and direct sunlight causes them to fade, so they must be replaced periodically. This process is called molting, and it happens to all birds. The molting period and the sequence in which this takes place varies among the different groups of birds; but, in adult individuals, it can happen once a year, after the mating season, which is the period when feathers deteriorate the most. Migratory birds must keep their flight feathers in good condition, and they molt before starting their migrations to areas where they spend the winter.

Hoopoes are a good example of the use of plumage merely as adornment. The crest can be raised in times of alarm and during courtship. Some of the brighter colors can be good camouflage in the outdoors when the bird is trying to hide itself among tree branches or in shaded areas.

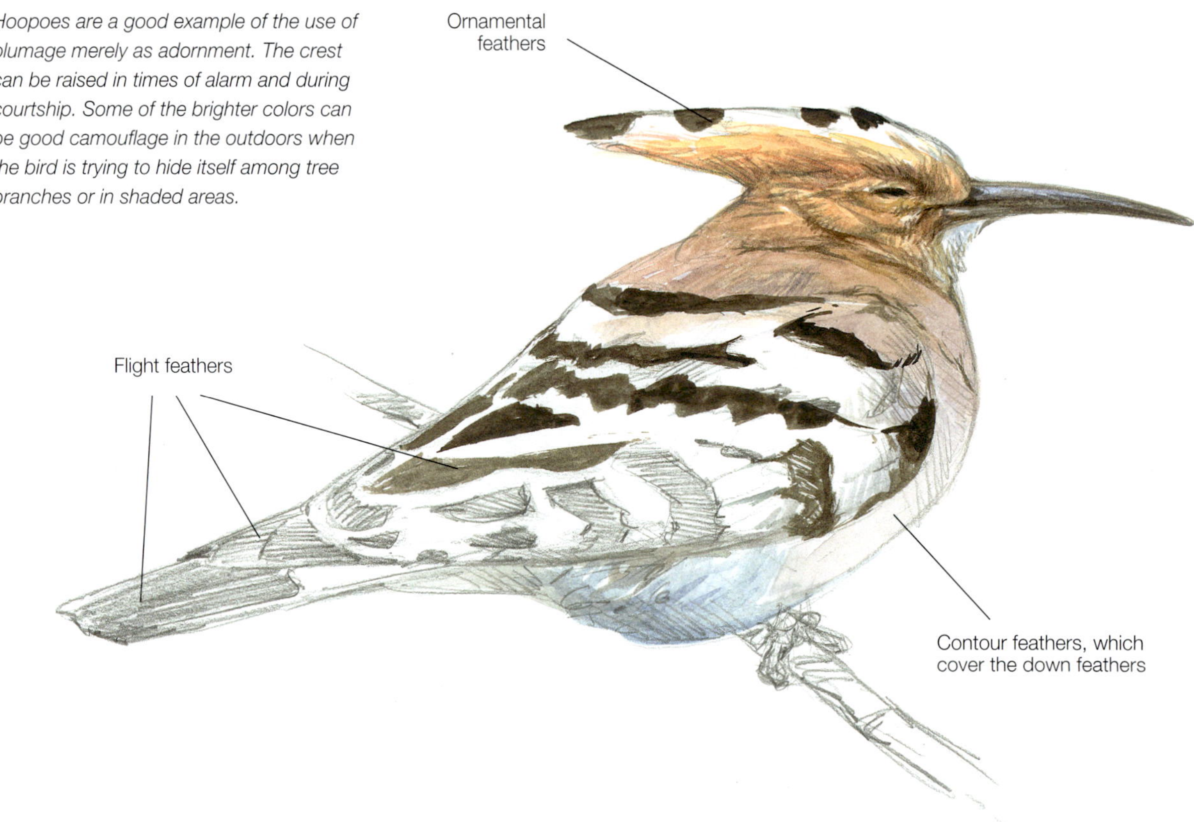

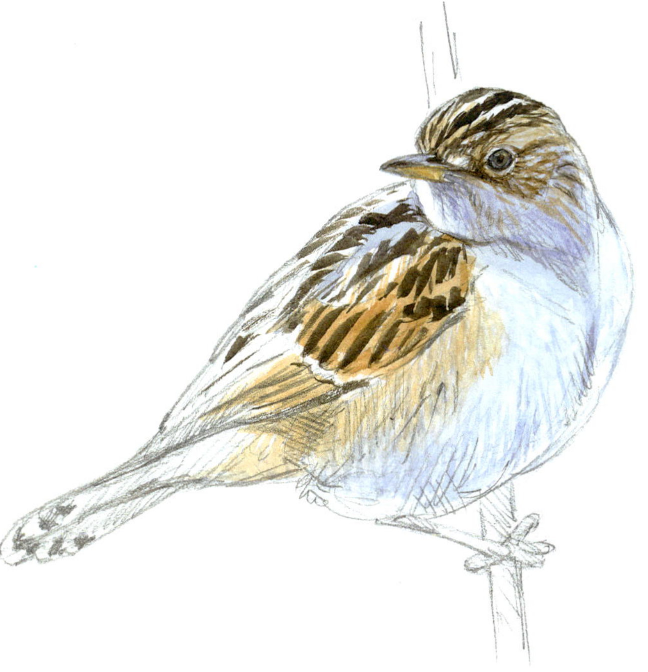

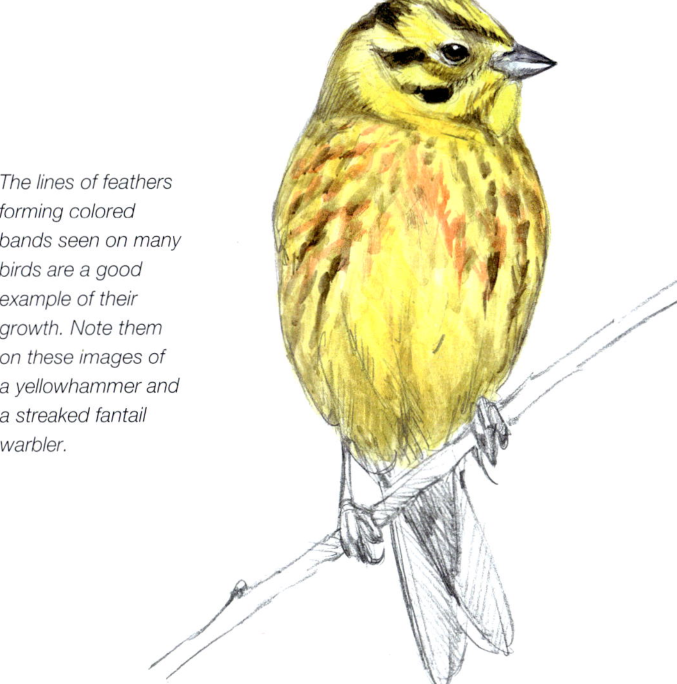

The lines of feathers forming colored bands seen on many birds are a good example of their growth. Note them on these images of a yellowhammer and a streaked fantail warbler.

THE FUNCTION OF COLOR

The coloring of the plumage fulfills many functions. In the first place, the melanin makes feathers more resistant to chafing; this is why nearly all birds have very dark tips on their flight feathers. Other functions include attracting a sexual partner and camouflage. It is possible for an individual bird to look different depending on the time of year and depending on whether it needs to look attractive or to pass unnoticed. In many species, there are also differences in color between the sexes. Finally, the color of the plumage can also be indicative of age, thus making it very clear to a possible mate that an individual is of reproductive age. This is more frequent among birds that live a long time.

Below are the names of different groups of bird feathers. The distribution of the groups of feathers on the birds follows very distinct patterns that can be easily observed on chicks that come out of the egg without feathers. The feathers are arranged following lines along the head, the back, the flanks, the breast, and the belly.

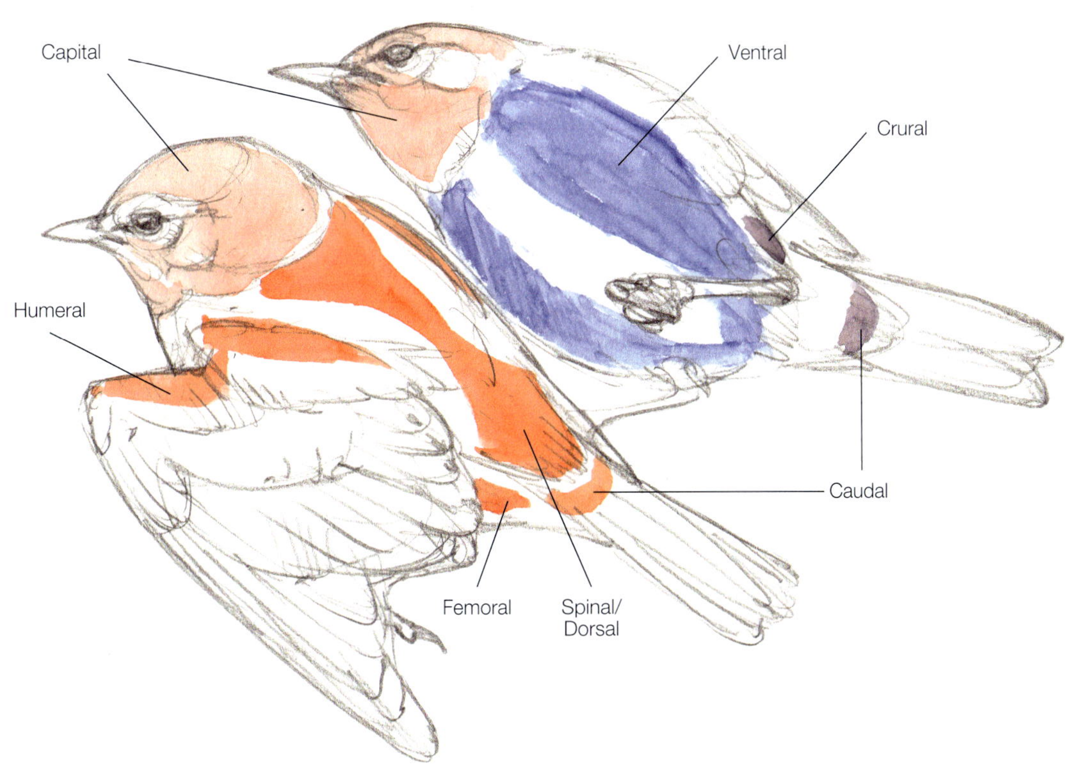

The forward extremities of birds have a very small surface area, as you may have observed if you have seen a plucked chicken. The flight feathers supply the surfaces that will sustain flight, arranged all along the rear edge of the wing. Their shape and size are related to the type of flight of the bird and its adaptation to soaring, maneuvering in small spaces, and beating its wings to sustain flight.

The pallid swift. It flies in open spaces while swerving rapidly.

Oars of Different Shapes

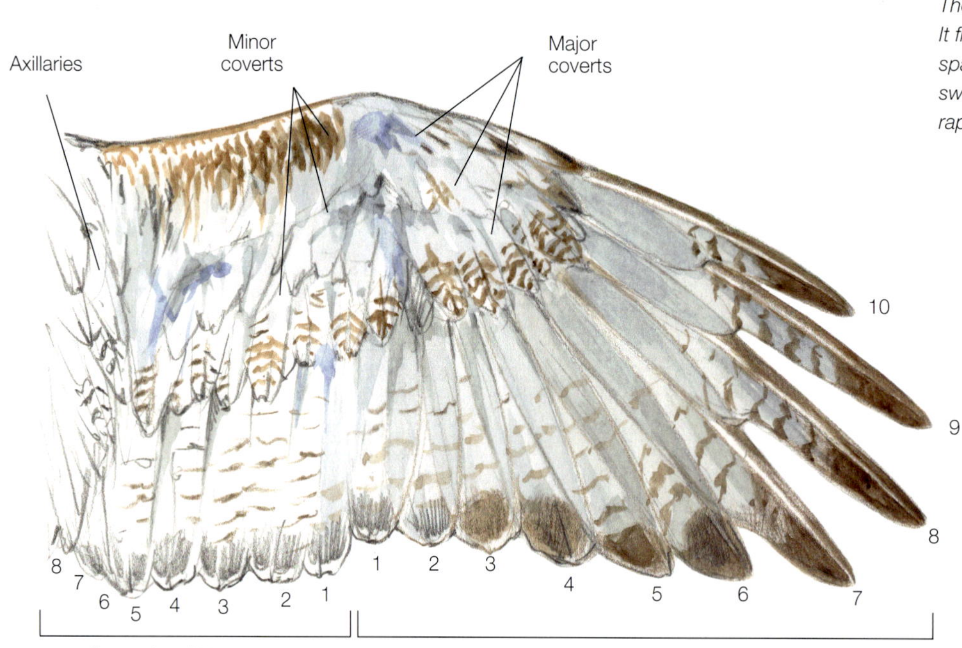

Spread wing showing the feathers it is composed of.

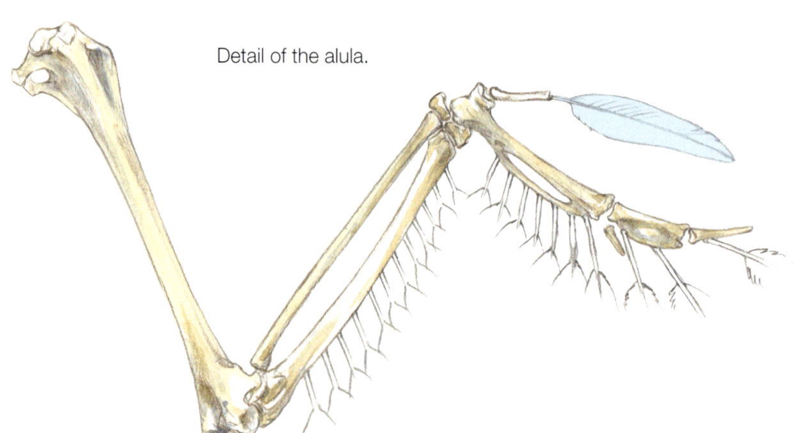

Detail of the alula.

COMPOSITION OF WING FEATHERS

Each wing consists of primary flight feathers and secondary flight feathers, and three layers of coverts, major and minor. Each primary flight feather is numbered as seen in the illustration, which is the order in which they molt in many species. Nearly all birds have ten primary flight feathers, but the number of secondary feathers ranges from 9 in passerines to 26 in swans.

THE ALULA

The alula, or "bastard wing," is a small group of feathers that are implanted in the first finger and fulfill the same function as the flaps on an airplane. When the bird is flying at a slow speed—for example, when it is landing or taking off—they are spread to avoid falling head first.

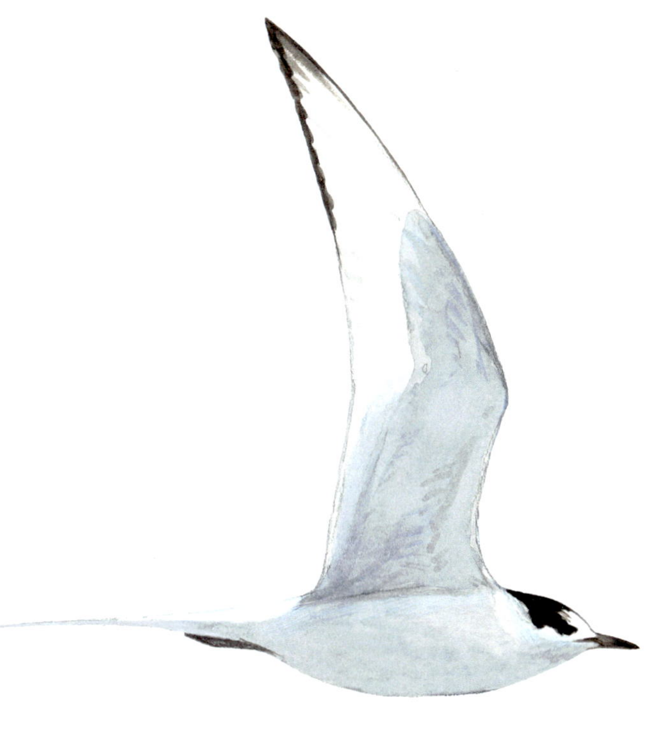

Arctic tern. Long distance migratory bird.

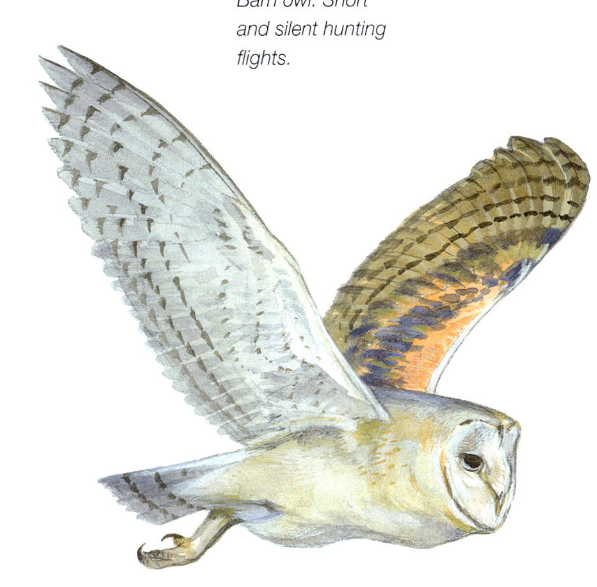

Barn owl. Short and silent hunting flights.

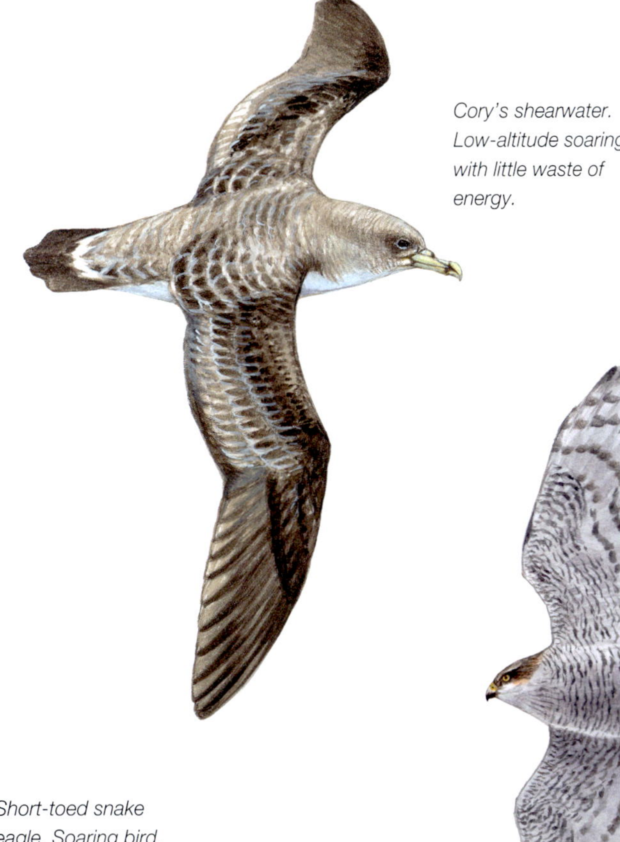

Cory's shearwater. Low-altitude soaring with little waste of energy.

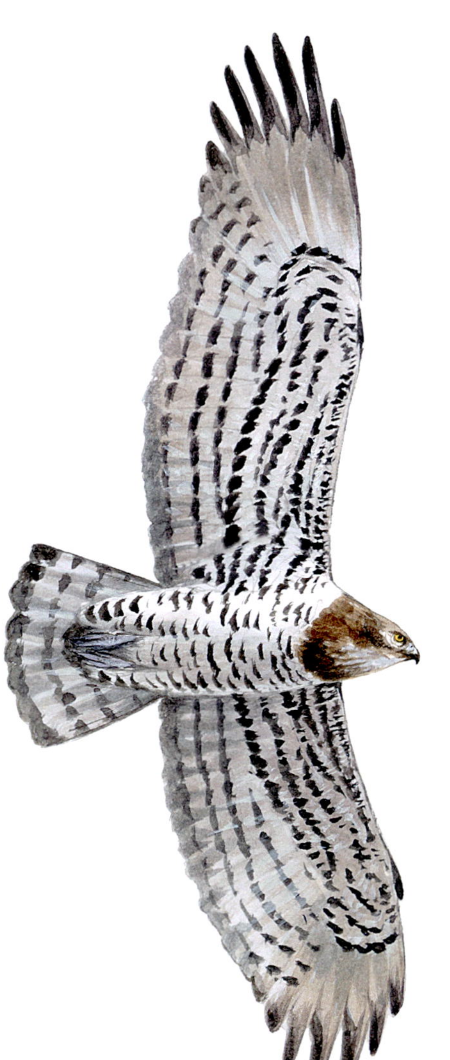

Short-toed snake eagle. Soaring bird.

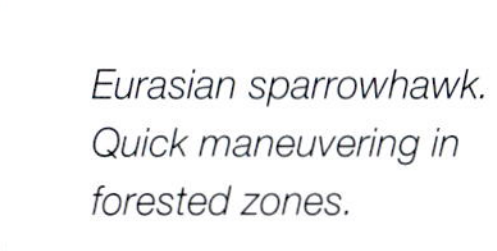

Eurasian sparrowhawk. Quick maneuvering in forested zones.

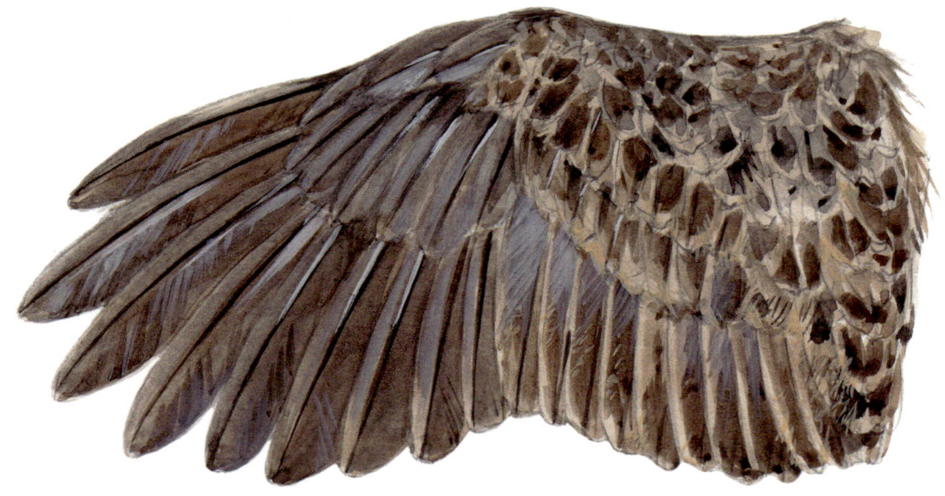

A realistic illustration of a wing shows different groups of feathers arranged in layers that, when folded, completely overlay each other.

FOLDING THE WINGS

Looking at a perching bird, it is difficult to understand the disposition of the feathers that form the wing, and this lack of information can cause you to draw a sort of jumble with no relation at all to reality.

The primary flight feathers fold up in a way similar to a fan, while the secondary feathers fold more like an accordion. The final shape of a folded wing nearly hides the primary feathers, which stick out in a greater or lesser degree depending on the proportions of the wing.

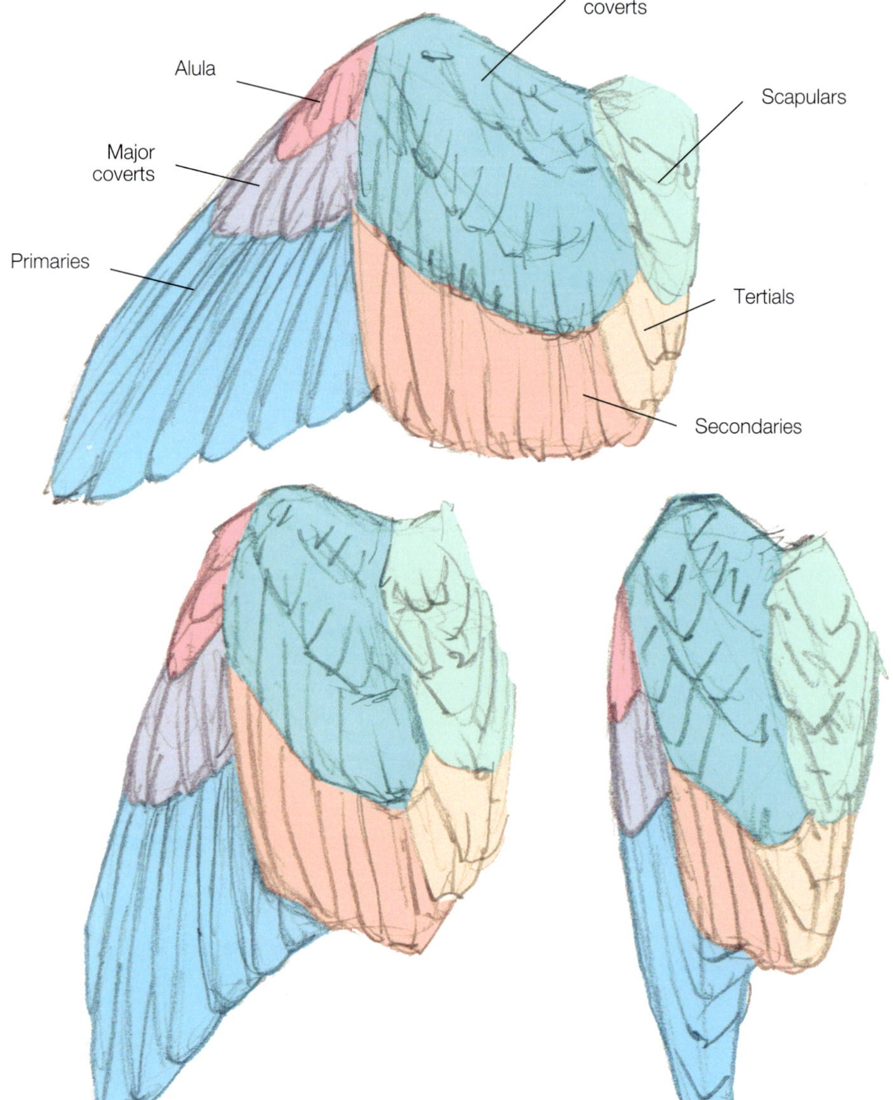

This sequence shows the progressive folding of a wing. Whether it is open or closed, the secondary feathers are parallel to each other. In an open wing, however, the primary feathers converge toward the area of the wrist.

The groups of feathers in the wing are not always easy to individualize on a bird drawn in the field. However, making a mental note of the basic distribution is essential for making quick decisive sketches.

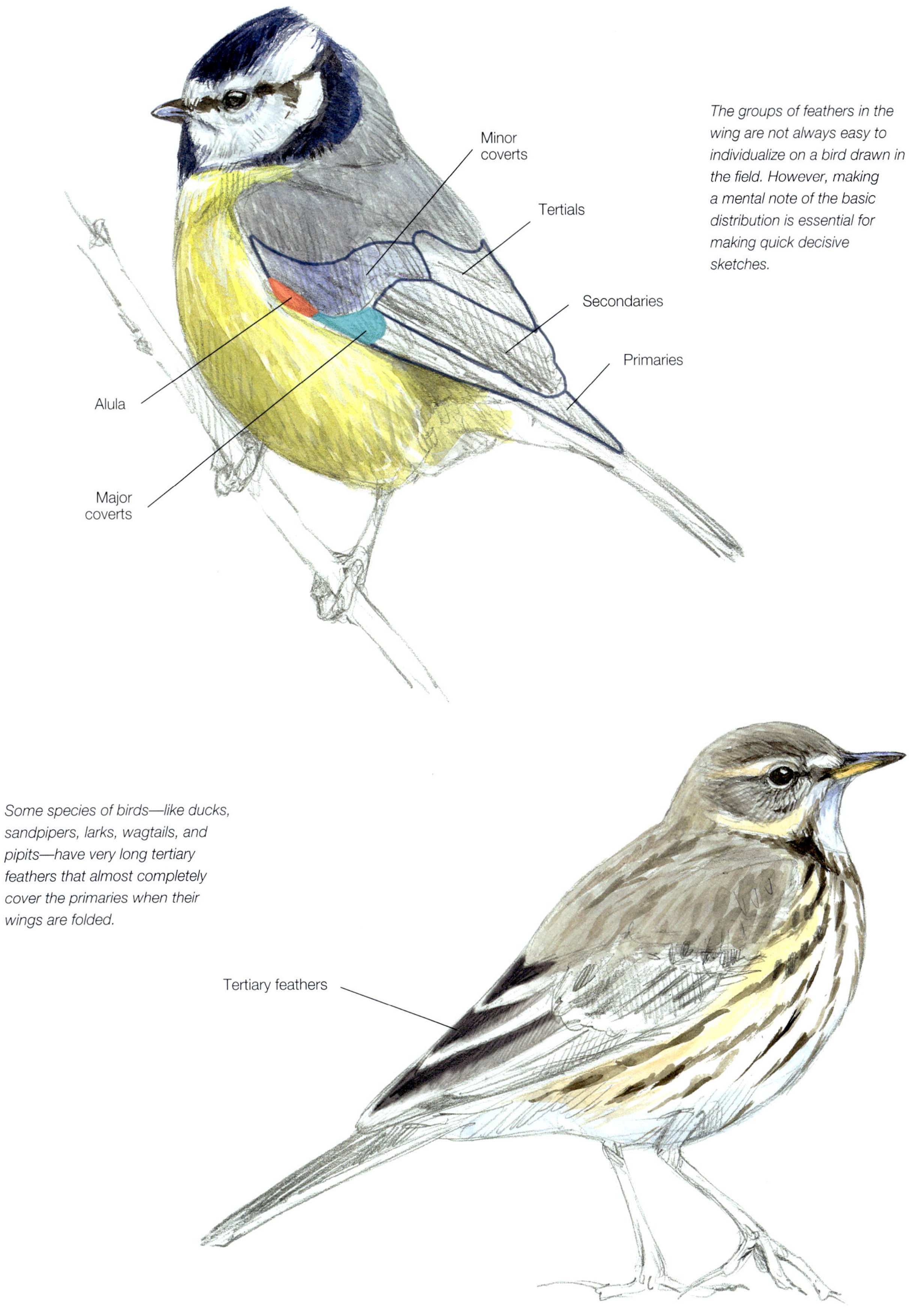

Some species of birds—like ducks, sandpipers, larks, wagtails, and pipits—have very long tertiary feathers that almost completely cover the primaries when their wings are folded.

The long-tailed tit is a small European bird with rounded shapes from which extends a very long tail. Seen from above, you can see that the central feathers lay over the exterior feathers.

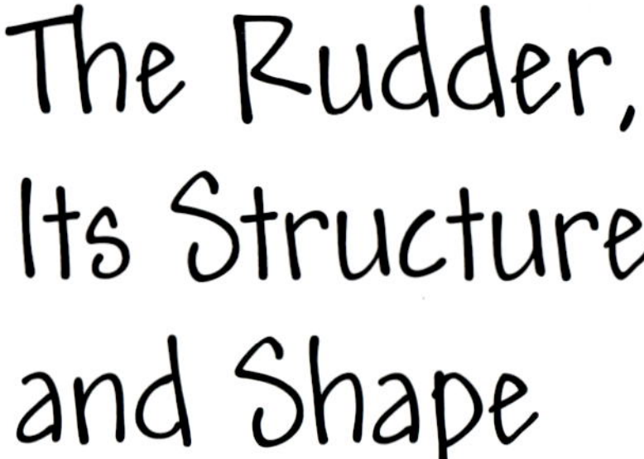

The Rudder, Its Structure and Shape

The tail fulfills the important role of stabilizing element and directional control, maintaining altitude when the bird is flying at slow speeds and during circling maneuvers. Its size has a strict relation to that of the wings and with the usual type of flight. It is long in species that maneuver quickly, like hawks and falcons, which also have wings with small surfaces and run the risk of losing altitude in such maneuvers. Small birds also require an efficient rudder to escape from these hunters. The largest soaring birds—like vultures, storks, and albatrosses—have very short tails in proportion to their wings.

Birds can continue to fly even if they have lost their tails, but at the expense of a great loss of maneuverability.

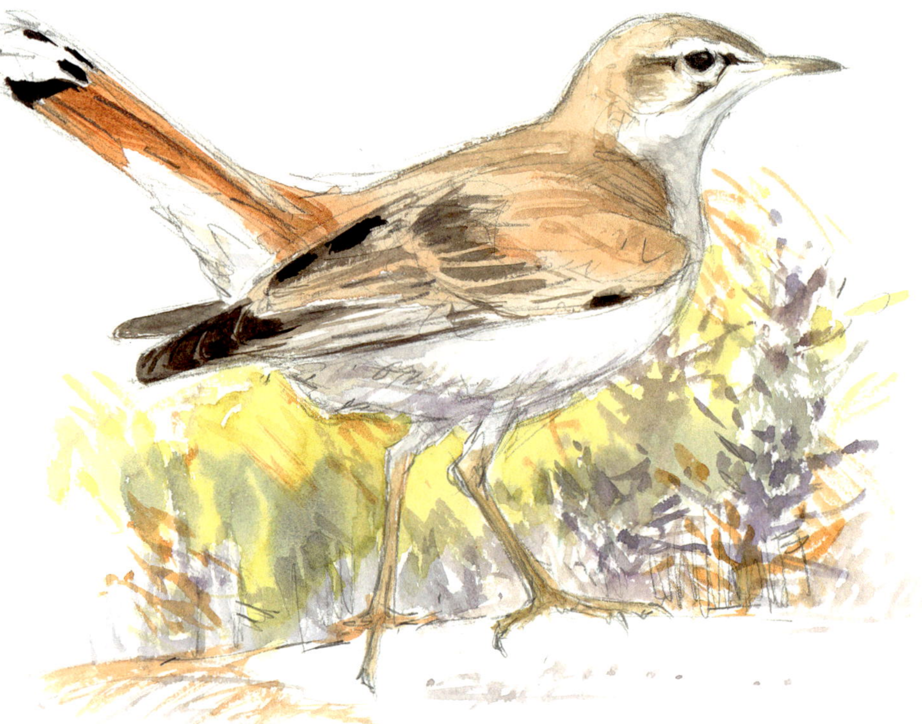

The tail can be used to communicate a bird's mood to its fellows. Sometimes, its coloring is hidden and can only be seen when the bird raises its tail or spreads it to express alarm when there is danger.

THE ARRANGEMENT OF THE FEATHERS

The feathers of the tail, twelve in many species, open in the shape of a fan in a way that the central ones, seen from above, lay over the outside feathers. The shape of the edge depends on the relative lengths of the feathers.

OTHER FUNCTIONS

The tail also fulfills an ornamental function. In male peacocks, roosters, and pheasants, for example, it constitutes such an exaggerated adornment that maintaining it requires a high cost in terms of energy. Its good condition is an indicator to females of the health and good genes of the males, and it is used in many courtship ceremonies. Although not as extreme as peacocks, male jays have longer caudal tails than the females.

Finally, another function of the tail is to serve as a third point of support for some climbing birds, among them woodpeckers and treecreepers.

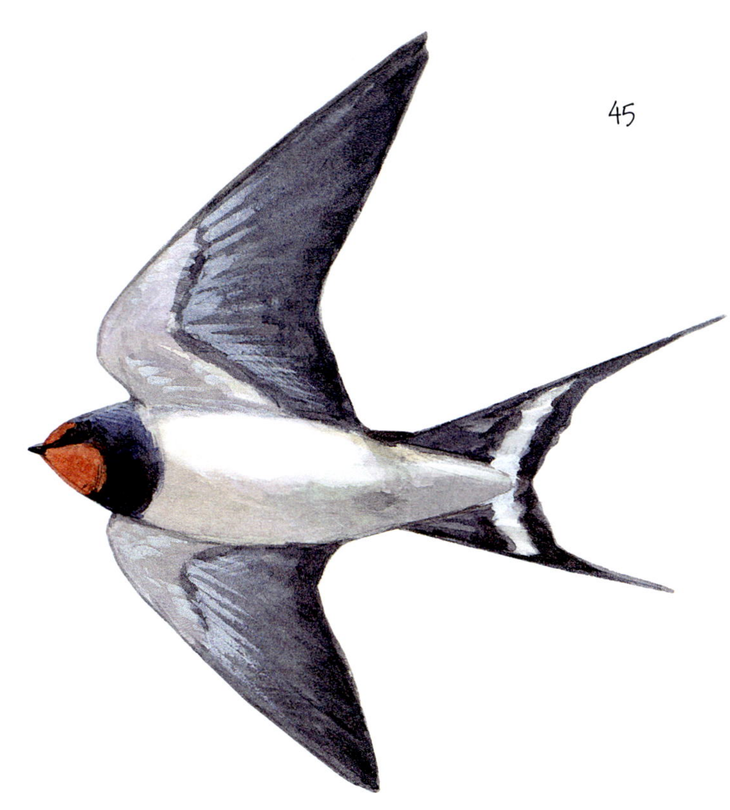

Swallows are usually used as an example of what was previously said, because the tail feathers of the males are longer than those of the females. This does not favor maneuverability in flight, but females prefer males that have this ornament in perfect condition, which keeps this genetic trait in the species.

Pheasants, like roosters, were originally Asiatic birds of the forests and plains, which is why they have handsome colors and adornments that help them find each other in the thickets.

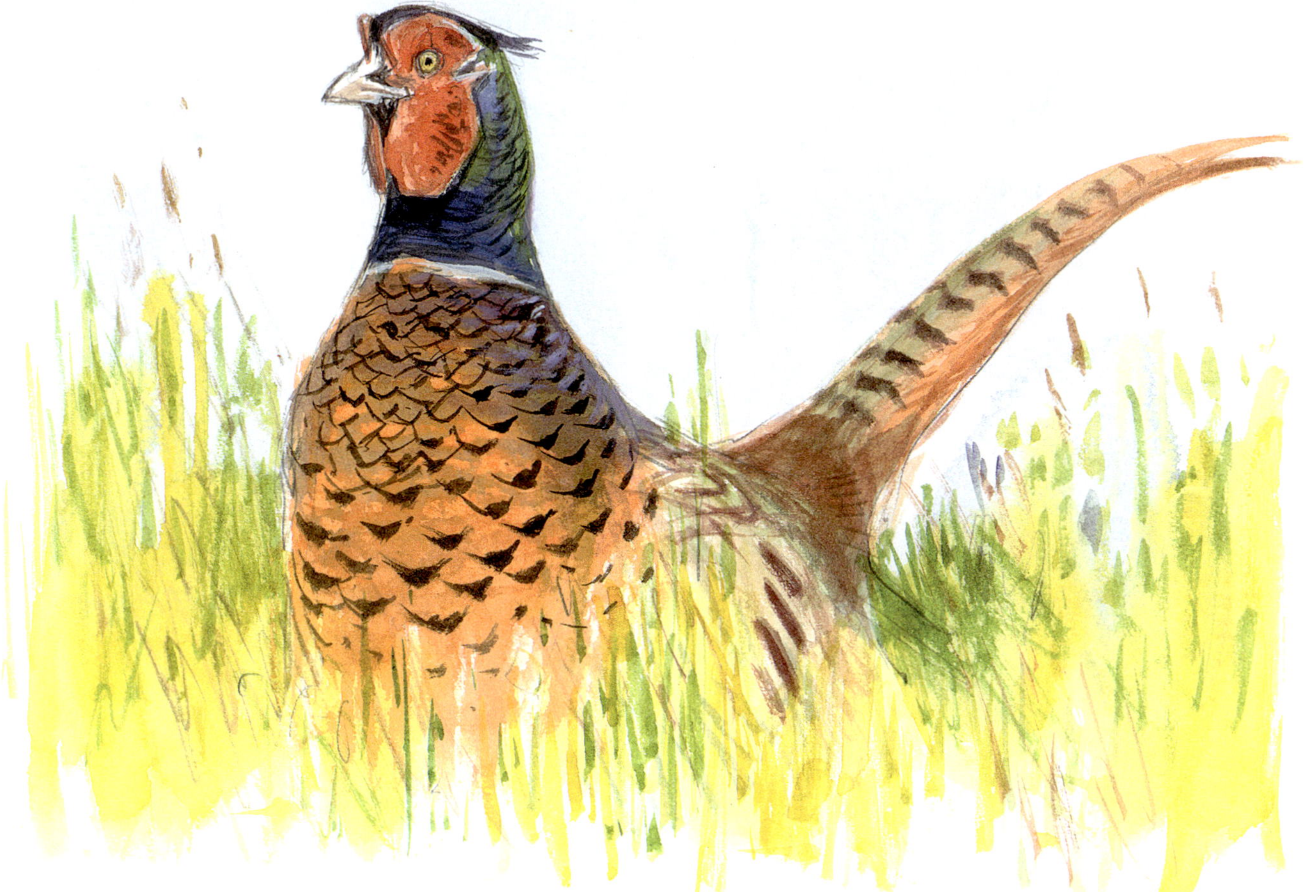

The feathers of the head are distributed in the same way on all species of birds except, of course, on those that have a bare or nearly bare head, like some species of vultures and galliformes (e.g., turkeys, grouses, and chickens). These species usually have brightly colored skin and even fleshy combs.

Other attractive adornments are large beaks, sometimes very large, of the hornbills, birds of the same family as the small kingfishers.

The feathers on the head are often small or look like small hairs, like those in front of or around the eyes.

Decoration on the Head

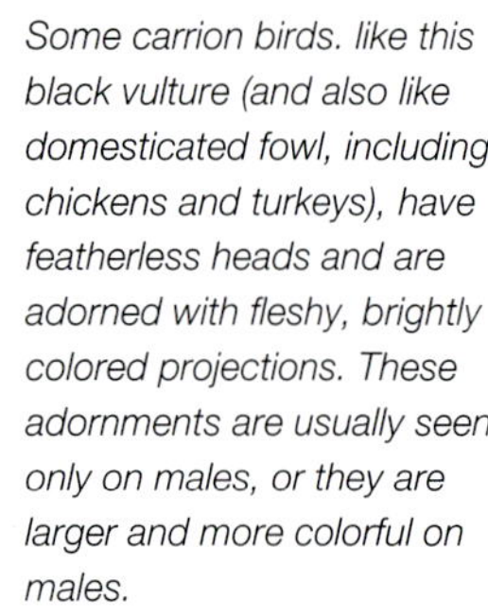

Some carrion birds. like this black vulture (and also like domesticated fowl, including chickens and turkeys), have featherless heads and are adorned with fleshy, brightly colored projections. These adornments are usually seen only on males, or they are larger and more colorful on males.

Recognizing the shapes of the different groups of feathers can be very helpful when you want to make a quick sketch of the head of a bird, whether in the field or in the studio.

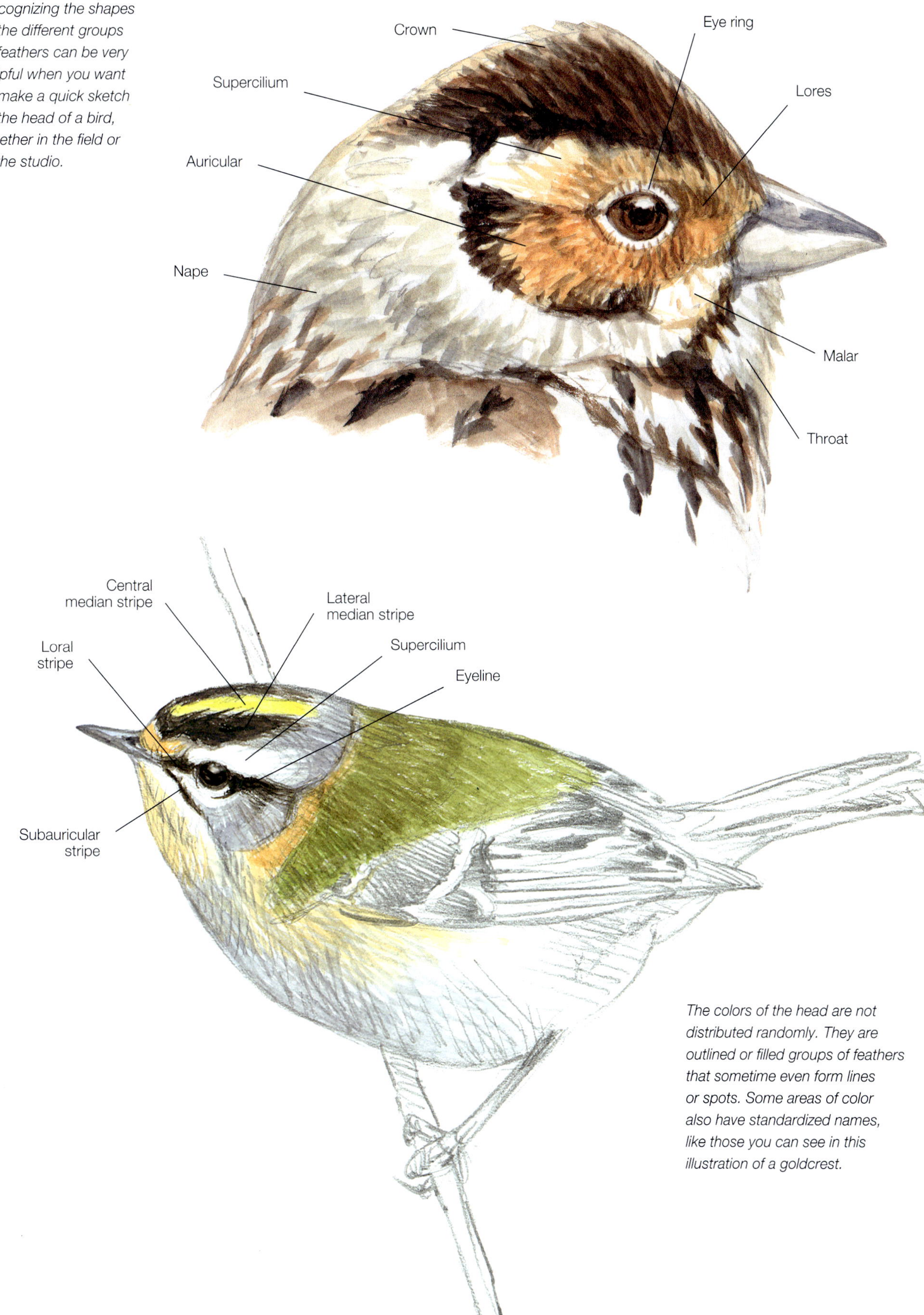

The colors of the head are not distributed randomly. They are outlined or filled groups of feathers that sometime even form lines or spots. Some areas of color also have standardized names, like those you can see in this illustration of a goldcrest.

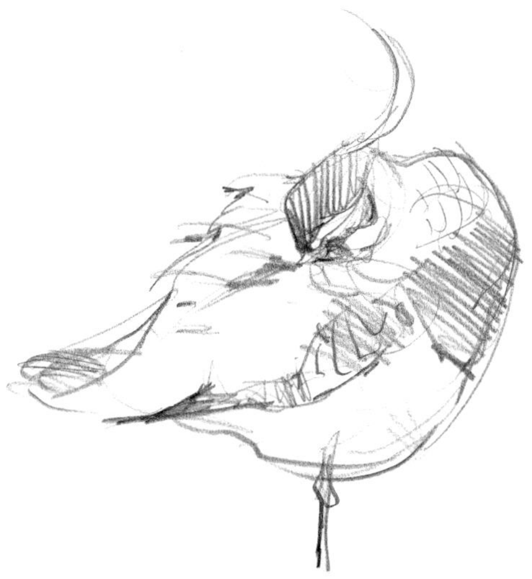

The Bird Moves
Observing Its Conduct

Drawing birds in movement is much easier if, after you have learned the basic details of their anatomy, you pay attention to their most habitual stances and the way in which they move. Among the wide variety of birds that includes such a large number of families, it is possible to recognize very similar habits—for example, those related to cleanliness. The greatest diversity is seen in courtship rituals.

Their conduct in the air and on land is so characteristic of a species that it is almost possible to identify birds, even in situations of poor light. The way they pose, walk, flap their wings, and the collection of typical stances of a species is what English-speaking ornithologists call "jizz."

JUAN VARELA
SKETCHES OF EGRETS (*GARZETTA GARZETTA*)
WATERCOLOR, 8.5 x 12 INCHES (22 x 30 CM)

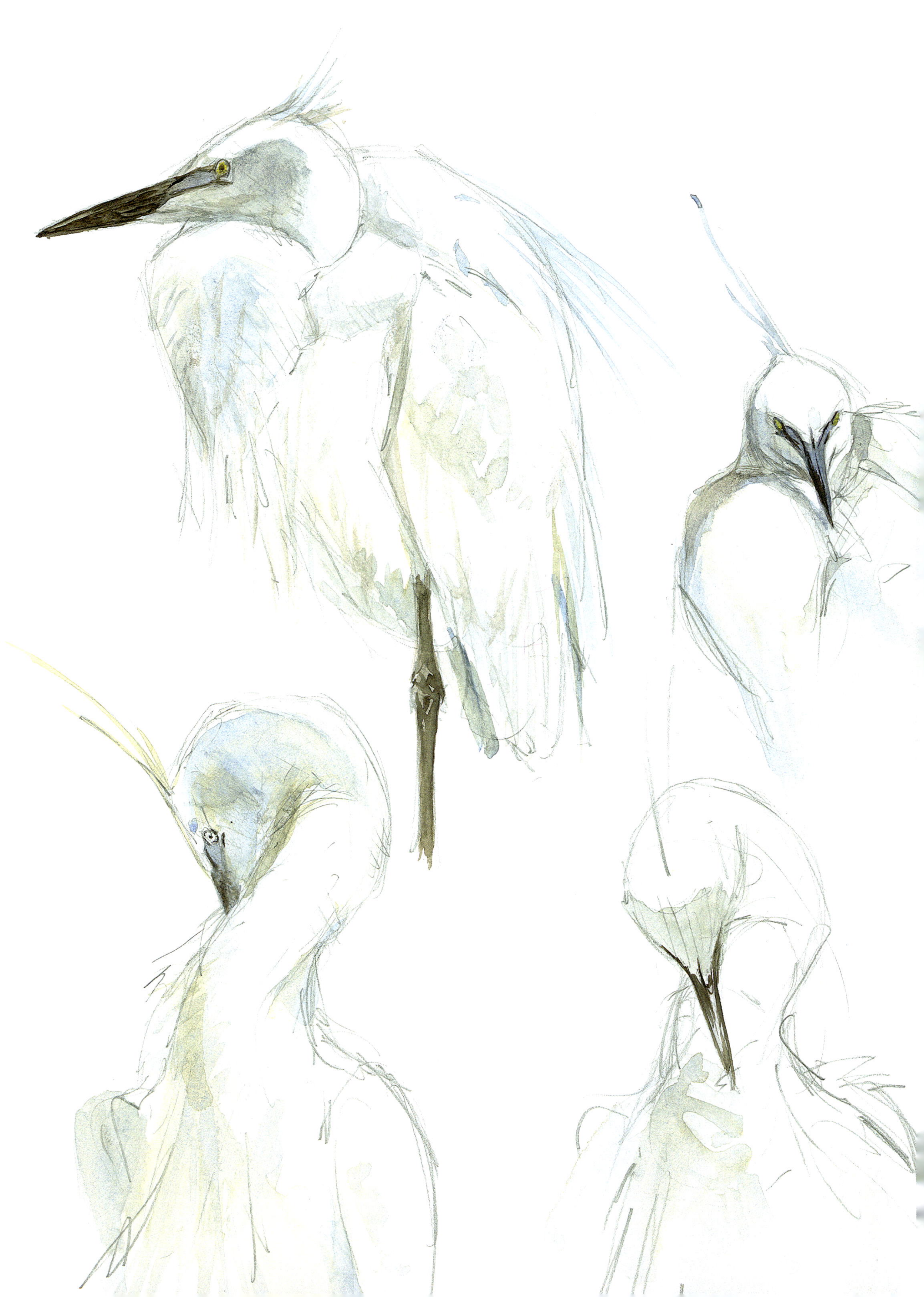

Resting

Most passerines sleep perched on a branch with their heads resting on their breasts or on one "shoulder." A large number of species, especially those with long necks—like the storks, herons, and ducks—sleep with their heads facing backward, resting on their backs, often half hidden among the feathers. Birds do not sleep very soundly; sometimes, they even rest with their eyes open or half open. They are able to relax just one side of the brain while the other stays alert. The ability to control this resting mechanism is exclusive to birds. Some, like swifts, can sleep during flight while using this system.

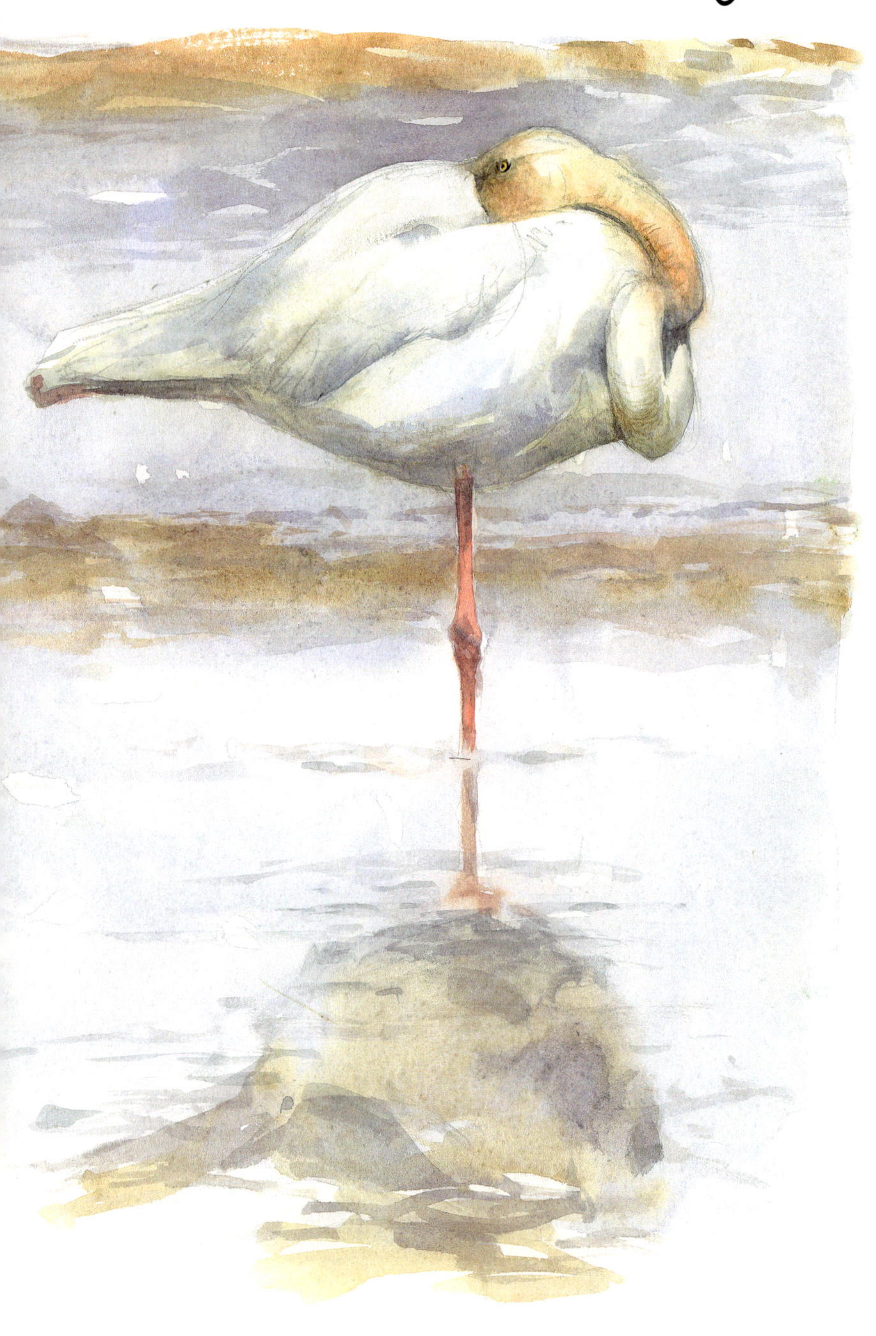

This study of a flamingo in the field shows the challenges of drawing this species at rest. Making sketches of it when it is active helps you to better understand its movements. Notice how the raised leg sticks out behind the tail. Many long-legged birds maintain their balance on one leg when they are resting, alternating every once in a while.

This greenfinch is perching on a branch. Smaller birds usually sleep in groups.

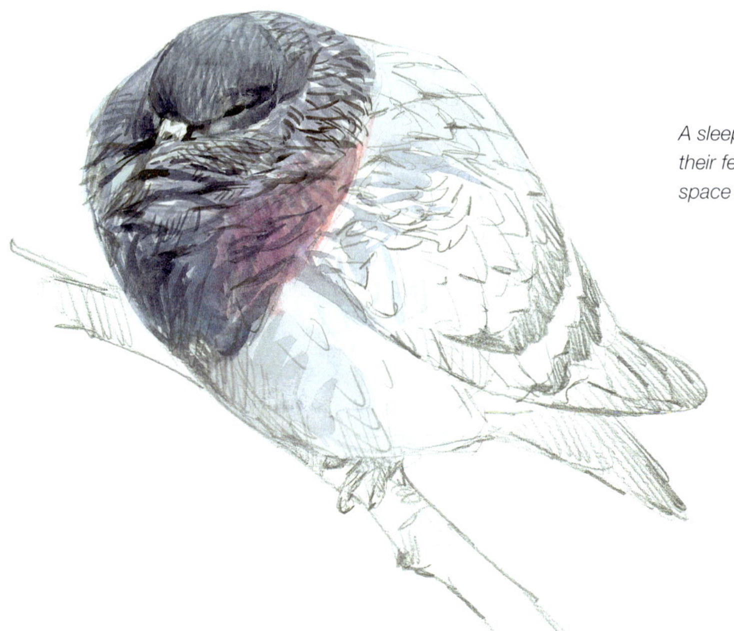

A sleeping pigeon. Generally speaking, birds usually fluff their feathers when they sleep to create an insulating air space that discourages the loss of heat.

A common pochard taking a nap. Diurnal birds can doze off at various times of day, not just at night.

PROTECTING SLEEP

When birds sleep, they look for perches where they will be safe from predators. In the winter, they can form roosts in trees where hundreds sometimes gather. Duck, seagulls, and long-legged birds can doze on the water or hidden in the brush. When grouped, they better maintain their heat, and they are protected from possible attacks by predators.

There are interesting cases, like that of a species of swift, which gathers in the hundreds to rest inside enormous empty tree trunks.

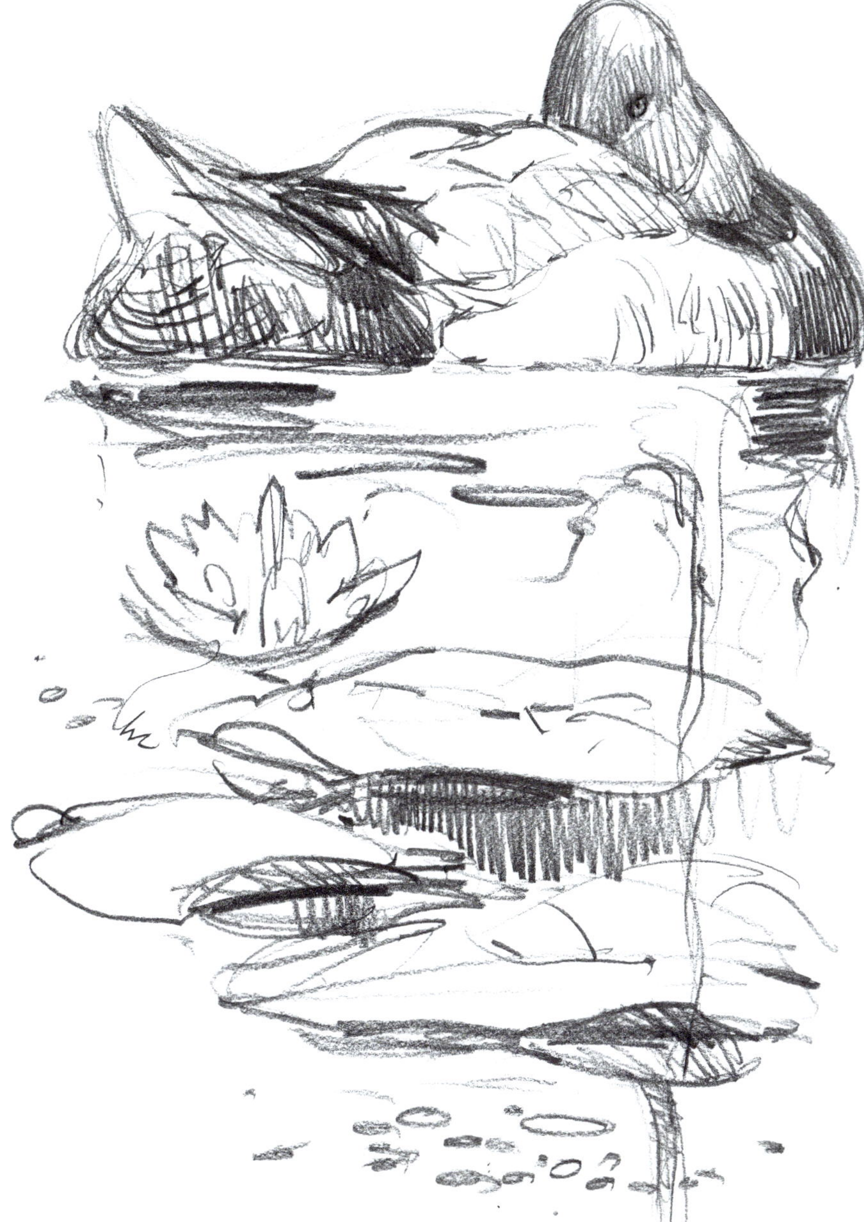

Diet

The need to acquire food is the origin of many adaptations in conduct and anatomy. Food sources that are available to birds are tremendously varied: grass, seeds, insects, and all types of food of animal origin, including carrion. Carnivorous birds need strong beaks and claws to hold, kill, and cut their prey into pieces, and their tools and the way they capture their prey vary depending on their size and species. Their hunting techniques are varied as well—from stalking to pursuing, there is a whole range of possibilities.

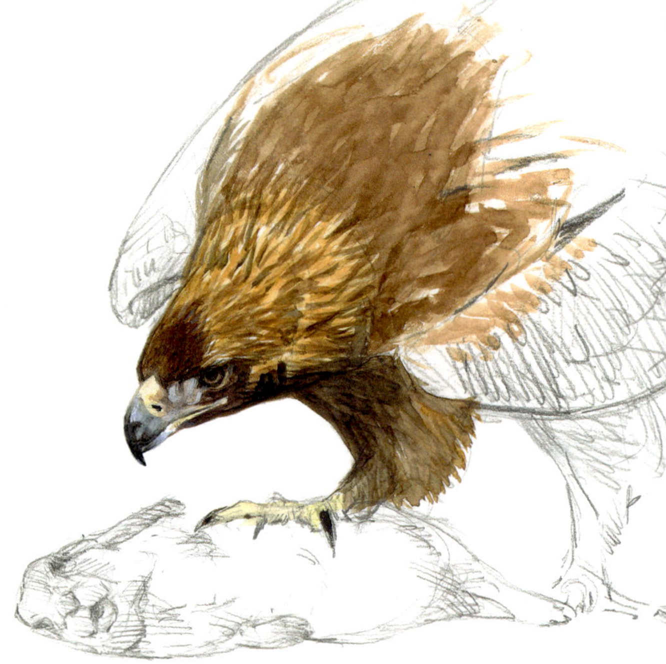

This golden eagle is a species of predator with a strong beak and sharp claws.

VEGETARIANS

The gathering of vegetable nourishment also leads to an enormous variety of systems and organs, because grazing is not the same as eating berries from a tree. Many species can change their diets depending on seasonal availability; some go from eating insects to pecking at autumnal fruits when the former become scarce. Just a few examples will be enough to give you an idea of the wide range of differences.

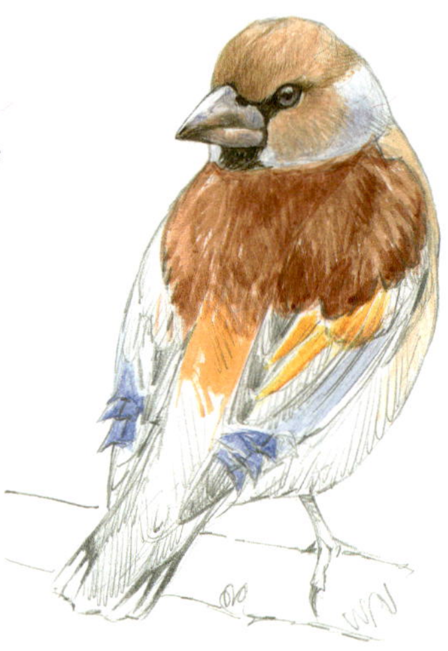

The hawfinch eats seeds, some of them with shells as hard as the pit of a cherry.

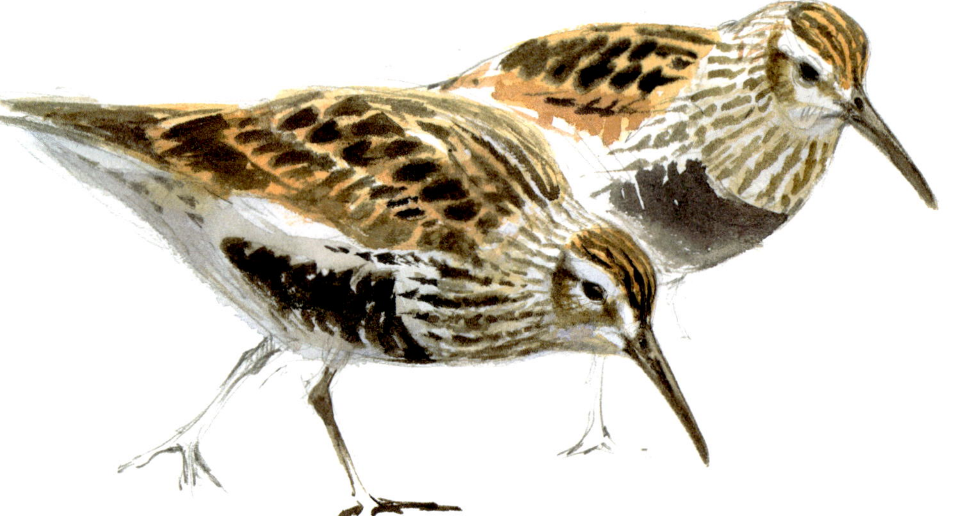

The dunlin pecks in the mud with its long beak to catch small mollusks.

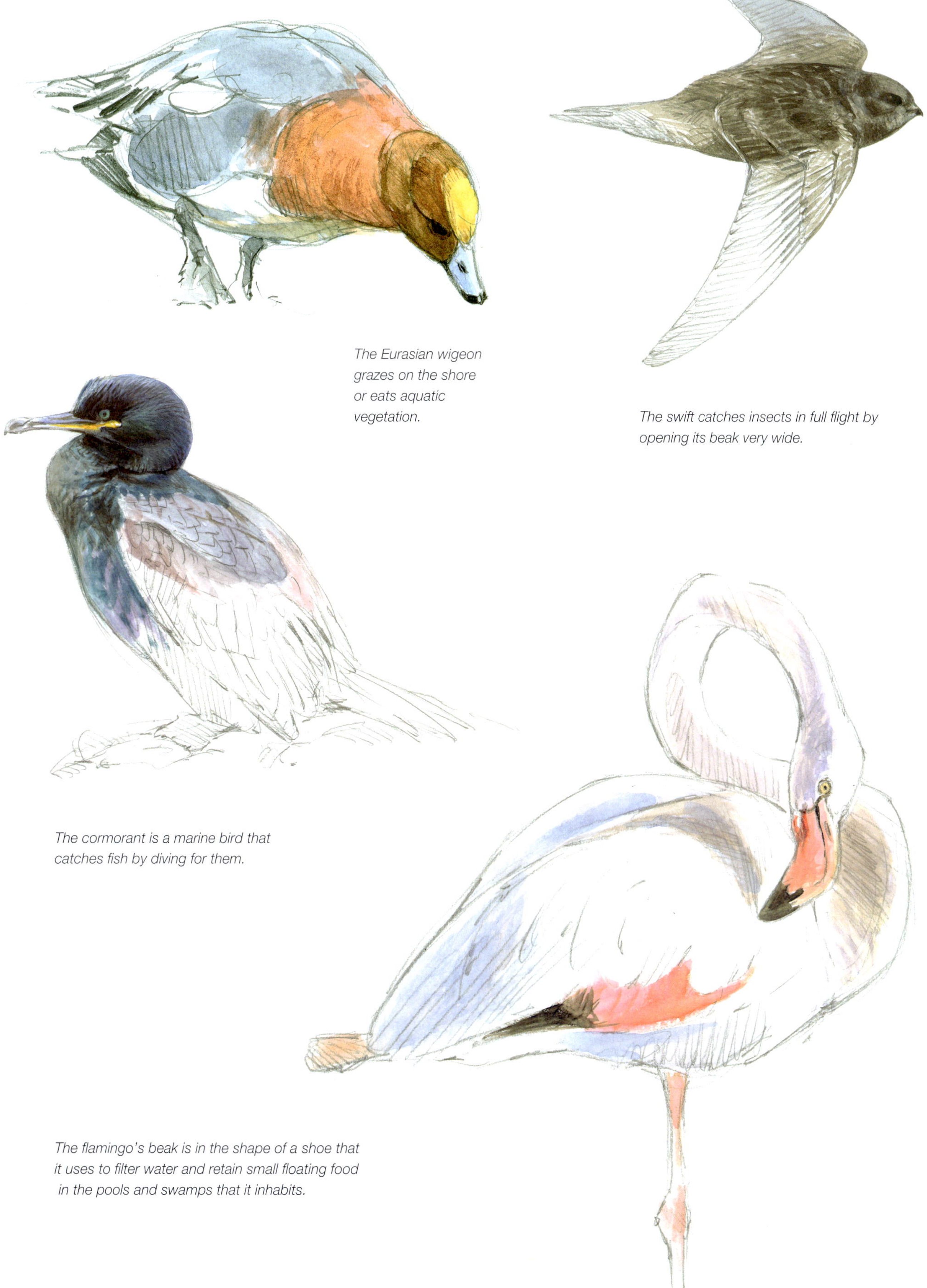

The Eurasian wigeon grazes on the shore or eats aquatic vegetation.

The swift catches insects in full flight by opening its beak very wide.

The cormorant is a marine bird that catches fish by diving for them.

The flamingo's beak is in the shape of a shoe that it uses to filter water and retain small floating food in the pools and swamps that it inhabits.

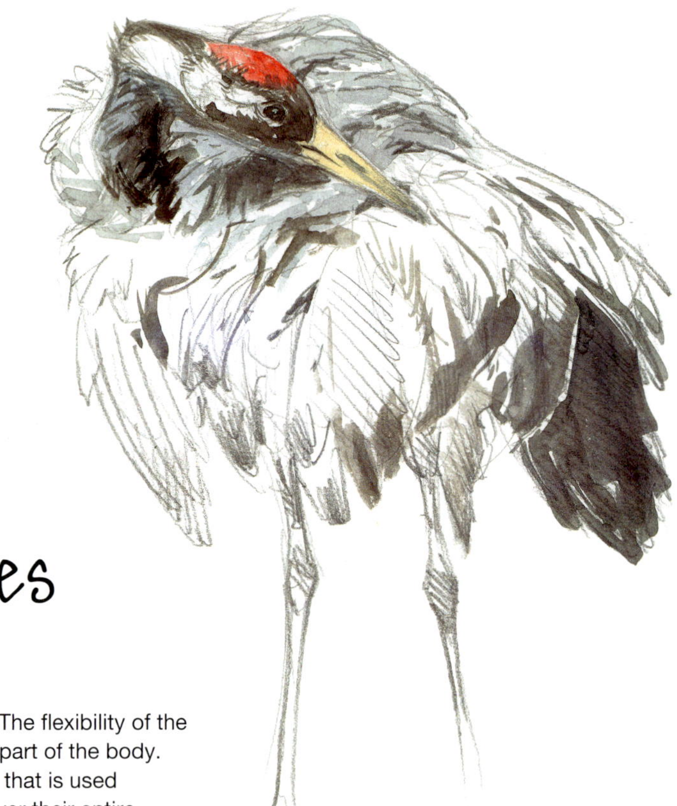

Keeping the feathers clean and free of parasites is of vital importance to birds, because plumage that is in good condition conserves body heat and is of utmost importance for flight. A large part of the daily activity of a bird is spent between eating and caring for its feathers, to which it dedicates long hours. For this reason, you can recognize a sick and weak individual, because it has abandoned its personal hygiene.

Caring for Themselves

WAYS OF CLEANING THEMSELVES

Cleaning behavior follows a ritual that is very similar in all birds. The flexibility of the neck allows them to twist it and stretch it to reach almost every part of the body.

All birds have a gland in the pigostyle, or tail, that secretes oil that is used to coat feathers. Birds take the oil in their beaks and spread it over their entire bodies to make them waterproof. Only a few birds that have to wet their feathers by diving, like cormorants, lack this behavior. Other common cleaning behaviors include water baths and dust baths to eliminate parasites.

A crane obtaining oil from the gland on its tail.

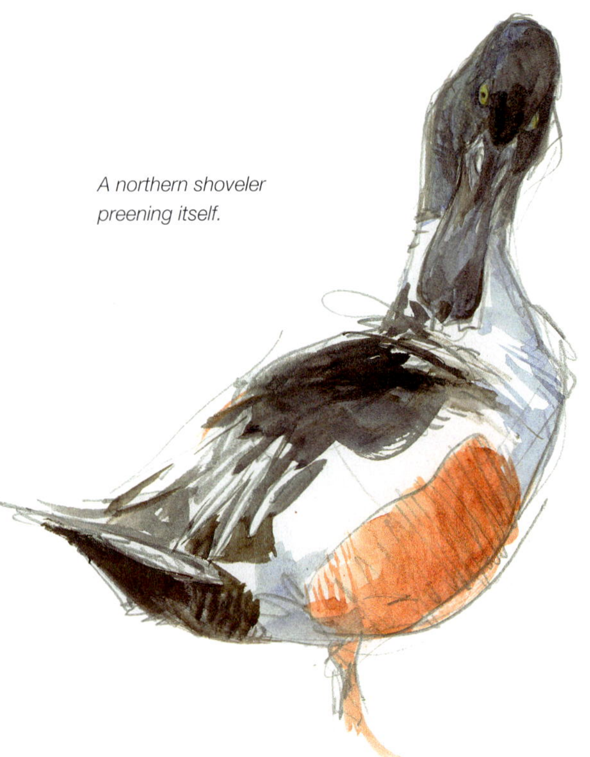

A northern shoveler preening itself.

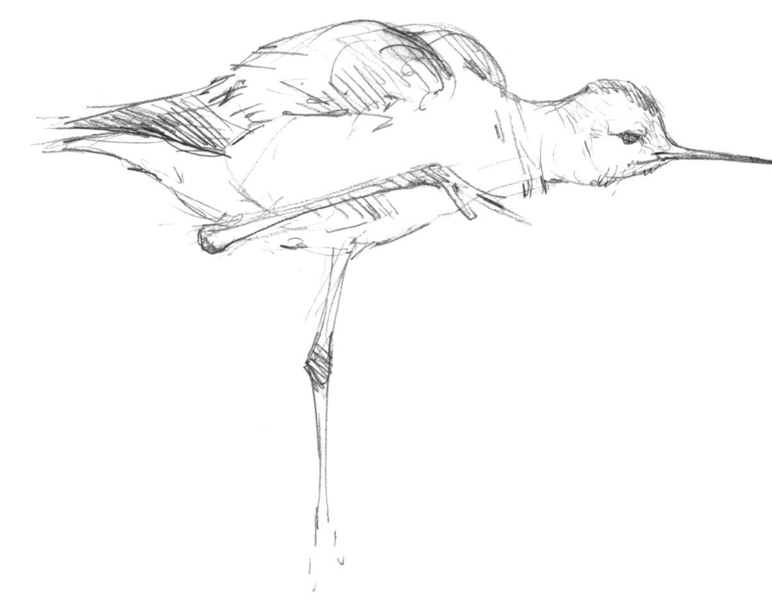

A black-winged stilt scratching itself. Birds frequently scratch their heads, which probably helps eliminate parasites and loose feathers. Some species always do this over their wings and others do it from underneath, the latter being more common in birds that do not perch in trees.

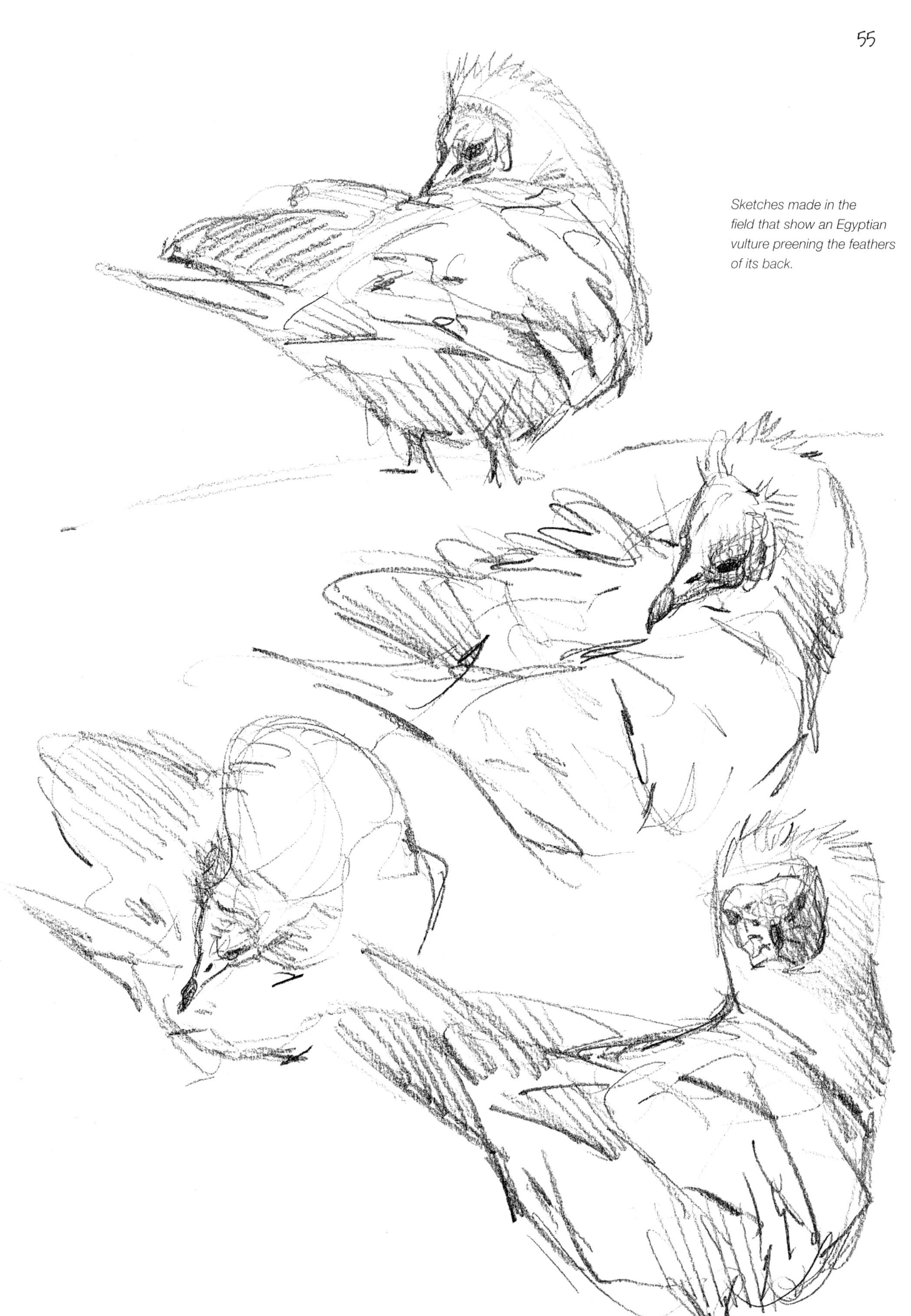

Sketches made in the field that show an Egyptian vulture preening the feathers of its back.

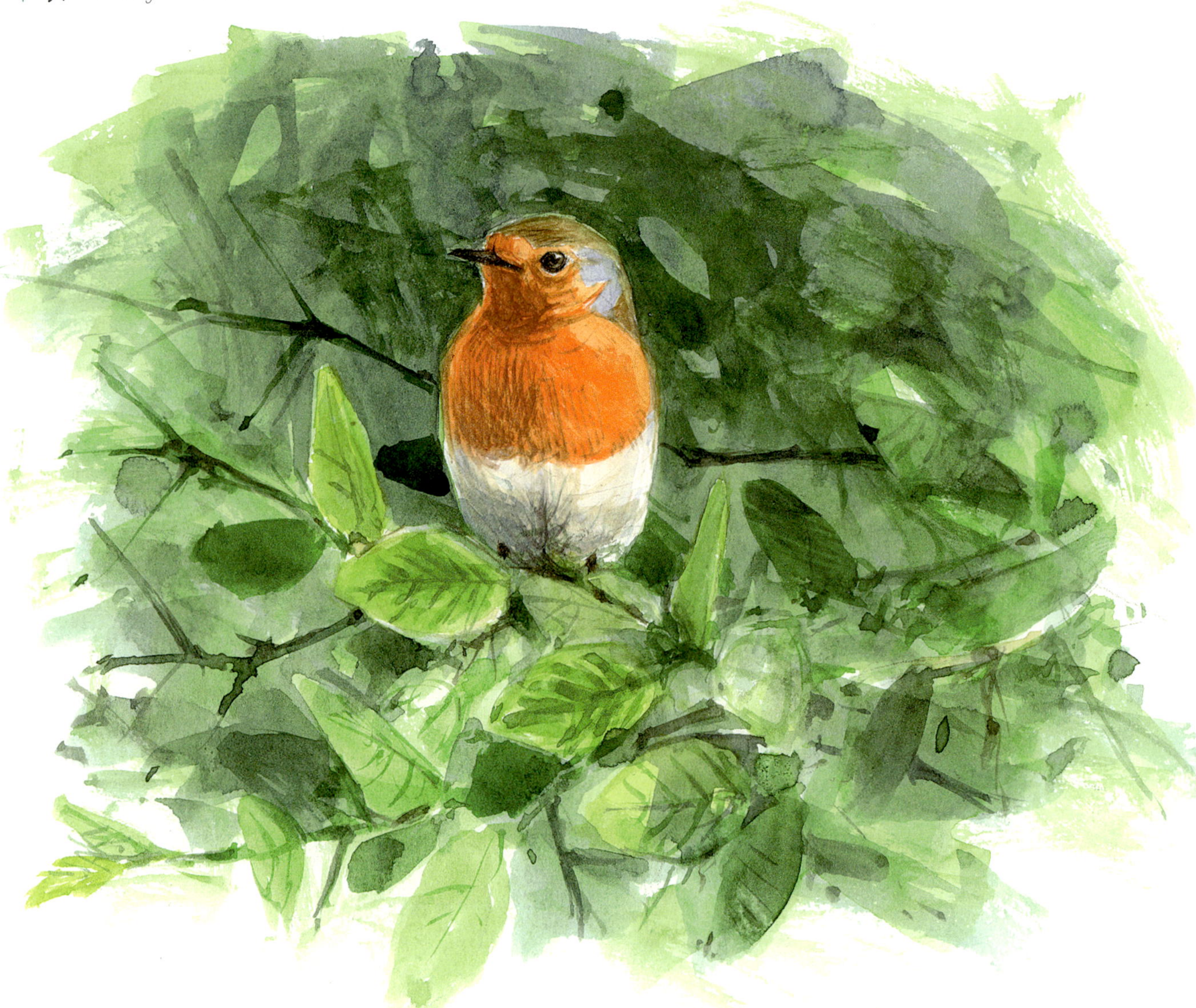

Elaborate Courtships

This European robin exhibits its attractive breast during mating season to attract females and chase other males away from its territory.

One of the most striking behaviors of birds involves courtship. Normally, it is quite an elaborate conduct in which the male usually takes a more active role, but this is not always the case. The wooing can take place on the ground, in the branches of a tree, where wood grouses do it; in flight, where birds of prey do it; and, in the water, which is preferred by quite a few species of aquatic birds, among them the great crested grebe. The songs of birds are also, in part, a form of courtship.

Sometimes, the male will present a gift to the female: the common tern, for example, will offer her a fish and the great crested grebe will take her some seaweed. The forms of courtship are almost as varied as the number of species, because one of courtship's functions is to keep similar species from mating. The most elaborate wooing is done by the male birds of paradise.

This illustration is of a male pigeon courting a female—erect, with its chest puffed out and dragging its open tail, a very common scene in any park or city center.

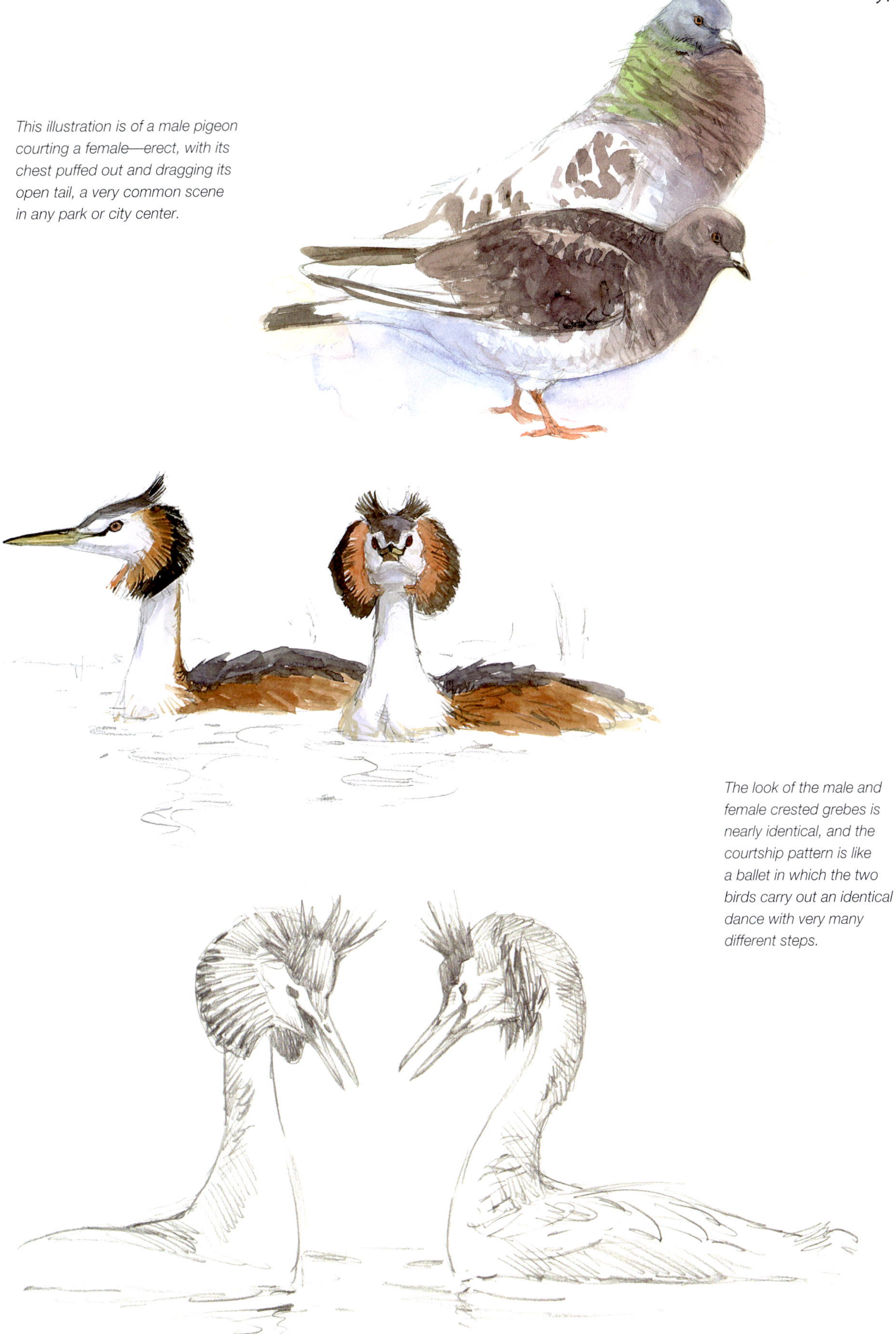

The look of the male and female crested grebes is nearly identical, and the courtship pattern is like a ballet in which the two birds carry out an identical dance with very many different steps.

The External Form

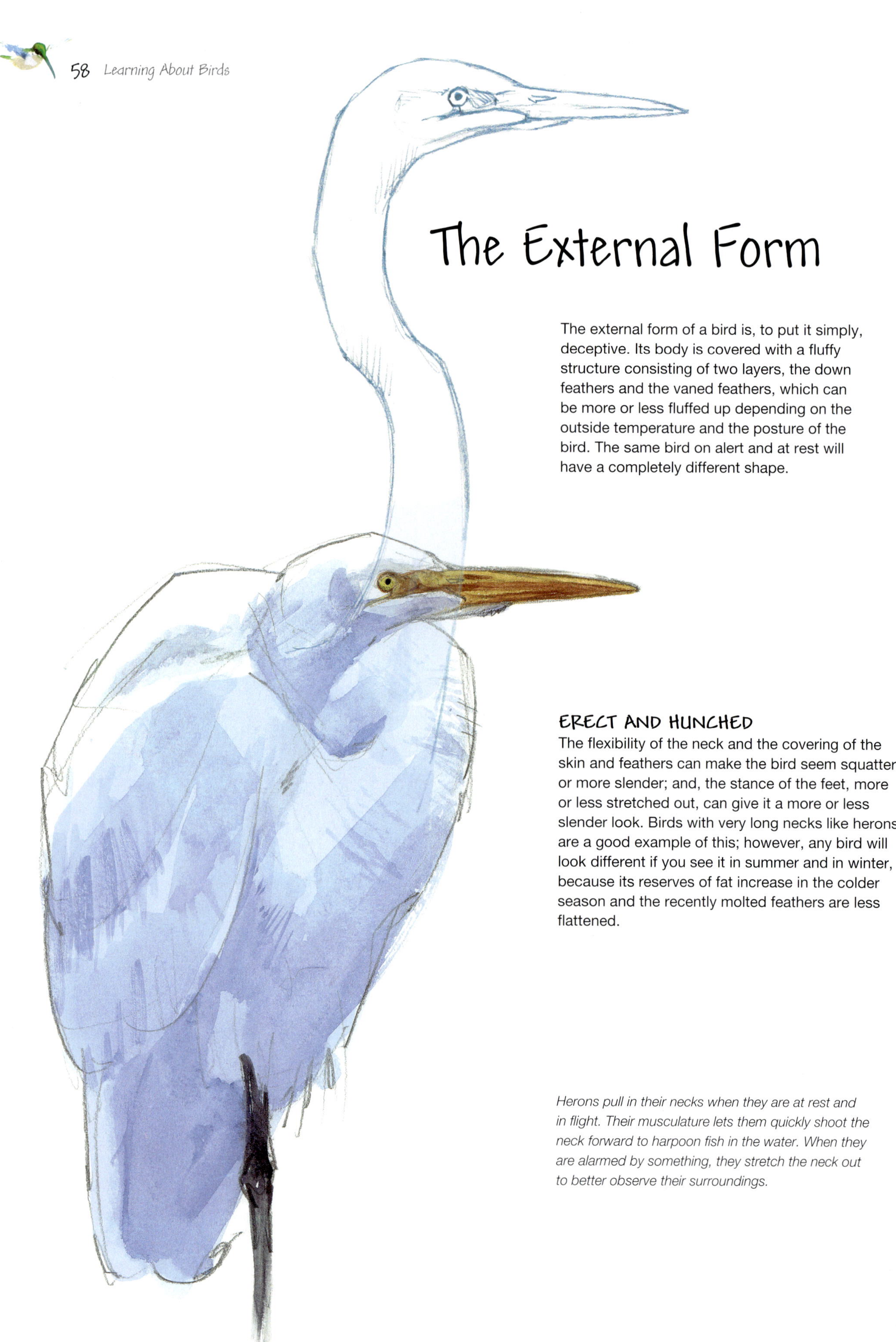

The external form of a bird is, to put it simply, deceptive. Its body is covered with a fluffy structure consisting of two layers, the down feathers and the vaned feathers, which can be more or less fluffed up depending on the outside temperature and the posture of the bird. The same bird on alert and at rest will have a completely different shape.

ERECT AND HUNCHED

The flexibility of the neck and the covering of the skin and feathers can make the bird seem squatter or more slender; and, the stance of the feet, more or less stretched out, can give it a more or less slender look. Birds with very long necks like herons are a good example of this; however, any bird will look different if you see it in summer and in winter, because its reserves of fat increase in the colder season and the recently molted feathers are less flattened.

Herons pull in their necks when they are at rest and in flight. Their musculature lets them quickly shoot the neck forward to harpoon fish in the water. When they are alarmed by something, they stretch the neck out to better observe their surroundings.

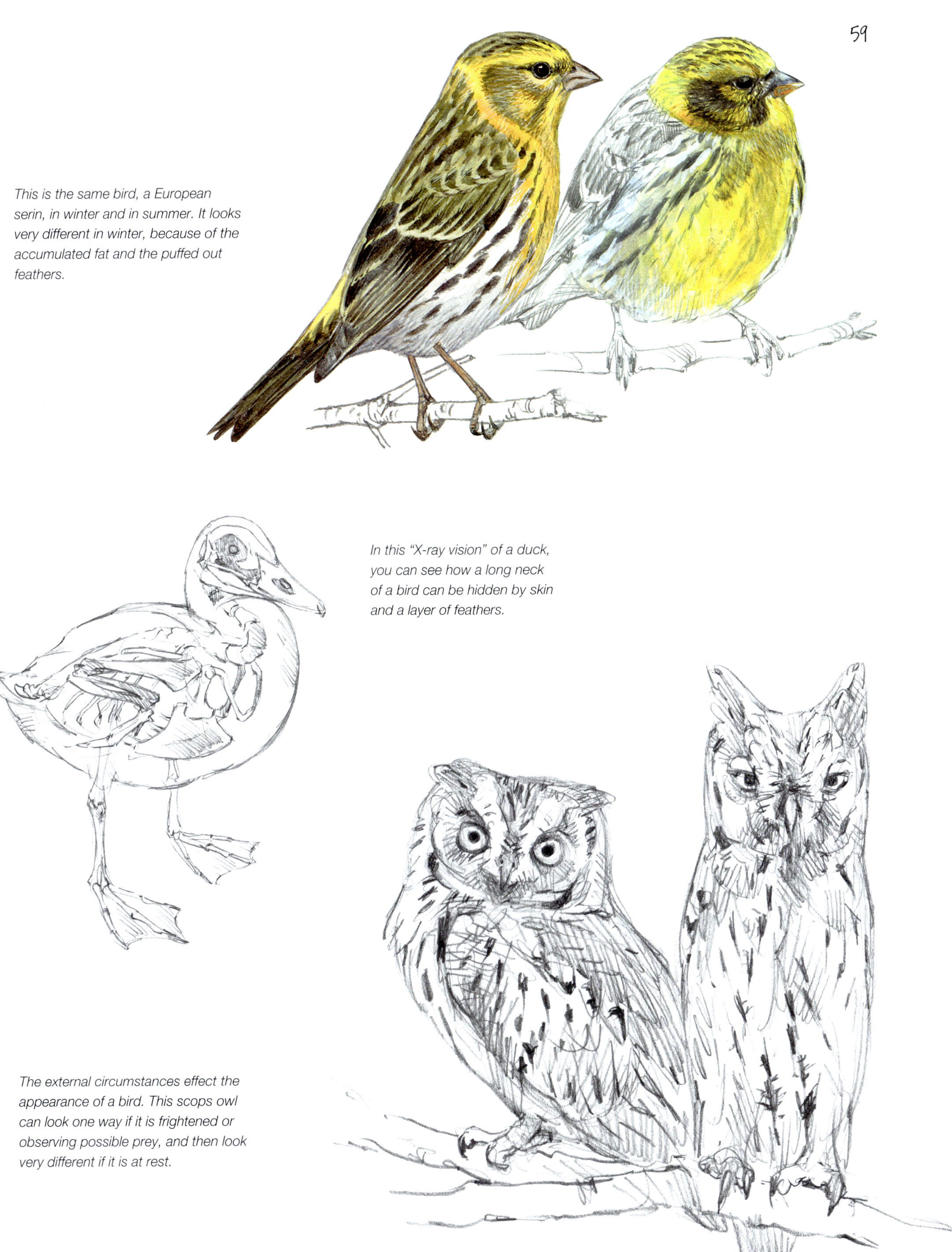

This is the same bird, a European serin, in winter and in summer. It looks very different in winter, because of the accumulated fat and the puffed out feathers.

In this "X-ray vision" of a duck, you can see how a long neck of a bird can be hidden by skin and a layer of feathers.

The external circumstances effect the appearance of a bird. This scops owl can look one way if it is frightened or observing possible prey, and then look very different if it is at rest.

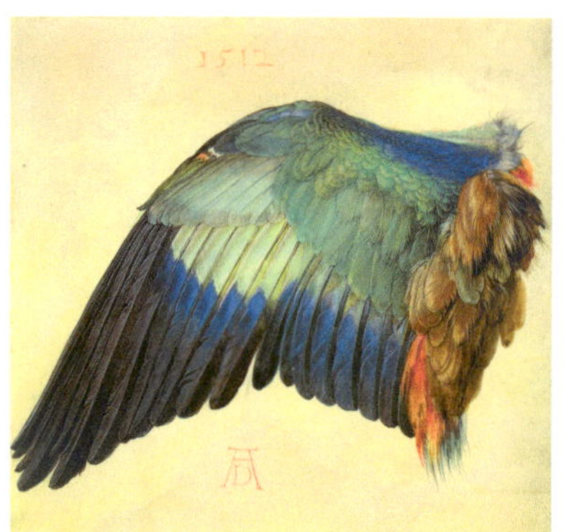

The Art of Flying
Working With Foreshortening

One of the most famous works or the Renaissance painter Albrecht Durer (1471–1528) is a watercolor of the wing of a blue roller. Flight is what defines birds, even though it is true that some species lost this ability as they evolved.

Correctly drawing a bird in flight is not an excessively difficult task, as long as you avoid getting into complicated foreshortening. Yet it is true that a foreshortened view is something that distinguishes a good draftsman. It is not just a matter of proportions and anatomy; here, we enter into problems of perspective, a subject that we will explain in the following pages so that you will be able to understand the functioning of a bird in flight.

JUAN VARELA
GOLDEN EAGLE
OIL ON PAPER, 12 x 15.75 IN (30 x 40 CM)

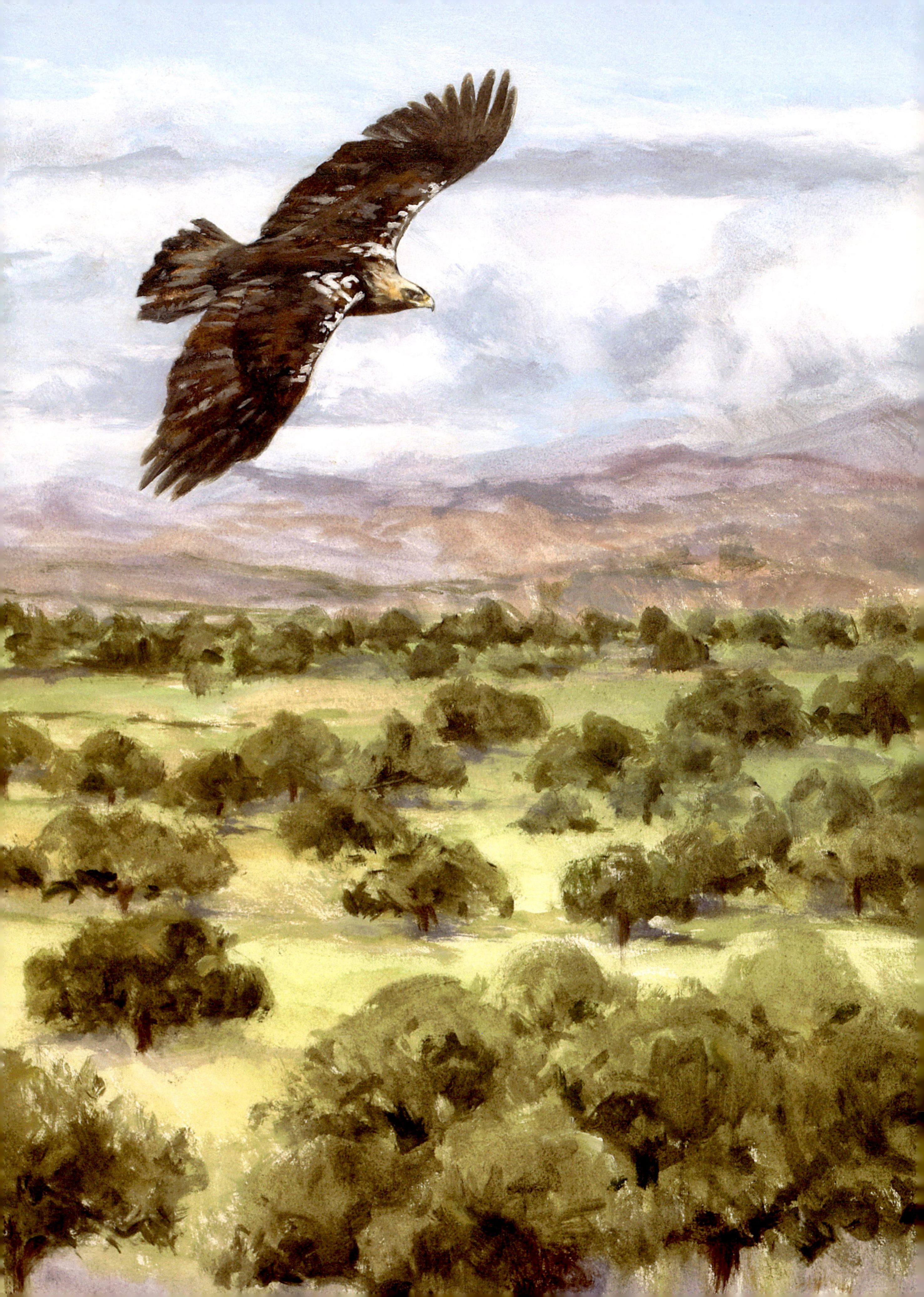

Proportions and Shapes

When you observe different species of birds in flight, you will see proportions and shapes that clearly respond to the type of flight and the movements these species make. Long, wide wings, generally associated with short tails, belong to soaring birds that are able to take full advantage of air currents to climb and then glide until they find a new thermal draft.

Short, rounded wings allow agile maneuvers in tight spaces, while long, narrow wings help gliding at low altitudes—for example, above a field of grain or over an ocean. There are numerous combinations that reflect the successive adaptations to needs like quick hunting maneuvers or long migratory flights.

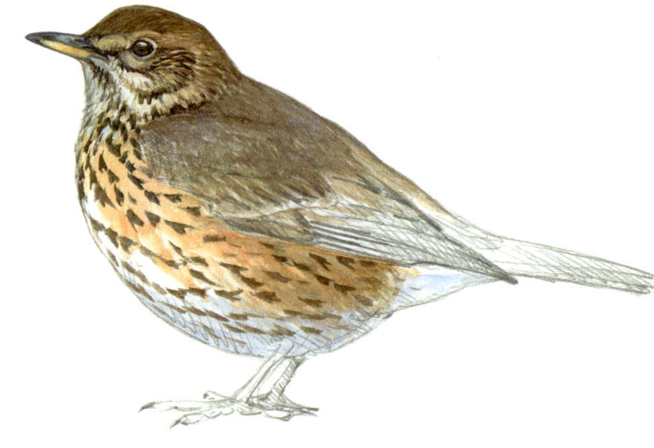

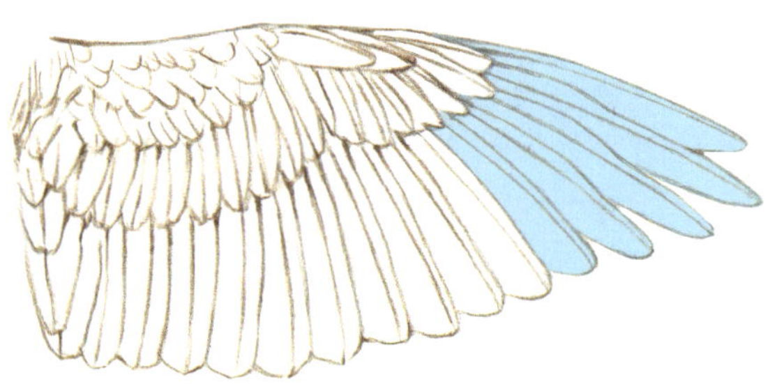

The edges of the wing with "fingers" are usually associated with many small birds that need to fly and maneuver at low speeds, like the thrush.

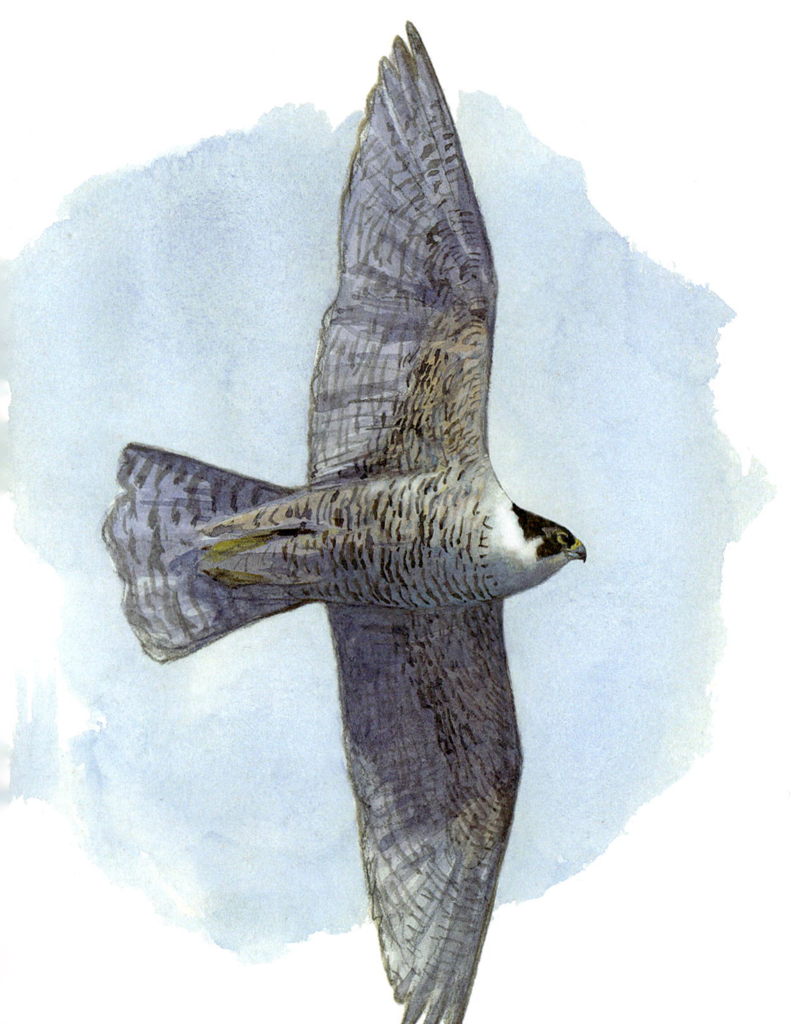

Birds with sharp edges on short wings, like falcons and swallows, belong to species with quick wing strokes and short periods of gliding in open spaces. Seabirds have similar habits: quick takeoffs, faster flight, and tolerance for long trips. Falcons have an extra line of covert feathers.

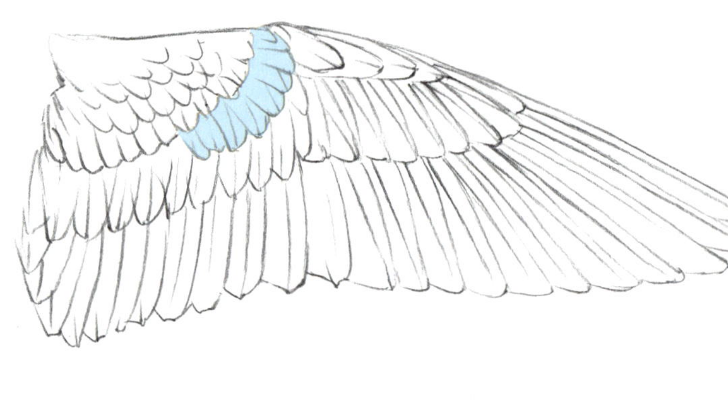

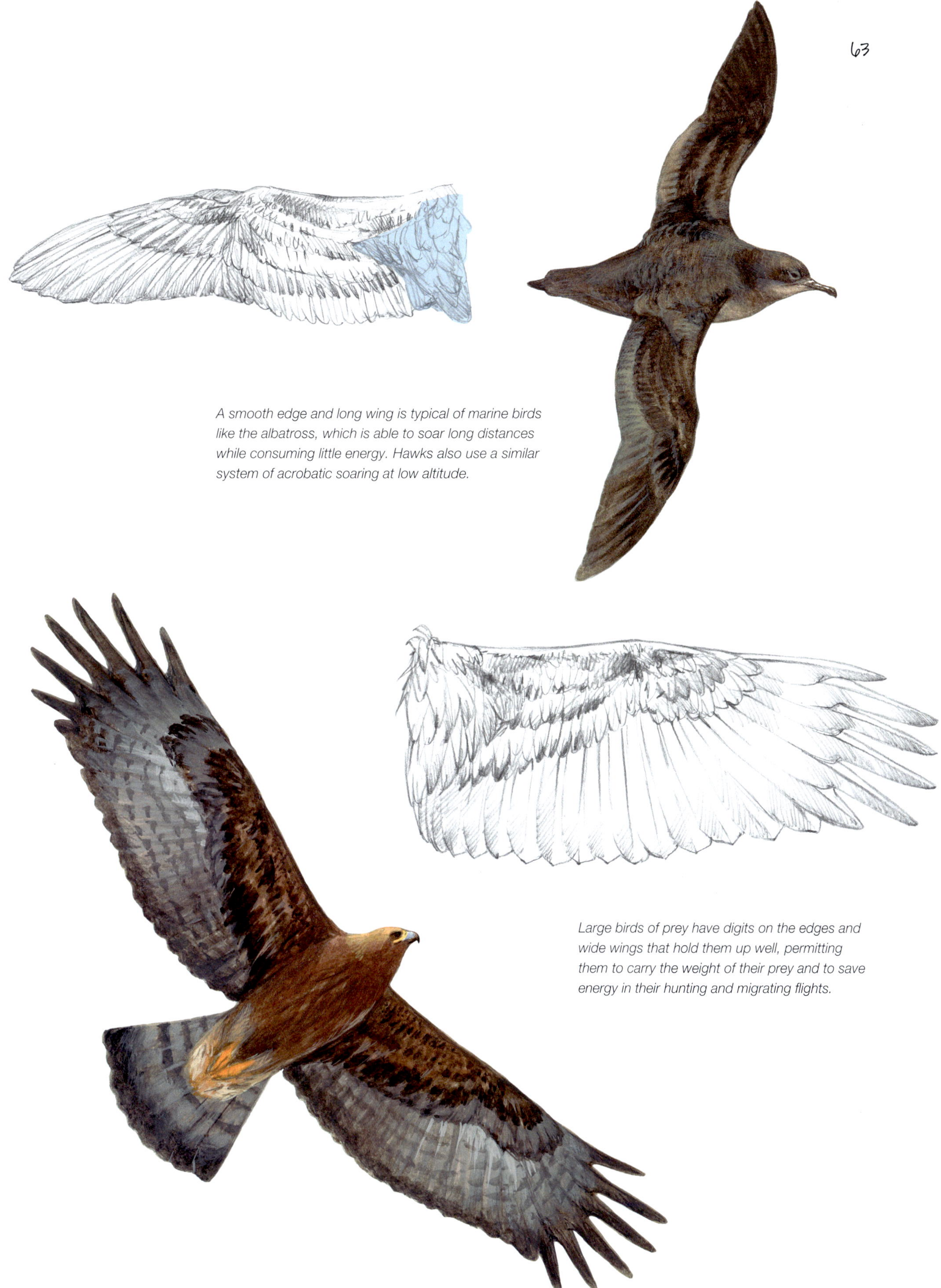

A smooth edge and long wing is typical of marine birds like the albatross, which is able to soar long distances while consuming little energy. Hawks also use a similar system of acrobatic soaring at low altitude.

Large birds of prey have digits on the edges and wide wings that hold them up well, permitting them to carry the weight of their prey and to save energy in their hunting and migrating flights.

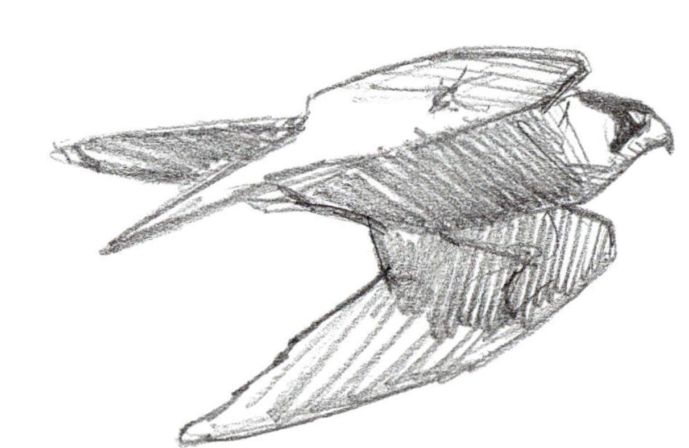

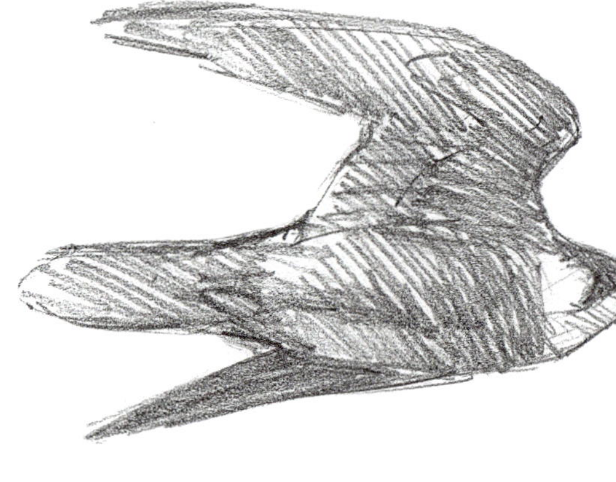

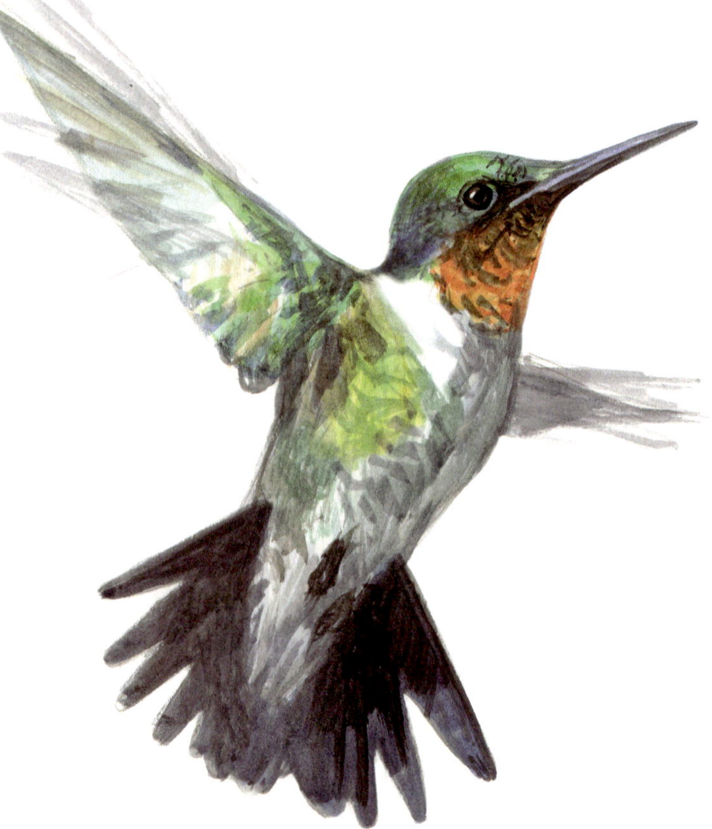

Some species of hummingbird can flap their wings up to 80 times per second. The way in which they flap their wings allows them to hover in the air to sip from a flower.

Mechanisms of Flight

Birds, like airplanes, stay in the air thanks to the power of the lift gained by forward motion. This is achieved by flapping the wings, alternating with gliding, or soaring on the currents of air of different temperatures. Only the largest birds soar all of the time, because it is necessary to have a minimum amount of body weight to glide on the wind during a long journey.

HANGING IN THE AIR

A third system of flight consists of hovering—that is, staying suspended at a fixed point in the air. This can be achieved in two ways: flying into the wind at the same speed as the wind is blowing, like kestrels, or flapping the wings at high speed in a figure eight motion that allows backward flight, like humingbirds.

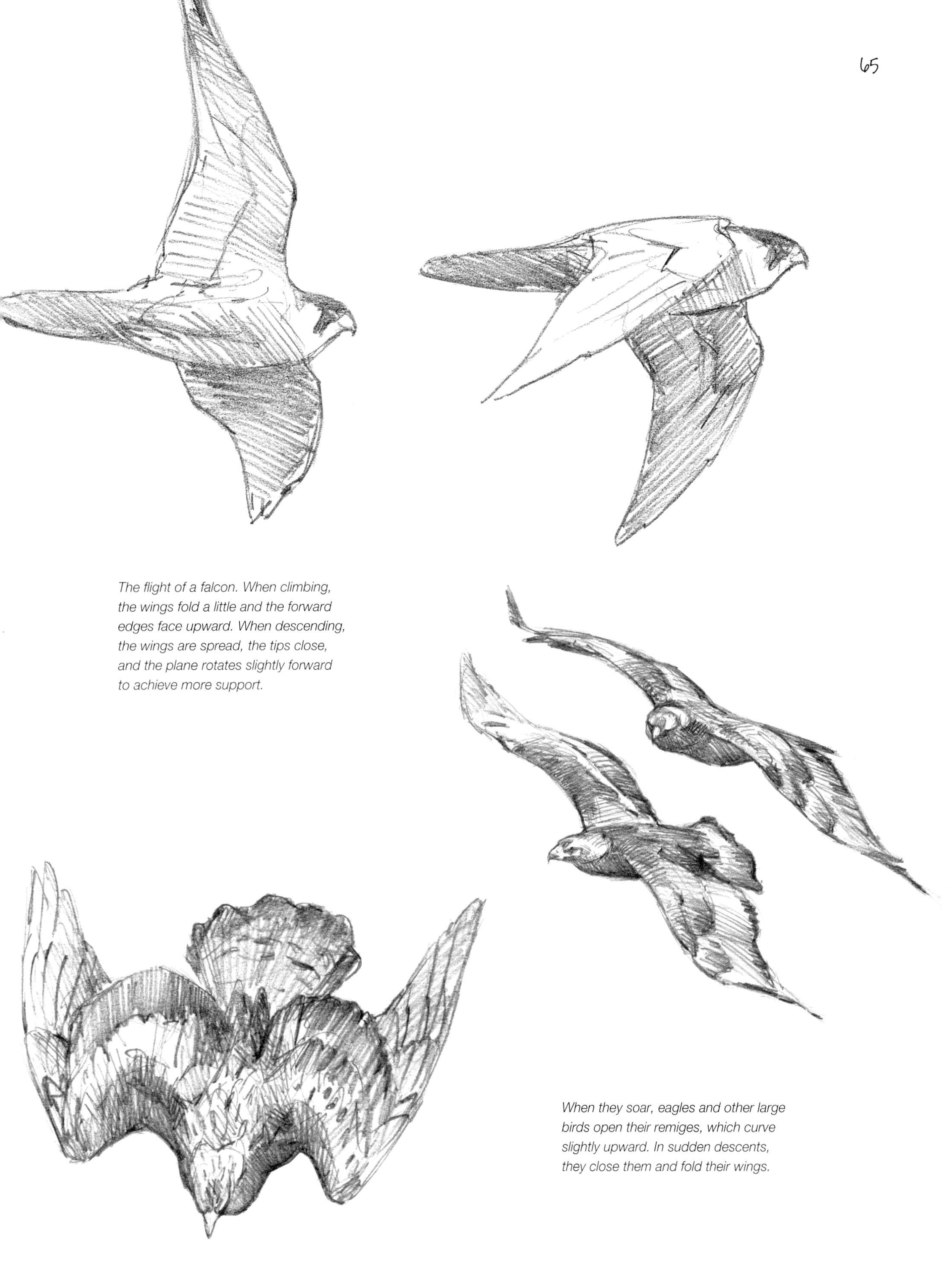

The flight of a falcon. When climbing, the wings fold a little and the forward edges face upward. When descending, the wings are spread, the tips close, and the plane rotates slightly forward to achieve more support.

When they soar, eagles and other large birds open their remiges, which curve slightly upward. In sudden descents, they close them and fold their wings.

How They Look in Flight

Each species of bird has a very characteristic look when flying. It is not just the general proportions or the relative sizes of the wings and tails, but the movements. Species of birds whose colors or shapes are difficult to distinguish are often identified either by the way they fly or by their silhouette in the sky. When drawing a bird in flight, you must be very careful with proportions. Good ornithologists have an incredible eye for detecting errors like wings that are too short or a tail that is mistakenly long.

Many small birds, among them the European green woodpecker and the goldfinch, close their wings or fold them for an instant during flight, causing an up and down motion in their trajectories.

HOW THEY FLY

The frequency of flapping and alternating with the gliding phase, the way it holds its wings, as well as the type of motion (whether the flight path is direct or zigzag), says a lot about the identity of a bird as observed from the ground. These and other details are important to keep in mind when drawing a particular species.

The griffon vulture soars with its wings raised in the shape of a V, while the black vulture curves them downward. This is a very reliable characteristic for differentiating between these two very similar birds of prey from the ground.

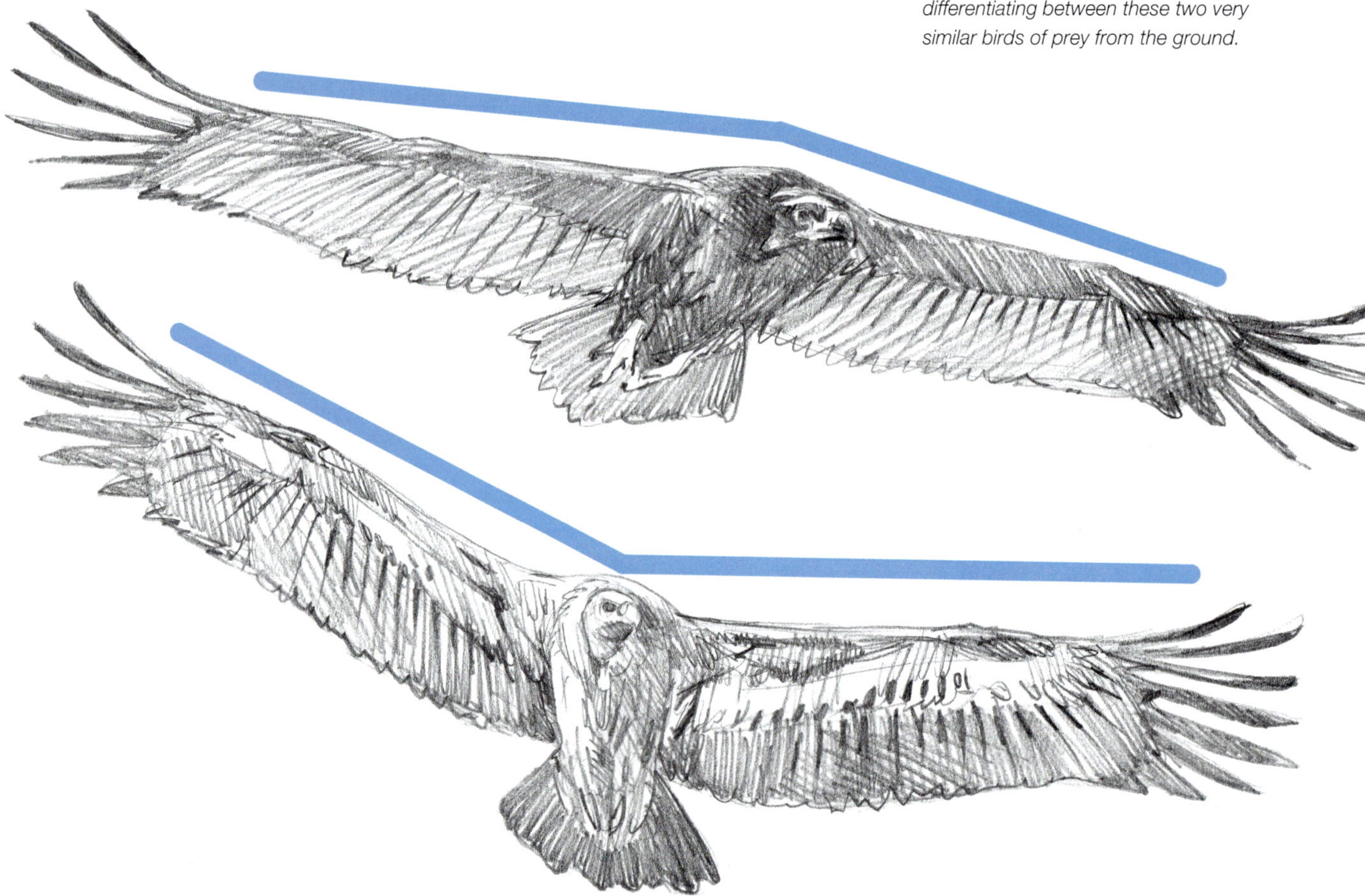

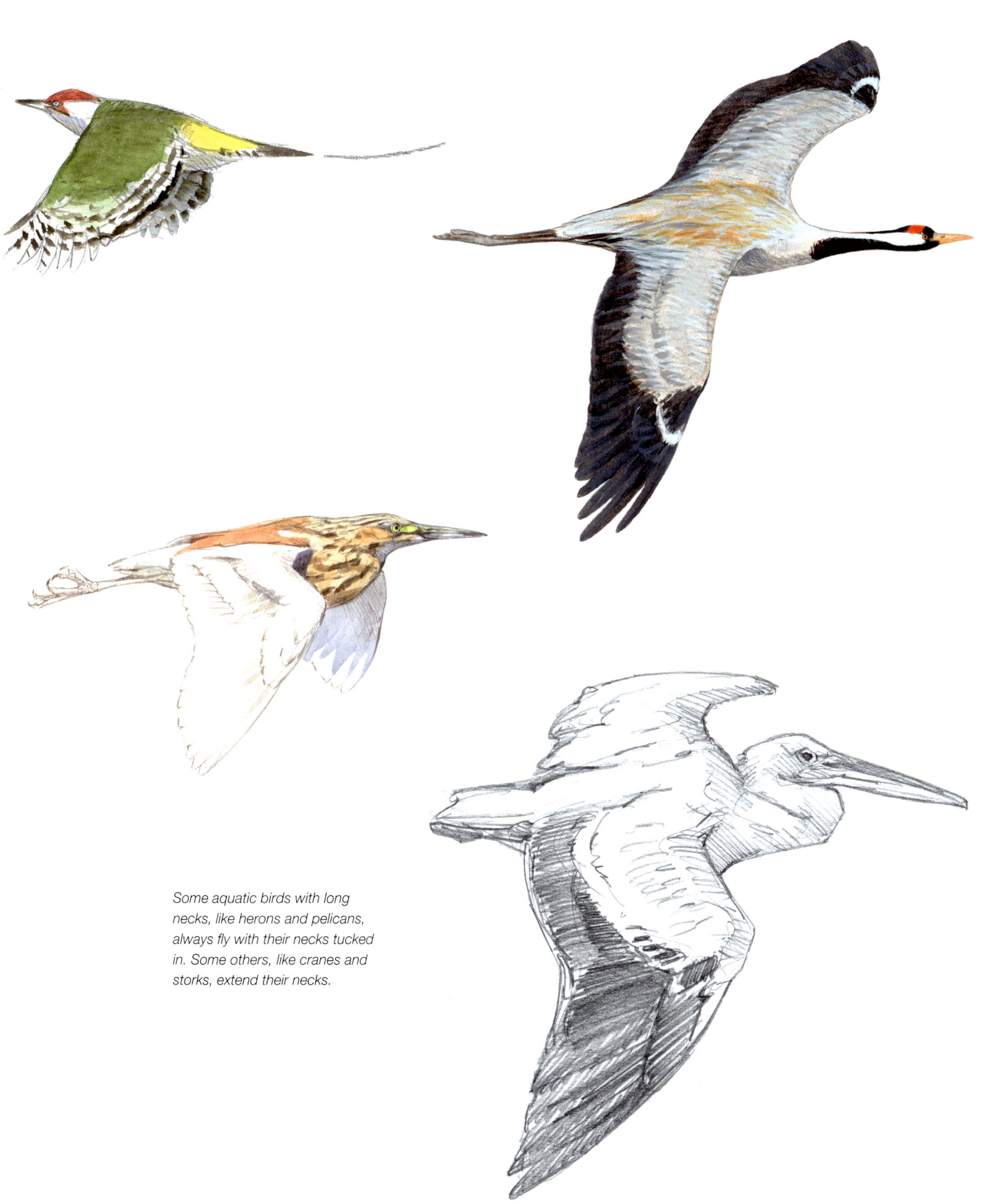

Some aquatic birds with long necks, like herons and pelicans, always fly with their necks tucked in. Some others, like cranes and storks, extend their necks.

The Parts and the Whole

JUAN VARELA
ROBIN
WATERCOLOR, 10.5 x 14.5 (27 x 37 CM)

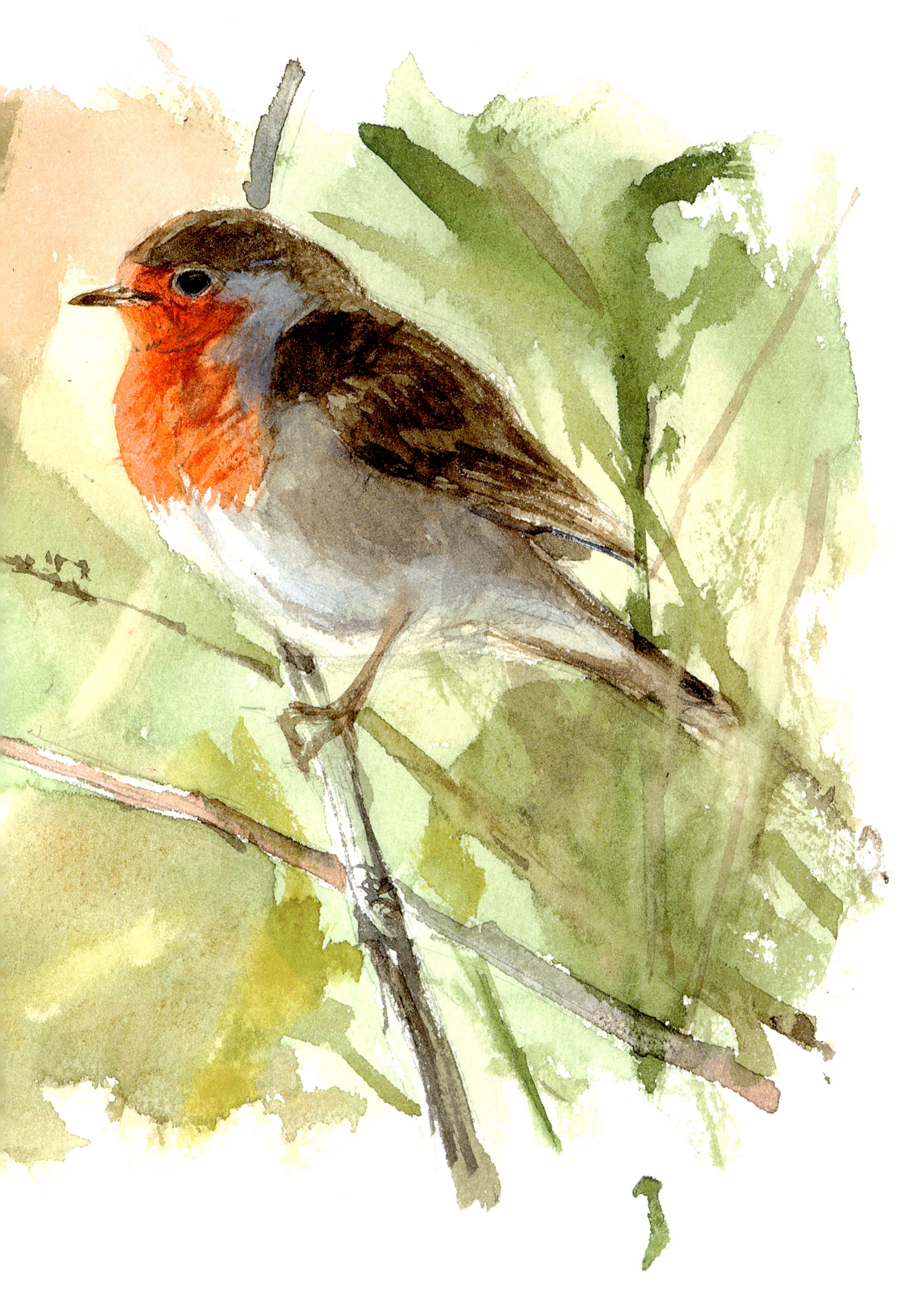

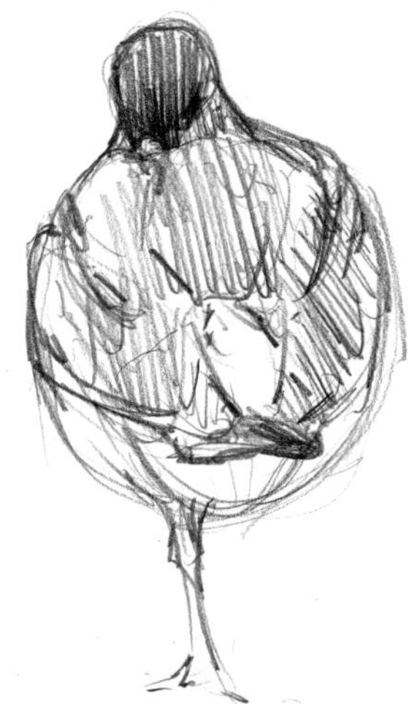

From Head to Foot
Where Do We Begin?

The head and its proportions, the gaze, and certain other details are what first attract a viewer's attention to a drawing, whether it is a bird or any other living being. Occasionally, small errors will go unnoticed i f the expression of the bird is well rendered. For this reason, many artists, after blocking in the whole bird, will begin by drawing the head, in the belief that, if they are able to start well, they will be able to move on to the next steps with more confidence.

JUAN VARELA
SKETCH OF A BALD EAGLE
WATERCOLOR, 10.5 x 14.5 (27 x 37 CM)

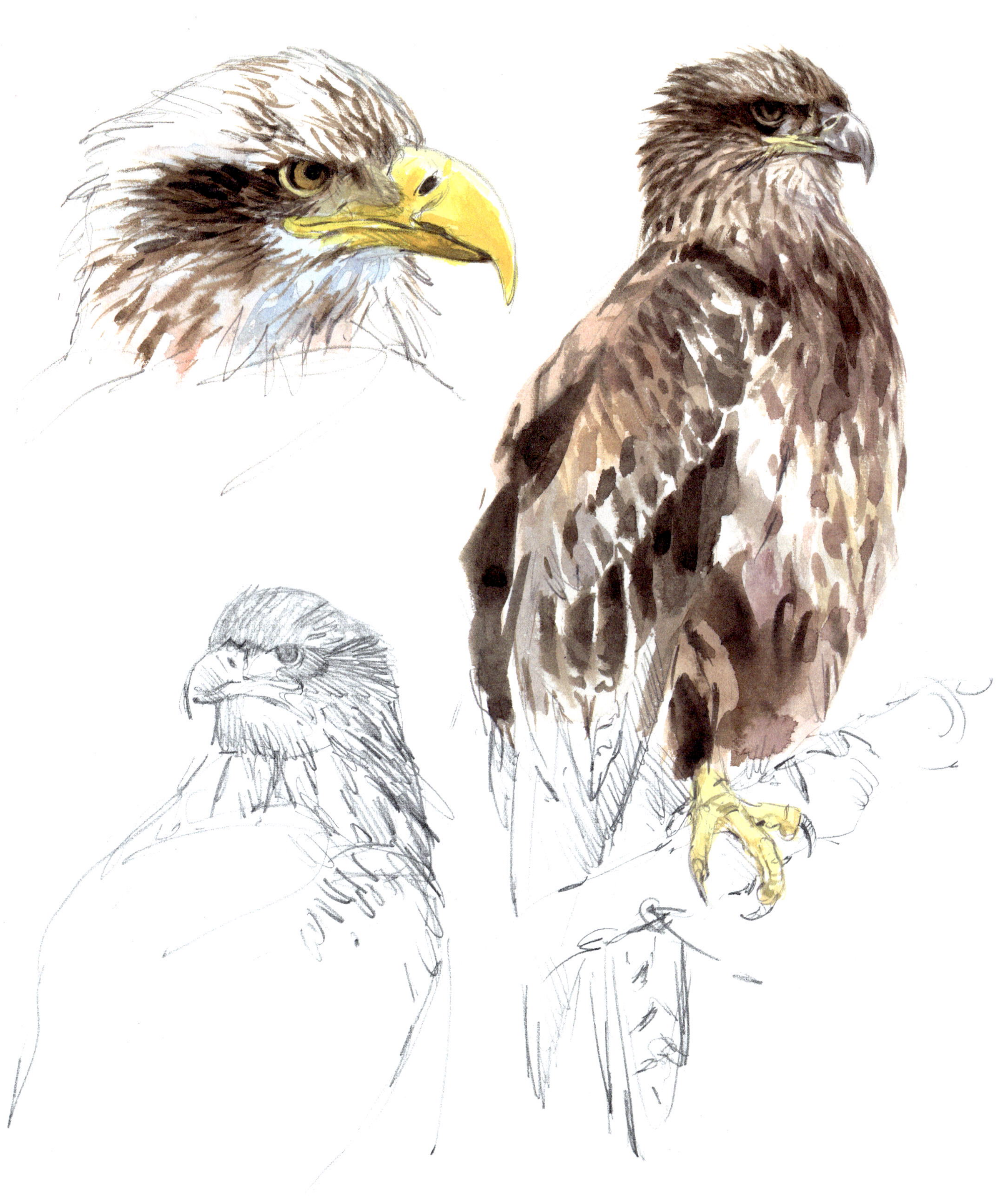

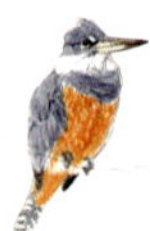

A Matter of Proportions

The shape of the head and the proportions among the different parts vary notably from one species to another. Species that are very near each other and with similar characteristics can differ in small details—for example, in the shape and size of the beak—or in certain colored markings, all of which is related to way of life, eating habits, and habitat. A bird's beak, for example, says much about its life and identity. Errors in its shape and size are less accepted by meticulous ornithologists than a lack of precision in other areas, including small deviations in the general coloring of its plumage.

THE EYES

The eyes of mammals are located quite far above the mouth, but this is not the case with birds. Many inexperienced artists tend to place a bird's eyes too high, when in reality, in most species, they are only slightly above the mouth line of the beak.

Birds' eyes are set into a circle of bony plates; and because they are not spherical, like those of mammals, they have very little mobility. In reality, birds have to turn their heads to see anything that is not within their field of vision. Many species have a very limited frontal field of vision; and, to see well, they have to cock their heads to the side. Birds of prey, however, have eyes in a more frontal position, which allows them to calculate distances very well, but their lateral vision is limited. Unlike the "prey" birds, they do not need to continually scan their surroundings to avoid being hunted.

In many species of birds, the eyes are just a little higher than the line of the beak. Creating a correct expression on a bird requires carefully measuring the distance from the eye to the beginning of the beak and to the top edge of the head.

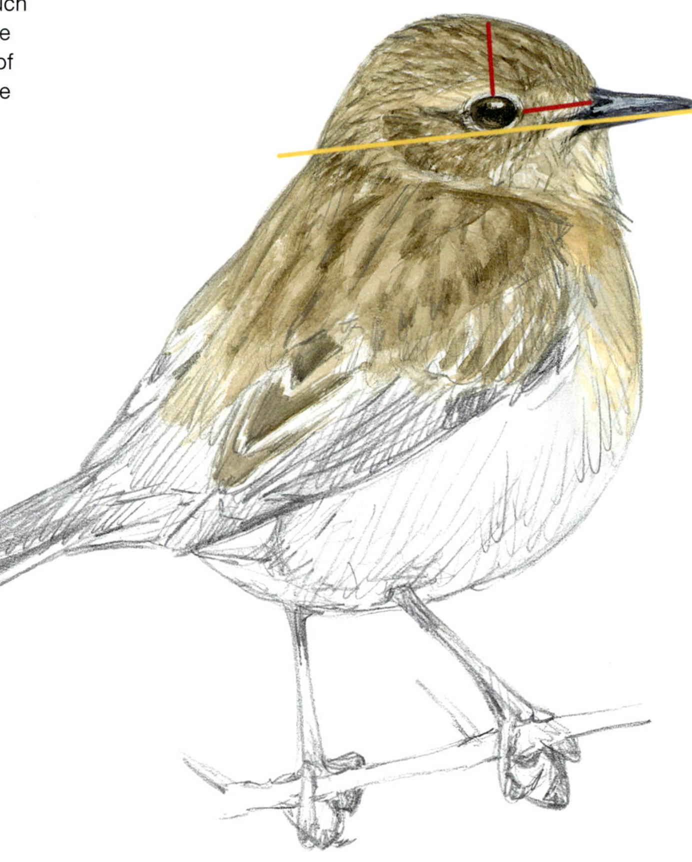

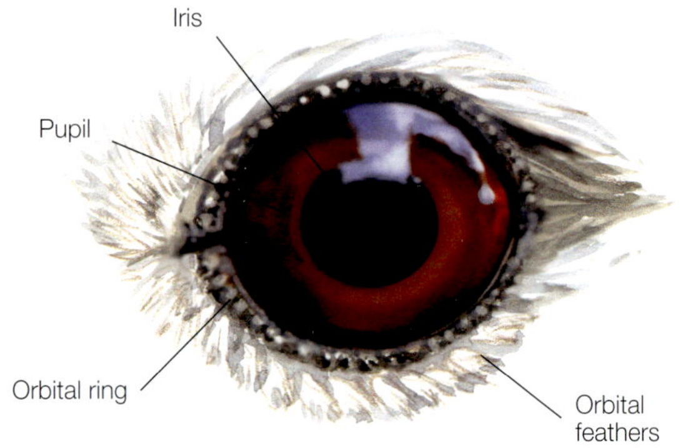

The color of the pupil varies according to the species, and it can even change during the lifetime of the bird. The artist must keep this detail in mind. In nearly all species, the upper eyelid is immobile; only the lower one closes for sleeping. There is a third eyelid underneath the others, the nictating membrane, which moves across the eye horizontally to moisten the cornea.

Location of the eye of a duck compared with that of a passerine (above) and a heron (below). In hunting birds—for example, birds of prey—the position of the eyes is more or less frontal and near the edges of the beak.

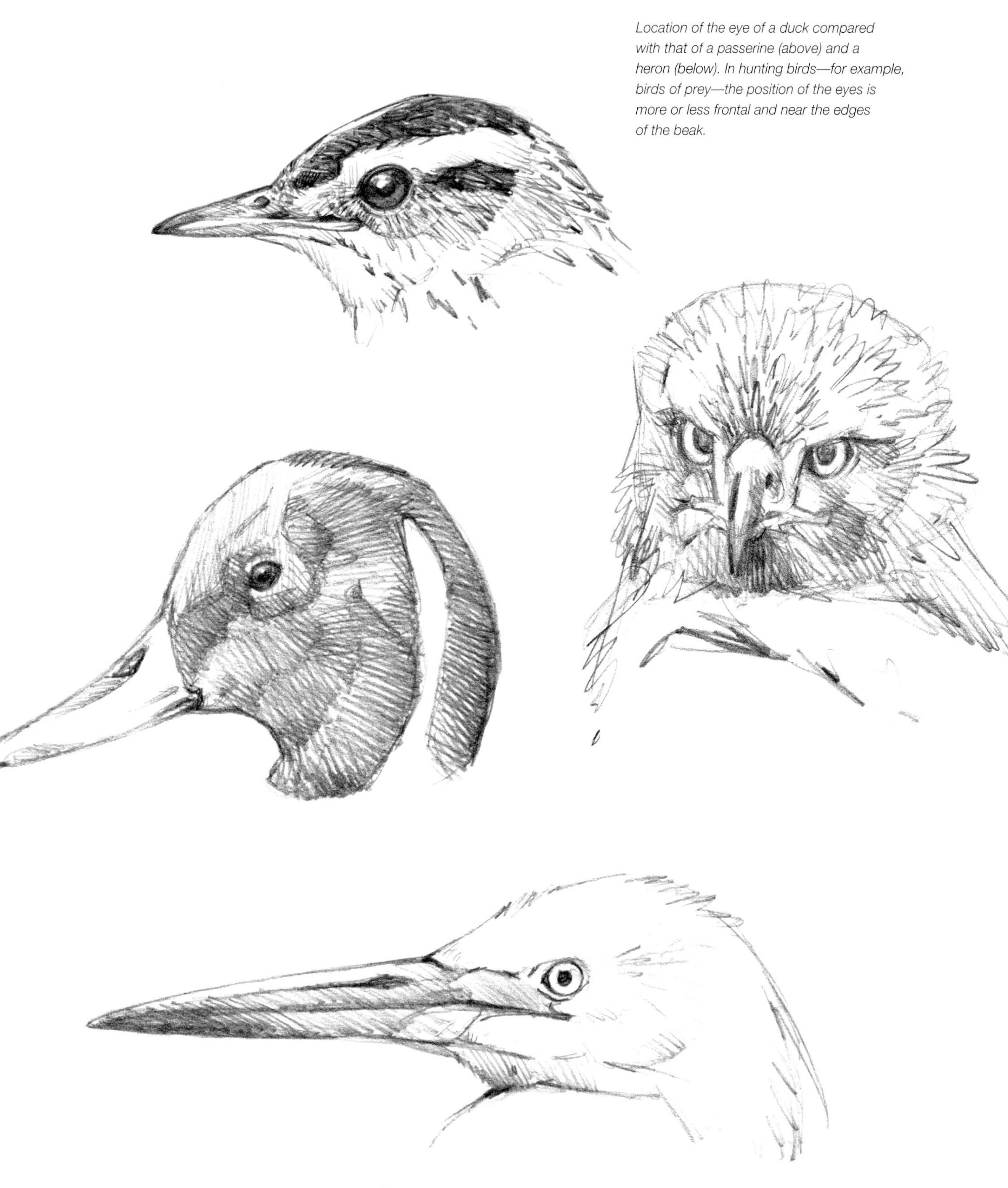

The representation of the open beak is usually quite a challenge for beginners at drawing birds, because they tend to make the articulation visible. But, in reality, it is behind the eye and underneath the skin, which makes it impossible to see. Excepting parrots and, in smaller numbers, *Anatidae* (ducks, geese, and swans), most birds' lower jaws have a large angle of movement, while the upper jaws only have a bit of flexibility. This is greater in chicks, whose skulls are not yet very bony. Although it seems obvious, you should remember that birds do not have teeth of any kind; however, in some cases, the edges of beaks are serrated, and this makes them better able to cut grass or make sure that any slippery fish will not get away.

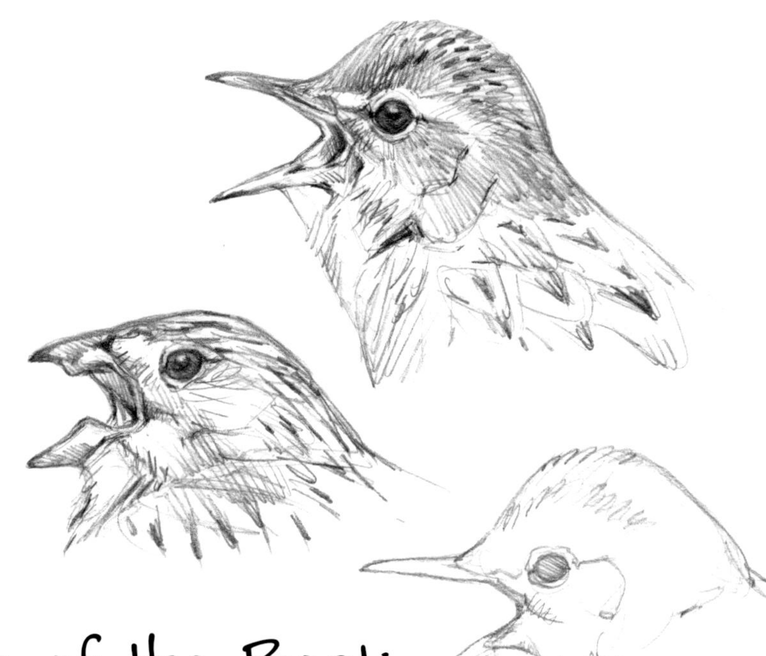

The Articulation of the Beak

In small birds, like this warbler and this yellowhammer, which have large orbital cavities, the articulation of the beak is located behind and below the eye. For this reason, the open beak never forms a visible angle.

THE TONGUE

The tongue corresponds to the shape of the beak, and it fulfills a very special function. Parrots, for example, have a fat, round, and very moveable tongue that they can use to extract grains and seeds to easily manipulate them, and this tongue also allows them to articulate words. Woodpeckers and hummingbirds have very long tongues; the woodpecker's tongue has a spearlike tip with small barbs, which is used to extract insect larvae from trees, while hummingbird tongues are perfectly adapted for sipping nectar from flowers, even difficult to reach nectar found at the base of the pistil.

Generally, tongues are not very visible, and it is not usually necessary to draw them.

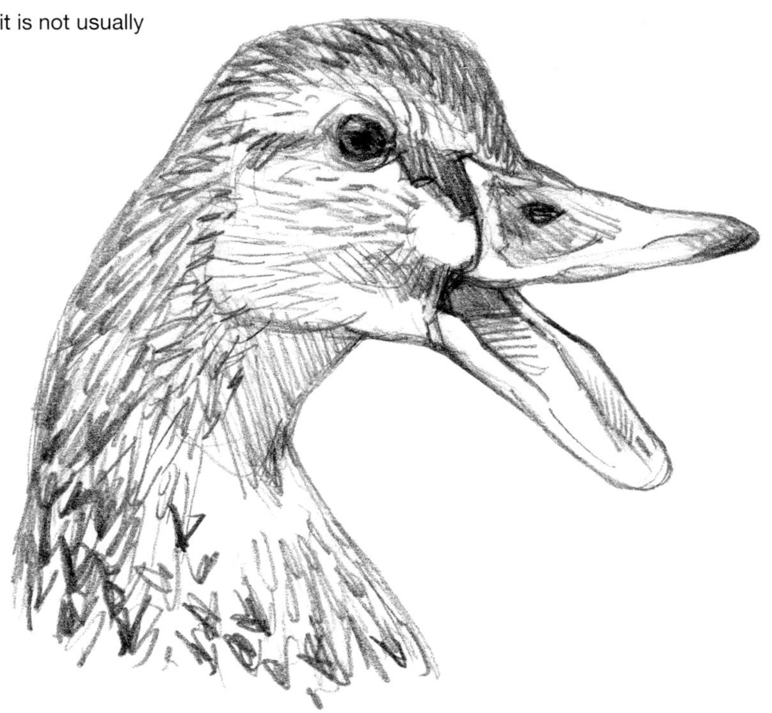

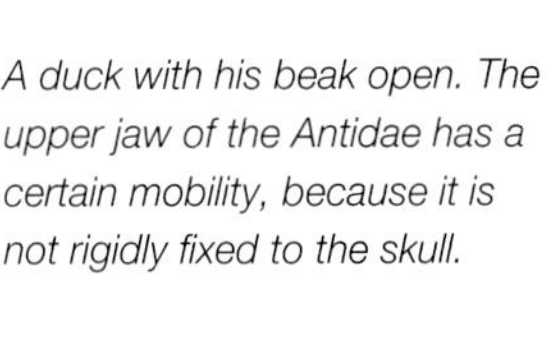

A duck with his beak open. The upper jaw of the Antidae has a certain mobility, because it is not rigidly fixed to the skull.

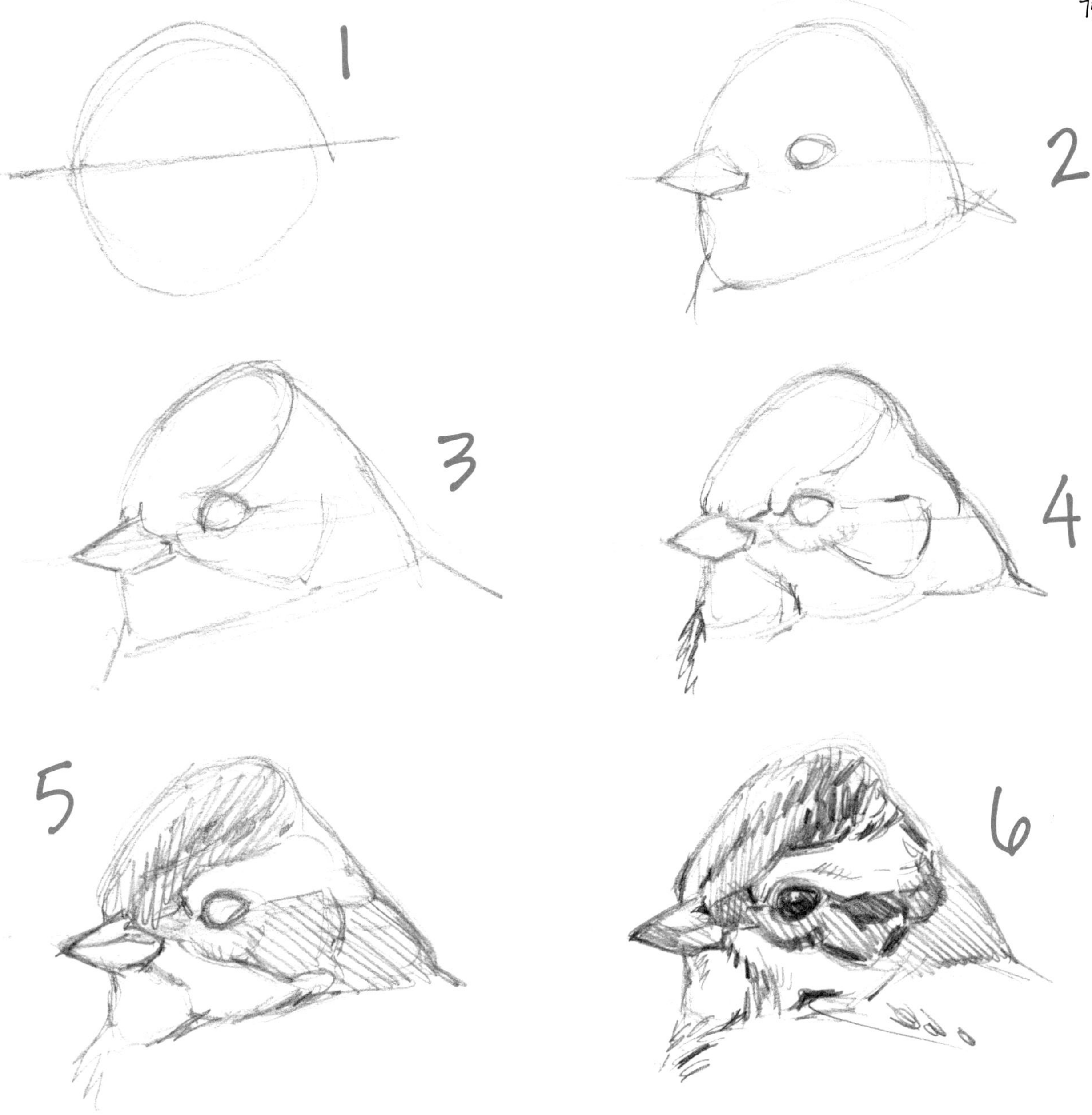

The groups of feathers that cover the head create a series of very recognizable outlines that help the different elements fit together and create the correct proportions.

1. First, draw the approximate outline of the head and a horizontal line to use as a reference for locating the eye and the beak.

2. When placing these two elements, you must keep in mind that the eye sits above the line of the beak, and that it is necessary to carefully calculate the separation between them.

3. Draw the outlines of the main groups of feathers. In this case, the bird has a prominent crest that is quite different from the rest of the feathers of the head. A triangle defines the auricular feathers and the small lines underneath the eye.

4. After detailing the groups of feathers, start working on the other details: the outline of the back of the head, the chin, and the line that begins at the lower angle of the beak and runs along the cheek.

5. Now it is time to apply color or to shade the middle ones with a pencil.

6. To finish up, you now add the areas of darkest color. The shape of the head depends on the posture and on the greater or lesser extension of the neck.

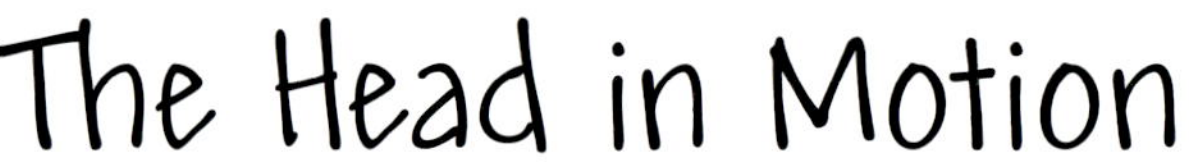

The Head in Motion

Drawing the expression of an animal requires a certain amount of skill, because this is the first thing that a viewer notices. It is even more difficult when you are trying to draw it from the front or at angles that are much different from a simple side view. The beak seen from in front or halfway between a front and side view requires a skilled representation of light and shadow to create a true impression of three dimensions.

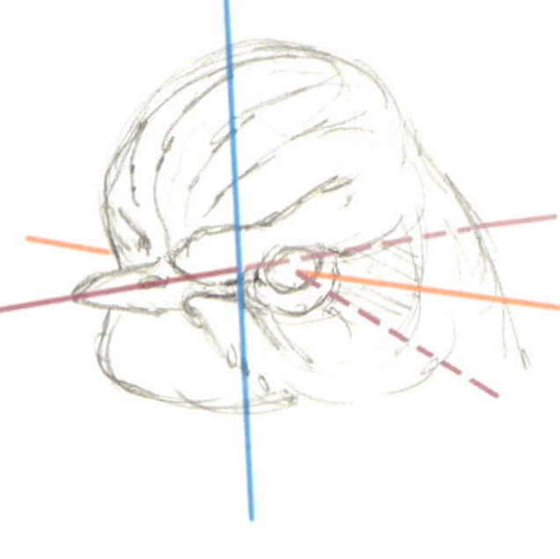

HOW TO DRAW THE EYES

When the head rotates from a side profile to a frontal or near frontal position, you see much better the different placements of the eyes and the angle formed between them and on the horizontal plane.

In the following illustrations, you will see how the shapes of the eyes and the relative distance from the line of the beak will vary according to the angle from which you see them.

You might think that birds look in the same direction as their beaks; however, many species have a very limited frontal field of vision. This view is sacrificed in exchange for greater range of vision on the sides. Some of herbivore mammals are in the same situation, gazelles for example.

In herons, the plane of the eyes is inclined toward the ground and toward the front, so that, when they walk in pools, they are looking downward and can better calculate the distance for spearing their prey.

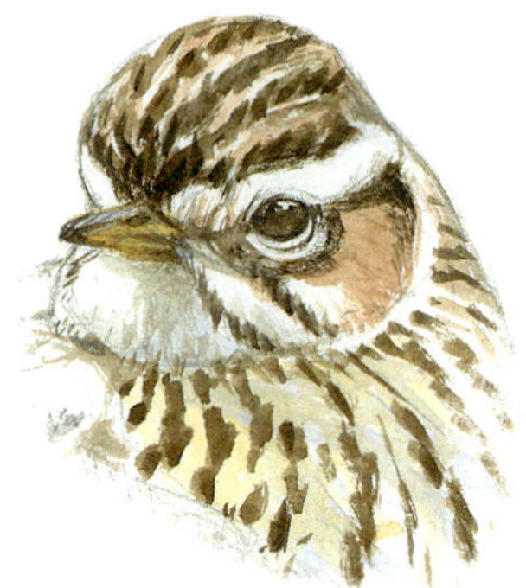

Woodlark *(Lullula arborea)*

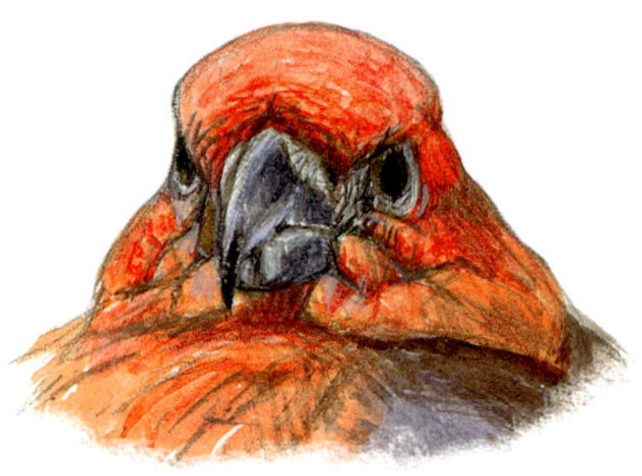

Red crossbill *(Loxia curvirostra)*

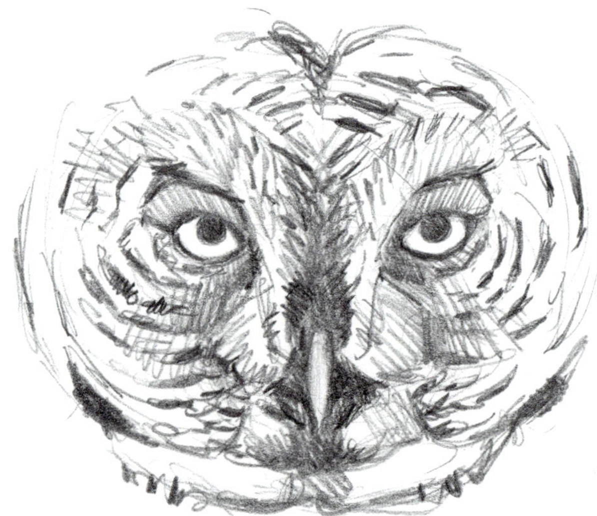

Owls can rotate their heads 180 degrees. However, because their eyes are on an extremely frontal plane, they cannot see what is happening behind their backs, unlike other birds, such as the blackbird, for example.

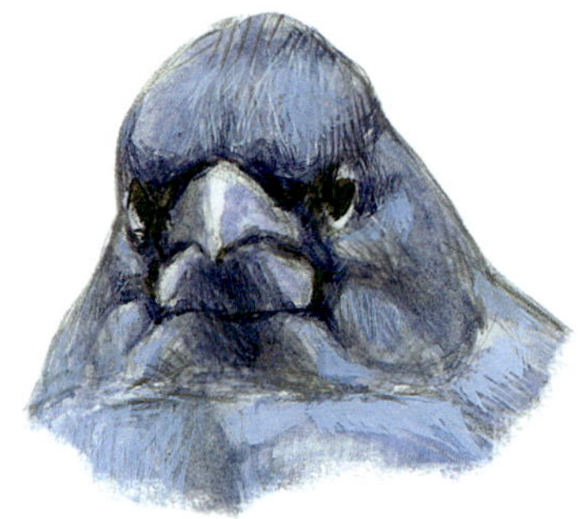

Blue chaffinch *(Fringilla teydea)*

When representing the head, you can imagine three axes on which it moves: one at the height of the eyes, another in line with the beak, and the third perpendicular to them both. Rotating these imaginary axes will give you different perspectives of the head. The eyes will be at a slight angle to the vertical line.

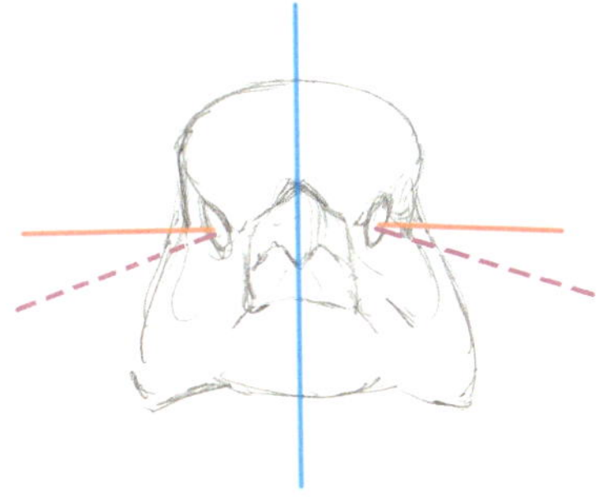

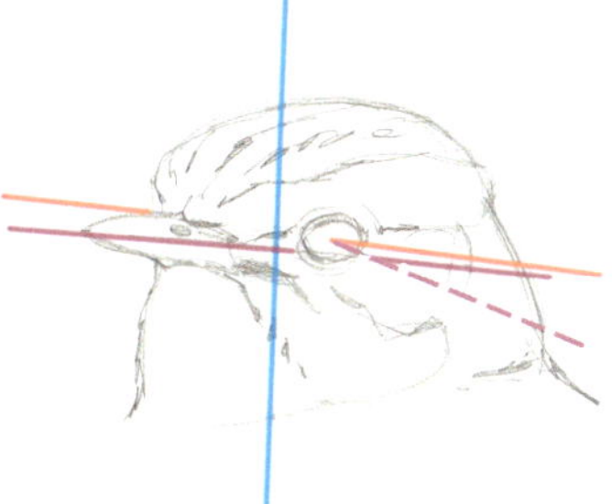

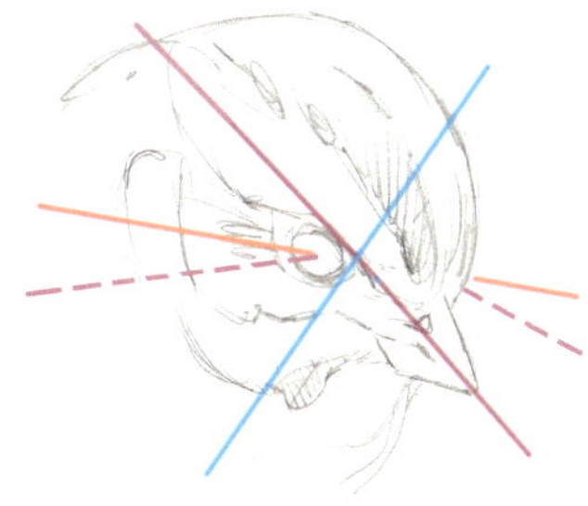

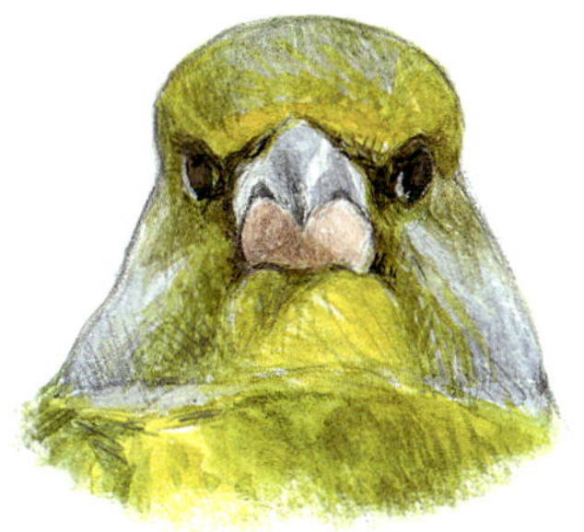

Greenfinch *(Carduelis chloris)*

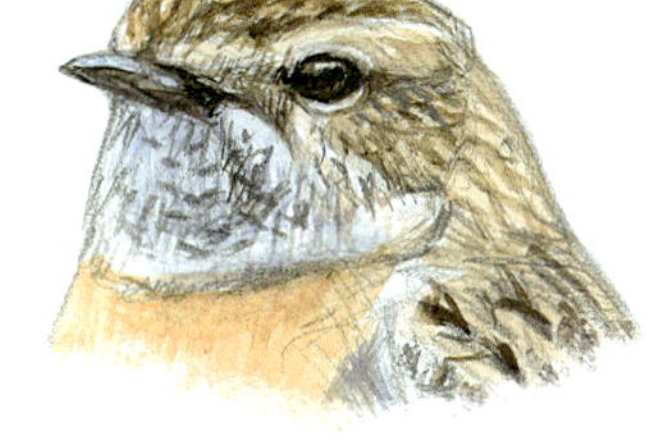

Canary Islands stonechat *(Saxicola dacotiae)*

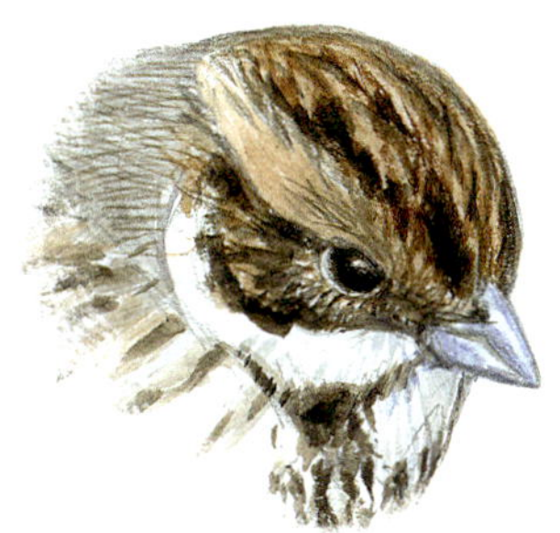

Common reed bunting *(Emberiza schoeniclus)*

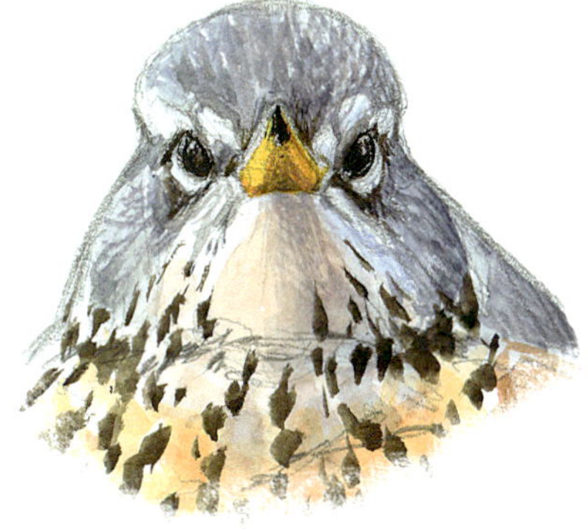

Fieldfare *(Turdus pilaris)*

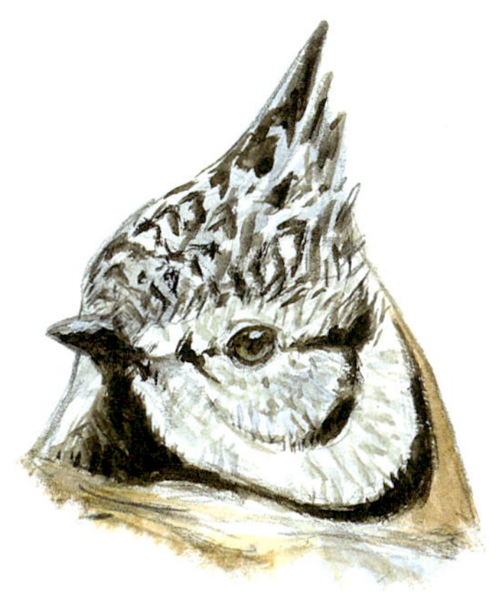

European crested tit *(Lophophanes cristatus)*

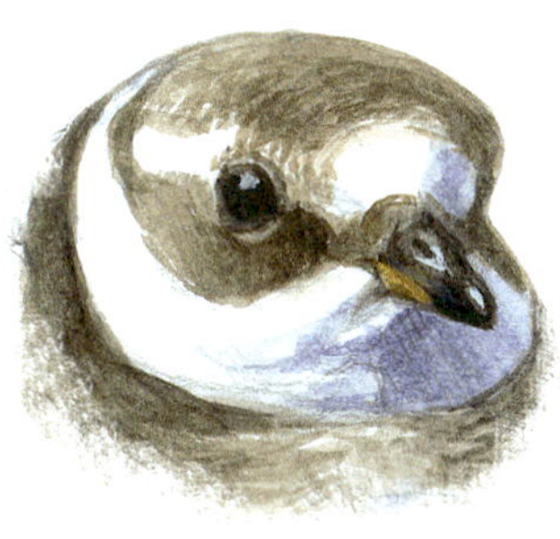

Common ringed plover *(Charadrius hiaticula)*

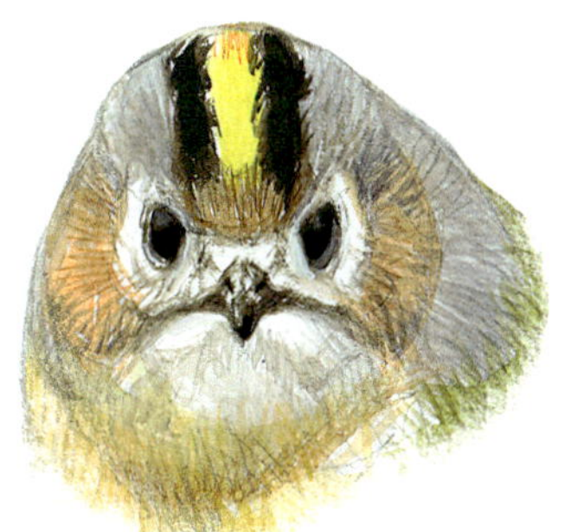

Common firecrest *(Regulus ignicapulla)*

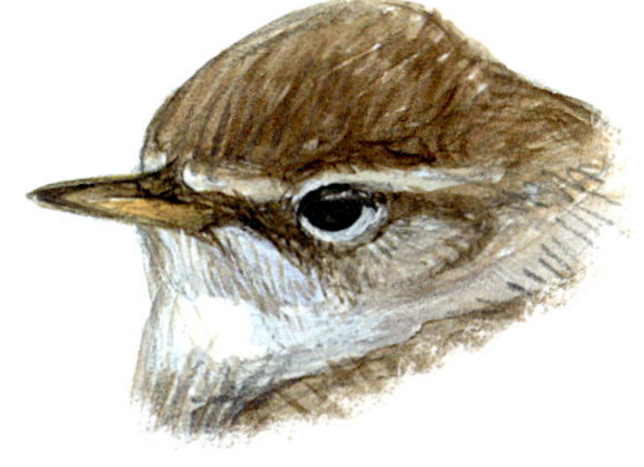

Cetti's warbler *(Cettia cetti)*

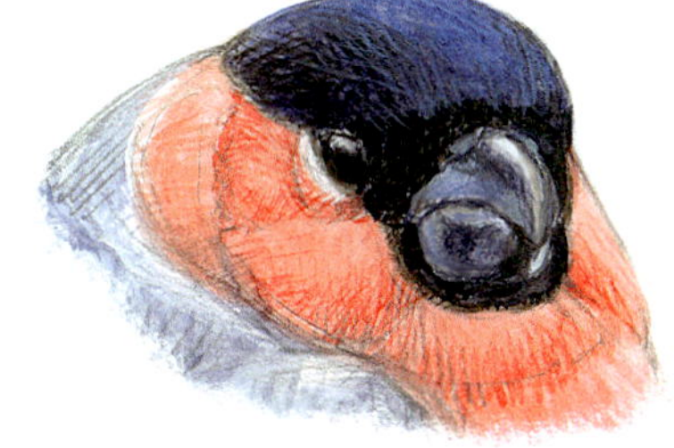

Bullfinch *(Pyrrhula pyrrhula)*

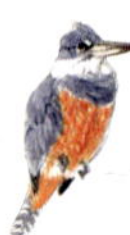

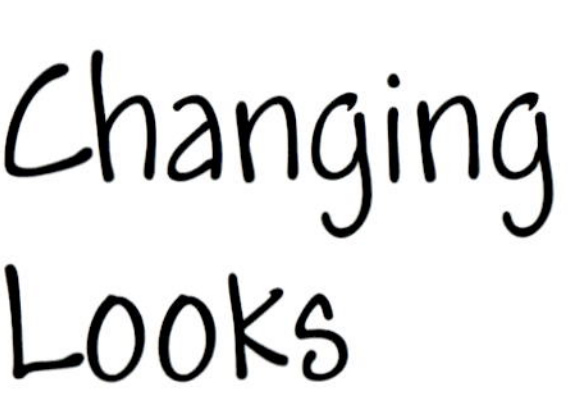

Changing Looks

Drawing birds does not just consist of representing the correct shape, coloring, and proportions of a species. Individualizing the subject and giving it a personal touch involves choosing an angle and a specific pose or attitude for the model. Even when you are making a schematic scientific illustration, behind the drawing there is something more than good artistic technique. Under that lies the preliminary choices of the artist based on his or her observations in the field or in the graphic references he or she has at hand. A single reference may be misleading if it shows the bird in a pose that is not very common for its species.

Remember that the covering of feathers changes the shape of the bird—in this case, the shape of its head, depending on the external temperature, its state of alarm, and seasonal changes. Even the coloring of the plumage can change the perception of its silhouette, and this supposes an advantage when the bird must camouflage itself, because its lines and contrasts in color break up its outline against the background landscape.

The feathers on the forehead, even if there is not an evident crest, can stand up. Many species of owls have a couple of groups of feathers that look like ears that they can raise when they wish. In other cases, the decorative feathers of birds, among them the herons, are lost or become less visible in winter, because at this time of year, they are not useful for attracting a mate, and maintaining them is a waste of energy.

The blue jay has an erect crest. This group of feathers can be used as a signal to others of its species.

The grebes have such different plumage in summer than in winter that they can be mistaken for different species.

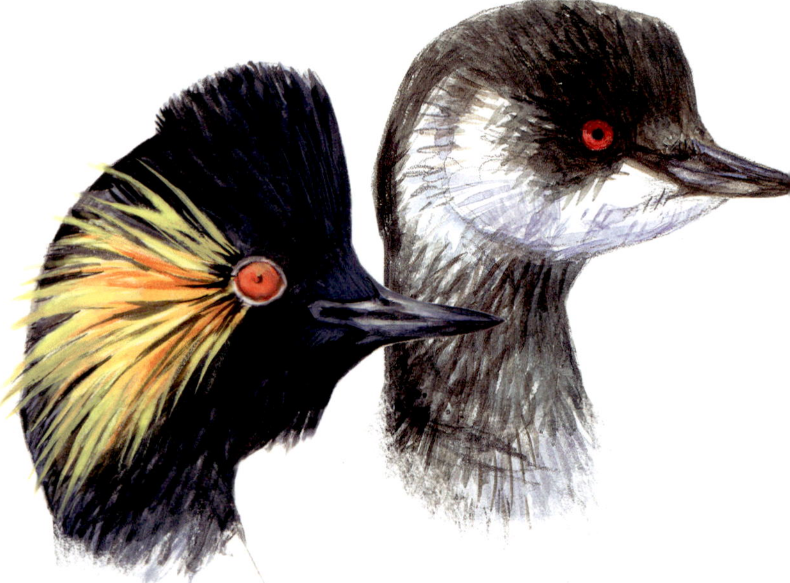

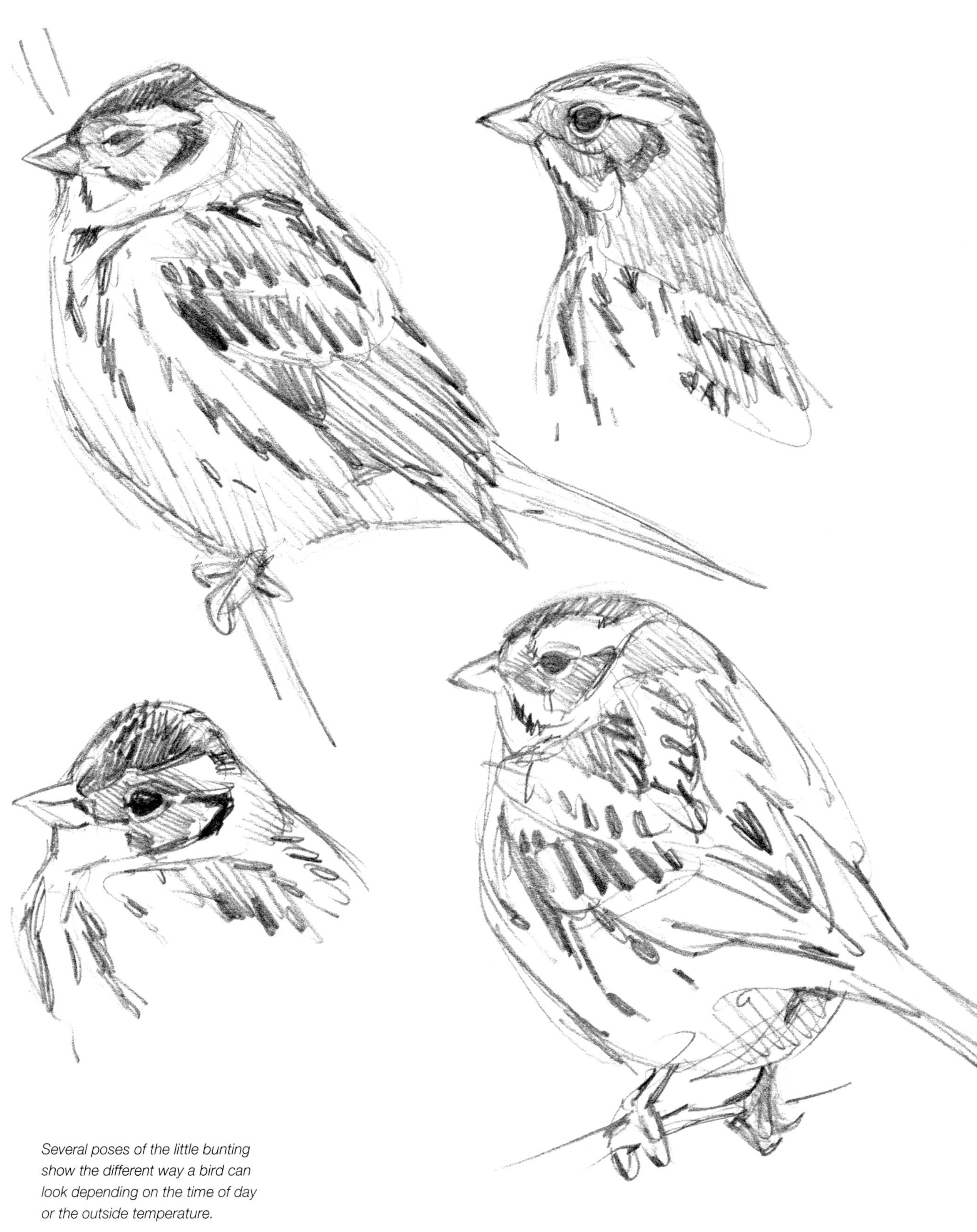

Several poses of the little bunting show the different way a bird can look depending on the time of day or the outside temperature.

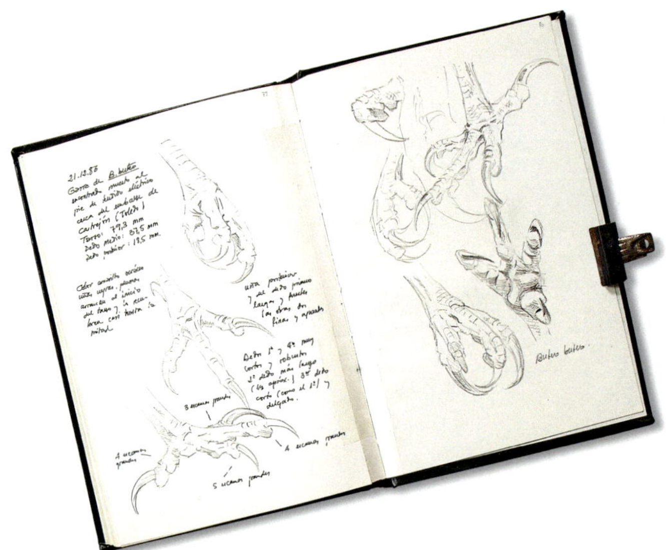

How to Draw the Feet

Accuracy and Perspective

For many artists, realistically representing the feet of a bird is the most difficult part of the job. Not only must the feet give the impression of supporting the bird in a balanced, and many times dynamic, manner, but they must also convincingly represent the parts of the feet that are in contact with the ground or the branches they are on, giving the impression of standing on the ground or grasping a branch. Additionally, you will again be facing the challenge of creating an accurate perspective rendering in accordance with the rest of the body.

On top of this, the shapes of birds' lower extremities are varied and adapted to many different functions, like swimming, hunting, and even handling food.

JUAN VARELA
STONECHAT IN WINTER
WATERCOLOR, 10.5 x 14.5 INCHES (27 x 37 CM)

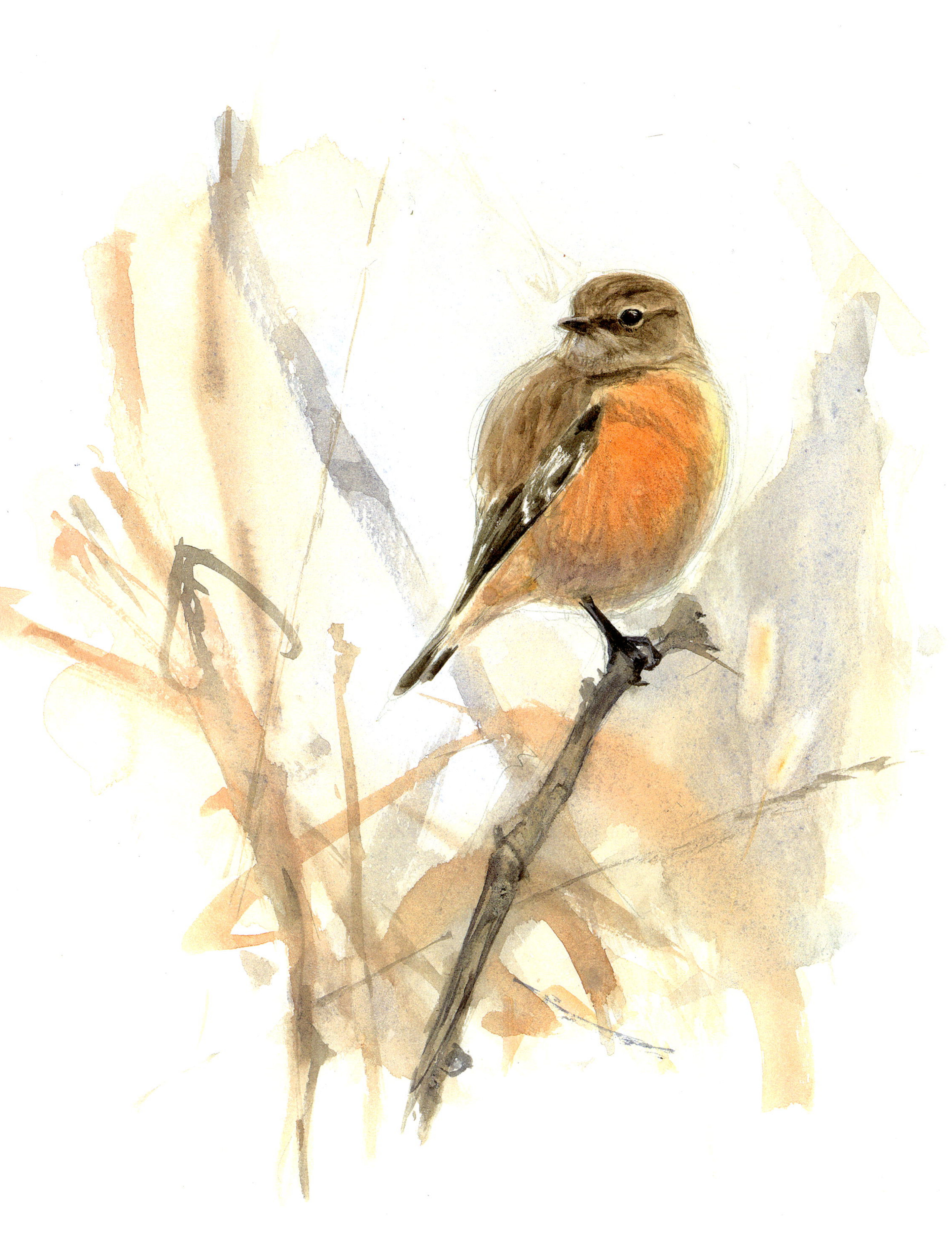

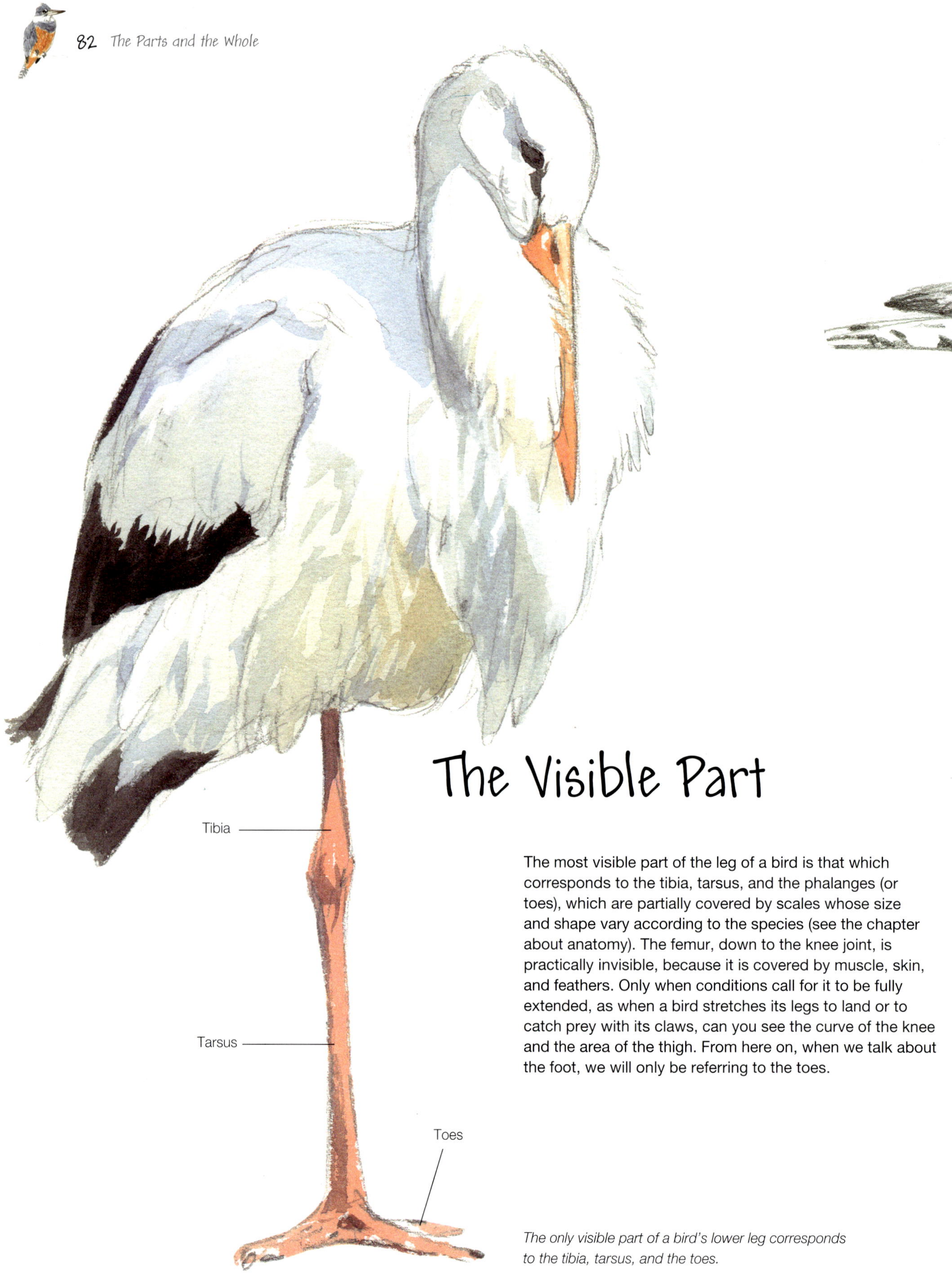

The Visible Part

The most visible part of the leg of a bird is that which corresponds to the tibia, tarsus, and the phalanges (or toes), which are partially covered by scales whose size and shape vary according to the species (see the chapter about anatomy). The femur, down to the knee joint, is practically invisible, because it is covered by muscle, skin, and feathers. Only when conditions call for it to be fully extended, as when a bird stretches its legs to land or to catch prey with its claws, can you see the curve of the knee and the area of the thigh. From here on, when we talk about the foot, we will only be referring to the toes.

The only visible part of a bird's lower leg corresponds to the tibia, tarsus, and the toes.

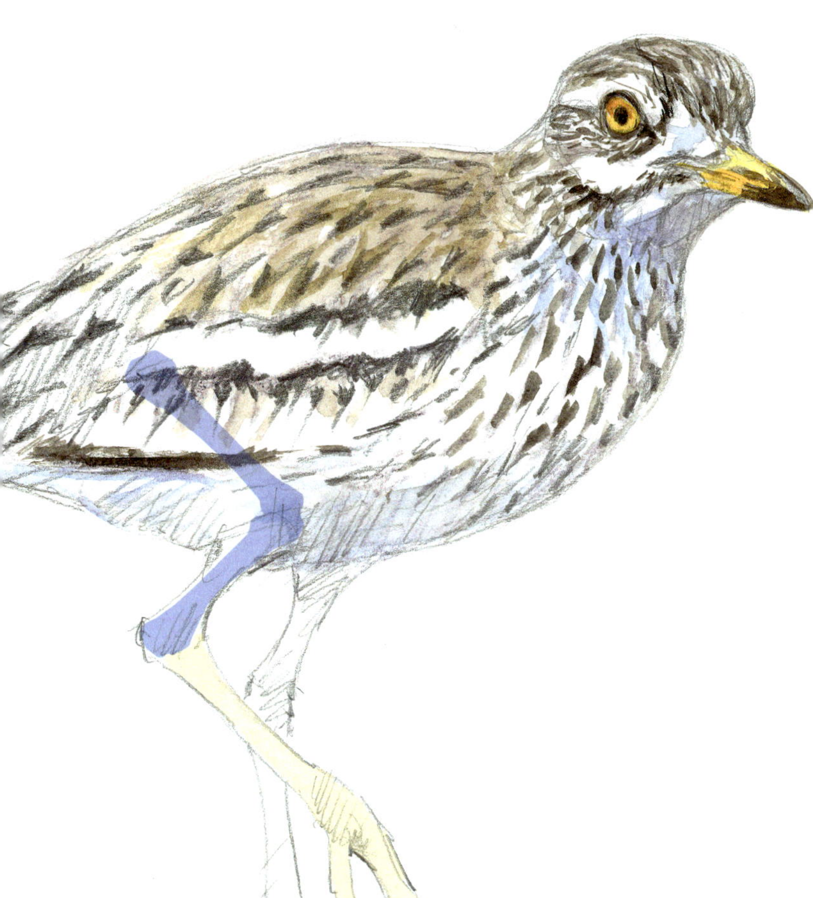

Notice the different placement and length of the legs of a swimming bird, like this Humbolt penguin, and a running bird, like this stone curlew.

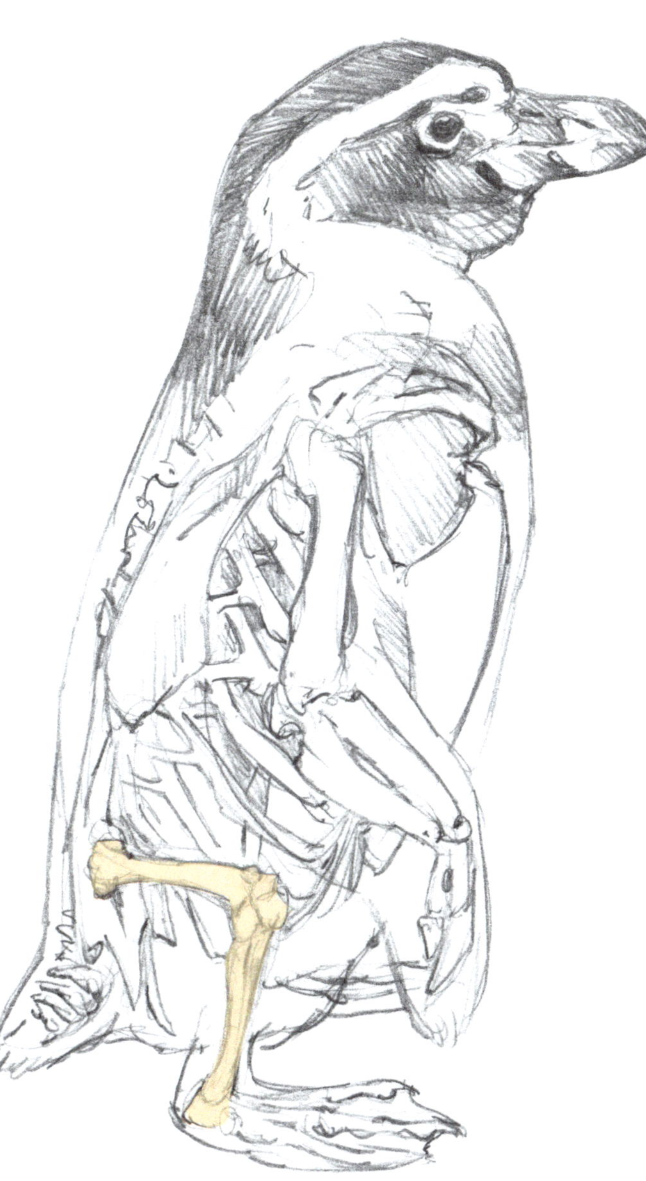

THE PLACEMENT

The location and length of a bird's legs are closely related to its way of life. Just observe a penguin or a cormorant and compare them with a blackbird or a heron. You will immediately see that the placement so far to the back and the short legs of the first two birds are meant for swimming under water and diving. Penguins actually propel themselves with their wings and hide their legs to lessen their drag in the water. Cormorants, on the other hand, kick their feet to move forward.

A duck or a goose will also have its legs farther back, but not as far as the above two species. A duck or goose walking always looks somewhat clumsy. It is obvious that the compromise between being able to walk around on land, and at the same time, be well adapted to swimming is not an easy one.

Birds' Feet

All birds have between two and four toes on each foot. Ostriches only have two, which are very strong and adapted for running. Swifts, however, have four toes, and all of them point forward, which allows them to hang on to rock faces and buildings. In many birds, the fourth toe is opposable and shorter—evolution probably has given them this form so they can perch on tree branches and for balancing when they walk. When it comes to aquatic birds, many species have lost their "thumbs," because they do not need them for hanging on to tree branches.

The toes usually have small pads or callouses underneath the joints that help birds to grasp. These pads are especially visible in birds of prey, which also have strong, curved claws. The word "falcon" actually comes from the Latin word *faix*, or "sickle," which has the same curved shape as the bird's claws.

TOES OR FINS

Almost all aquatic birds have some kind of membrane, or expansions of their feet, which help them to swim. Some of them have webs that connect all their toes and others, like coots, have small lobes that increase the supporting surface so they can walk on aquatic vegetation. Certain aquatic birds, like the jacanas and swamphens, however, walk across floating vegetation with the help of their very long toes. Generally, the web-footed birds only have three toes, with the exception of cormorants, which have four long toes connected by a single membrane that creates a large surface that helps them dive.

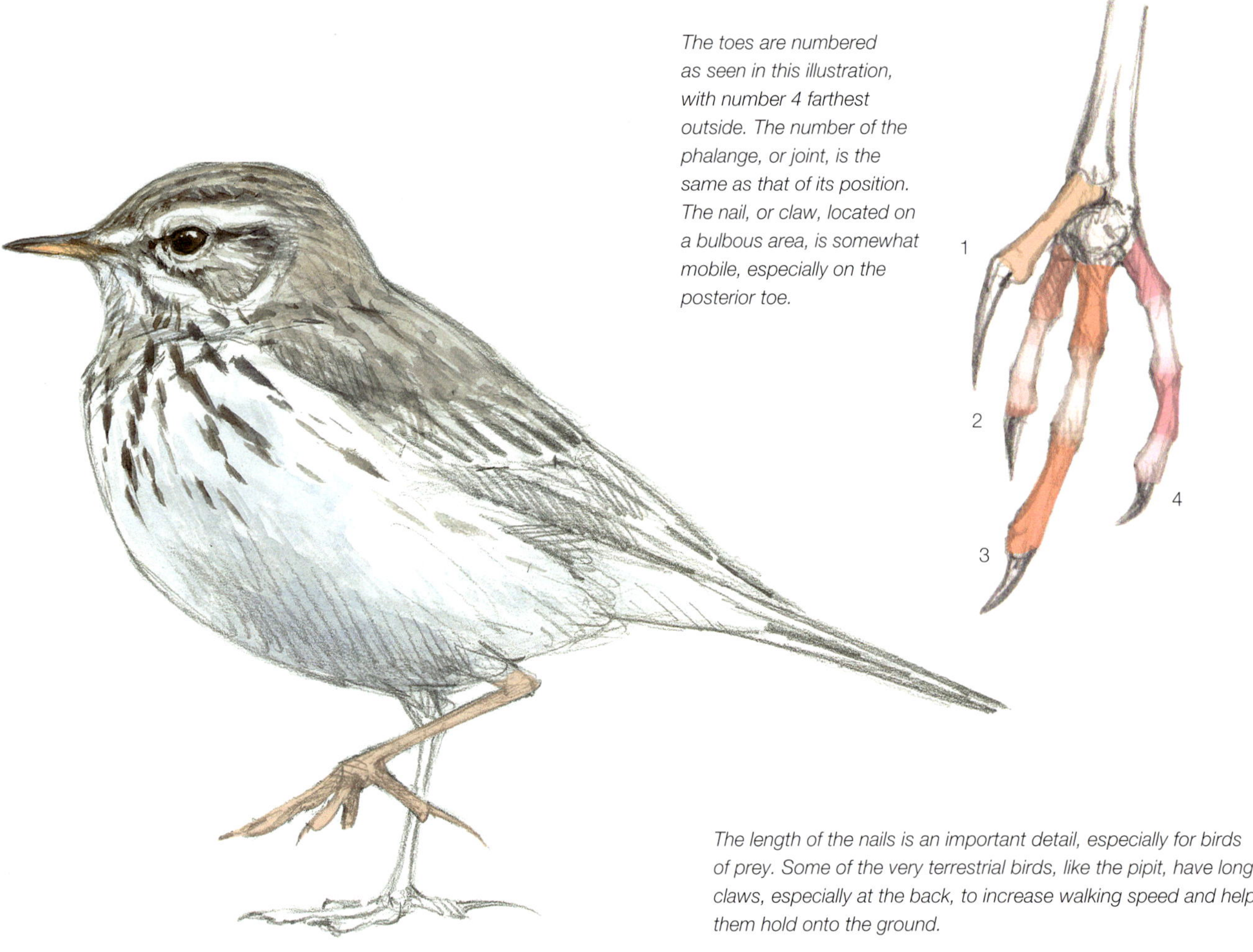

The toes are numbered as seen in this illustration, with number 4 farthest outside. The number of the phalange, or joint, is the same as that of its position. The nail, or claw, located on a bulbous area, is somewhat mobile, especially on the posterior toe.

The length of the nails is an important detail, especially for birds of prey. Some of the very terrestrial birds, like the pipit, have long claws, especially at the back, to increase walking speed and help them hold onto the ground.

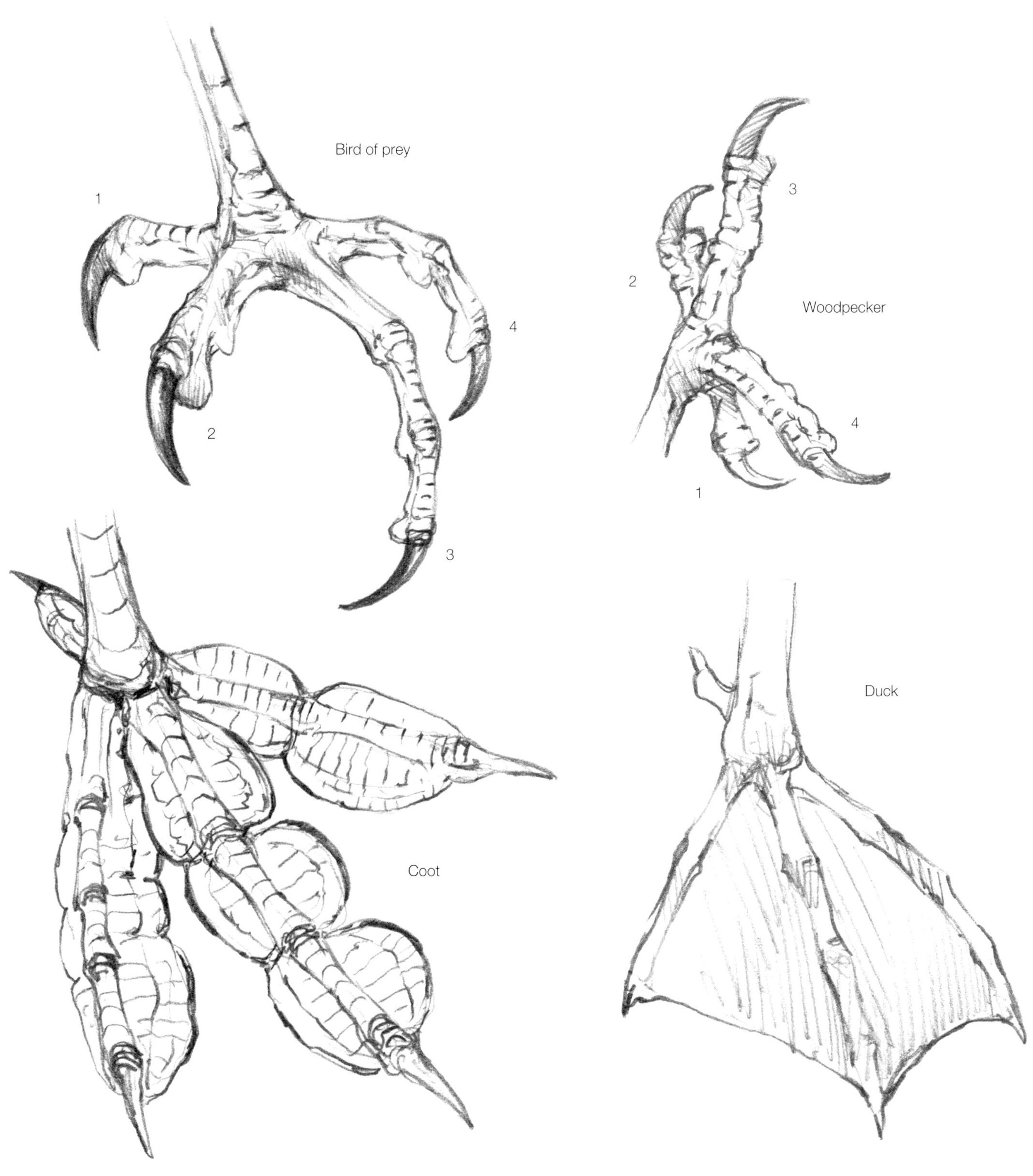

Many birds of prey have a more robust inner toe with a strong claw. Woodpeckers, parrots, cuckoos, ospreys, and owls, among others, have two opposable toes, numbers 1 and 4, for climbing and to better grasp their prey.

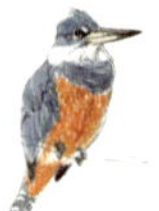

Many good drawings of birds lose their realism because the feet do not seem to be hanging onto a branch or rock, or even to be well planted on the ground. Sometimes, it happens that the perspective of the feet does not coincide with the rest of the bird. To draw feet well, you must remember that each toe has a different number of phalanges, and therefore the curvature of each one must be different. The posterior toe has only a single phalange, so it does not curve and it only bends where it meets the tarsus. The nail has its own independent articulation separate from the joint at the tarsus.

The Importance of the Grasp

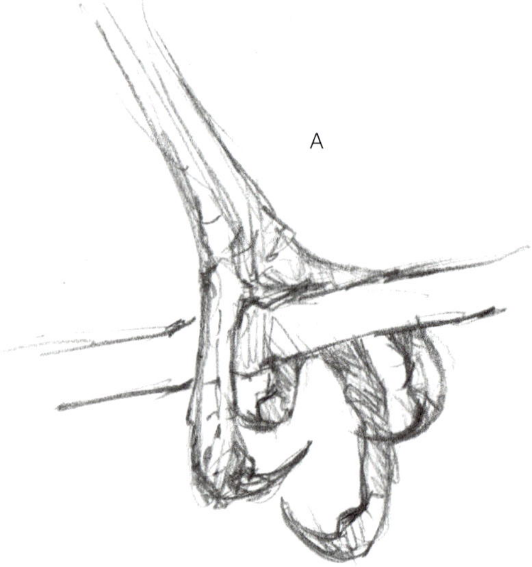

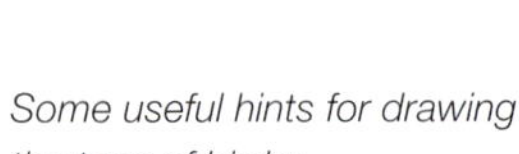

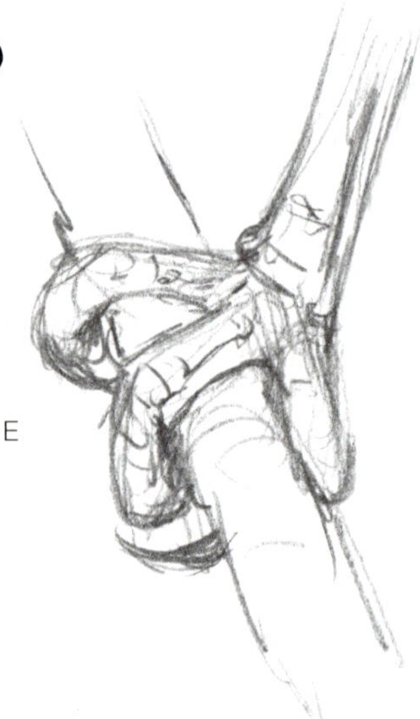

Some useful hints for drawing the toes of birds:
When the leg is extended, the toes do not close and the bird must stay in a balanced pose (A). Bending the leg forces the flexor tendons to close the toes with no energy spent (B). The middle and internal toes bend in a more angular manner, because they have fewer and longer articulations than the exterior toe (C). The interior toe can be more separated when the bird perches on a steeply inclined branch or when hanging on a littler tighter (D). Some birds have opposable toes; but, even those that do not sometimes place one toe on the other side of the branch. This detail makes the drawing a bit more artistic and less orthodox (E). It is important to draw an accurate rendering of the foot placed on the ground so that it corresponds to the rest of the body.

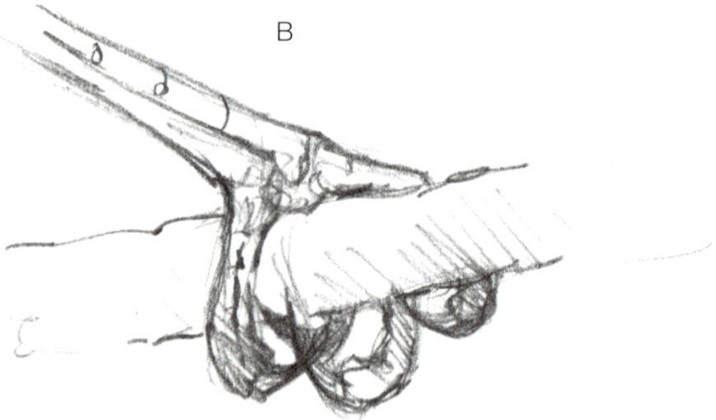

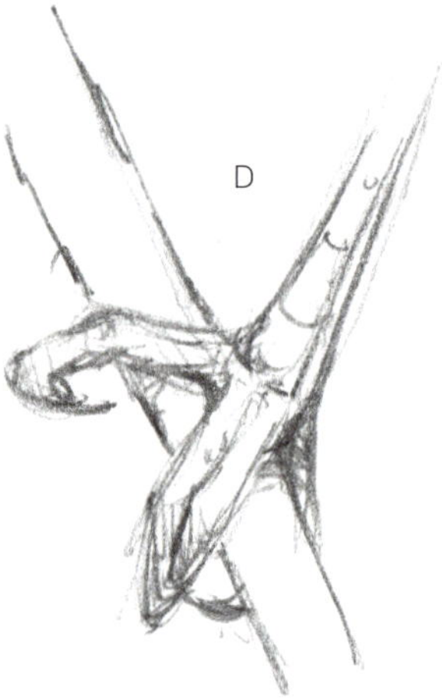

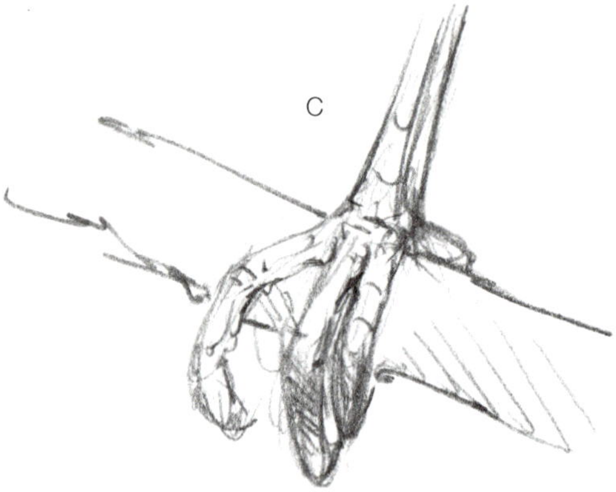

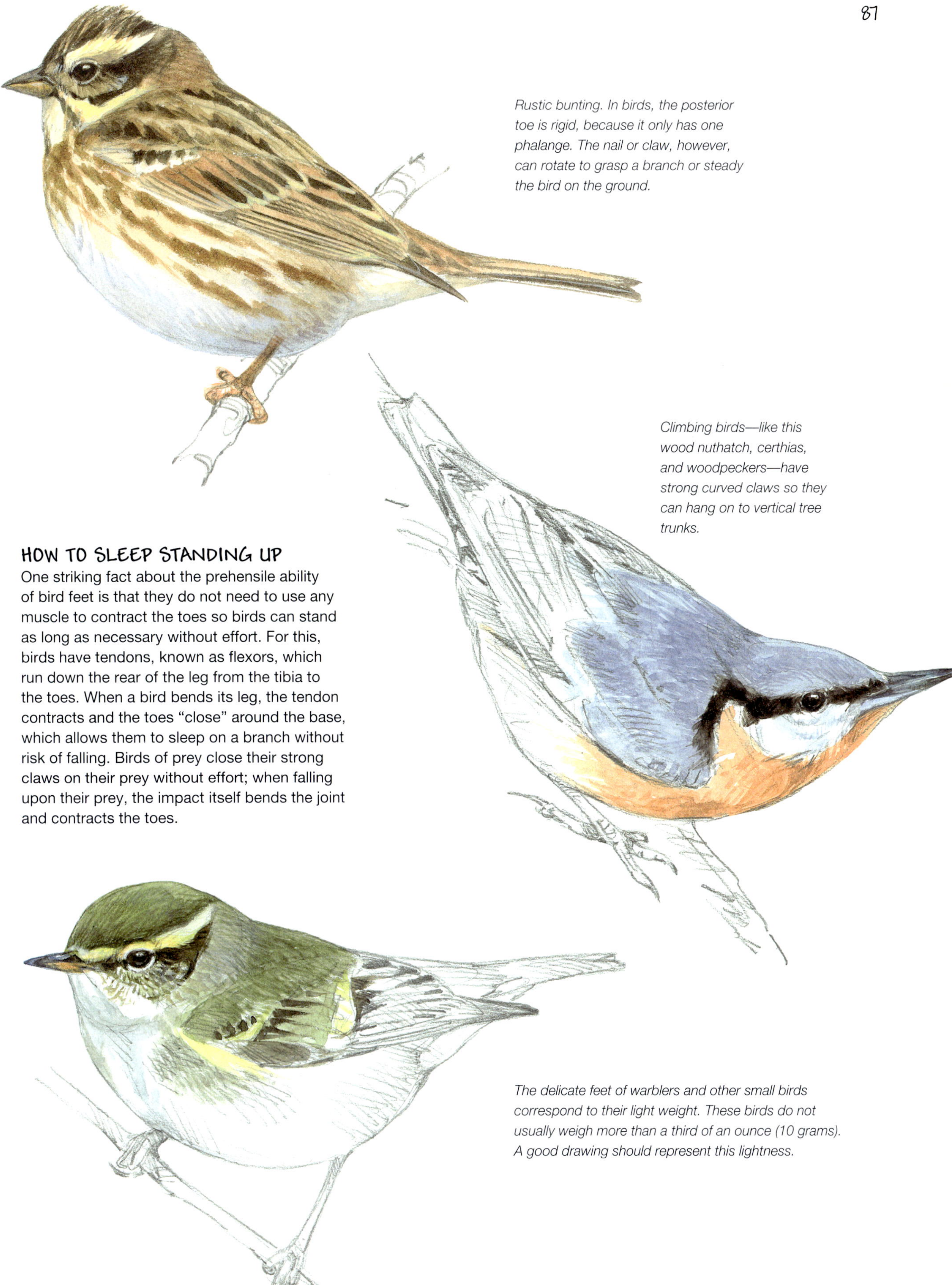

Rustic bunting. In birds, the posterior toe is rigid, because it only has one phalange. The nail or claw, however, can rotate to grasp a branch or steady the bird on the ground.

Climbing birds—like this wood nuthatch, certhias, and woodpeckers—have strong curved claws so they can hang on to vertical tree trunks.

HOW TO SLEEP STANDING UP

One striking fact about the prehensile ability of bird feet is that they do not need to use any muscle to contract the toes so birds can stand as long as necessary without effort. For this, birds have tendons, known as flexors, which run down the rear of the leg from the tibia to the toes. When a bird bends its leg, the tendon contracts and the toes "close" around the base, which allows them to sleep on a branch without risk of falling. Birds of prey close their strong claws on their prey without effort; when falling upon their prey, the impact itself bends the joint and contracts the toes.

The delicate feet of warblers and other small birds correspond to their light weight. These birds do not usually weigh more than a third of an ounce (10 grams). A good drawing should represent this lightness.

How to Balance a Bird

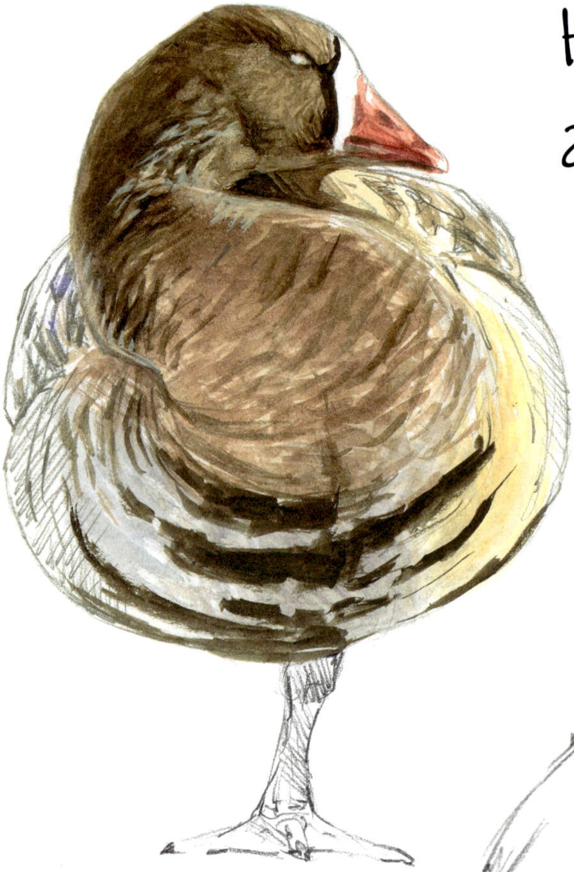

This greater white-footed goose stands on a single leg, maintaining its center of gravity directly over it.

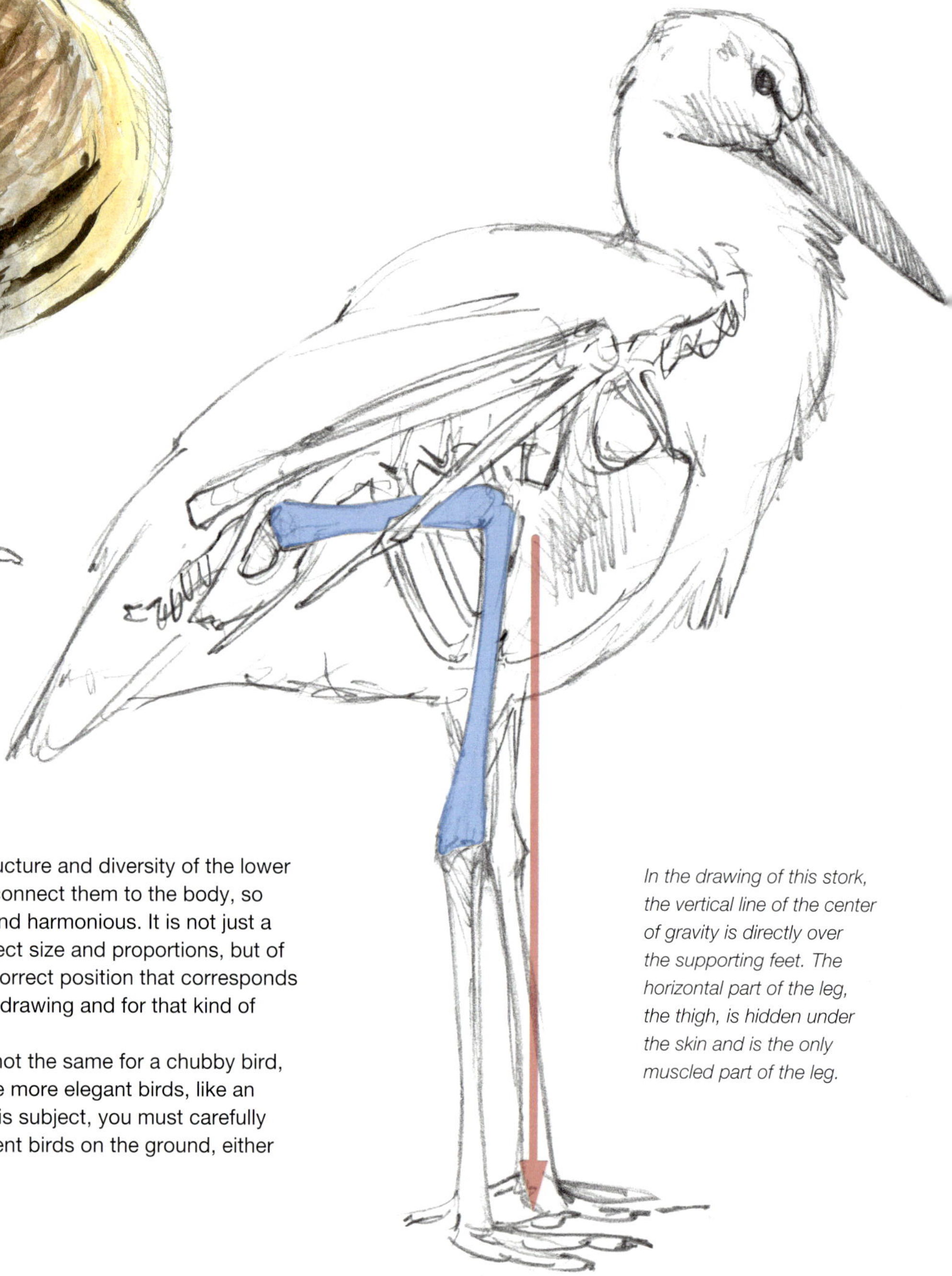

Now that you understand the structure and diversity of the lower extremities of birds, it is time to connect them to the body, so that the whole will be balanced and harmonious. It is not just a matter of giving the legs the correct size and proportions, but of anchoring them and finding the correct position that corresponds to the movement reflected in the drawing and for that kind of bird.

The harmony of movement is not the same for a chubby bird, like a goose, as it is for one of the more elegant birds, like an egret. To become familiar with this subject, you must carefully observe the movements of different birds on the ground, either in the field or in videos.

In the drawing of this stork, the vertical line of the center of gravity is directly over the supporting feet. The horizontal part of the leg, the thigh, is hidden under the skin and is the only muscled part of the leg.

While a bird is running, its body is in dynamic balance, and its center of gravity can be momentarily displaced until the leg supports it.

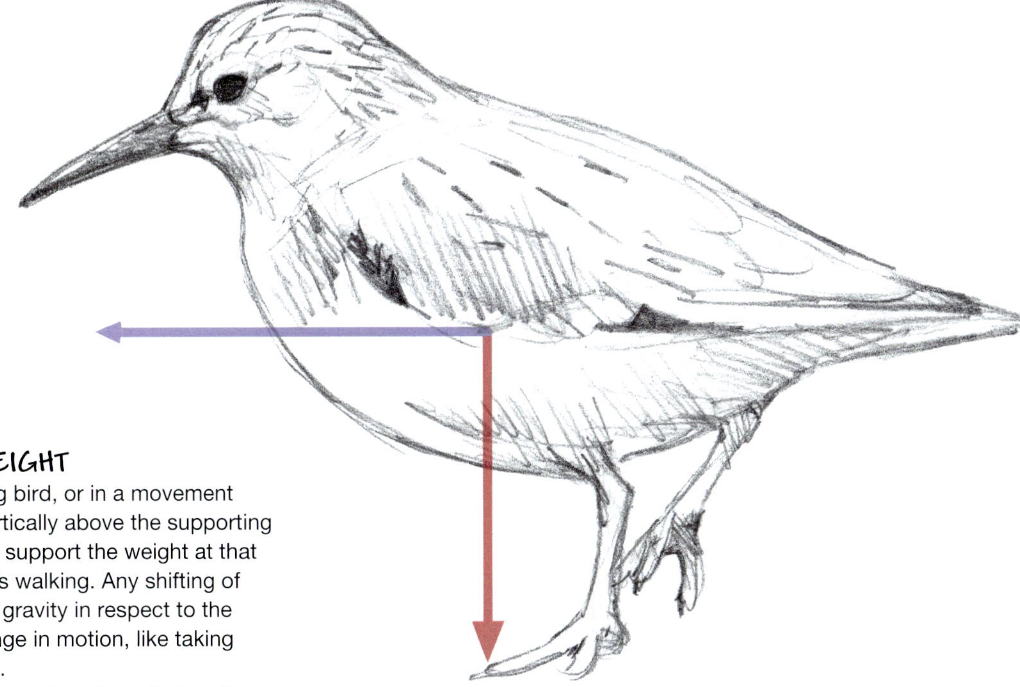

THE CENTER OF THE WEIGHT

The center of gravity in a resting bird, or in a movement that is not forced, is located vertically above the supporting point of the foot or the feet that support the weight at that moment, or between them if it is walking. Any shifting of weight away from the center of gravity in respect to the vertical will be related to a change in motion, like taking flight, starting to run, and so on.

Calculating the vertical of this center of gravity is not difficult; it is more a question of the artist's experience, because it varies according to the bird's position and the observer's point of view. The center will be found in the densest part of the body, where the major part of the bird's weight is concentrated.

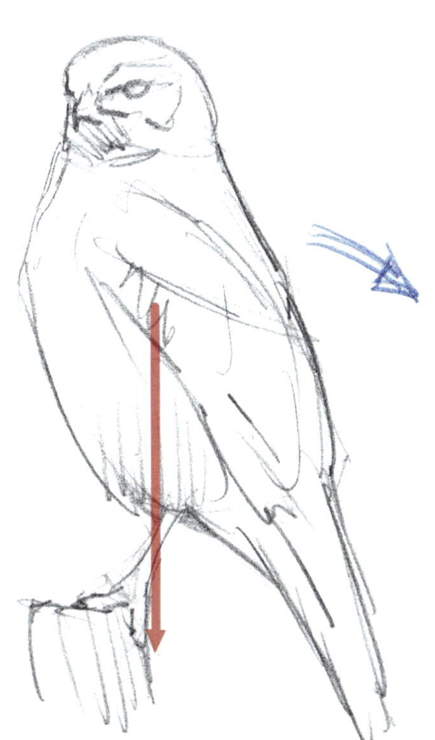

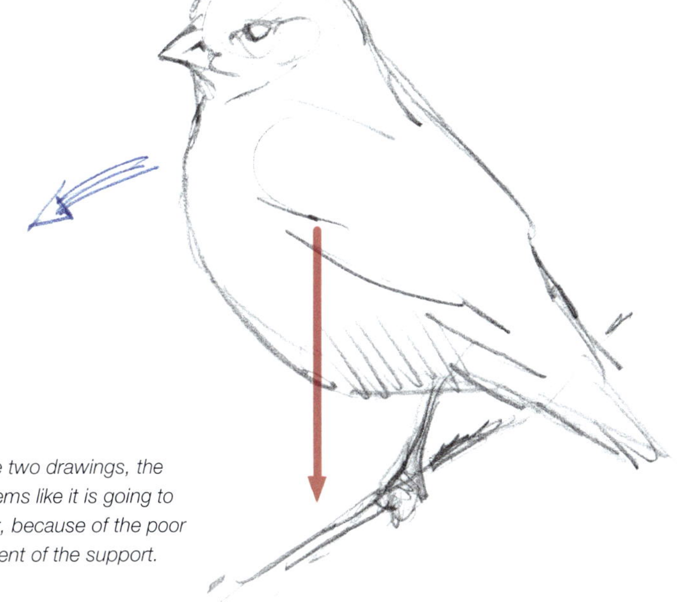

In these two drawings, the bird seems like it is going to fall over, because of the poor placement of the support.

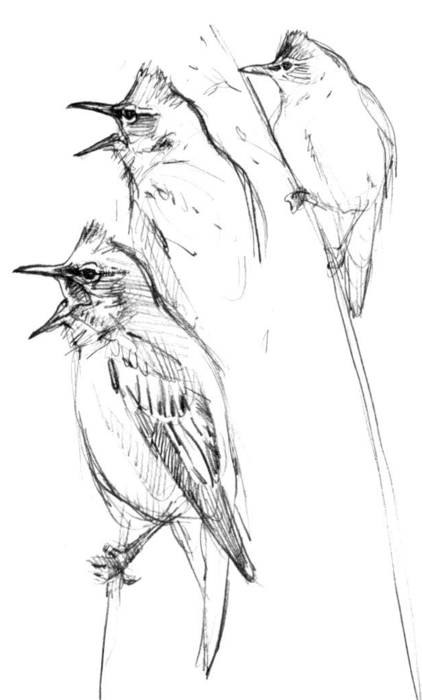

The Complete Bird
How to Represent Its Volume

To be successful at drawing birds as complete and mobile figures, you must study their anatomy, their conduct, and their great diversity. A good draftsman can quite accurately reproduce a bird from a photograph, or even from a living bird that stays more or less at rest; but, without intimate knowledge of birds, it will be difficult for him or her to understand what he or she is drawing.

The goal of the previous chapters is to offer the artist specific information that allows him or her to understand the form and movement of birds and to internalize these in such a way that he or she will be able to draw a bird in any possible pose. The following step is to practice a series of exercises for accurately representing the volume and perspective views of birds.

JUAN VARELA
AQUATIC WARBLER (*ACROCEPHALUS PALUDICOLA*)
WATERCOLOR, 8.25 x 12 INCHES (21 x 30 CM)

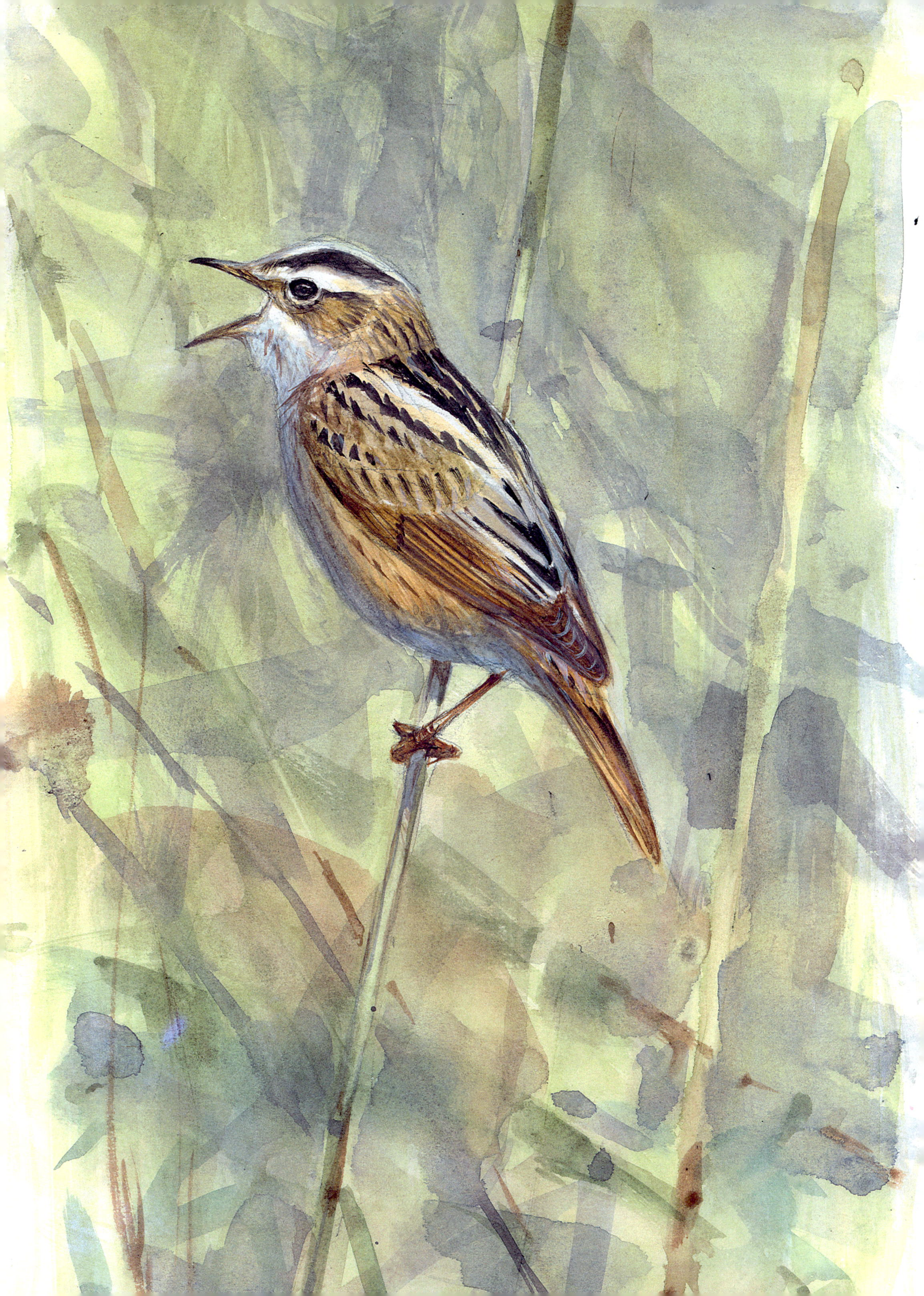

Being faced with drawing a complete bird will be easier after having studied its most complicated parts. Blocking in the bird requires solving two challenges: its proportions and its posture. Whether you are working in the field or using a photograph, you must start with a few simple lines to locate the essential elements: the head, the central nucleus of the body, the legs, and the tail. At this moment, you must start to carefully define the proportions, because later there is a risk of getting carried away with working on the details and losing the references of the relative sizes.

The most basic and traditional approach is to reduce all of the elements to small circles and lines.

How to Find the Shapes

1. A few lines will help you establish the approximate posture and the proportions of the bird. With practice, this system will not be necessary and you will be able to approach the drawing of the bird more directly.

2. These initial lines, generally very light, should be developed using shapes that indicate somewhat more energy and movement. It is typical to start at the head, locating the eye and the line of the beak to create clear reference points.

3. With a few later lines, you can block in the wings and tail, making sure their lengths are correct, the shape of the breast and the back, and the positions of the feet. The use of broken lines and varied widths will add liveliness and realism to the drawing. The addition of feathers will now be of great help in developing the shape of the head, the wings, and the back.

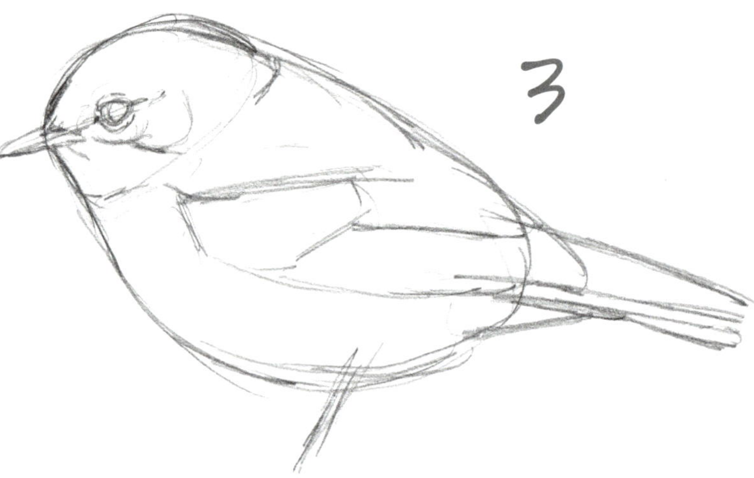

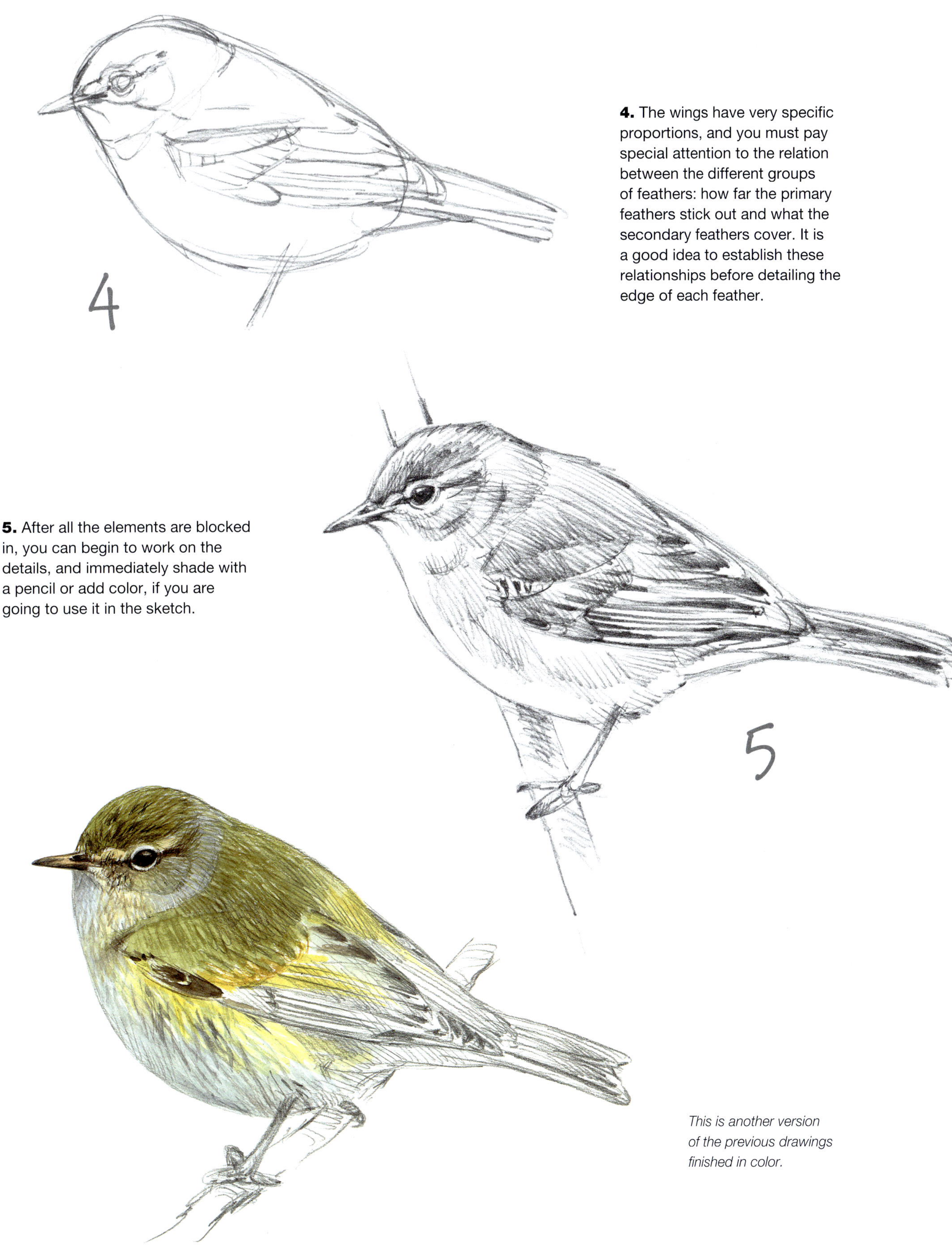

4. The wings have very specific proportions, and you must pay special attention to the relation between the different groups of feathers: how far the primary feathers stick out and what the secondary feathers cover. It is a good idea to establish these relationships before detailing the edge of each feather.

5. After all the elements are blocked in, you can begin to work on the details, and immediately shade with a pencil or add color, if you are going to use it in the sketch.

This is another version of the previous drawings finished in color.

A Way of Understanding Volume

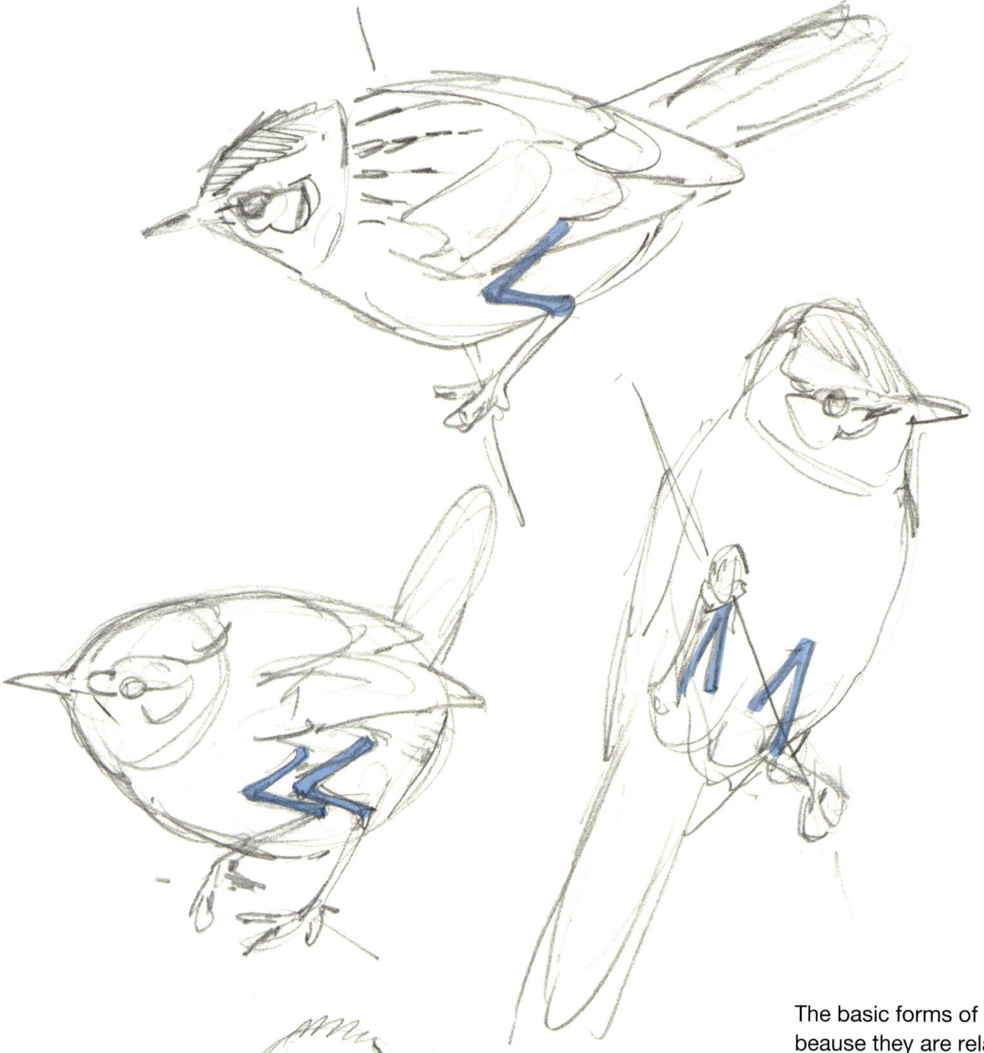

An interesting exercise is to try to concentrate the information that you see on the model in very simple lines, without getting into details other than the placement of the eyes, the feet, and the outlines of the wings. In this way, you will keep from getting bogged down in the details.

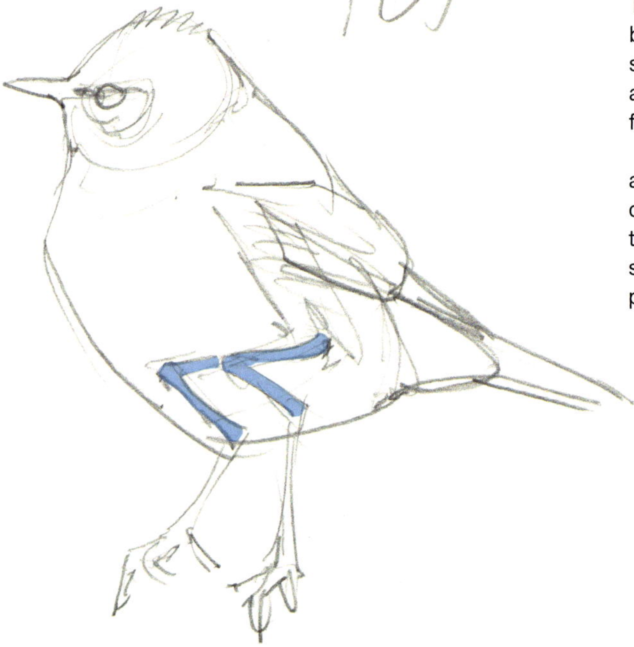

The basic forms of the body are well known by artists, beause they are related to the most basic geometrical shapes. Cylinders, spheres, and cones can define almost all parts of the body and are a good approach for understanding its volume.

A lot of imagination is required to see these shapes as transparent objects, so that all the different parts can be correctly placed in perspective. Practicing these examples is very easy, just like making small studies of light and shadow, which is necessary practice for making a successful drawing from nature.

The different parts of a bird's body are here reduced to three-dimensional geometric forms. One good exercise consists of taking photographs of birds and copying them while reducing their volumes to these shapes and imagining the placement of the legs, even those that can barely be seen.

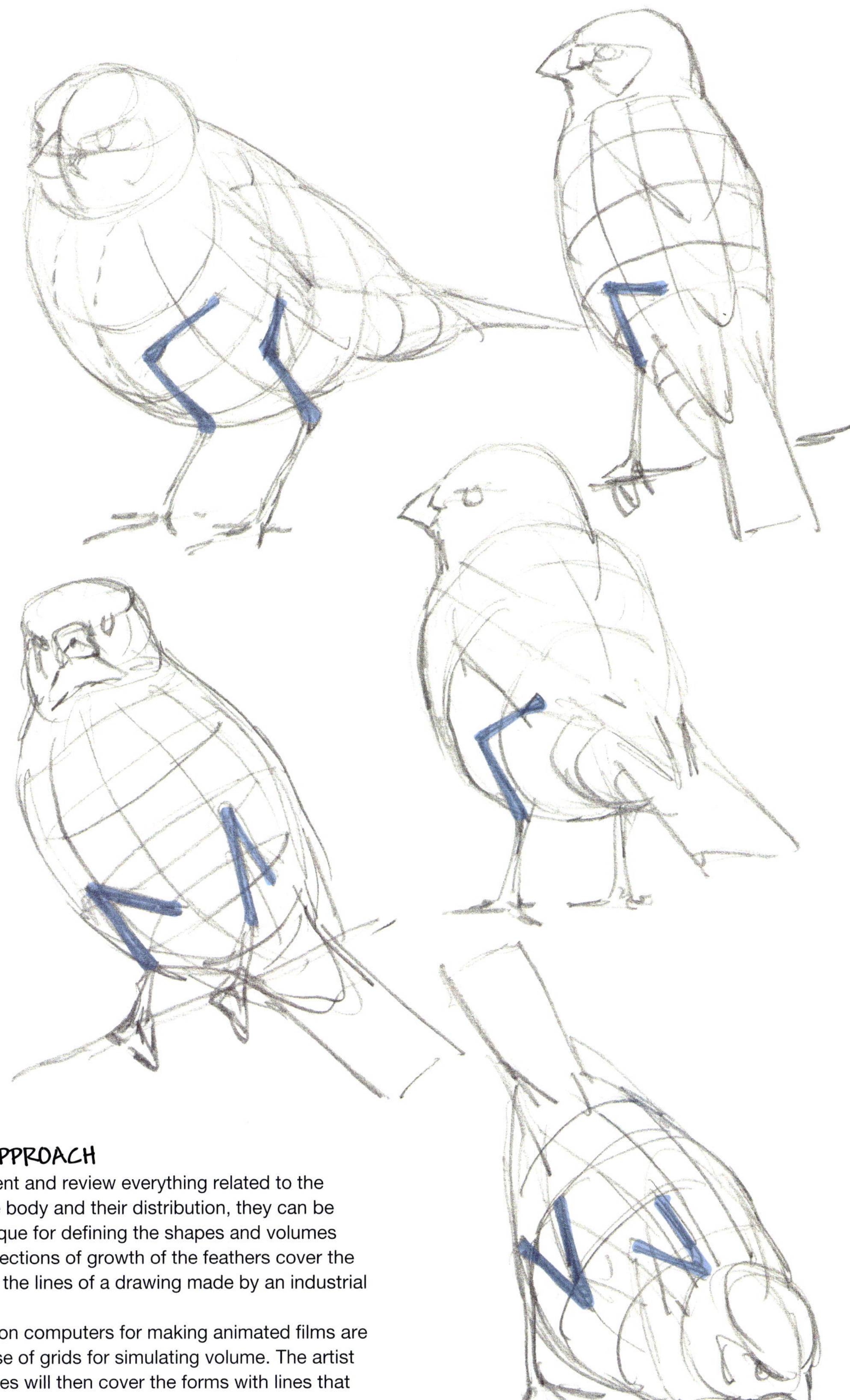

USING THE GRID APPROACH

If we go back for a moment and review everything related to the groups of feathers on the body and their distribution, they can be used as one more technique for defining the shapes and volumes of a bird, because the directions of growth of the feathers cover the body in the same way as the lines of a drawing made by an industrial designer.

The basic lines drawn on computers for making animated films are a good example of the use of grids for simulating volume. The artist responsible for the textures will then cover the forms with lines that imitate fur or feathers.

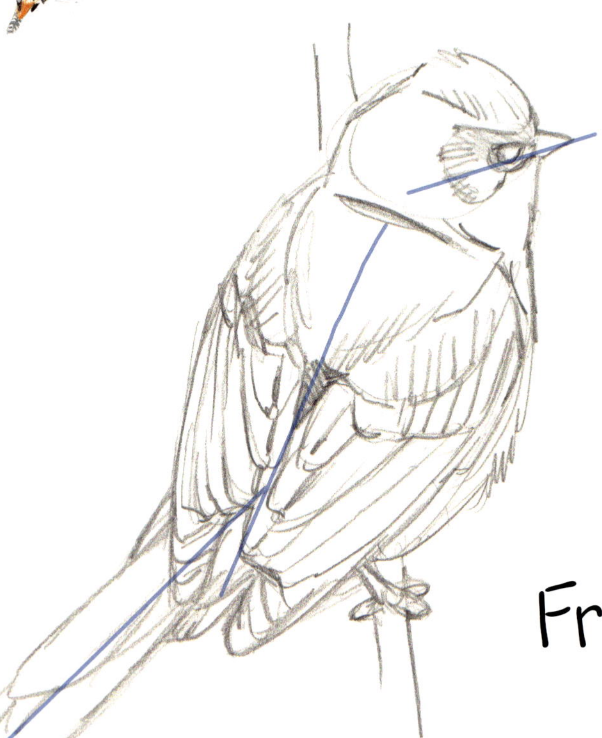

For many artists, drawing a profile portrait, whether of a person or an animal, is very simple. In this way, the shapes are simplified, the proportions are better calculated, and complicated views are avoided. Birds, however, are usually in constant motion and strike a wide variety of postures that an artist should be able to reproduce on paper. To do this, it is a good idea to study the greatest possible number of images, whether photographs or the drawings of other artists who reproduce birds in postures that are not so common. The goal is not just to copy the photo, but to understand the perspective, the balance, and other details, internalizing them, so that the each time the drawing flows more spontaneously.

From Any Angle

The centerline of the back separates the nearly symmetrical halves of the drawing, although the left side is partially hidden by foreshortening. The line of the tail is not a continuation of the back, and it helps make the figure more dynamic.

SIMPLIFYING THE LINE

On this page, we show a variety of the passeriform (or passerine) species in different poses that are not, at first, easy to draw. To make them more understandable, they have been reduced to just the essential lines—that is, to those that indicate the edges of the different groups of feathers and that the artist uses in a preliminary sketch to later guide the placement of additional details. As you can see, they go a step farther than the sketch of circles used to block in the drawing.

The blue lines define the angles formed between different parts of the body in respect to the vertical and horizontal axes. You can achieve somewhat more liveliness and movement in the drawing as long as you keep these angles in mind.

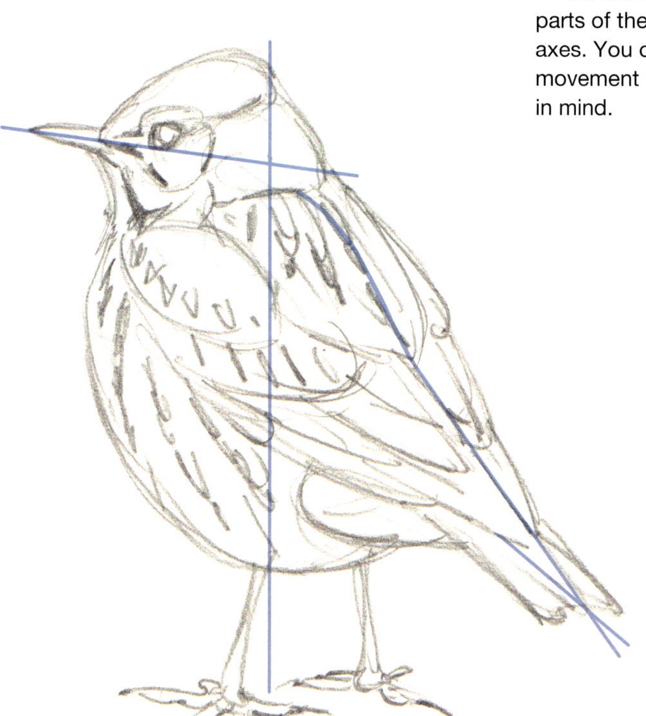

This more aesthetic pose is not too difficult, but you must be careful with its balance. The line of the tail forms a different angle with the horizontal than that of the back, because it begins at a lower point. All of the feather groups are represented by circular lines.

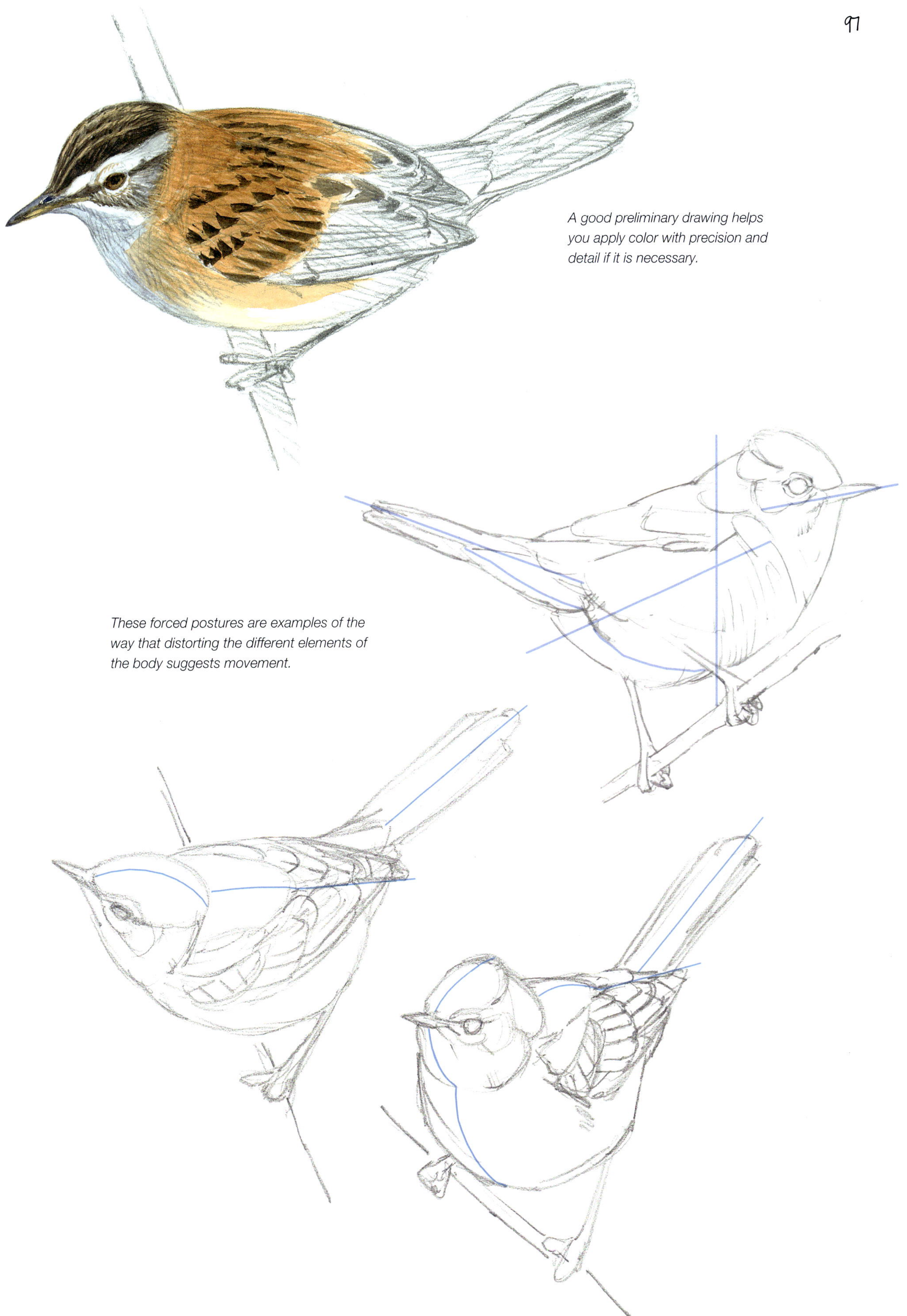

A good preliminary drawing helps you apply color with precision and detail if it is necessary.

These forced postures are examples of the way that distorting the different elements of the body suggests movement.

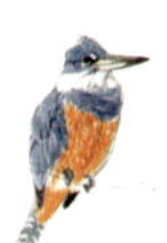

Birds on the Ground

Not all birds move across the ground by walking. Some move with short hops, like the sparrow, for example. Generally, birds that spend a large part of their lives on the ground, like wagtails, walk to move around, because it is the way that uses the least energy. Magpies usually hop when moving large distances, because they move forward more quickly, even though they use more energy; but they walk if they have to cover a very short distance.

When it comes to the artist, the way that the bird moves should be reflected in the drawing. A sparrow should never be depicted walking, with its legs in a V-shape, but sandpipers, which are great walkers, should be, because they find their food as they cover great distances while pecking in the mud.

Small land birds have long feet, and usually long claws that help them run on hard terrain.

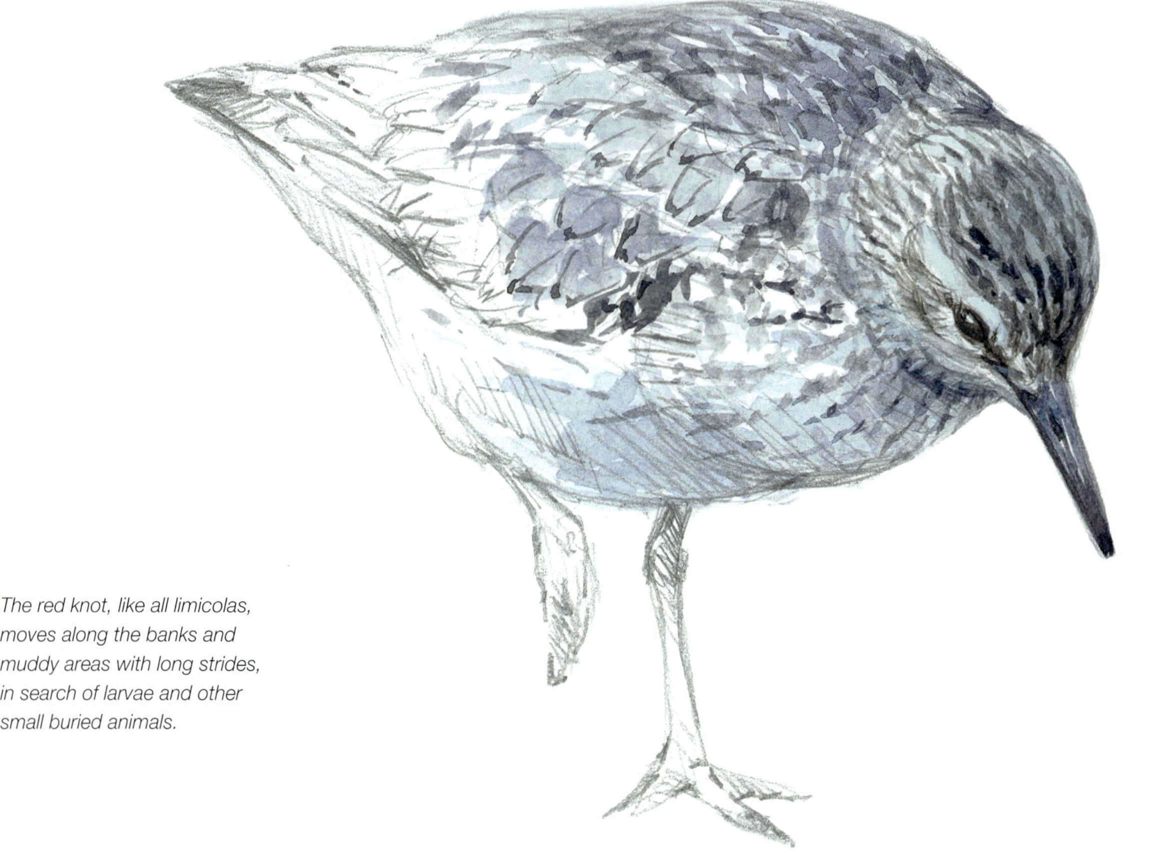

The red knot, like all limicolas, moves along the banks and muddy areas with long strides, in search of larvae and other small buried animals.

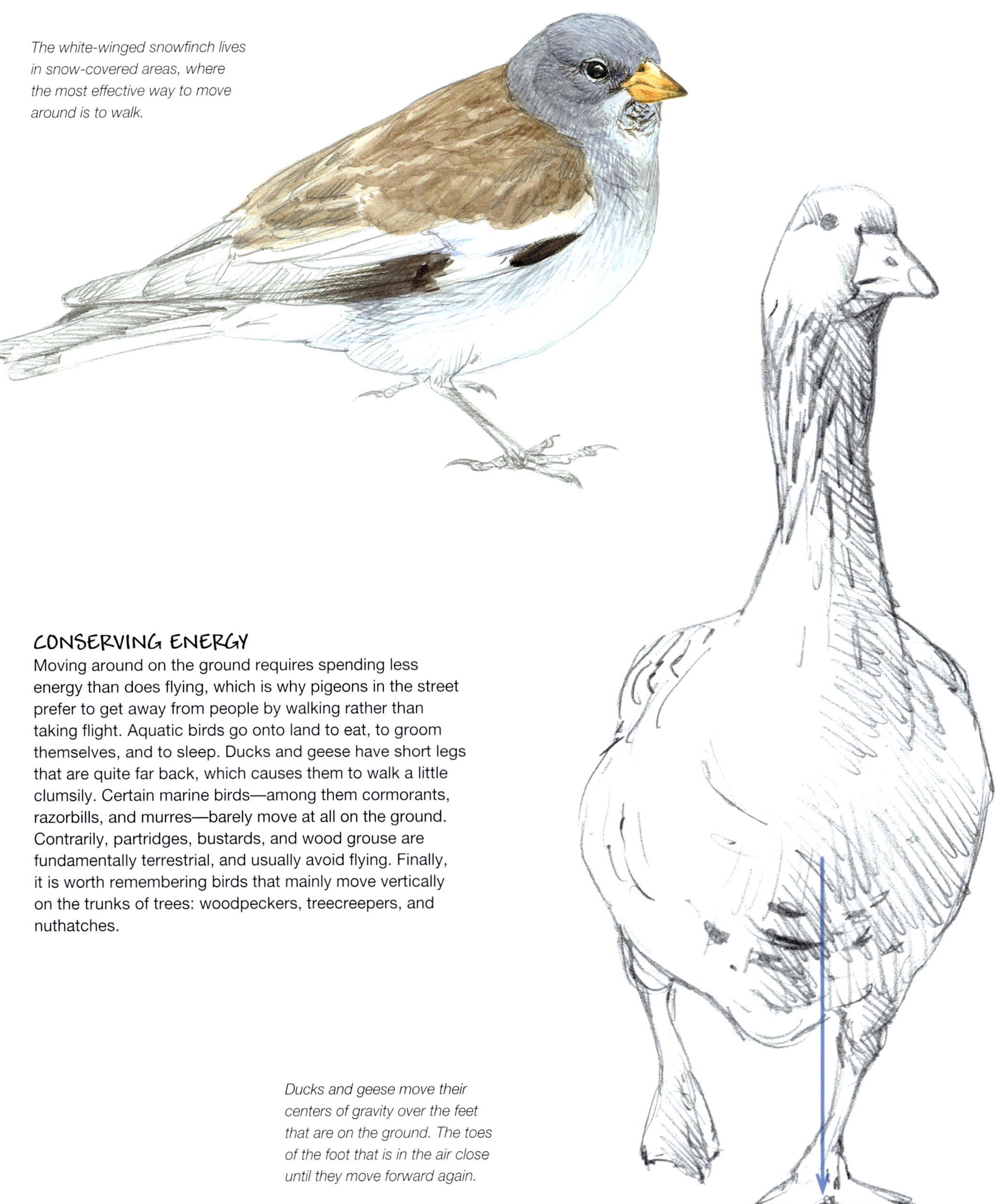

The white-winged snowfinch lives in snow-covered areas, where the most effective way to move around is to walk.

CONSERVING ENERGY

Moving around on the ground requires spending less energy than does flying, which is why pigeons in the street prefer to get away from people by walking rather than taking flight. Aquatic birds go onto land to eat, to groom themselves, and to sleep. Ducks and geese have short legs that are quite far back, which causes them to walk a little clumsily. Certain marine birds—among them cormorants, razorbills, and murres—barely move at all on the ground. Contrarily, partridges, bustards, and wood grouse are fundamentally terrestrial, and usually avoid flying. Finally, it is worth remembering birds that mainly move vertically on the trunks of trees: woodpeckers, treecreepers, and nuthatches.

Ducks and geese move their centers of gravity over the feet that are on the ground. The toes of the foot that is in the air close until they move forward again.

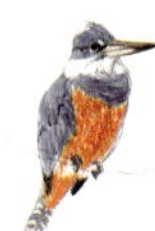

Birds in the Air

Drawing a bird in flight brings up a series of complications that must be considered and cleared up one by one. On the one hand, you must correctly illustrate the proportions and habitual attitude of the species; the posture of flight is sometimes a characteristic that should be kept in mind. On the other hand, it is necessary to approach drawing the point of view from different angles, with the added problem that the wings are flexible and the curvature is not always easy to describe in perspective. A third aspect to consider is the position of the whole body, depending on the type of flight: soaring, flapping, ascending, or diving.

As you can see, as soon as you depart from the simple scheme of a bird in a plane that is perpendicular to your line of sight, everything becomes quite complicated.

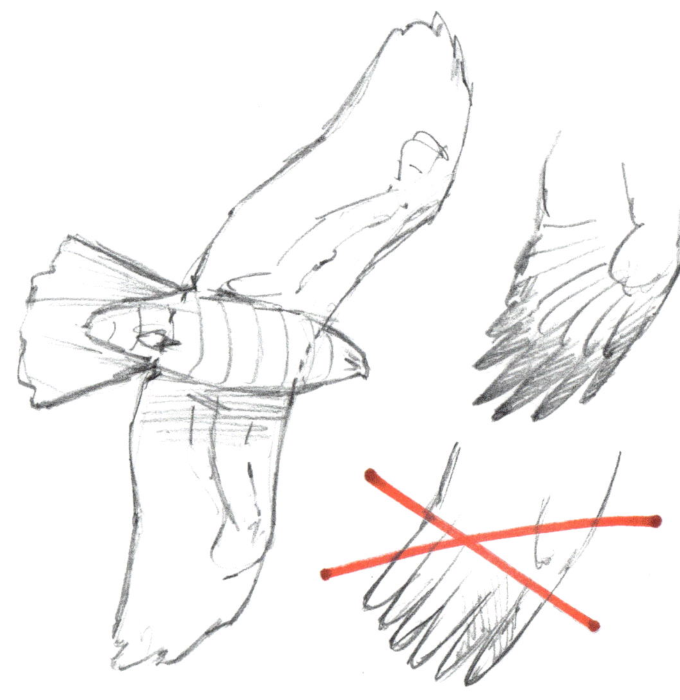

The forward edge of the wing can be blocked in with a continuous line. Depending on the position of the bird, the joint of one of the wings can be hidden by the body. It is a common error to draw the primary feathers as if they were a brush, because they actually open like a fan.

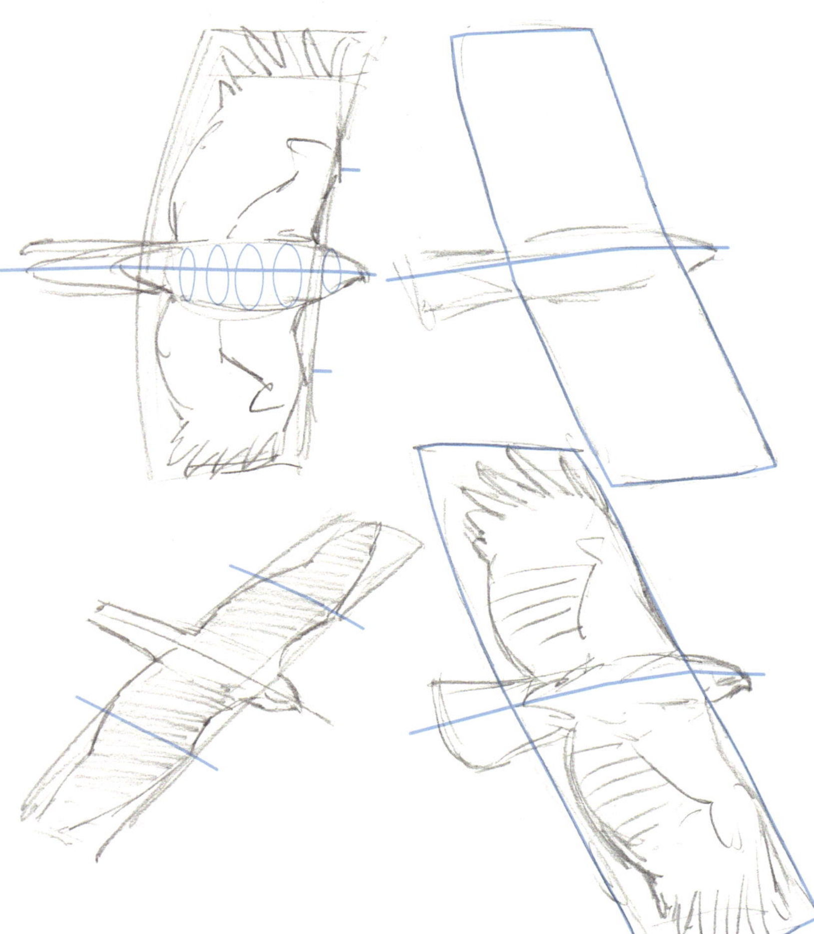

THE BASIC STRUCTURE

In the same way that a drawing of a bird on the ground can be based on a structure of circles, a bird in flight can be constructed with "scaffolding" lines that enclose the final sketch. This scaffolding is easier to rotate in space and allows you to better block in the proportions from the first moment. In the following images, we will only show birds of prey, because they better illustrate the peculiarities of flight.

Establishing some guidelines will create a frame where you can begin adding the general shape of the bird. A rectangle scheme works well for the normal posture of a bird soaring. From the first lines, you must establish accurate relationships among the length of the body, the wings, and the tail. The relation between the length of the "hand" and the total wing will also vary.

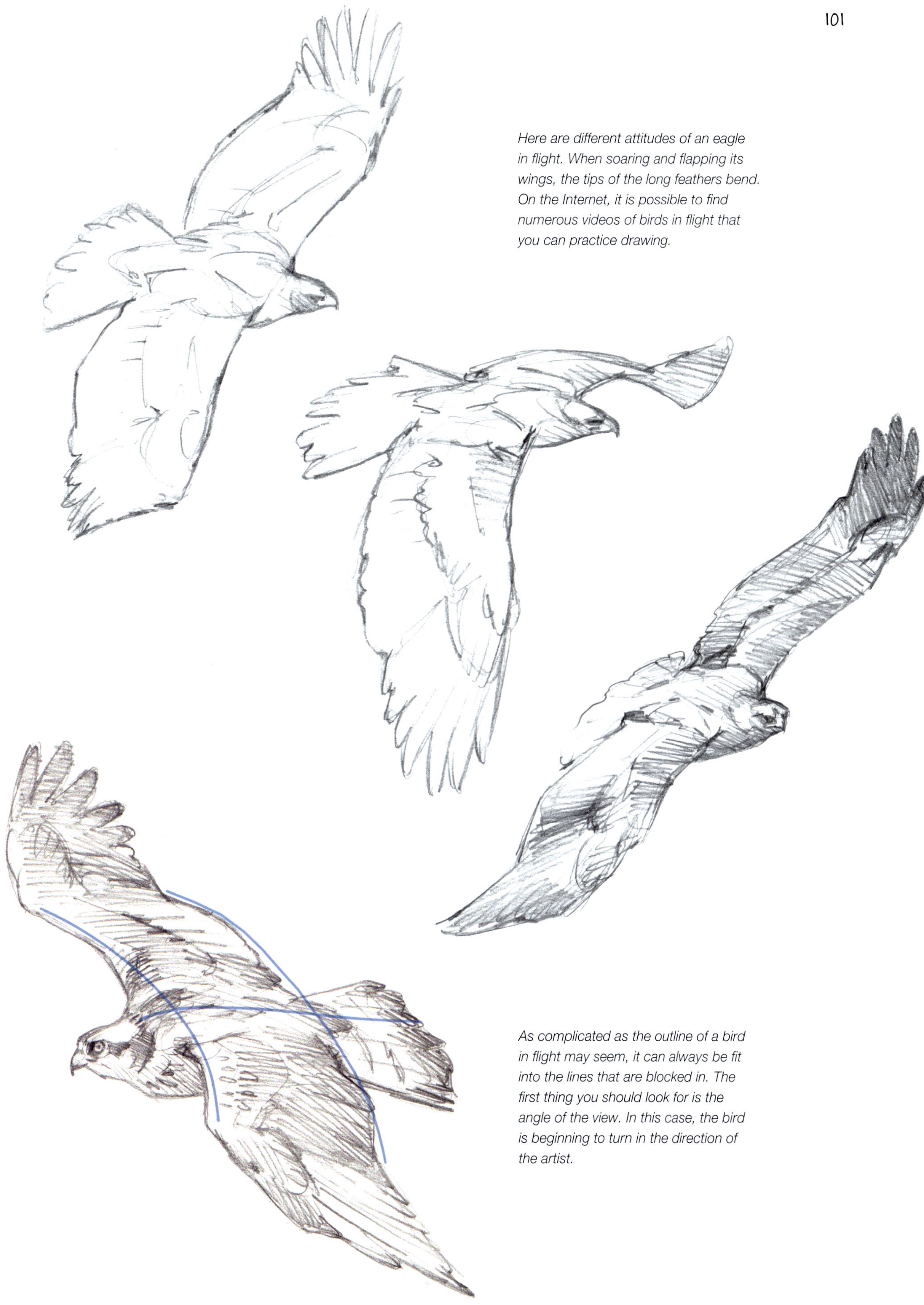

Here are different attitudes of an eagle in flight. When soaring and flapping its wings, the tips of the long feathers bend. On the Internet, it is possible to find numerous videos of birds in flight that you can practice drawing.

As complicated as the outline of a bird in flight may seem, it can always be fit into the lines that are blocked in. The first thing you should look for is the angle of the view. In this case, the bird is beginning to turn in the direction of the artist.

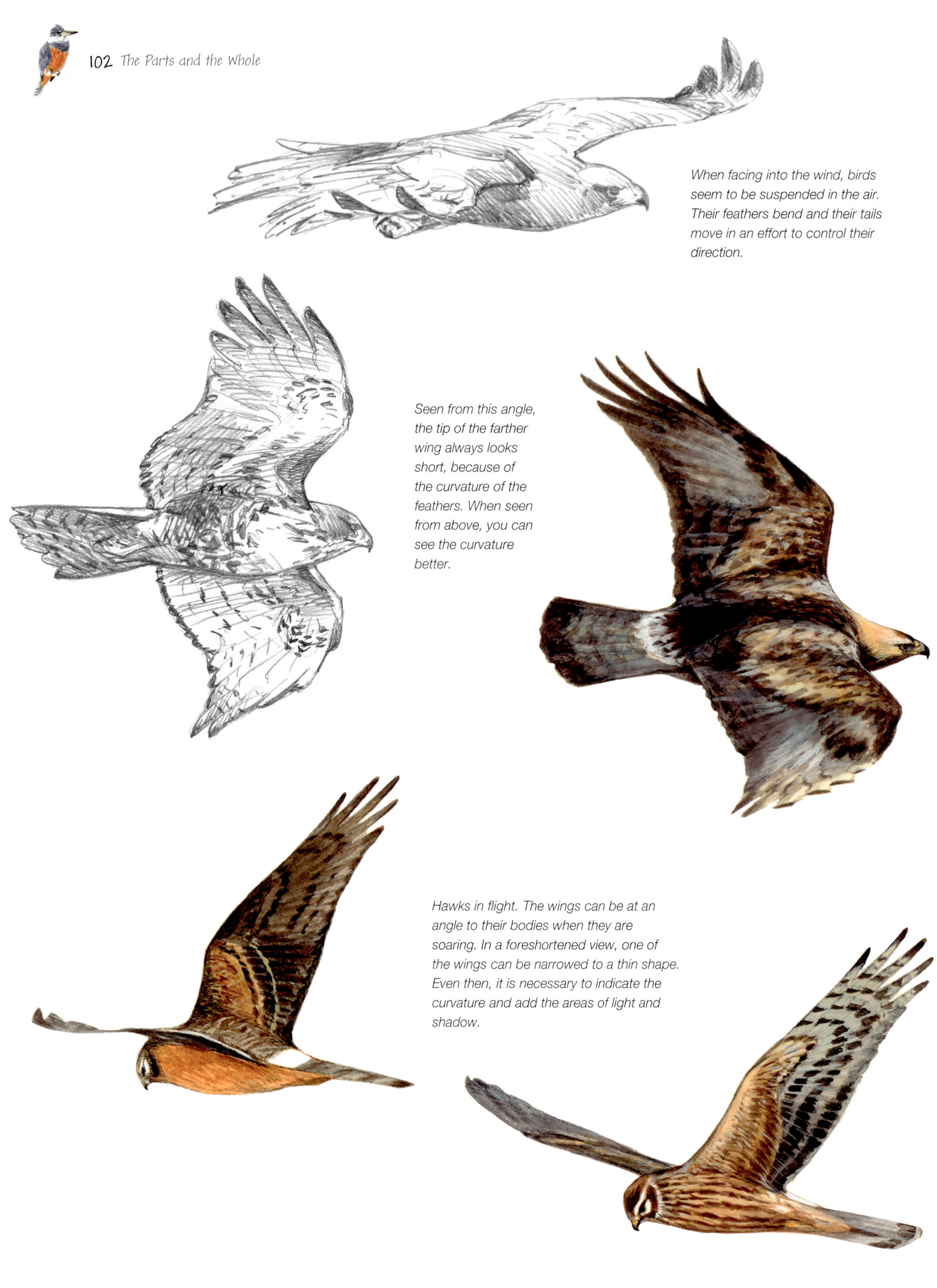

When facing into the wind, birds seem to be suspended in the air. Their feathers bend and their tails move in an effort to control their direction.

Seen from this angle, the tip of the farther wing always looks short, because of the curvature of the feathers. When seen from above, you can see the curvature better.

Hawks in flight. The wings can be at an angle to their bodies when they are soaring. In a foreshortened view, one of the wings can be narrowed to a thin shape. Even then, it is necessary to indicate the curvature and add the areas of light and shadow.

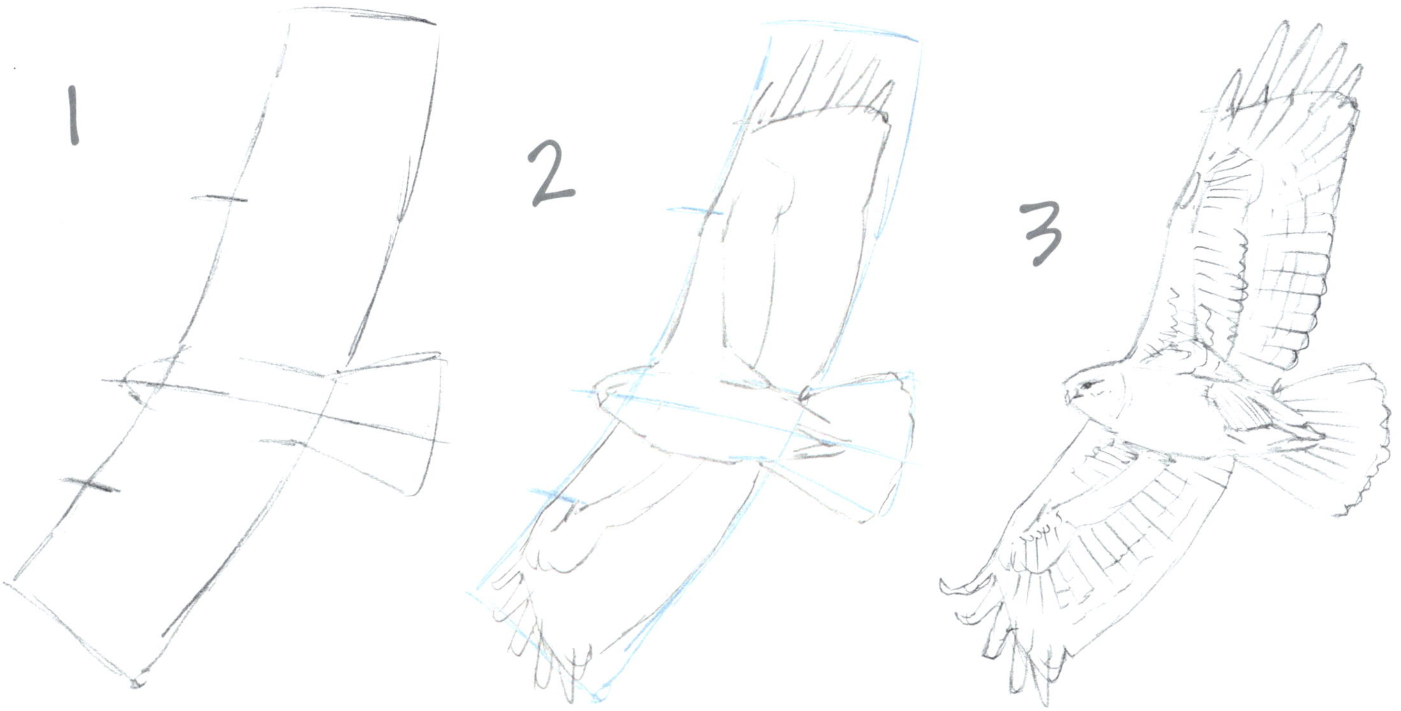

1. Lay out the guidelines as close as possible to the proportions and posture of the bird you are drawing. Here the lines would work for views from either above or from below.

2. Accurately define the outlines of the bird based on groups of feathers. The small reference marks indicate the points where the wings bend.

3. You must draw the feathers of the wings and tail individually, remembering that almost all birds have ten primary feathers and ten in the tail. Add detail to the face and erase the lines that you used for blocking in the drawing.

4. If you do not plan to color the drawing with watercolor or a similar medium, you can start shading the medium tones first, preserving the white areas.

5. Finish the work by adding dark tones to the plumage, such as on the tips of the wings and on the bars on the feathers. You should also touch up some of the final details and remove any leftover lines from the initial sketch.

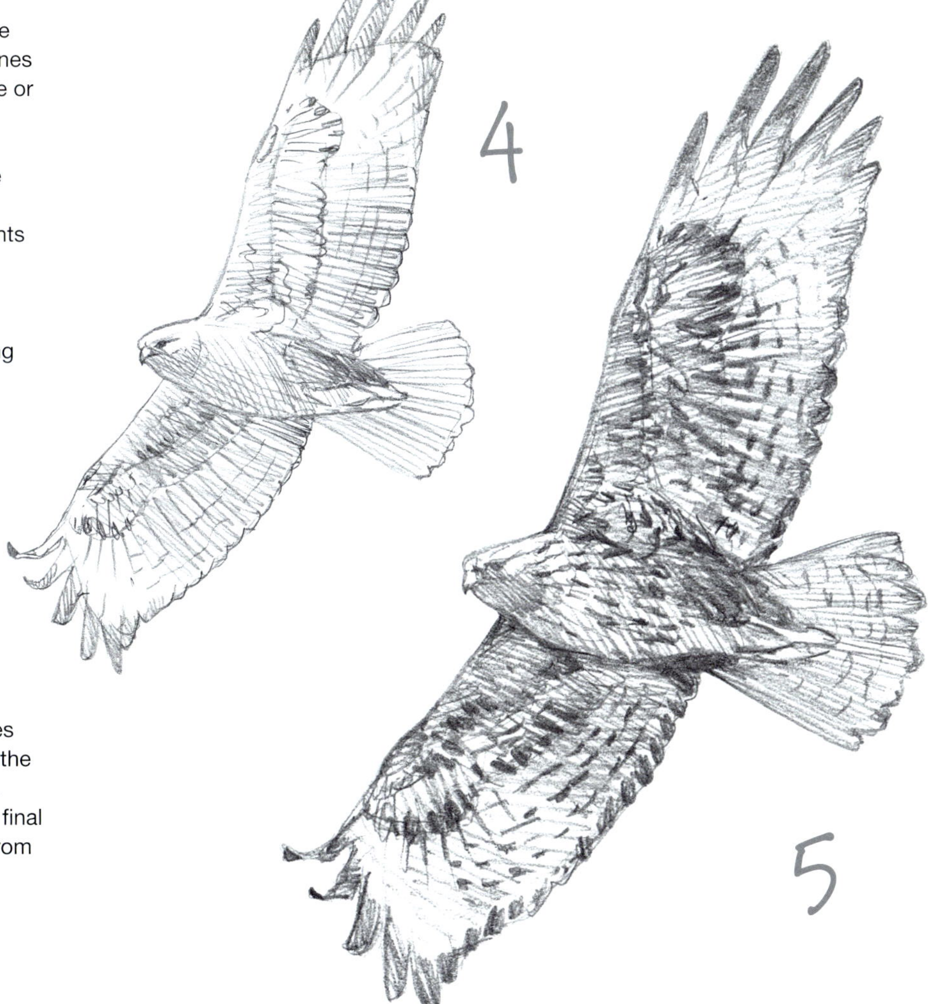

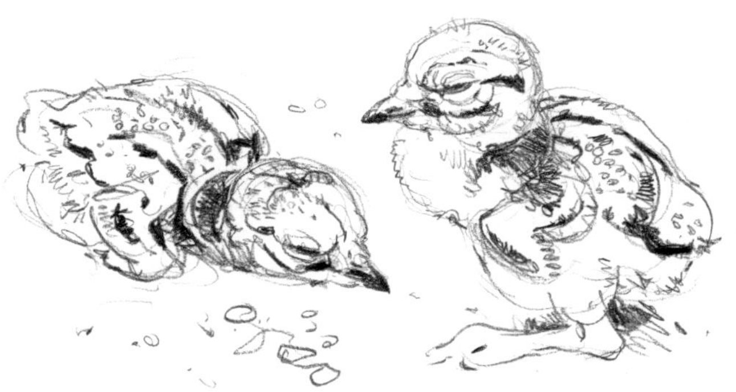

Birds and Time
Growth and the Seasons

The way birds look changes throughout the year and throughout their lifetimes, and it can also be different because of their sex. They molt to renew plumage that has worn out and been discolored by the sun, but they can also change so that they can hide during the season that they are most vulnerable, which, outside of the tropics, coincides with the wintertime.

An expert illustrator of birds should be aware of these details and be able to accurately draw and paint the variations of their feathers. If the landscape plays an important part in the painting, the plumage of the bird should correspond to the landscape—for example, it should have winter plumage if the trees do not have leaves.

JUAN VARELA
EUROPEAN PENDULINE TIT
WATERCOLOR, 10.5 x 14.5 INCHES (27 x 37 CM)

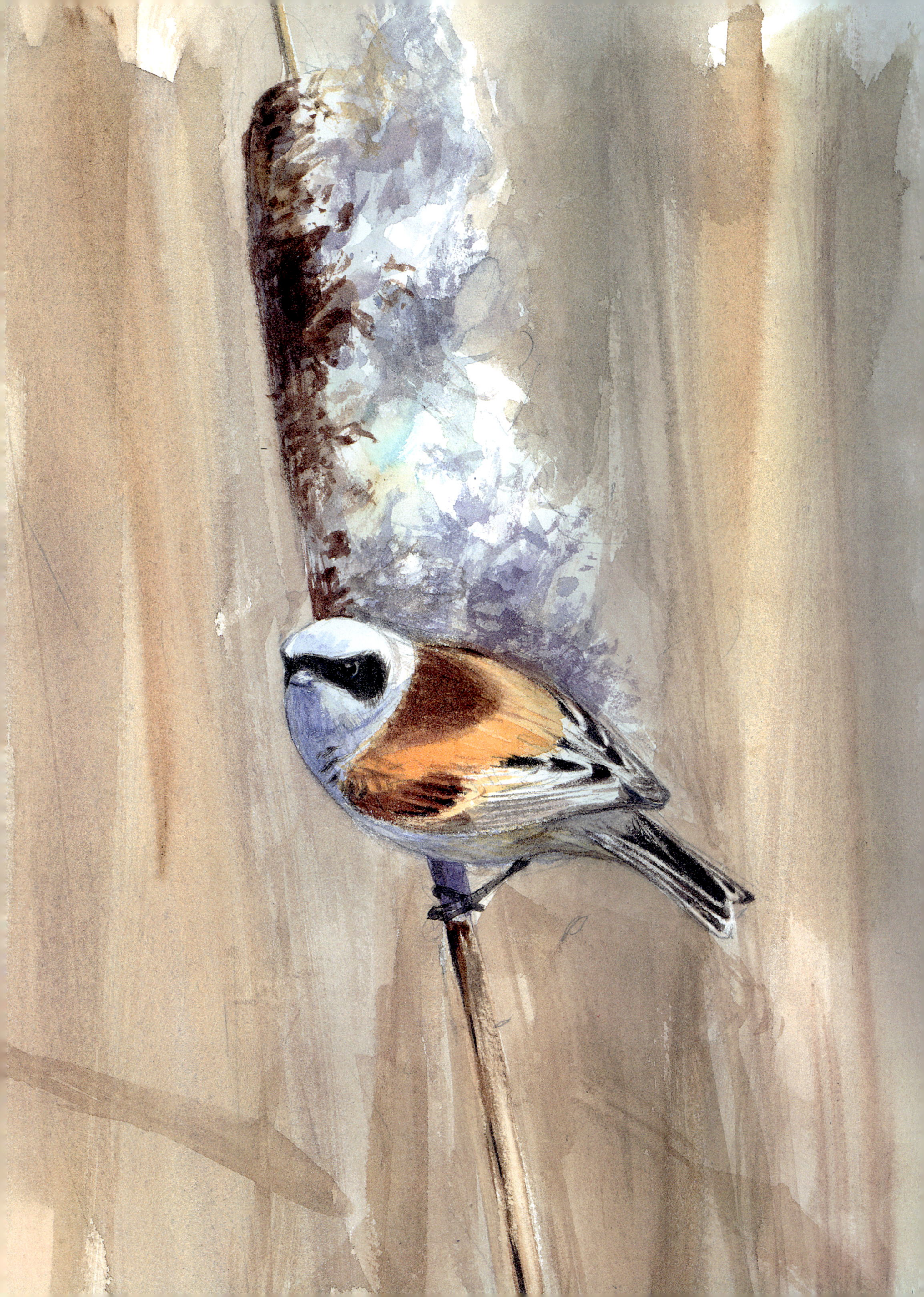

Juvenile Plumage

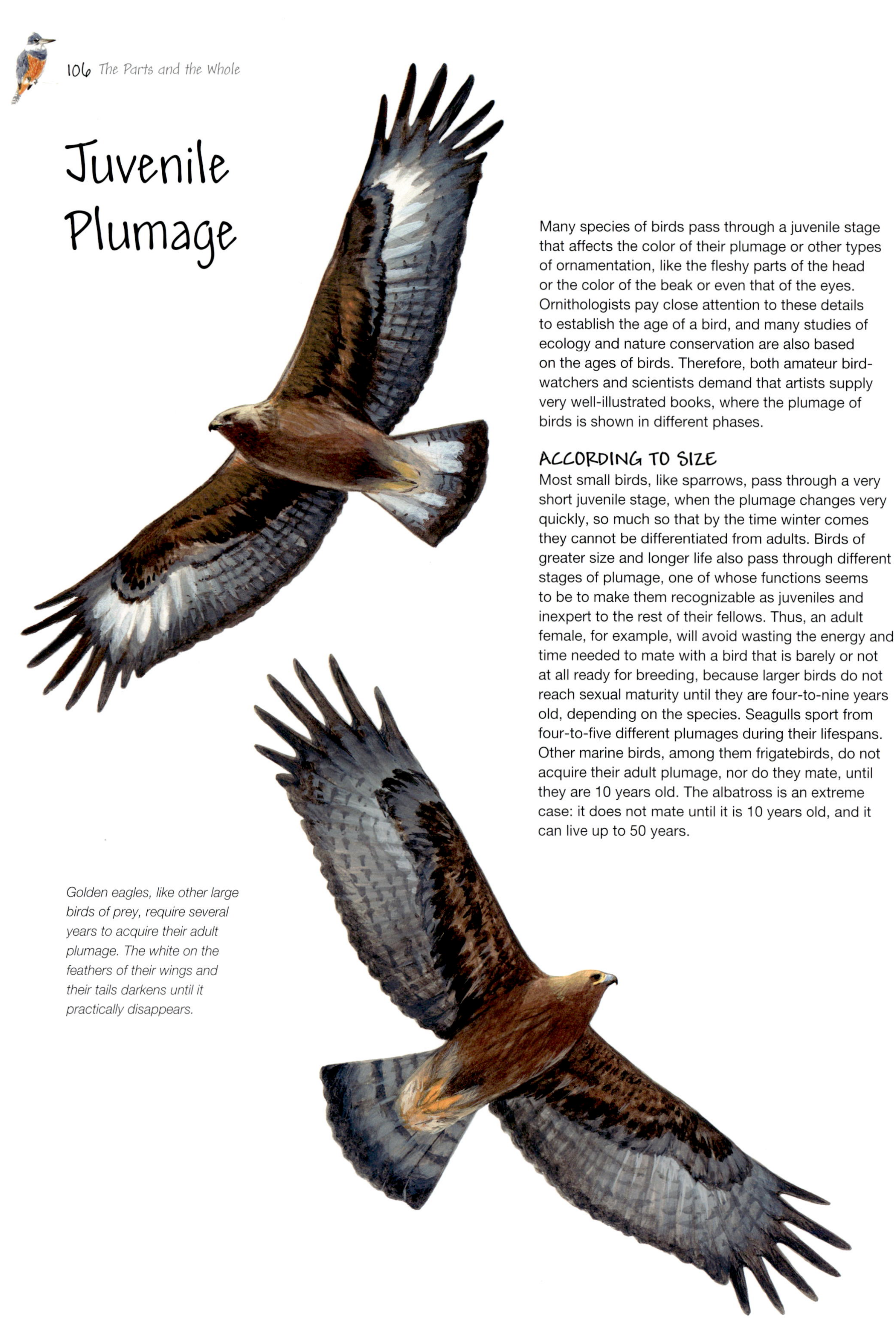

Many species of birds pass through a juvenile stage that affects the color of their plumage or other types of ornamentation, like the fleshy parts of the head or the color of the beak or even that of the eyes. Ornithologists pay close attention to these details to establish the age of a bird, and many studies of ecology and nature conservation are also based on the ages of birds. Therefore, both amateur bird-watchers and scientists demand that artists supply very well-illustrated books, where the plumage of birds is shown in different phases.

ACCORDING TO SIZE

Most small birds, like sparrows, pass through a very short juvenile stage, when the plumage changes very quickly, so much so that by the time winter comes they cannot be differentiated from adults. Birds of greater size and longer life also pass through different stages of plumage, one of whose functions seems to be to make them recognizable as juveniles and inexpert to the rest of their fellows. Thus, an adult female, for example, will avoid wasting the energy and time needed to mate with a bird that is barely or not at all ready for breeding, because larger birds do not reach sexual maturity until they are four-to-nine years old, depending on the species. Seagulls sport from four-to-five different plumages during their lifespans. Other marine birds, among them frigatebirds, do not acquire their adult plumage, nor do they mate, until they are 10 years old. The albatross is an extreme case: it does not mate until it is 10 years old, and it can live up to 50 years.

Golden eagles, like other large birds of prey, require several years to acquire their adult plumage. The white on the feathers of their wings and their tails darkens until it practically disappears.

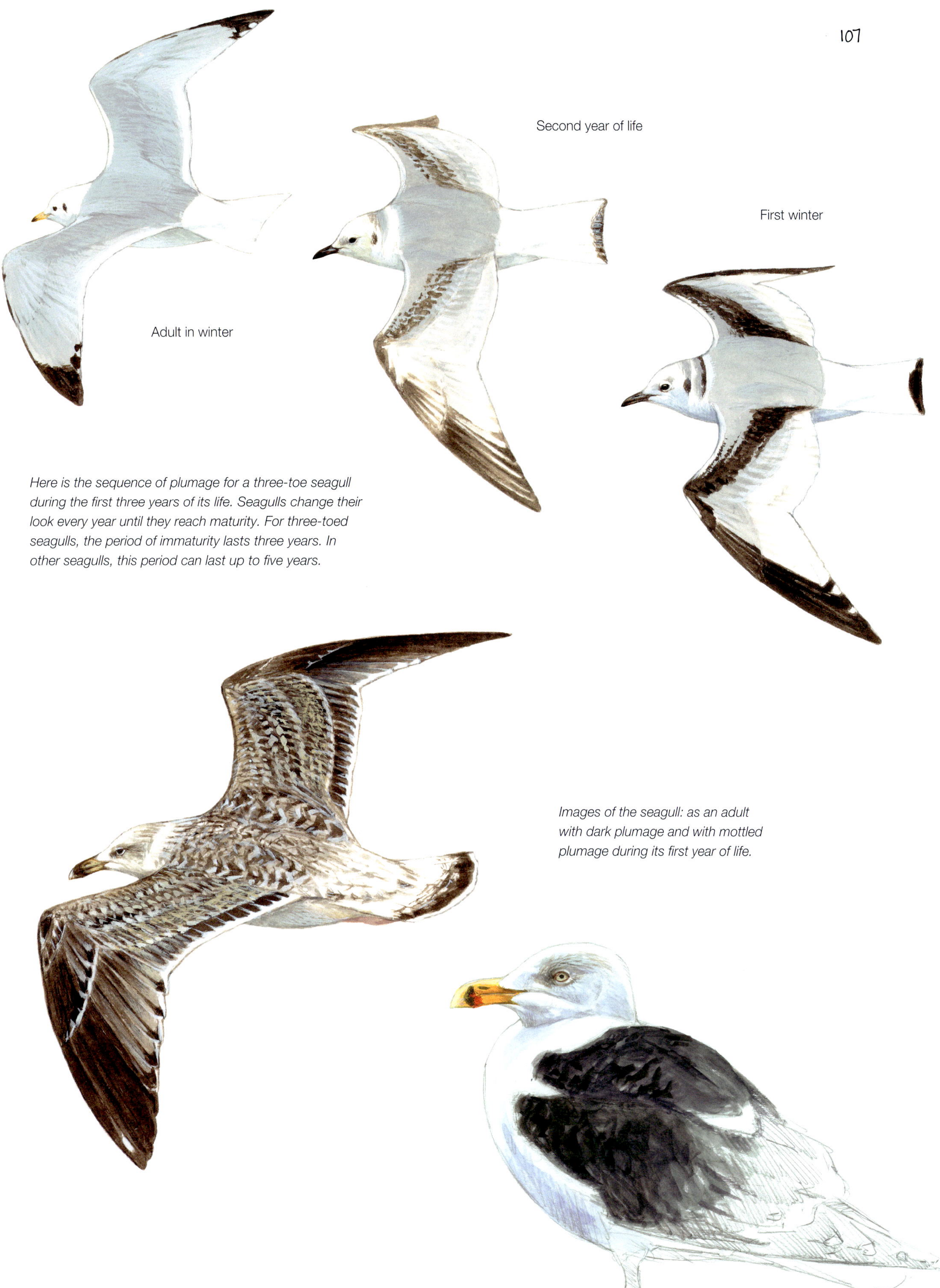

Here is the sequence of plumage for a three-toe seagull during the first three years of its life. Seagulls change their look every year until they reach maturity. For three-toed seagulls, the period of immaturity lasts three years. In other seagulls, this period can last up to five years.

Images of the seagull: as an adult with dark plumage and with mottled plumage during its first year of life.

Seasonal Plumage

For the parts of the planet where there are notable changes of season and birds only mate during the warm months, many species change their plumage with the annual rhythm. With this, they renew that which was damaged during the previous busy period; and, in some species, birds shed the attractive colors that were used for courting and take on more discrete coloring. The rock ptarmigan becomes as white as the snow of their environment, and waders acquire gray tones, which are more discreet in proximity to the coast. In the spring, you can see flocks of waders, for example, with transitional plumage in between the discrete winter tones and the colors of the upcoming mating season.

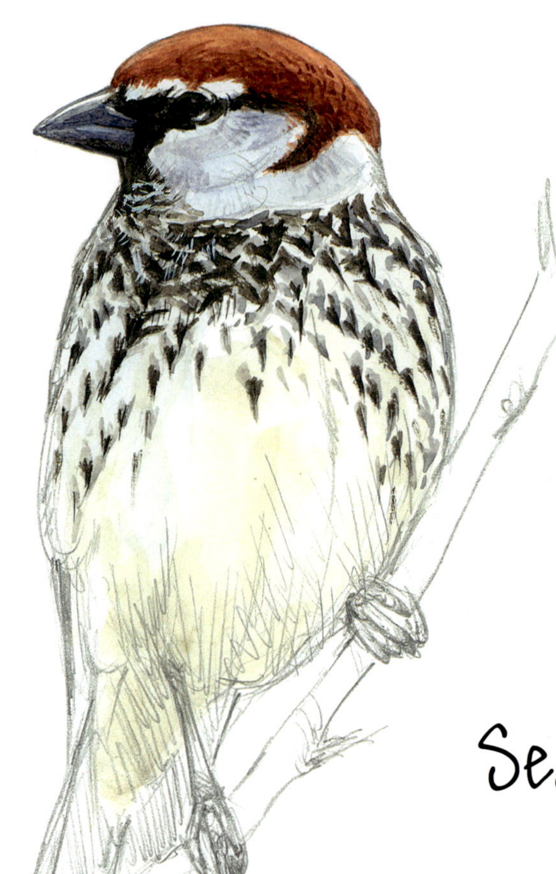

The black marks on the breast of the Spanish sparrow begin appearing from the wear and tear of the light edges of the feathers that hide the dark center of the inner ones.

During the molting period, ducks suddenly lose many of their flight feathers, rendering them quite defenseless, and they acquire a mottled look that is known as the "eclipse" plumage, which is not as attractive. During the rest of the year, they maintain a constant coloring.

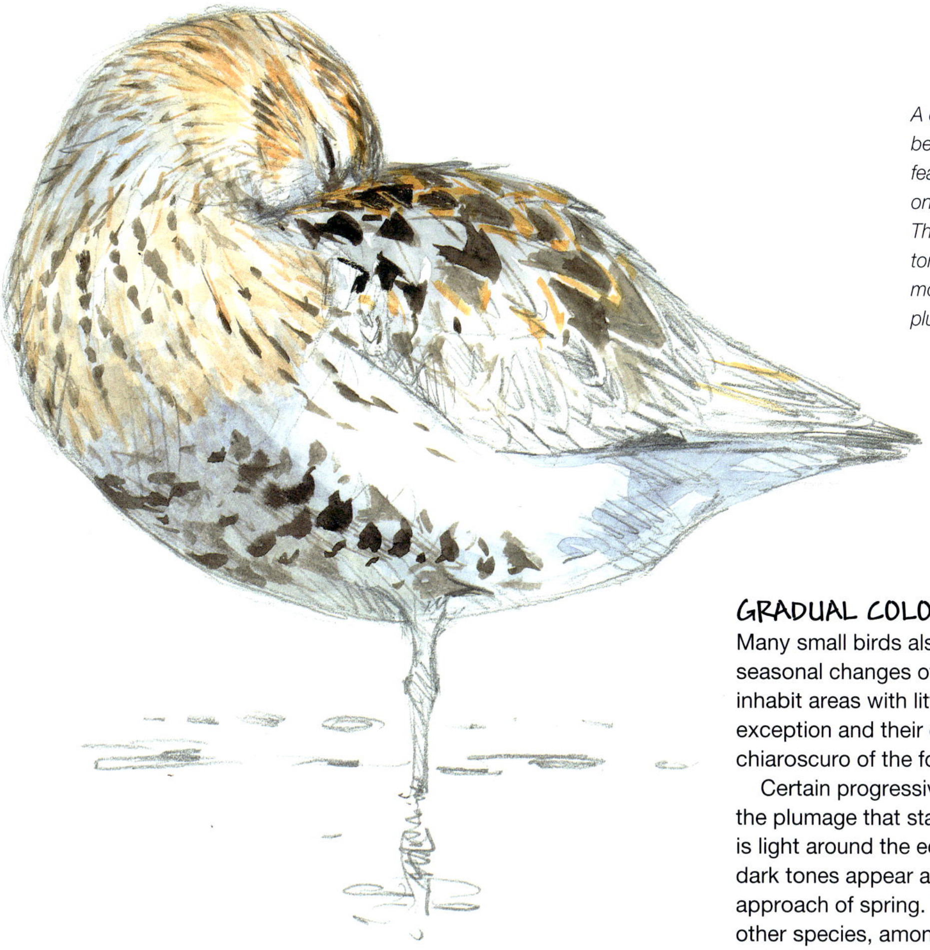

A dunlin in its transitional plumage between winter and summer. The feathers that form the black patch on the belly are beginning to appear. The back is losing its uniform gray tone and is acquiring the more mottled breeding or nuptial plumage.

GRADUAL COLOR

Many small birds also lose their coloring with their seasonal changes of plumage. Tropical birds that inhabit areas with little change in climate are an exception and their coloring helps hide them in the chiaroscuro of the forests.

Certain progressive changes in color are due to the plumage that starts growing in the winter, which is light around the edges and dark in the center. The dark tones appear as the edges wear off with the approach of spring. This is the case of sparrows and other species, among them linnets, which turn red with the arrival of spring.

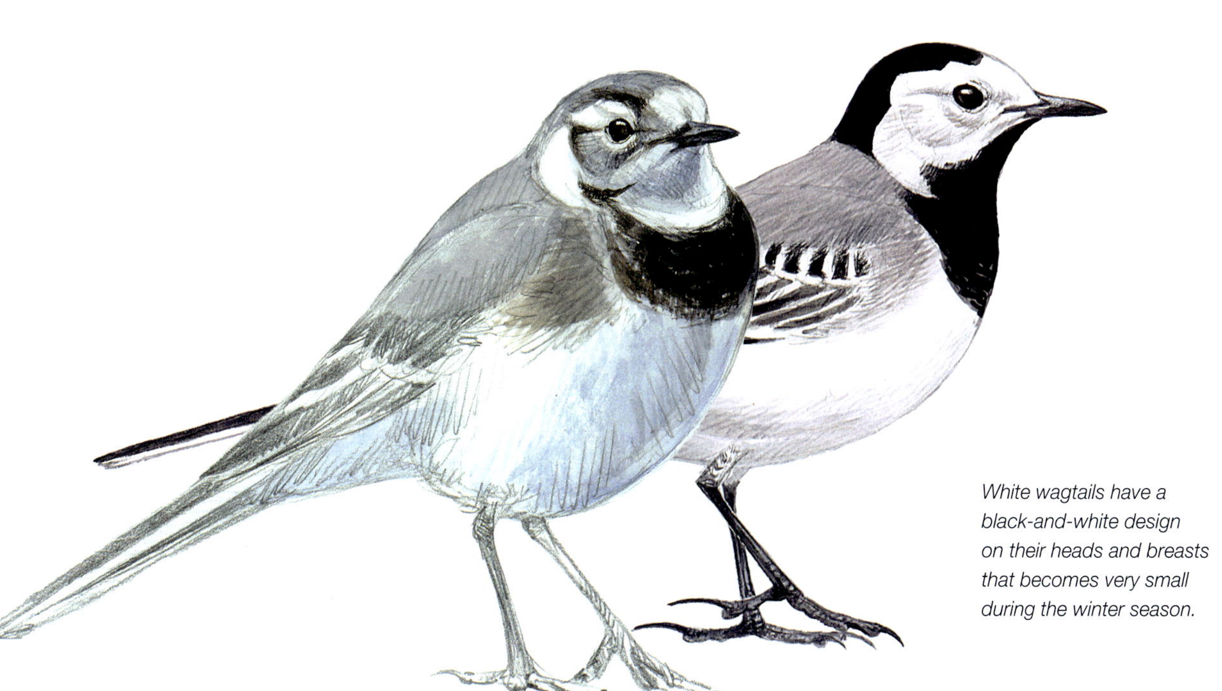

White wagtails have a black-and-white design on their heads and breasts that becomes very small during the winter season.

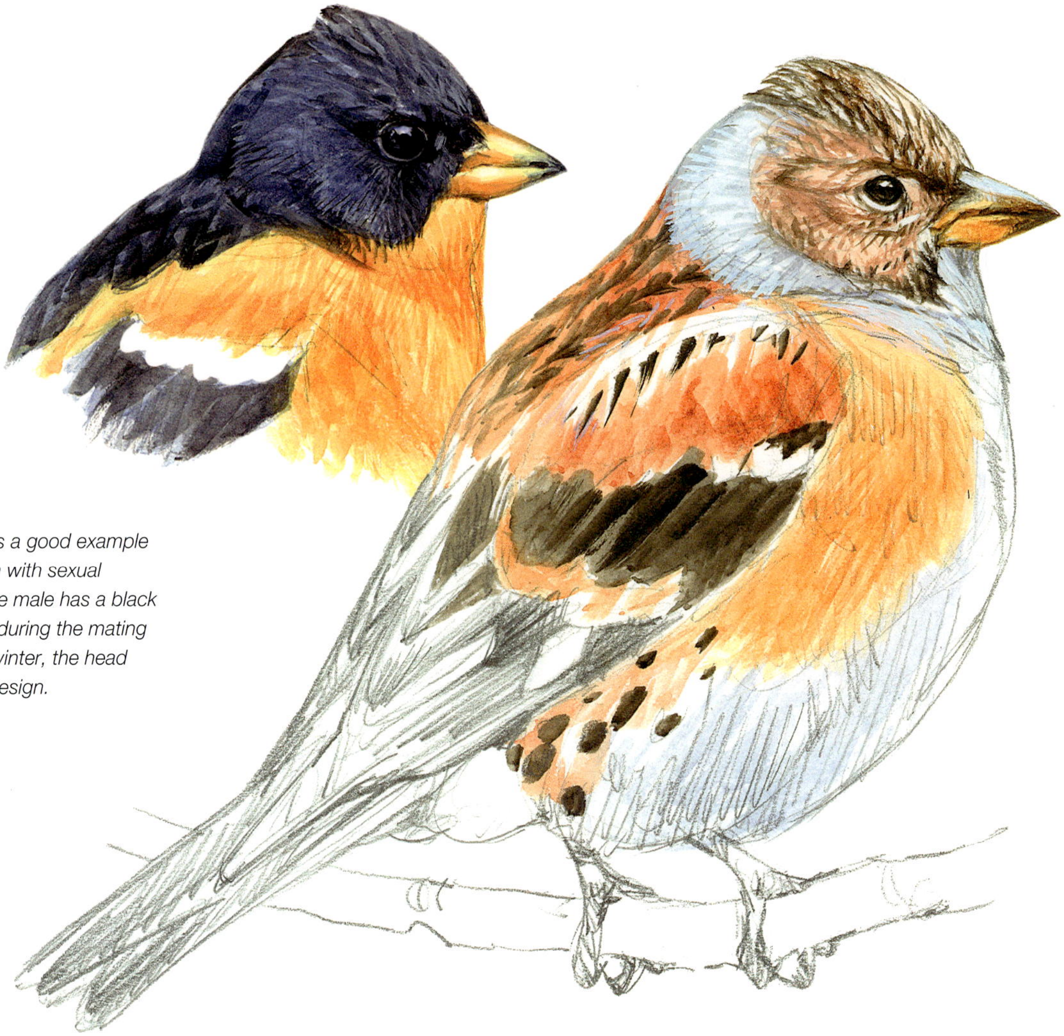

The brambling is a good example of a passeriform with sexual dimorphism. The male has a black head and back during the mating season. In the winter, the head has a spotted design.

Sexual Differences

Not all species of birds show differences between the sexes in the plumage, or at least the differences are minimal. In some species, it is a question of size; the females of some birds of prey, like falcons, are larger than the males. In others, the differences are more noticeable: brighter colors on the males, feather adornments or caruncles on the head or the tail, and more striking adornments like the red sacks on the throat of the frigate bird. In this group, there are not usually great sexual differences: male seagulls, terns, gannets, albatrosses, pelicans, puffins, cormorants, and others are very similar to the females. Almost all species of ducks shown striking sexual differences; this also occurs in many passeriforms, in the Galliformes, and, especially in birds of paradise, a family of birds in New Guinea.

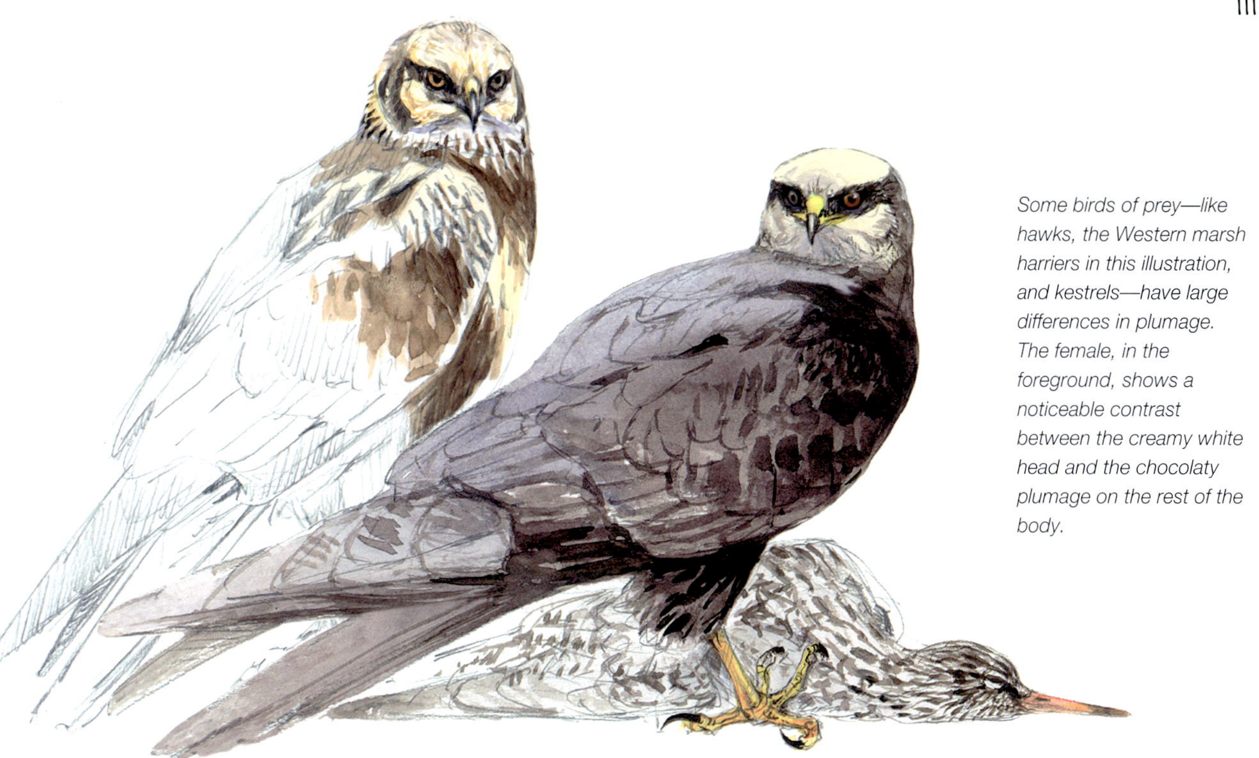

Some birds of prey—like hawks, the Western marsh harriers in this illustration, and kestrels—have large differences in plumage. The female, in the foreground, shows a noticeable contrast between the creamy white head and the chocolaty plumage on the rest of the body.

ADVANTAGES AND INCONVENIENCES

Generally speaking, sexual dimorphism is attributed to the different function of each member of the pair in reproduction. In the species in which the males are more colorful and attractive, they usually play a very limited role in raising the chicks. Basically, they build nests and impregnate females. Producing such ornamentation uses a great amount of energy and their bright colors make them more visible to predators, which leads to a higher mortality rate. In species whose males are more discretely colored, there is a greater collaboration between both sexes in raising the chicks.

In the Phalaropes, the dimorphism is reversed. The female is more attractive than the male, because she is the one that courts and he takes charge of incubating the nest and raising the chicks. Furthermore, the female will successively pair up with several males.

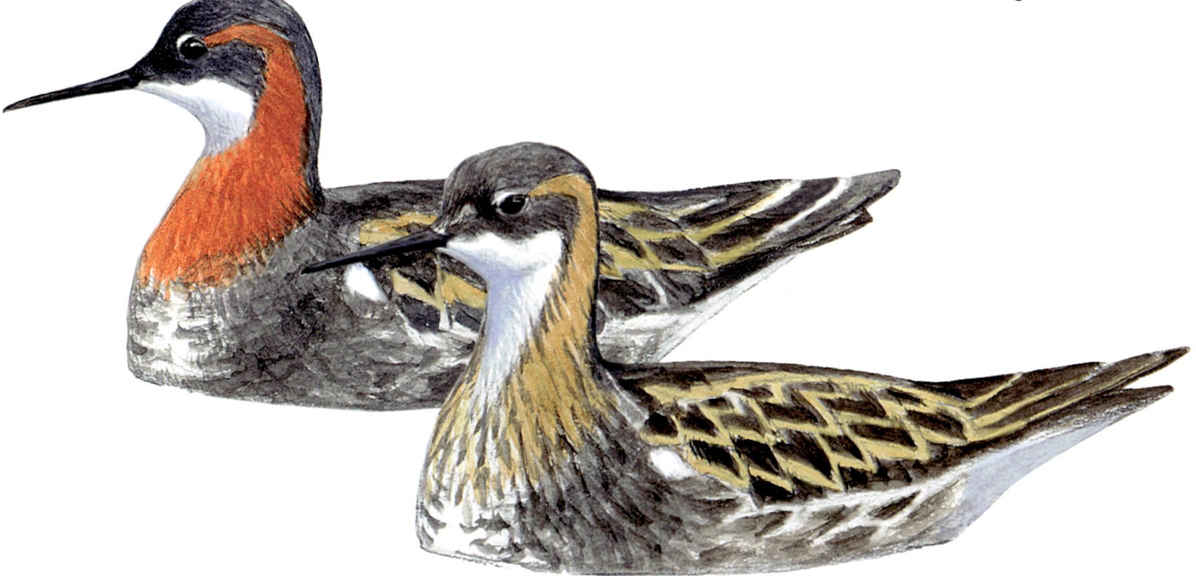

Kinds of Birds

TIM WOOTTON
GYRFALCON
WATERCOLOR ON PAPER, 27 x 19.5 INCHES (69 x 50 CM)

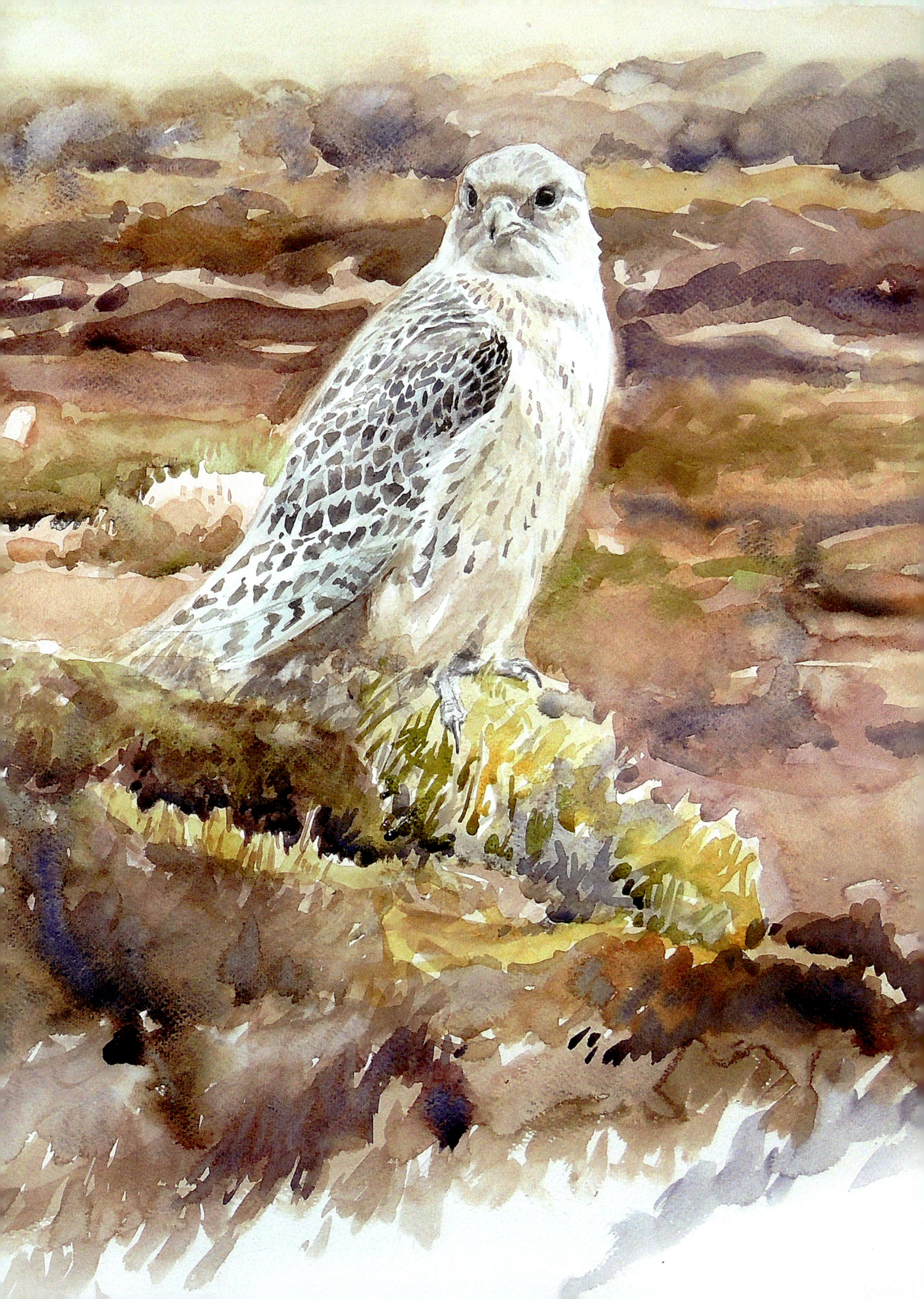

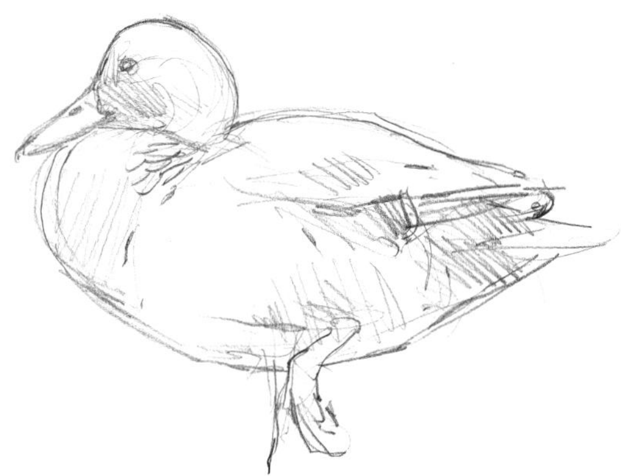

Aquatic Birds
Adaptation to the Environment

These birds make up a large group of species that, for the most part, depend on water for sustenance. Aquatic environments, whether marine or freshwater, supply many food sources, and certain groups of birds have adapted to living nearby. These adaptations have developed in several directions: some help getting from place to place, others with reproduction, and still others with the way of catching food.

Not all species have the same level of dependence on water. Birds that are strictly aquatic—gulls, gannets, terns, and so on—inhabit islands and coasts near the ocean, while many species of *Limicola* (sandpipers) and *Anatidae* (ducks and geese) are brought up in zones with tundra and only occupy the coasts and freshwater areas in winter.

TIM WOOTTON
ANADES SILBONES
WATERCOLOR ON PAPER, 27 x 19.5 INCHES (69 x 50 CM)

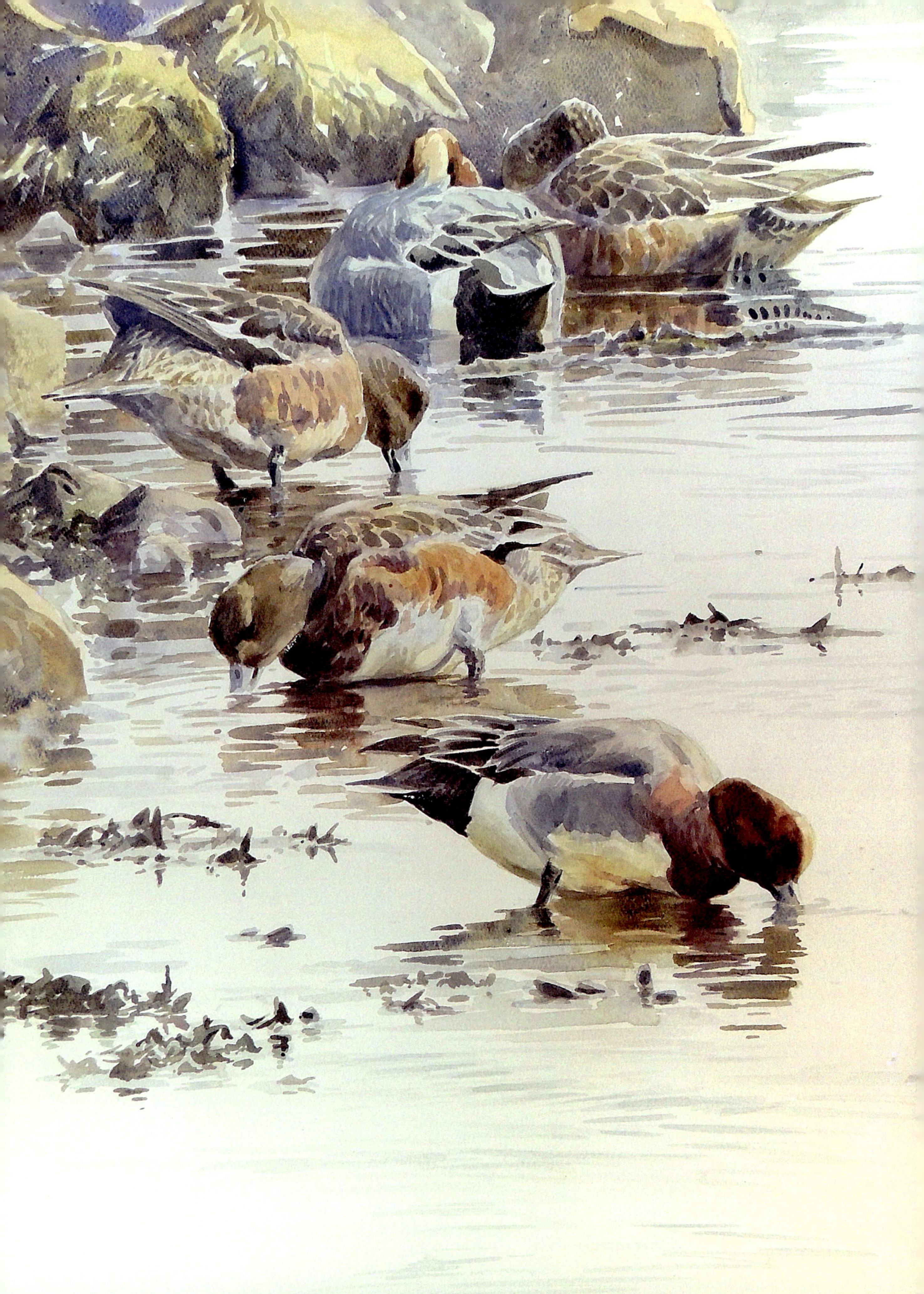

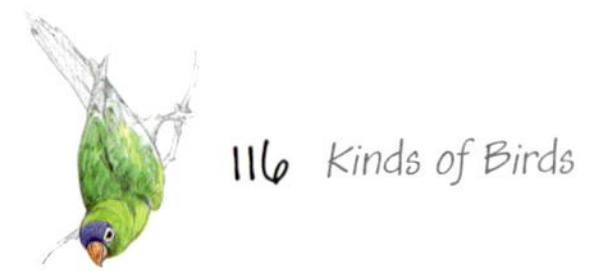

Ducks and Geese

A gadwall searching for food and a ring-necked duck resting. When aquatic birds are in the water, the wings are partially hidden by the plumage on the sides. The waterline is usually low, unlike that of the diving birds, whose plumage gets wet and sinks lower when they swim.

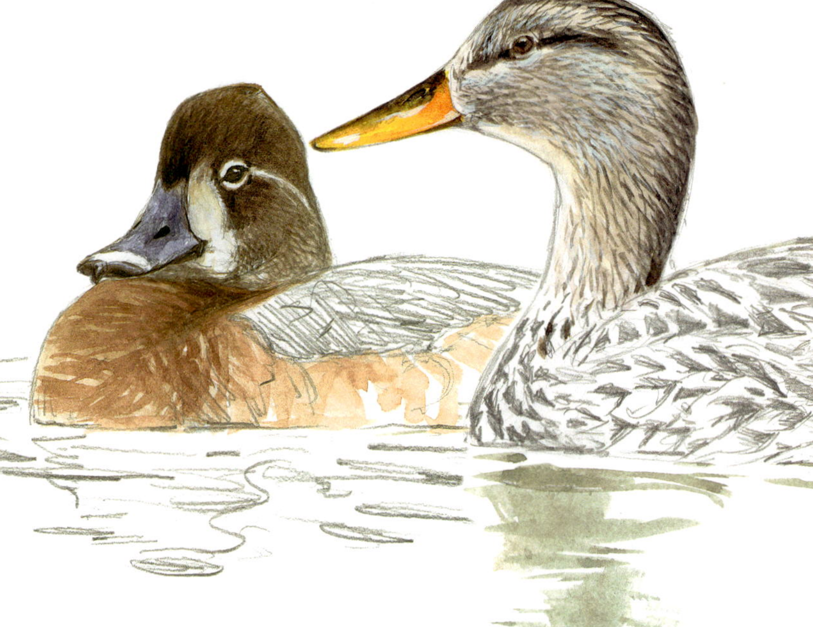

The *Anatidae* constitute a large group of birds, which includes all the ducks, geese, and swans. They all have in common the toes on their feet, joined by a membrane, and a more or less flat beak with somewhat serrated edges, which allows them to pull up grass and aquatic plants. Some species also feed on aquatic invertebrates and even fish (the mergansers, for example, which are ducks with exceptionally sharp and narrow beaks).

DETAILS YOU MUST KEEP IN MIND

The *Anatidae* are round in shape. These birds have a lot of body fat, which allows them to maintain their internal temperature in cold water. They have short tails and can barely maneuver when they fly. The duck species flap their wings rapidly. Larger species, like geese and swans, flap their wings slowly and deliberately. The surface area of their wings is greater, so they can support their weight more easily. Another common characteristic of *Anatidae* is the length of the neck, notable in all of them, but even greater in the swans and geese.

This is the wing of a Northern shoveler. The secondary feathers of many species of ducks have a white or iridescent band that is very visible in flight and sometimes when the bird is standing. In some species, these bands extend to the covert feathers.

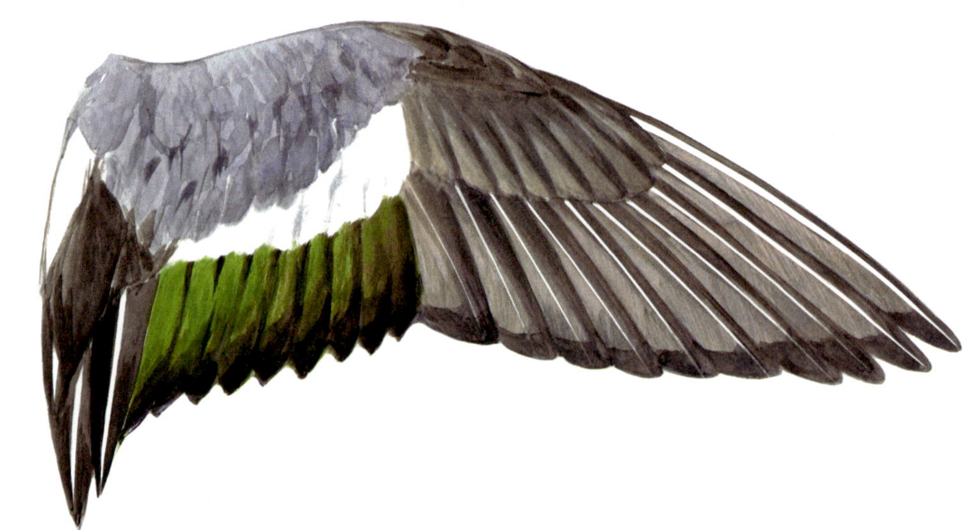

A mallard at rest. The sexual differences are more visible in ducks than in geese and swans, in which the differences between males and females can barely be seen. During a molting period in the fall, a time when they are the most defenseless, male ducks acquire a more subdued plumage, which is similar to that of the females.

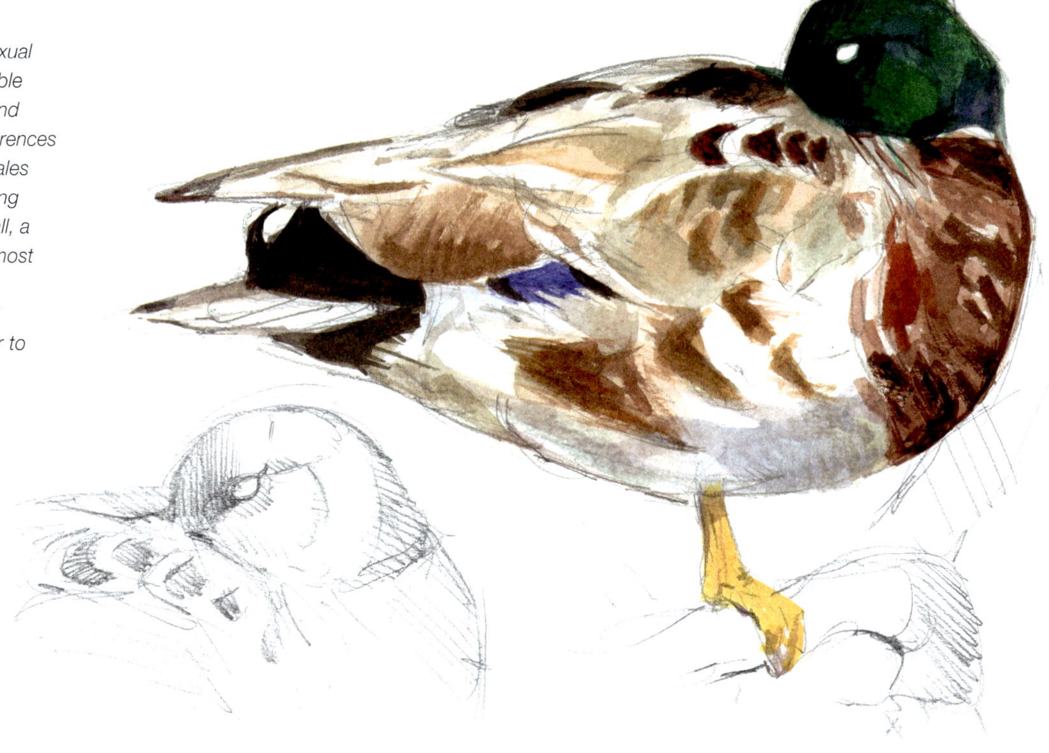

HOW TO RECOGNIZE THE PLUMAGE

When drawing *Anatidae*, you must keep in mind the diverse groups of feathers and their sizes. The scapulars form two large groups of feathers on both sides of the back and the tertials are very long, and sometimes they form striking patterns combined with the scapulars. The secondaries, on many species, form a band of color.

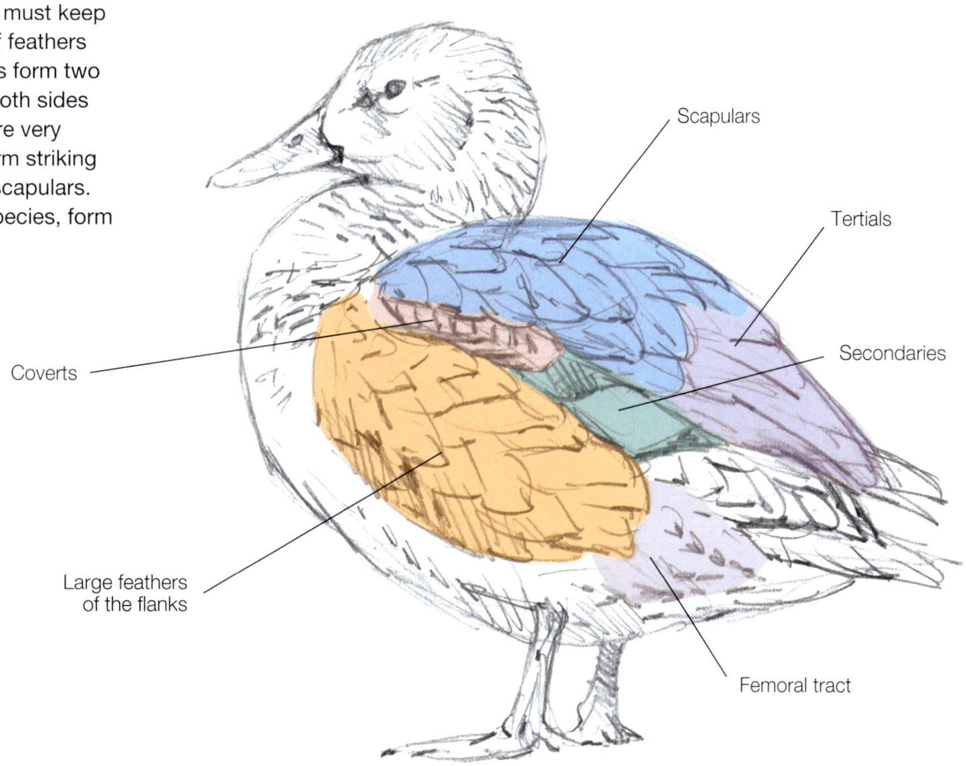

Scapulars
Tertials
Secondaries
Coverts
Large feathers of the flanks
Femoral tract

Arrangement of the feathers of an Anatidae.

The shape of the head and the beak, and the relationship between them, is very different among all species, and it is necessary to draw them correctly. Another detail that you must keep in mind is the line of separation between the beak and the head, which also varies, as you can see in the drawings.

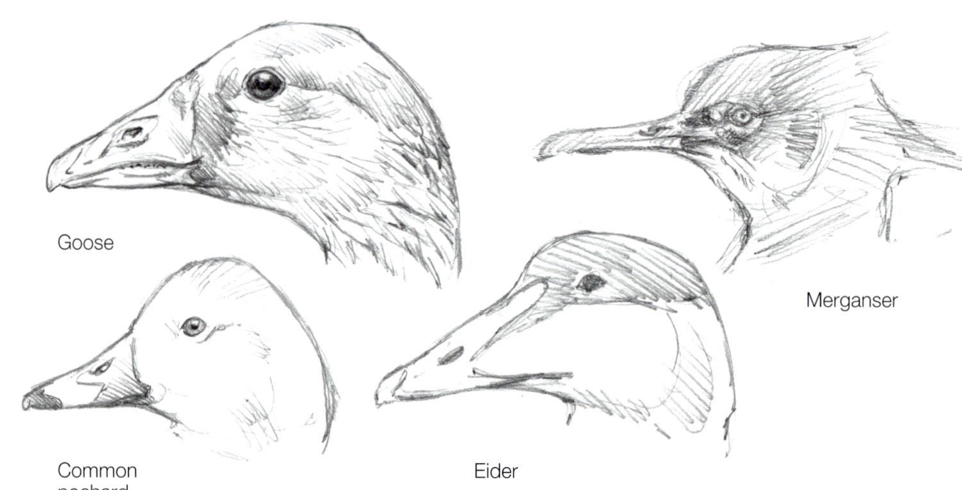

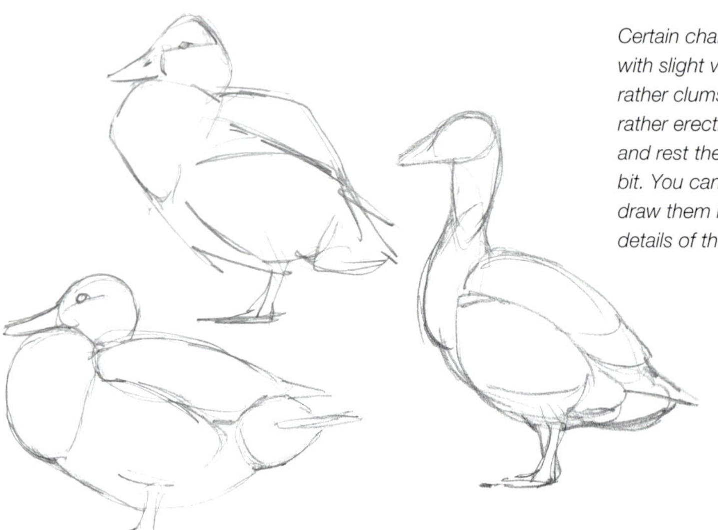

Certain characteristics of the Antidae are repeated in all species, although with slight variations. These are plump and short-legged birds that move rather clumsily on land. The legs are set back and cause the birds to walk rather erectly to balance their weight. Often, Antidae will pull in their necks and rest their heads on their backs, causing their breasts to stick out quite a bit. You can simplify their outline and stylize it in a few lines that will help you draw them more easily and adjust their proportions before getting into the details of their plumage.

The front view, or foreshortening of the beak, shown in this drawing, requires a little practice and much observation. You must keep in mind that the planes of the eyes look to the sides. Photographs and illustrations by other artists will help you understand the perspective.

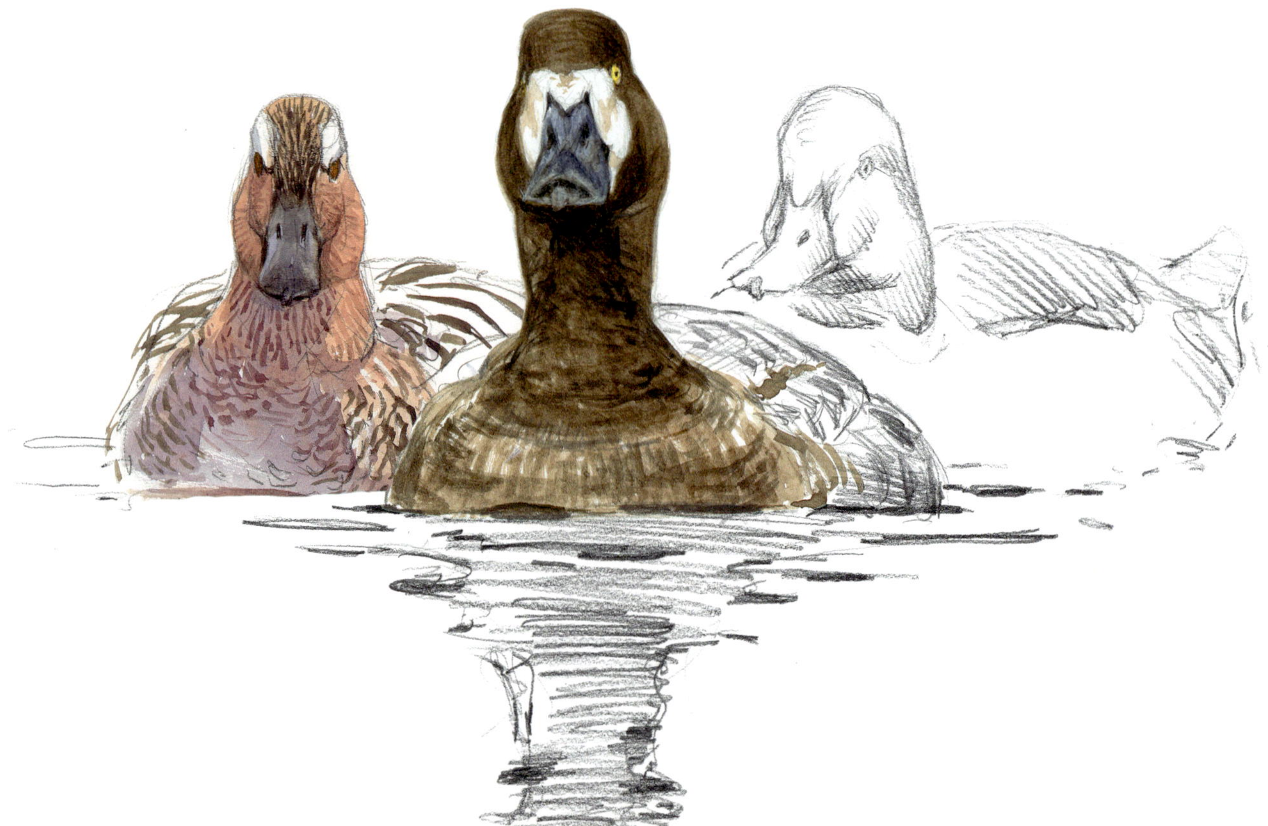

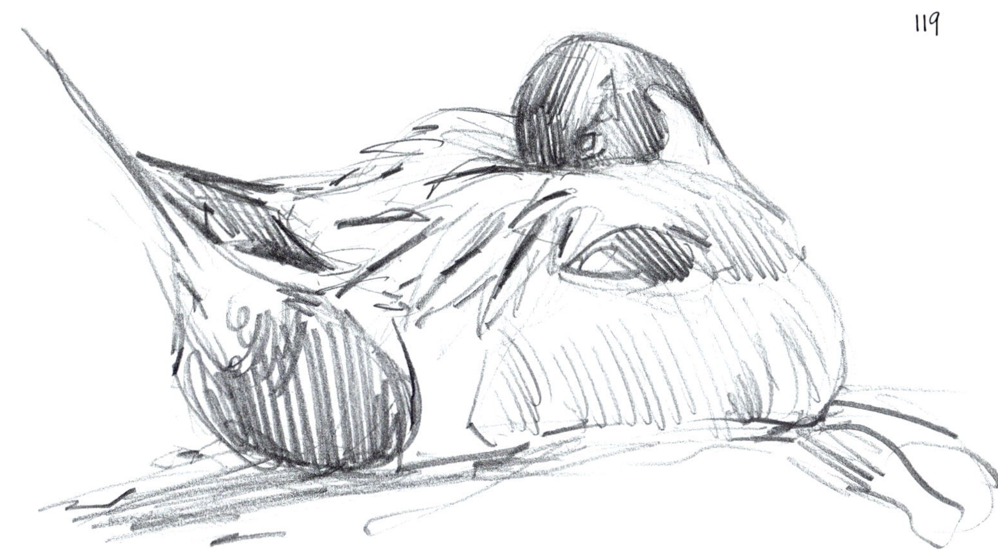

Ducks, like this Northern pintail, and the rest of the Antidae always sleep with their heads resting on their shoulders and hidden in their feathers.

Molting eiders at the end of July. Watercolor on paper, 27 x 19.5 inches (69 x 50 cm) by Tim Wootton. The composition, the light, and the poses of the birds are not the only striking thing about this painting. The fact that it illustrates a specific moment of molting plumage indicates a very careful study made in the field.

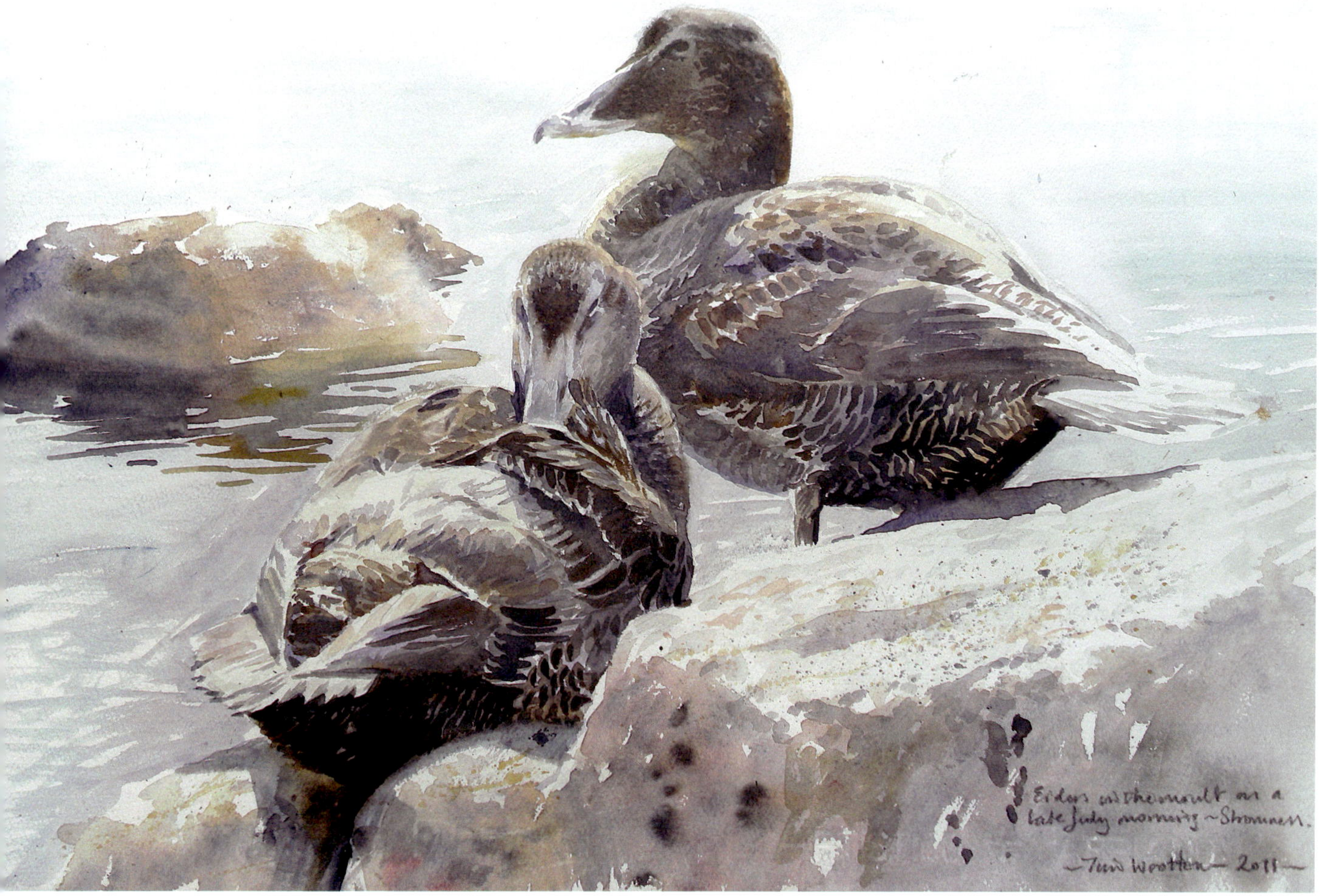

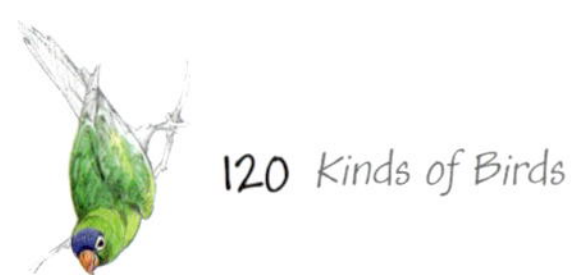

Long-legged Birds

Herons, storks, cranes, and flamingos are commonly referred to as long-legged birds. Other characteristics that they have in common are very long necks and the presence, except in the flamingos, of more or less long and pointed beaks that they use to eat seeds and catch fish, frogs, and other small animals. Flamingos primarily feed on the plankton that floats on bodies of saltwater, and their beaks have small plates that filter the water and retain the nutrients. Drawing long-legged birds usually presents some problems in describing the elegance of their movement, the relative proportions of their necks and legs in respect to their bodies, and the attitudes of hunting, walking, and resting. Flamingos have a more sinuously curving neck than herons, which have more apparent angles.

The structure of the legs and the toes of the long-legged birds varies depending on the habits of each particular species. Herons, in general, have longer toes than flamingos, storks, and spoonbills, and the small species that mainly live among tree branches have even longer ones. Their legs are proportionately shorter than those of their larger relatives.

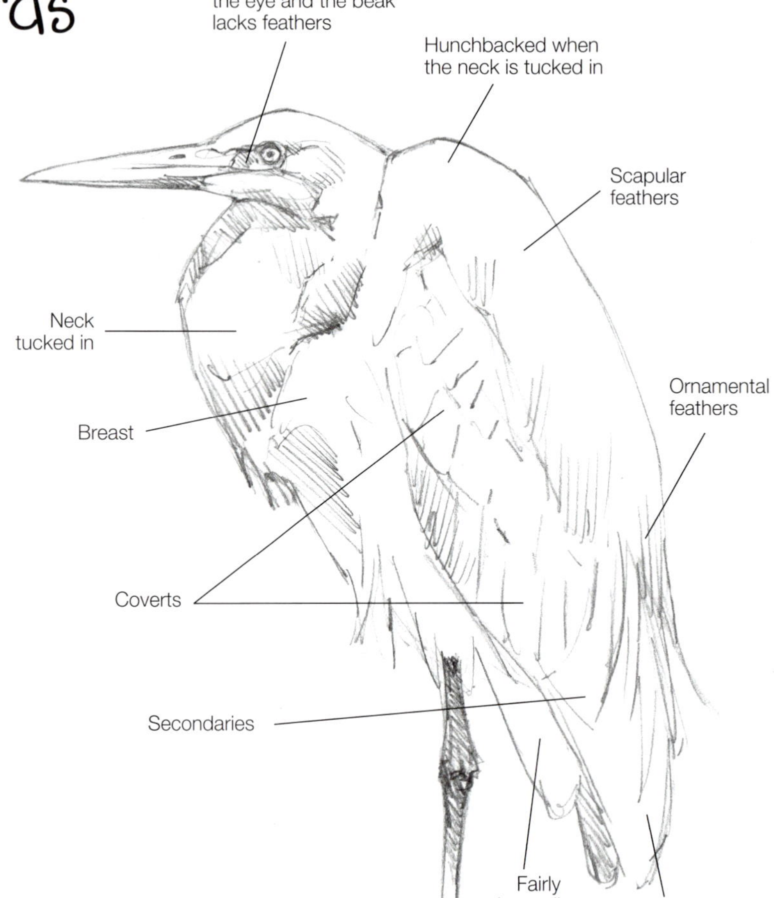

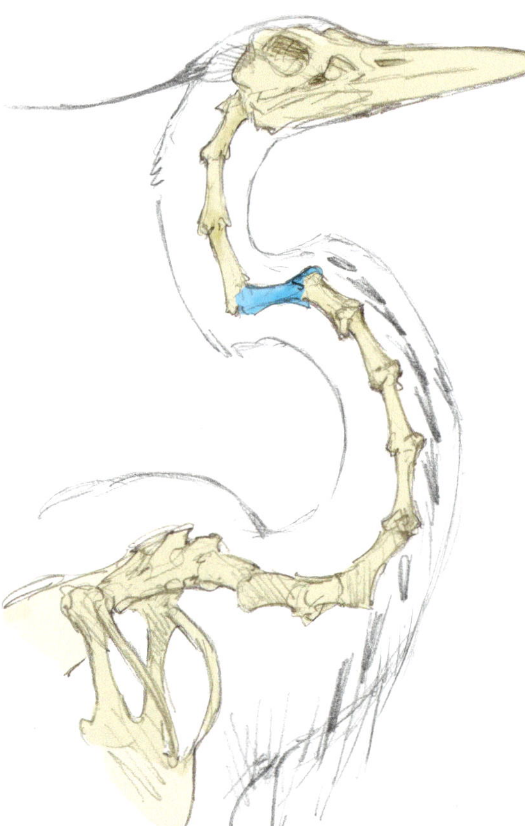

The extraordinary length of the neck of herons is not obvious when they are at rest or walking around with it tucked in. Many species have long ornamental feathers on their backs and their heads during mating season. Knowledge of the disposition of the feathers and the way that the bird tucks in its neck is essential for achieving a realistic drawing.

Herons have an angular neck because of special vertebrae connected to strong muscles that propel the neck forward to spear prey. This special arrangement allows them to fold their necks back on themselves.

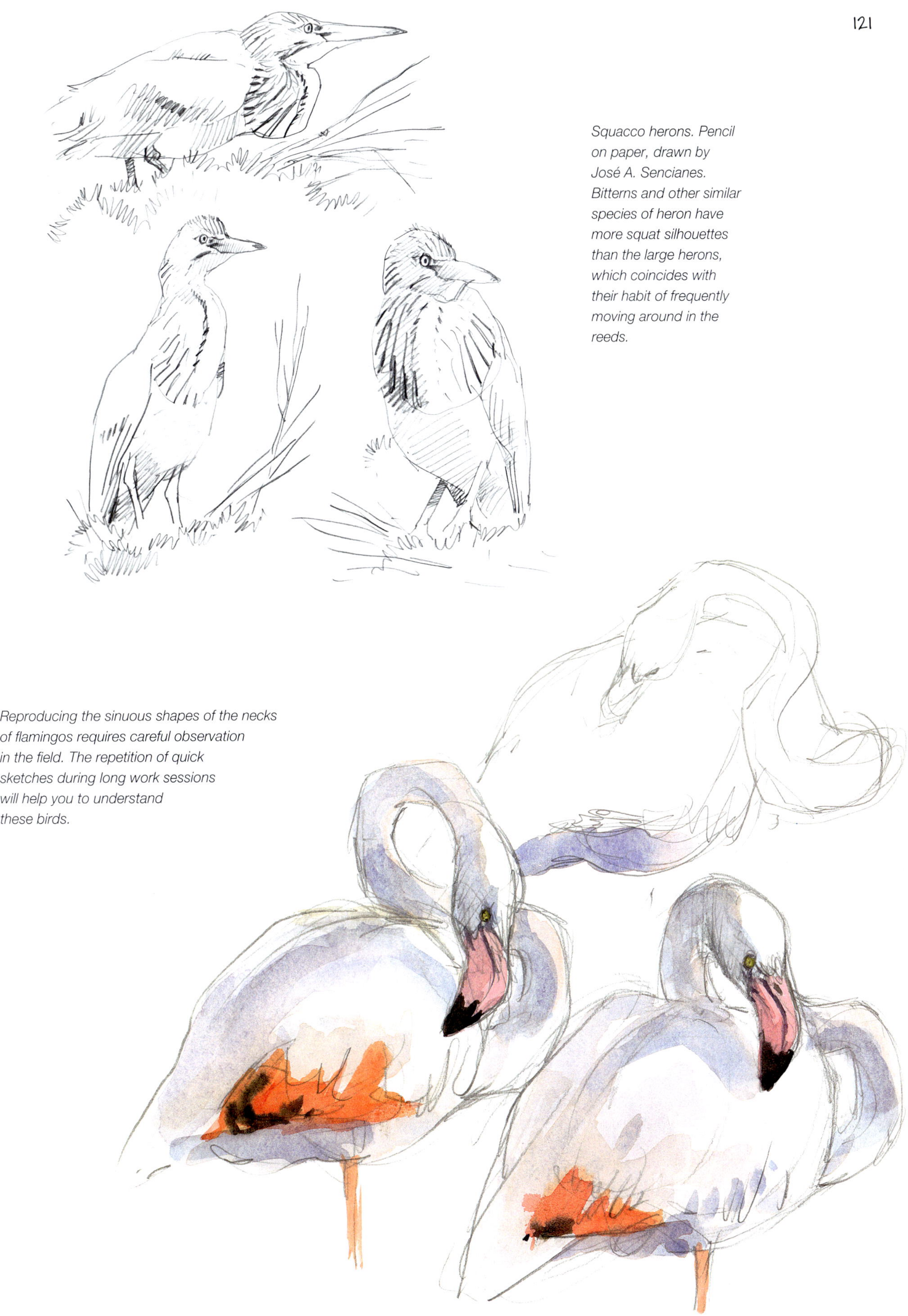

Squacco herons. Pencil on paper, drawn by José A. Sencianes. Bitterns and other similar species of heron have more squat silhouettes than the large herons, which coincides with their habit of frequently moving around in the reeds.

Reproducing the sinuous shapes of the necks of flamingos requires careful observation in the field. The repetition of quick sketches during long work sessions will help you to understand these birds.

Shorebirds

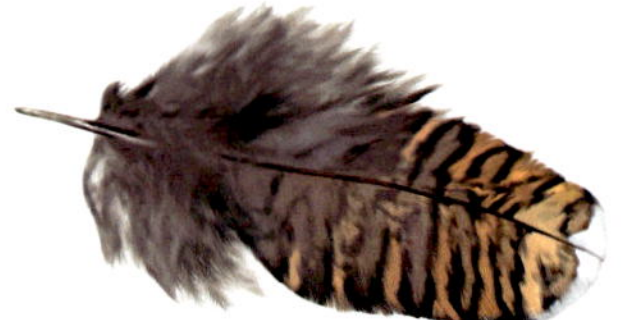

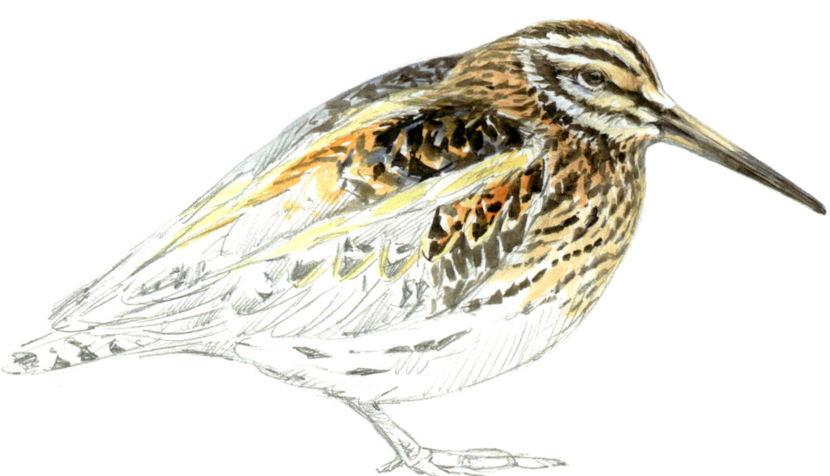

Shorebirds frequent muddy banks, silty intertidal zones, and other swampy areas in fall and winter, but many of them breed in open spaces, where they can see danger approaching, like the tundra of Northern Europe. There are exceptions to this—for example, the Eurasian stone-curlew, which lives permanently in arid zones or steppes, or the woodcock, which inhabits forested areas year-round. There are species of shorebirds all over the world, and some of them, like the bar-tailed godwit and certain dunlins, make migratory journeys between their breeding grounds and their wintering sites, sometimes up to 6,600 miles (11,000 km).

Correctly representing a specific species of limicole, like this jack snipe, requires careful drawing so that the coloring of the wings is believable. The areas of darkest color can even be previously shaded with pencil so it will not be lost when color is added. The light edges and some of the bright streaks on the feathers can be painted with gouache instead of leaving the paper white, because it is an opaque paint.

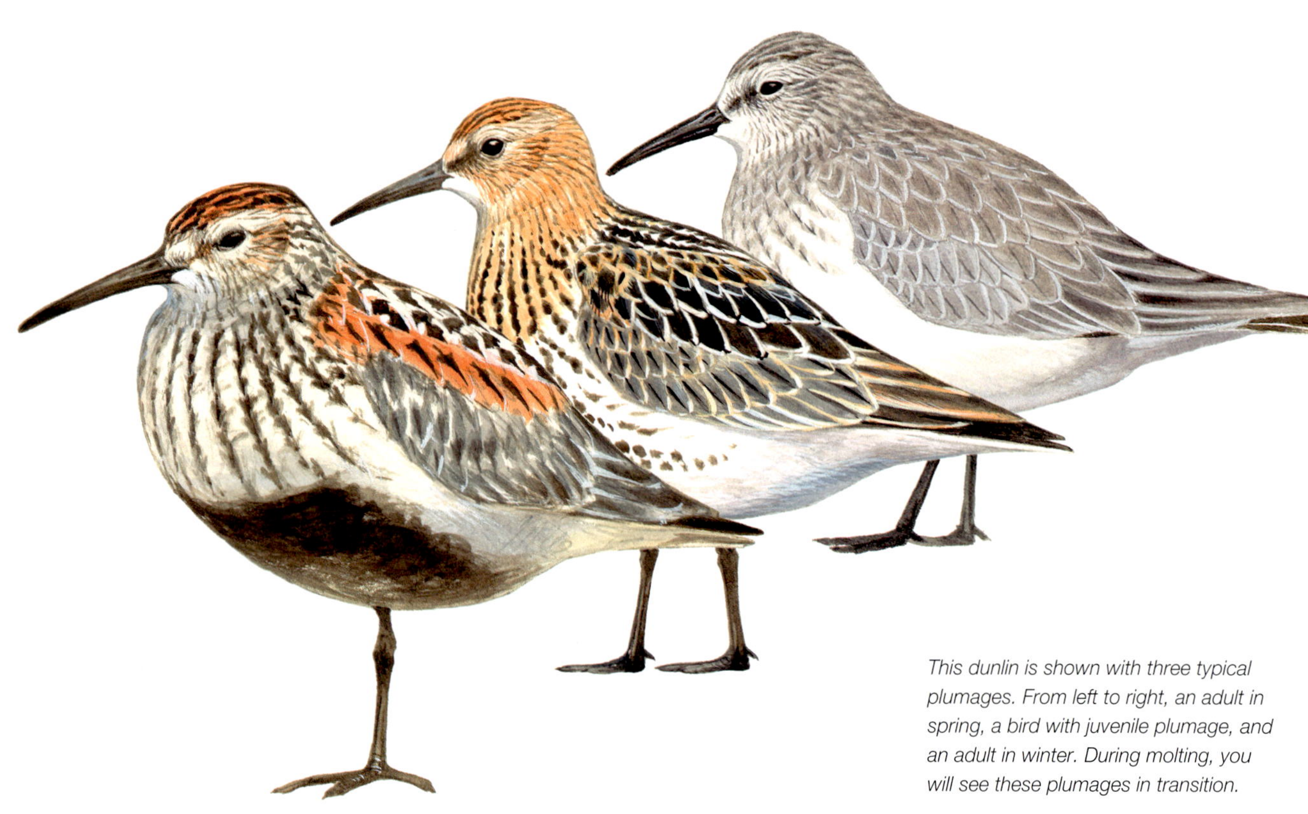

This dunlin is shown with three typical plumages. From left to right, an adult in spring, a bird with juvenile plumage, and an adult in winter. During molting, you will see these plumages in transition.

Many species have marks on their wings and tails, even on their winter plumage, which can help you identify them in flight. On the left in the illustration is a curlew sandpiper and, on the right, a dunlin.

MOTTLED PLUMAGE

A large number of species have very colorful plumage during mating season that they then lose with the coming of autumn. The bright colors are less noticeable on the ground in the tundra, which is covered with lichens. The discrete colors are more useful in the coastal zones in wintertime. For the artist and the ornithologist, the variety of plumages is very attractive, but difficult to understand and draw. Furthermore, the plumage of young birds is different from that of adults.

Not all species, however, are so complicated. Avocets, oystercatchers, lapwings, blackwing stilts, and several more sometimes have an iridescent sheen.

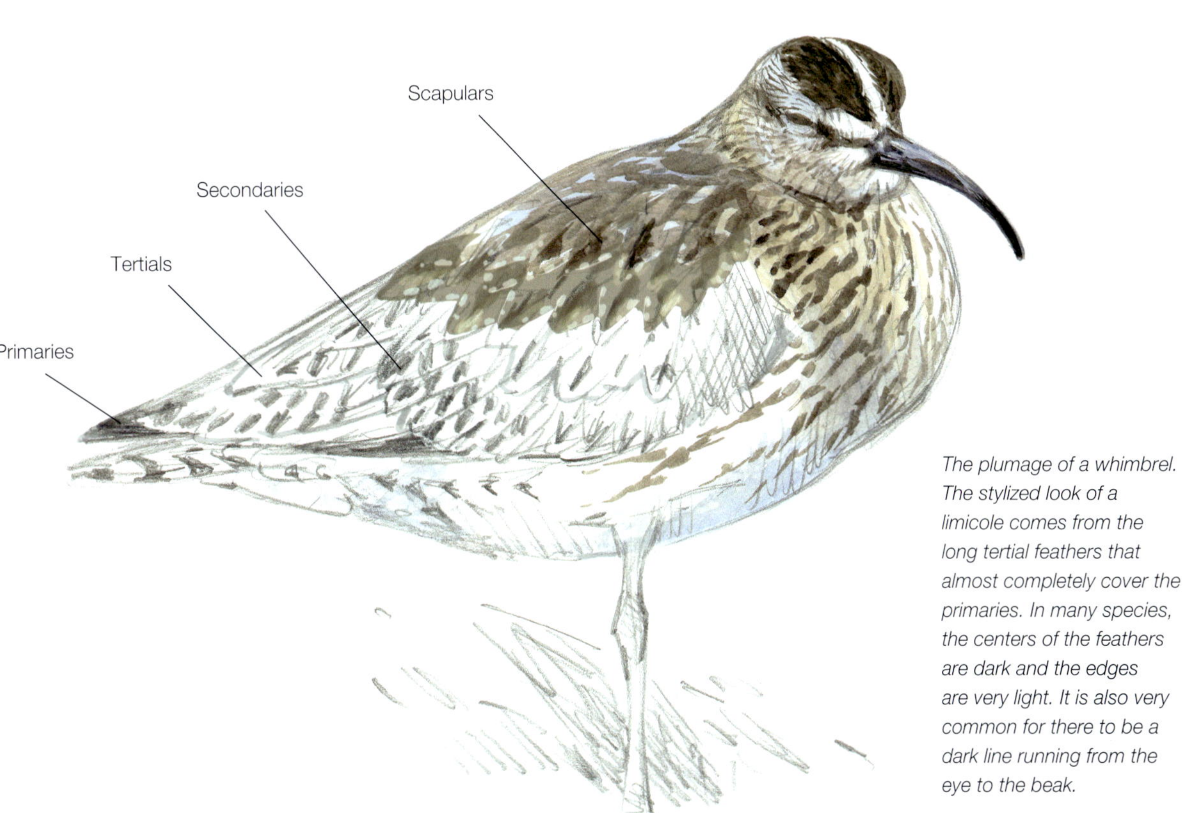

The plumage of a whimbrel. The stylized look of a limicole comes from the long tertial feathers that almost completely cover the primaries. In many species, the centers of the feathers are dark and the edges are very light. It is also very common for there to be a dark line running from the eye to the beak.

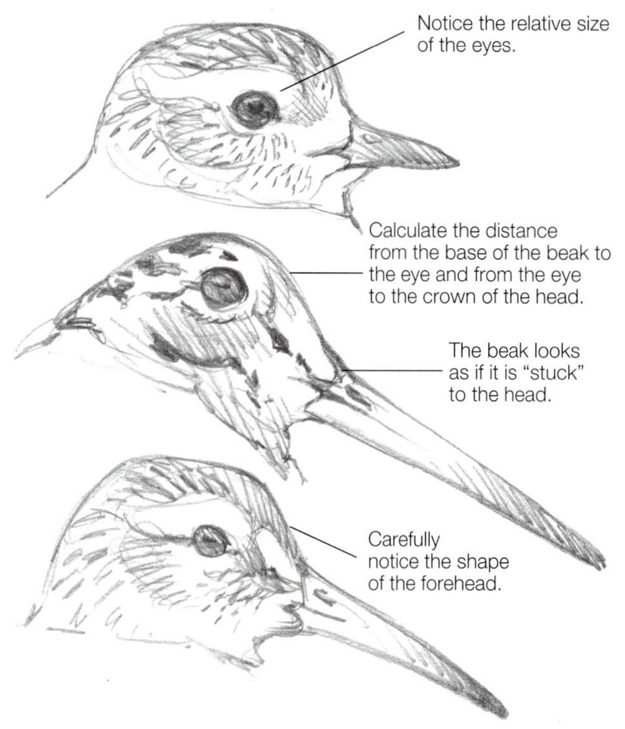

Shorebirds, or by their scientific name, limicoles, are usually very active, especially the small ones, which spend countless hours exploring the areas of low tide, swamps, salt marshes, and rice fields and pecking at the mud in search of small invertebrates. The fact that they travel in large flocks makes it easy to observe the birds in different postures and plumages and it also makes it easy to draw many different sketches. During the migration season, you will see birds with many diverse plumages, because some will still have their spring, juvenile, or fall plumages while others will have already molted completely, so this is a good time for understanding the molting process.

The shape of the head, the length of the beak, and the location and size of the eyes differ greatly among species and correspond to the way they eat. Careful observation of the birds in their natural environment will help you to understand the reasons for the variety of forms. In this illustration, from left to right, are shown the three most common forms: birds with short beaks, like crab plovers and ringed plovers; birds with long beaks, like snipes, bar-tailed godwits, and curlews; and birds with medium beaks, like various sandpipers and greenshanks.

The large group of limicoles encompasses species that are very different in size, color, and proportions. In this illustration are drawings, from bottom to top, of a Kentish plover, a common greenshank, and a bar-tailed godwit.

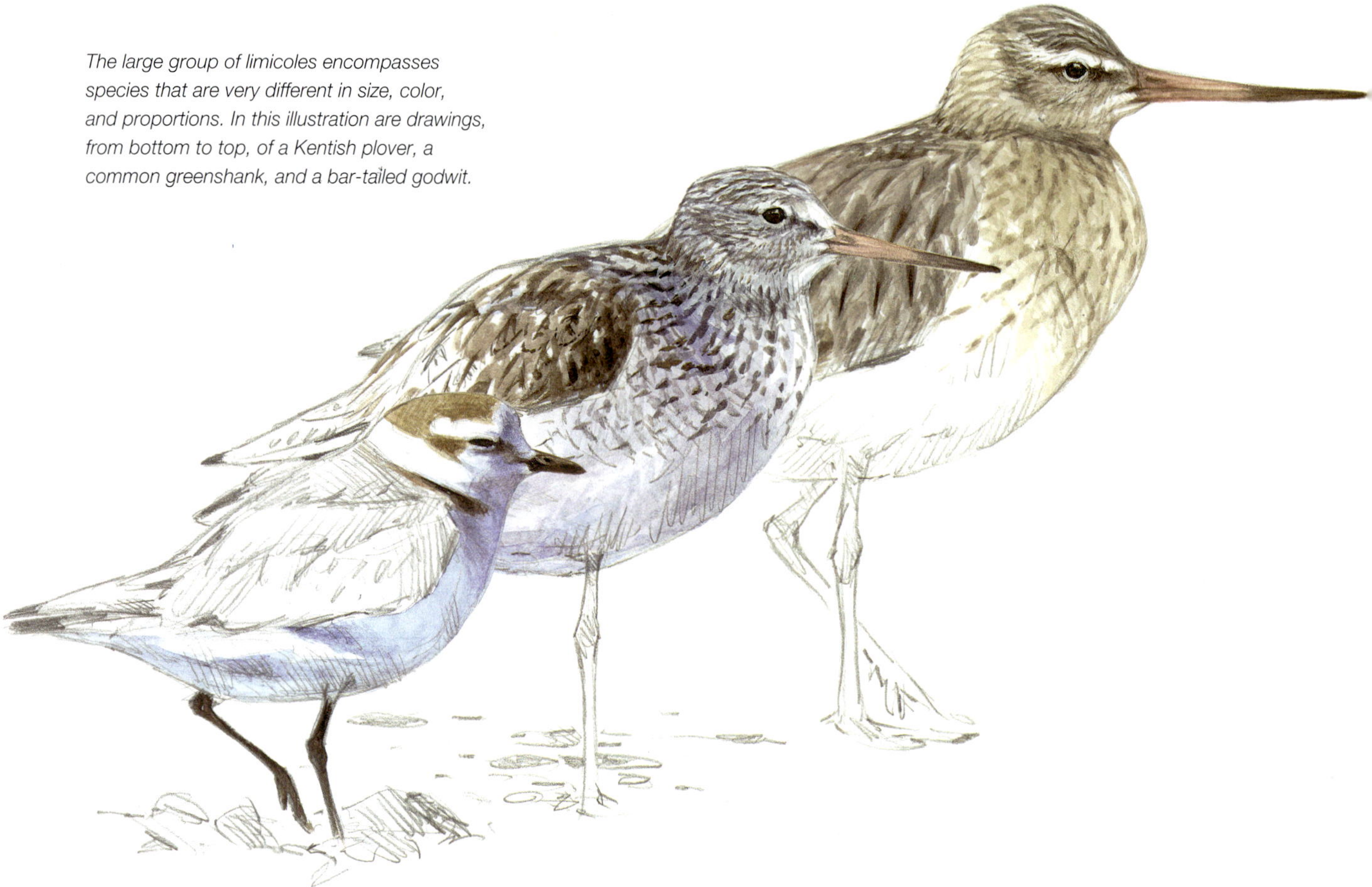

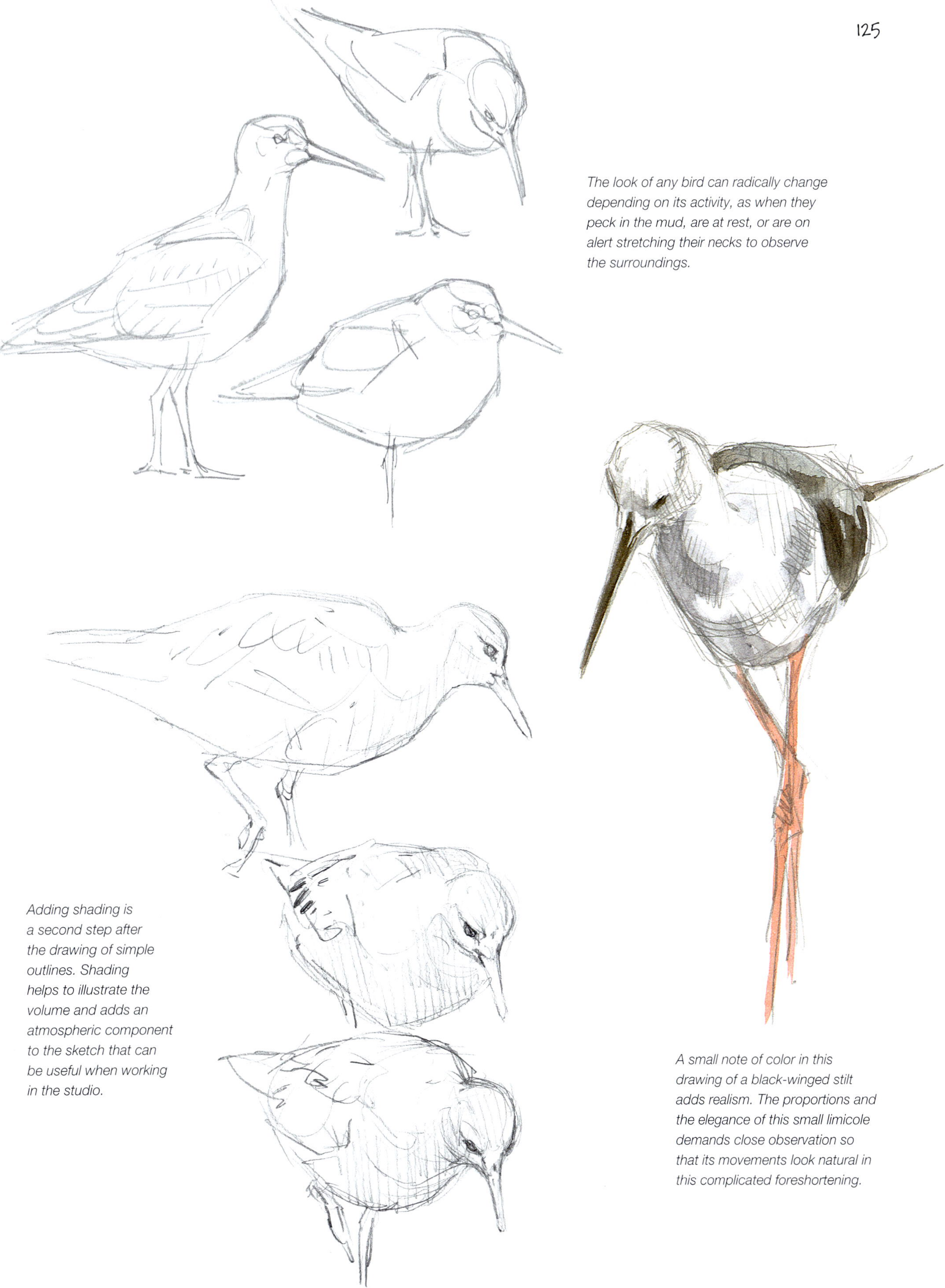

The look of any bird can radically change depending on its activity, as when they peck in the mud, are at rest, or are on alert stretching their necks to observe the surroundings.

Adding shading is a second step after the drawing of simple outlines. Shading helps to illustrate the volume and adds an atmospheric component to the sketch that can be useful when working in the studio.

A small note of color in this drawing of a black-winged stilt adds realism. The proportions and the elegance of this small limicole demands close observation so that its movements look natural in this complicated foreshortening.

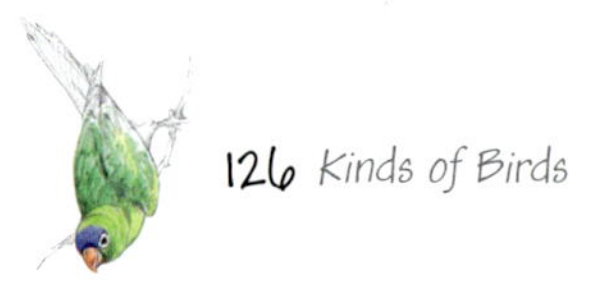

The sea provides many nutrients in the form of fish, mollusks, and other small animals, but they are quite dispersed and it is not easy to find and capture them, especially nowadays with overfishing and pollution affecting the marine environment so much. This explains why marine birds have long lives and few descendants, and why they take so long to reach maturity. They are usually bred on beaches and cliffs, often in colonies, especially where the waters are richest and with the least amount of human presence, like the coasts of the South Atlantic.

Penguins, seagulls, cormorants, shearwaters, gannets, albatrosses, and loons are typical representatives of marine birds.

Marine Birds

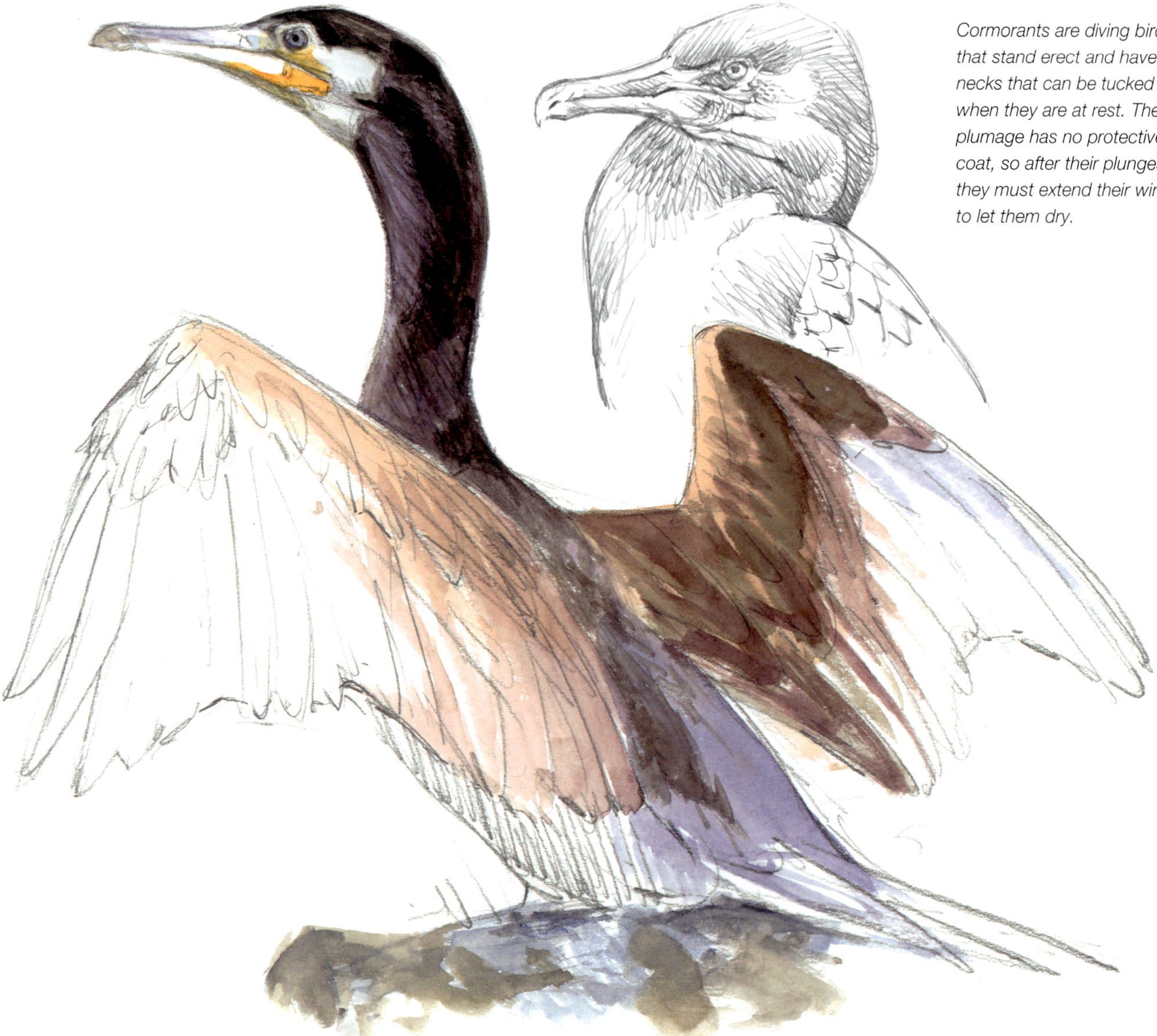

Cormorants are diving birds that stand erect and have long necks that can be tucked in when they are at rest. Their plumage has no protective coat, so after their plunges they must extend their wings to let them dry.

LIVING NEAR THE WATER

With the exception of penguins, who have lost the ability to fly, and their northern relatives, razorbills, who have very short wings, the rest of the marine birds share the trait of wings that are proportionately longer and narrower than those of other species—some as long as those of frigate birds and albatrosses and others a little less exaggerated, like those of cormorants.

The manner of catching fish, diving from high altitudes, has caused marine birds to have very stylized shapes and thin or hooked beaks with sharp edges, sometimes formed by several plates. In all of them, the toes are webbed, joined by membranes for swimming, and these birds are generally clumsy on land.

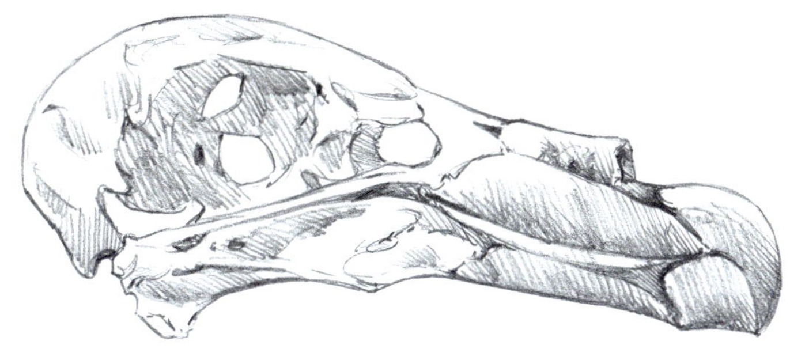

The beak of a fulmar. Shearwaters and albatrosses as well as cormorants and pelicans have beaks formed of plates. The first two species have a pair of small nasal tubes at the base of the beak.

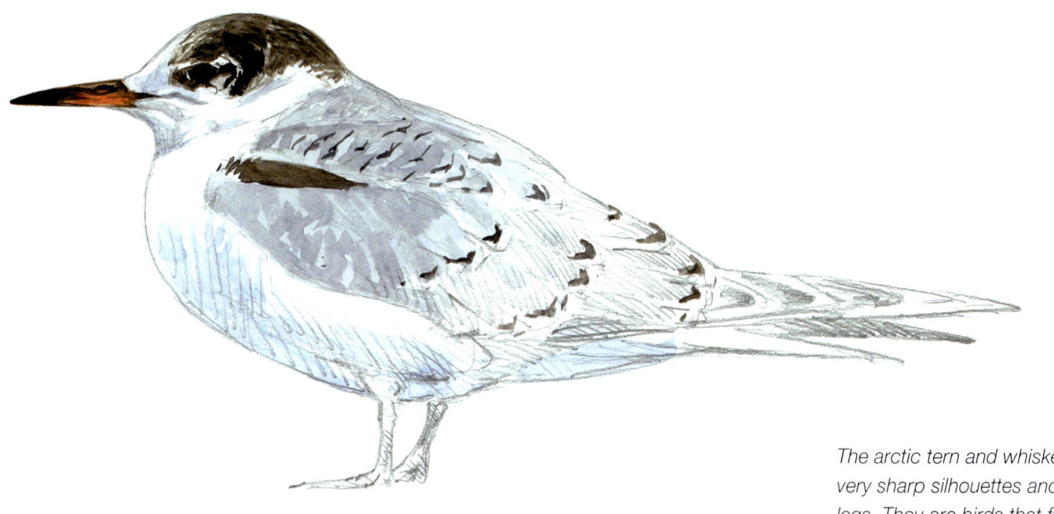

The arctic tern and whiskered tern have very sharp silhouettes and very short legs. They are birds that fly fast and maneuver with great agility.

This lesser black-backed gull has the plumage of a third year juvenile. Nearly all the species of marine birds have juvenile plumage until arriving at maturity. It is possible to calculate their age quite closely based on their coloring.

Seagulls, pelicans, cormorants, and gannets are some of the species that are commonly observed near areas inhabited by humans, because they form flocks during the winter or during the breeding season. In less accessible areas are concentrations of large flocks of razorbills, murres, puffins in the northern hemisphere, and different species of penguins south of the equator.

These concentrations provide a multitude of examples, plumages, and postures that will keep the artist occupied for hours.

Great northern loons drawn by Barry Van Dusen. Loons are solitary marine birds. In this collection of sketches, this artist from Massachusetts proves the saying "less is more." With a few lines, he represents family scenes of a female great northern loon and her chicks. A few notes of color and text alluding to the different kinds of plumage will serve as helpful information for later work in the studio.

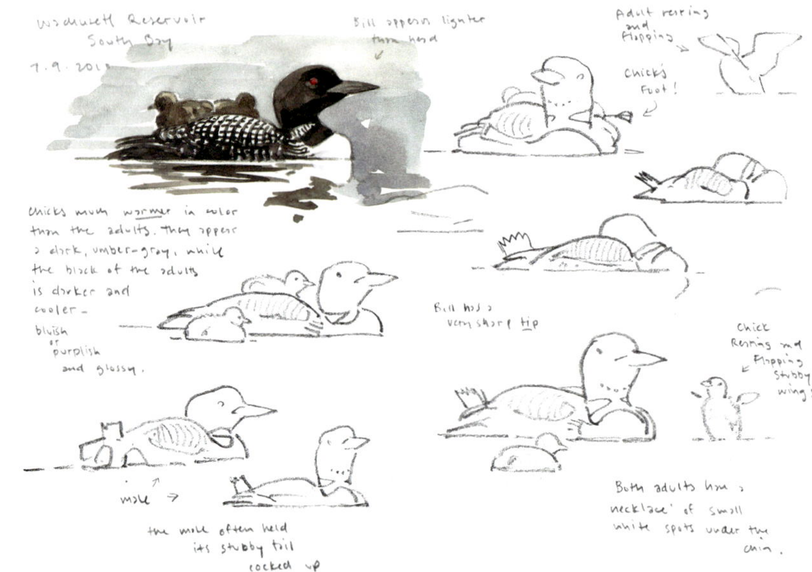

This lesser black-backed gull is a typical marine bird with many points in common with other members of the type. A large number of marine birds lack bright colors in their plumage, with only basic black and white and different shades of gray.

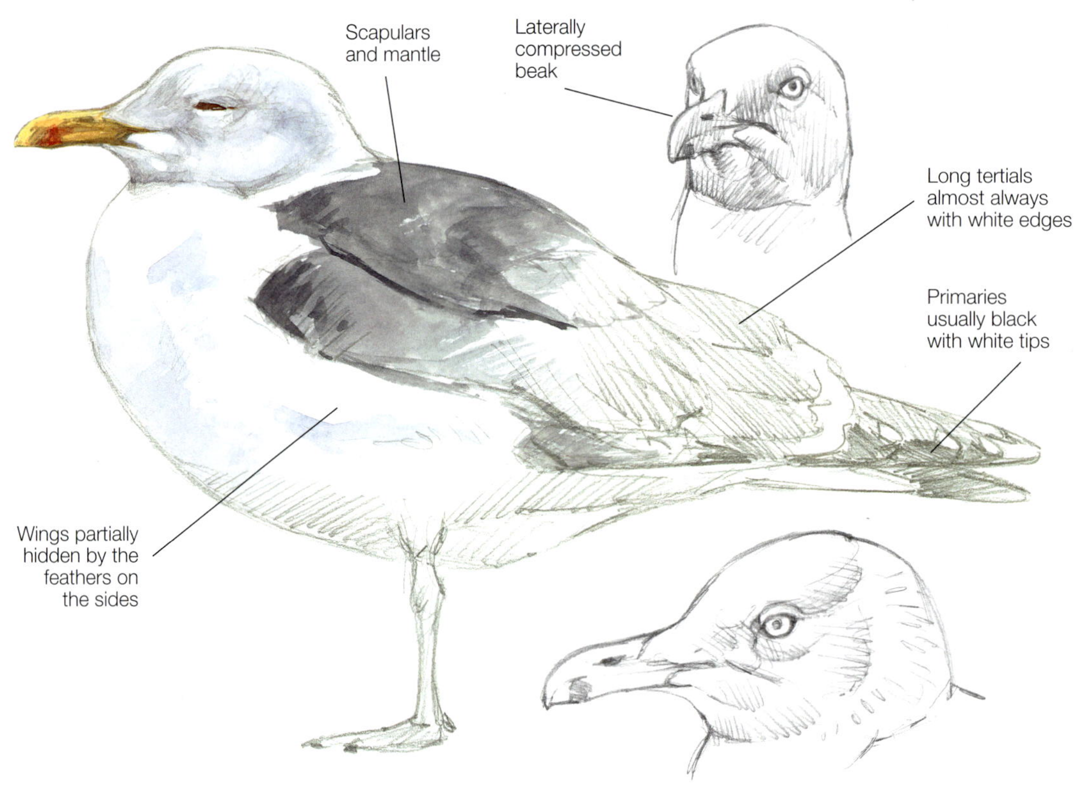

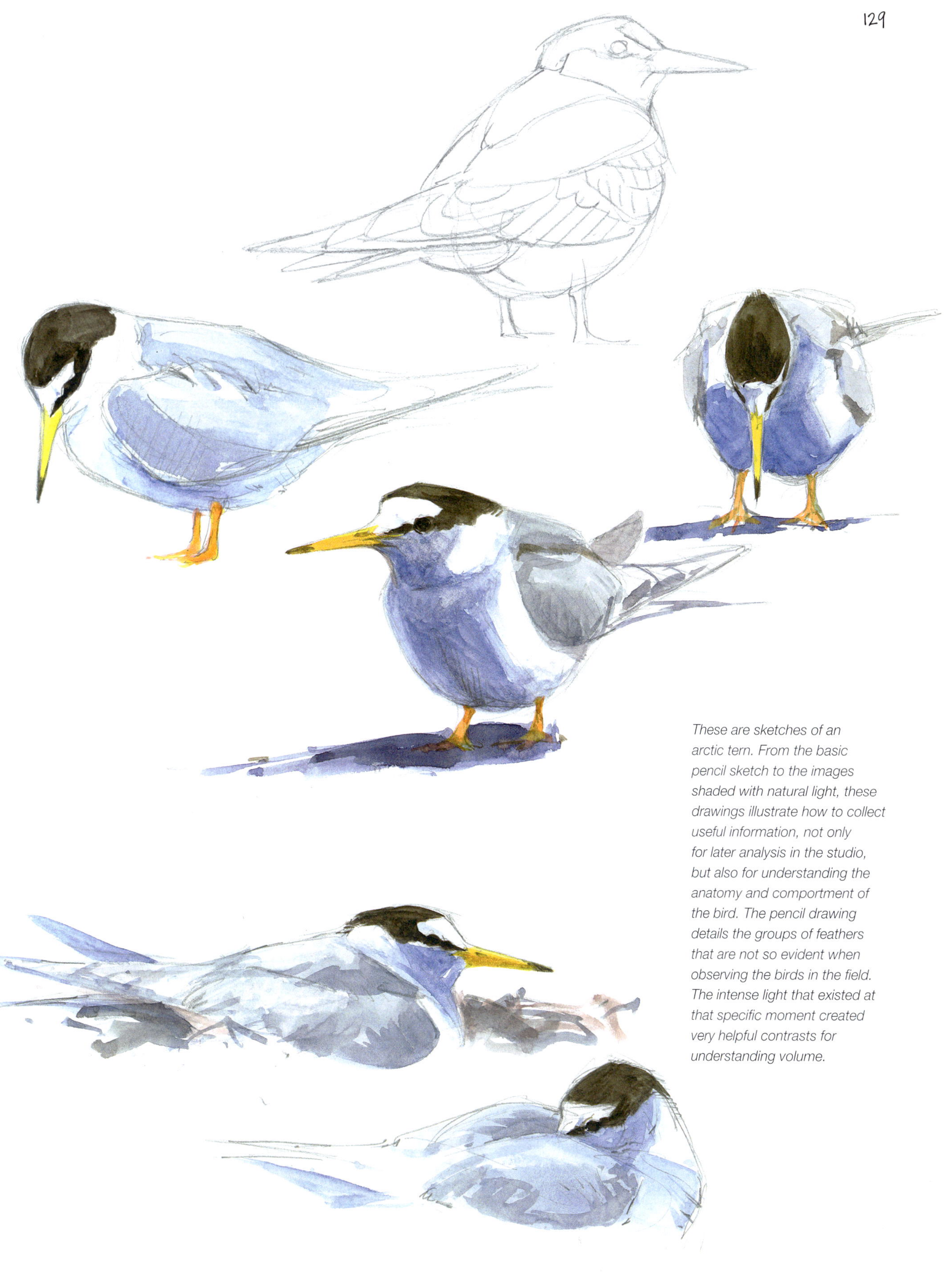

These are sketches of an arctic tern. From the basic pencil sketch to the images shaded with natural light, these drawings illustrate how to collect useful information, not only for later analysis in the studio, but also for understanding the anatomy and comportment of the bird. The pencil drawing details the groups of feathers that are not so evident when observing the birds in the field. The intense light that existed at that specific moment created very helpful contrasts for understanding volume.

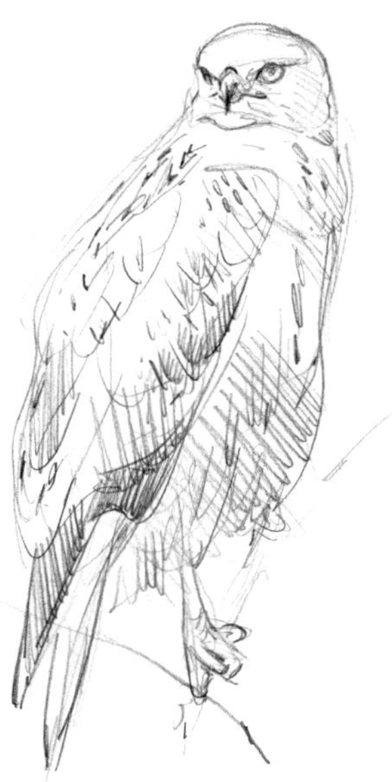

Land Birds
Some Fly and Others Do Not

The name "land birds" refers to the species that do not habitually use aquatic environments for survival. This large group can be subdivided into different parts to distinguish forest birds, mountain birds, steppe birds, and so on, but, for the artistic purposes of this book, it will be enough to briefly list some of the species that are most interesting from the aesthetic point of view and that might be in greatest demand from illustrators. It would be impossible to go into detail about the thousands of shapes and adaptations that have developed in these birds with the passage of time, from the striking birds of paradise and the hummingbirds to the ostriches and cassowaries, which are unable to fly.

ANTONIO OJEA
PAIR OF GRIFFON VULTURES
WATERCOLOR, 15.75 x 21.25 INCHES (40 x 54 CM)

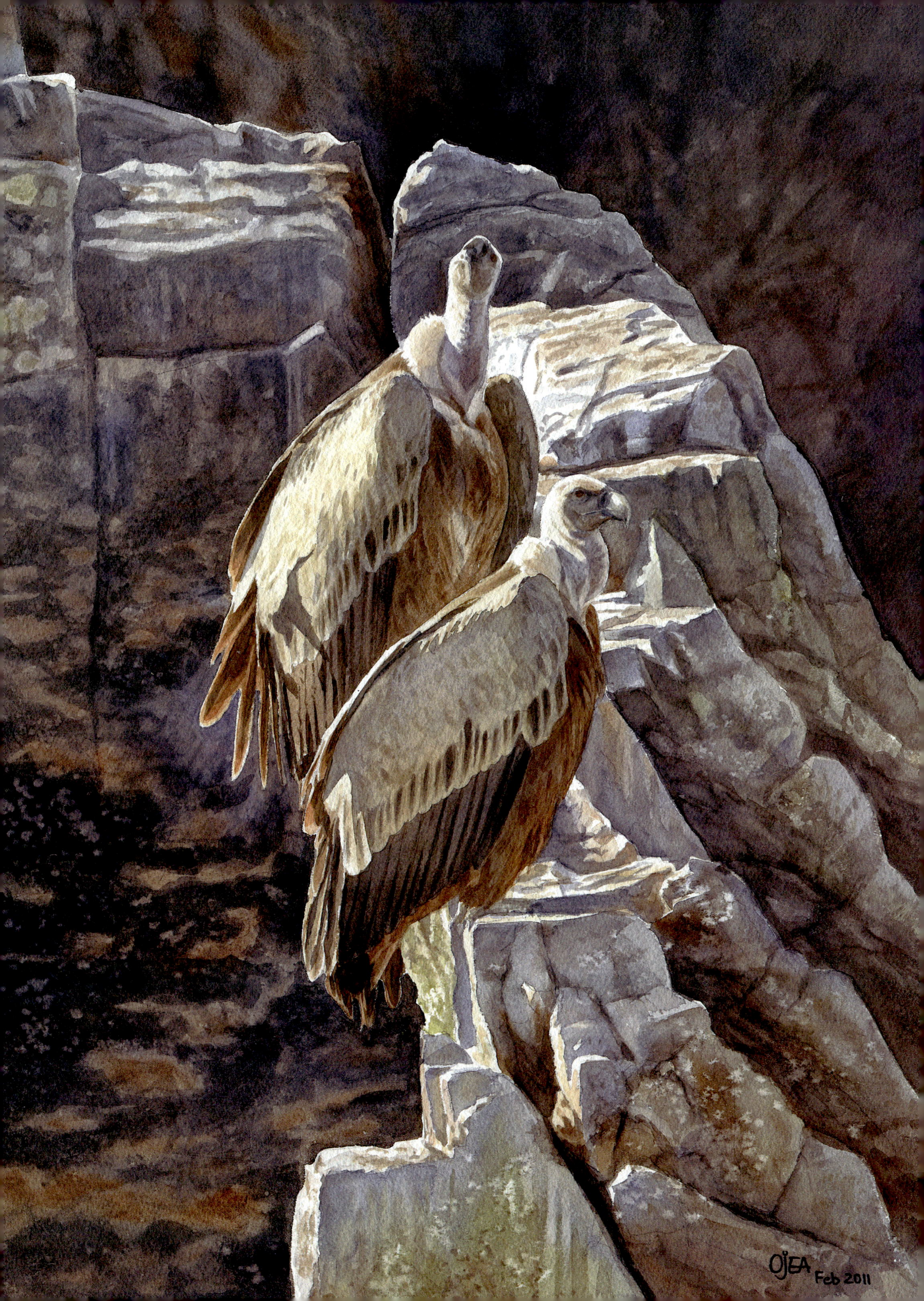
OJEA
Feb 2011

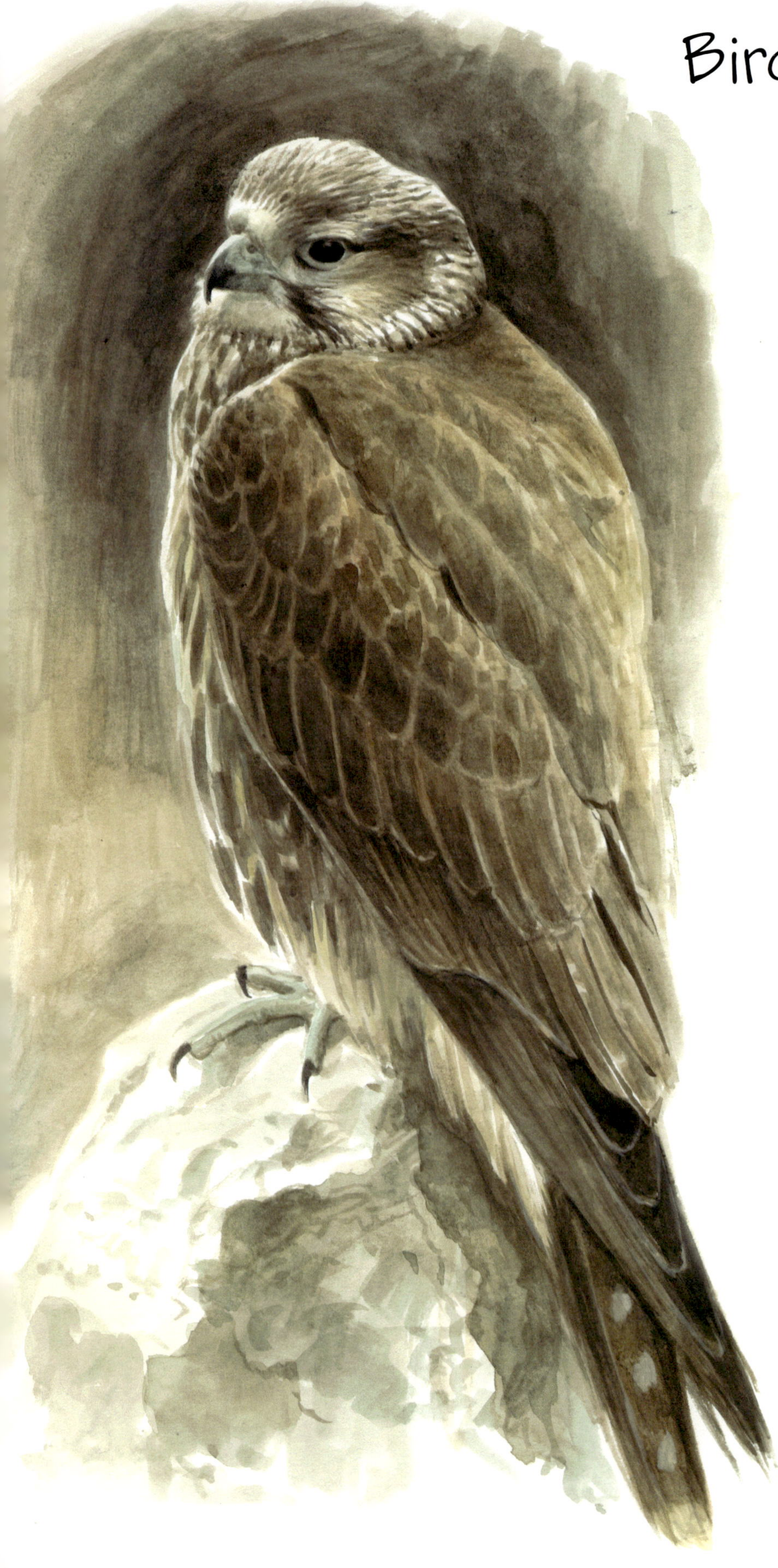

Birds of Prey

This is probably the group of birds that gets the most attention from fans of ornithology and from artists. The birds of prey are divided into several groups based on their morphology. On one side, the fast-flying falcons, of relatively small size and with narrow wings; on another are the eagles of various shapes, but generally large in size and with wide wings; a third group is made up of goshawks and related birds; and a fourth group includes the carrion birds like vultures that can soar for very long periods and that lack the characteristic sharp claws of the hunting birds.

INHABITANTS OF THE NIGHT

A review of the birds of prey would not be complete without mentioning a group of species that, although they do not belong to the same order as the previous birds, also catches prey for their food. The owls belong to what we call night hunters, which mainly eat rodents, small birds, and insects. Only the largest ones, like the European eagle-owl, are capable of catching larger size animals like rabbits. Not all of them are strictly nocturnal. Some are more active at dusk and others can scour the countryside during a large part of the day.

Saker falcon, 2007. Watercolor, 8.5 x 12.25 inches (22 x 31 cm), painted by Paschalis Dougalis. Zoological parks like the Hellabrunn in Munich offer many opportunities for drawing birds and other species of animals.

Northern hawk-owl, aplomado falcon, and bald eagle. The essential weapons of birds of prey are the claws and the beak, whose shape and size depend on the way they hunt and the type of prey. A striking characteristic, which is important to include in the drawing, is the nearly frontal position of the eyes, more so than even in the nocturnal birds.

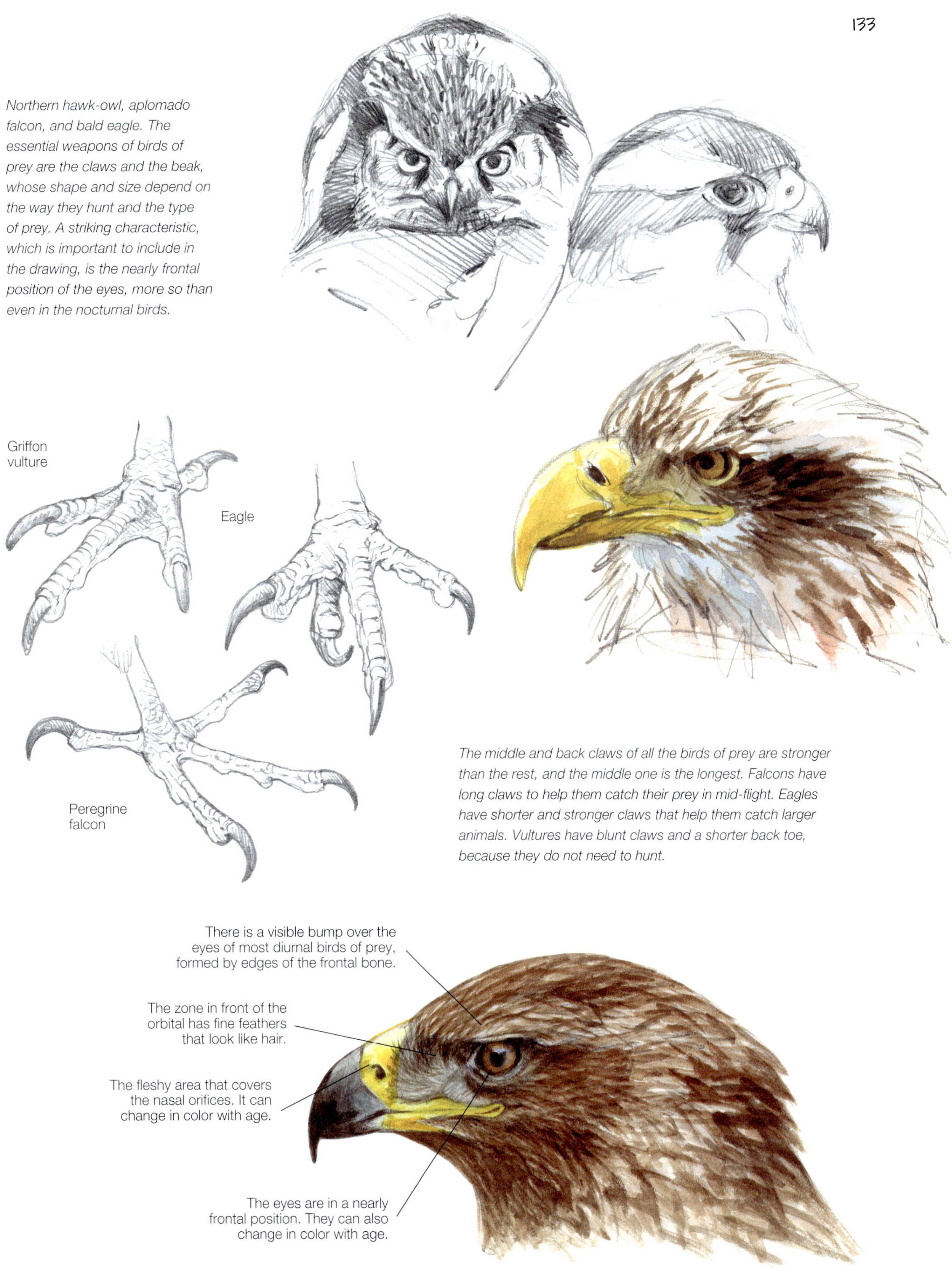

The middle and back claws of all the birds of prey are stronger than the rest, and the middle one is the longest. Falcons have long claws to help them catch their prey in mid-flight. Eagles have shorter and stronger claws that help them catch larger animals. Vultures have blunt claws and a shorter back toe, because they do not need to hunt.

Birds of prey, at least the diurnal ones, are relatively easy to observe from the ground, because of their size and their hunting habits. Many of them soar over their hunting grounds or perch on telephone poles or trees from where they can watch the ground. During mating season, they usually perform aerial acrobatics alongside their mates. These occasions allow you to observe them at your pleasure and make sketches in the field. The nocturnal hunters are seen more around dusk, especially during breeding time, when they must collect more food to feed their chicks. The head–body relationship in birds of prey varies according to the size of the bird. Small birds of prey, the falcons, usually have larger heads compared to the larger eagles. Nocturnal birds of prey have heads that are proportionately larger.

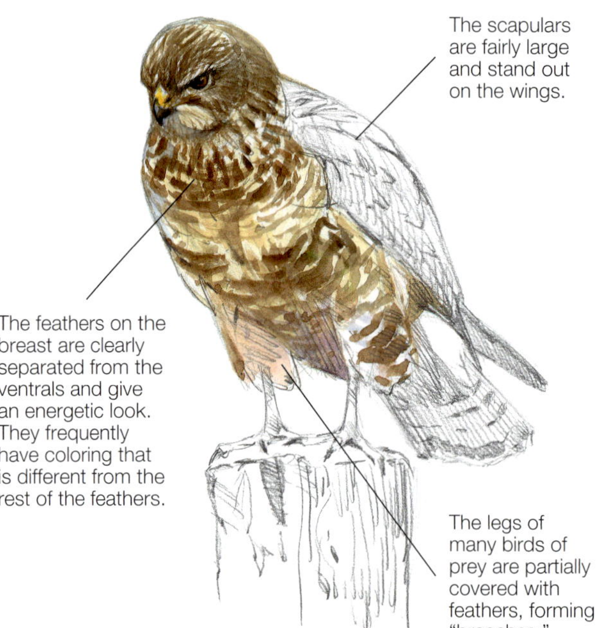

Particularities of the plumage of a bird of prey.

Birds of Prey in Flight

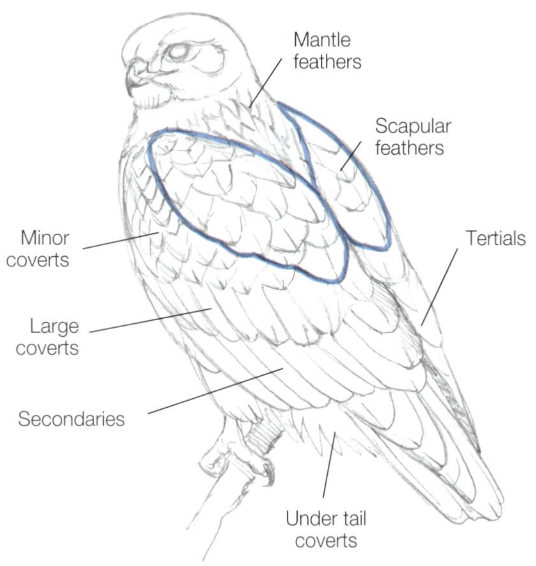

The scheme of the plumage of a common buzzard, a medium size bird of prey. In larger hunting birds, the soaring birds, the surface of the wing is greater and the secondary wing feathers are longer than those of falcons and other small birds of prey.

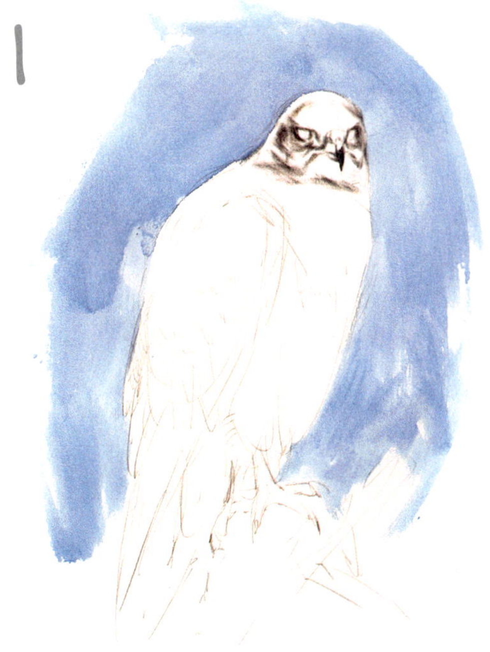

1. Black-chested buzzard-eagle. Water-base oil on paper, 12 x 16 inches (31 x 41 cm). Although this original was painted with water-base oil paint, the process would be very similar with watercolor or gouache. No more than five colors were used: yellow, red, ultramarine blue, and burnt umber. A little white was also applied here and there to create opaque tones.

Begin with a pencil drawing that, in this case, does not need a lot of detail, because the intention is to give the drawing a loose feeling. Lightly mark the features with a neutral tone, avoiding the areas that should have light colors. Paint the background to outline the bird.

2

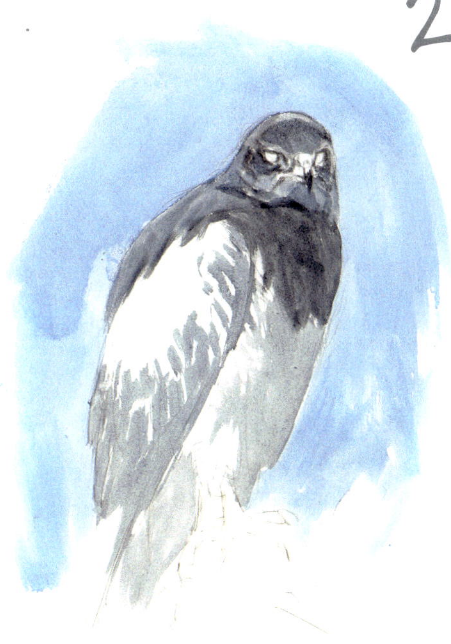

2. Add light washes to block in the main areas of color and the shadows. The first brushstrokes all indicate a certain direction.

3. Paint over with warmer colors and add some dark shadows, then start working on the features. The bird's stare must be well drawn. If necessary, you can use a mirror to be sure that the eyes are correctly placed. Draw the feet, which were only suggested.

3

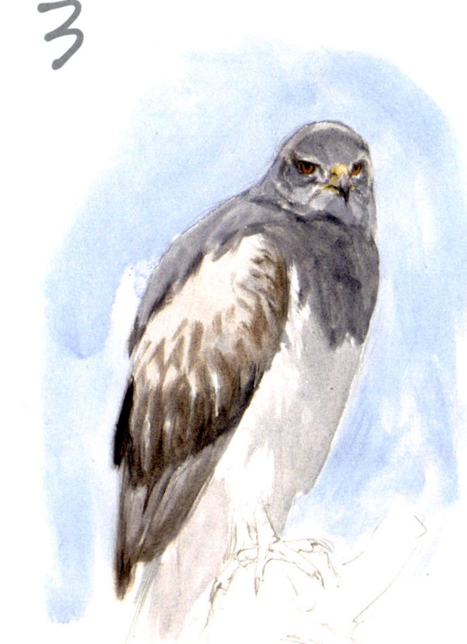

4. Suggest the direction of the plumage with darker short strokes. Add color to the feet, and, with opaque paint, draw some details on the wings.

4

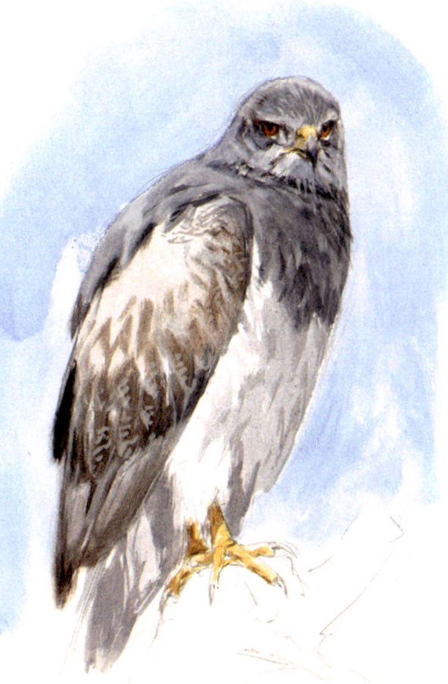

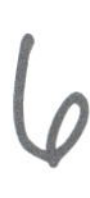

5

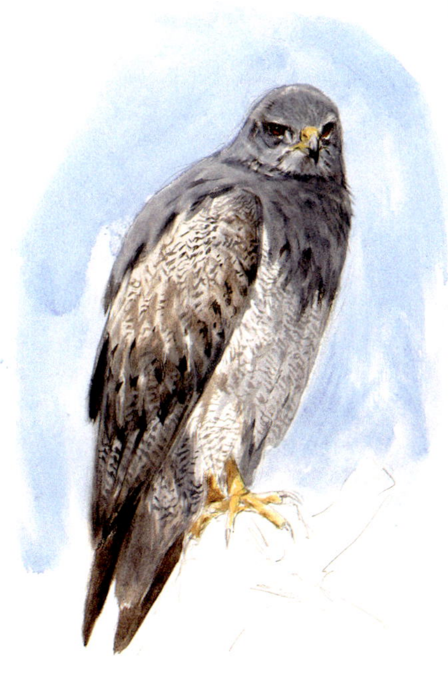

5. Draw the darker lines on the wings and ventral area in a somewhat loose manner. These lines should not be random, but should follow the line of the feathers. Continue with similar work on the lower part of the tail and the secondary feathers.

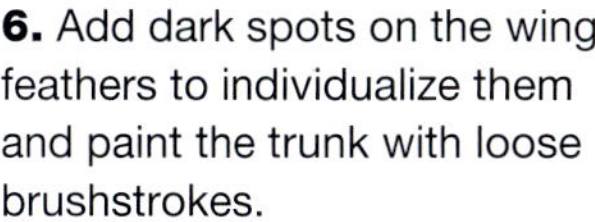

6. Add dark spots on the wing feathers to individualize them and paint the trunk with loose brushstrokes.

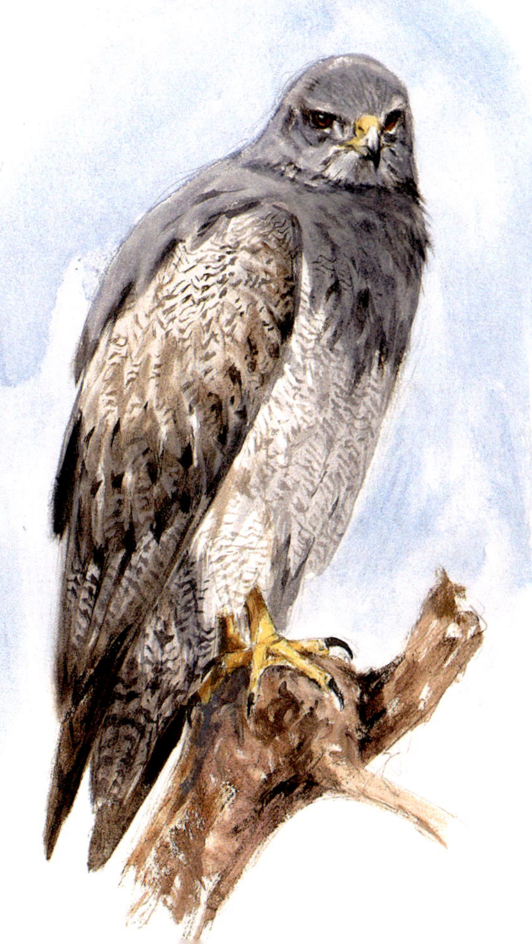

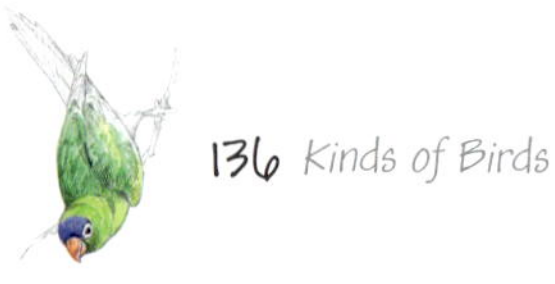

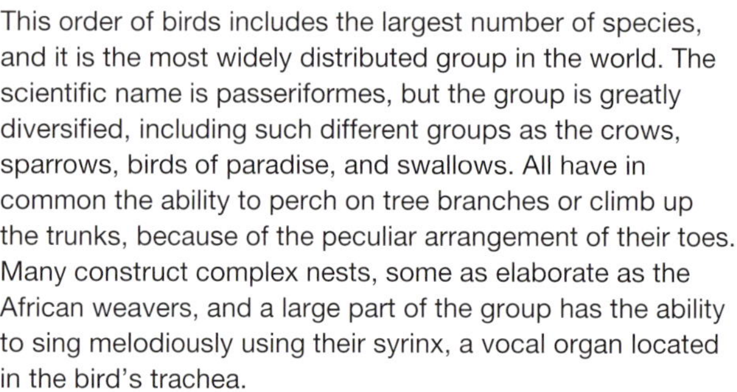

Dartford warbler. When you have a good drawing as a base, color can be added with more confidence. Notice that the brushstrokes were not applied haphazardly. On a light base, the dark brushstrokes follow the shapes of the feathers, and they are applied in a specific direction to "comb" the body of the bird.

Small Birds

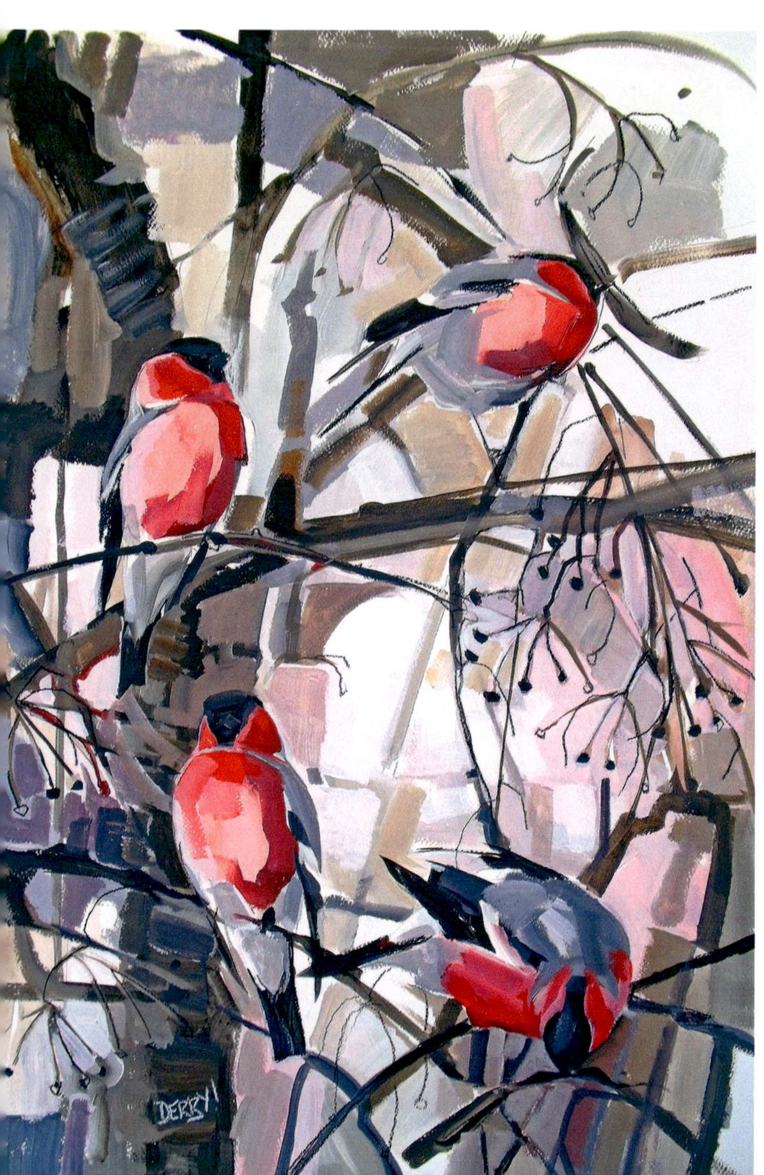

This order of birds includes the largest number of species, and it is the most widely distributed group in the world. The scientific name is passeriformes, but the group is greatly diversified, including such different groups as the crows, sparrows, birds of paradise, and swallows. All have in common the ability to perch on tree branches or climb up the trunks, because of the peculiar arrangement of their toes. Many construct complex nests, some as elaborate as the African weavers, and a large part of the group has the ability to sing melodiously using their syrinx, a vocal organ located in the bird's trachea.

OBTAINING THE MODEL

Small birds can present the most difficulties for the artist, at least when working in the field, because of their incessant activity and the challenge of getting close enough to them to observe their features. In these cases, photographs will help you become familiar with their proportions and details, but understanding their movements and conduct requires spending hours in the field, something that always turns out to be very entertaining.

To draw them in the field, it is a good idea to avoid detail and attempt to quickly capture their outlines and proportions. Later, you can add the necessary details in the studio, using photographs and videos. With practice, you will eventually be able to work with more accuracy in the field.

Eurasian bullfinch. Acrylic and oil pencil on paper, 19.5 x 27.5 inches (50 x 70 cm), painted by Nick Derry. Using a few sketches of live birds, this artist created a beautiful composition in the studio, in which he mixed media and his personal experiences. You can clearly see his firsthand knowledge of the postures of these birds.

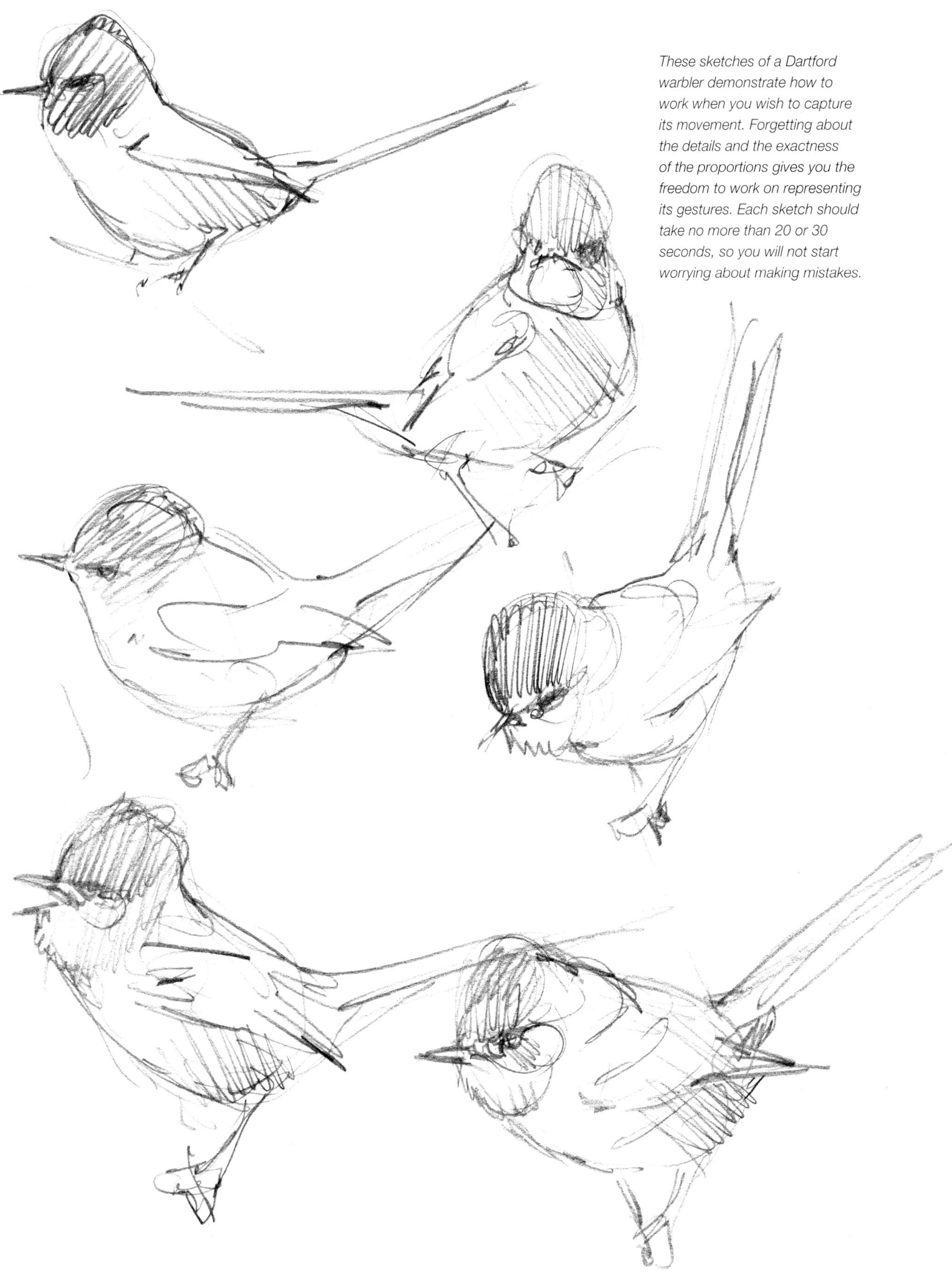

These sketches of a Dartford warbler demonstrate how to work when you wish to capture its movement. Forgetting about the details and the exactness of the proportions gives you the freedom to work on representing its gestures. Each sketch should take no more than 20 or 30 seconds, so you will not start worrying about making mistakes.

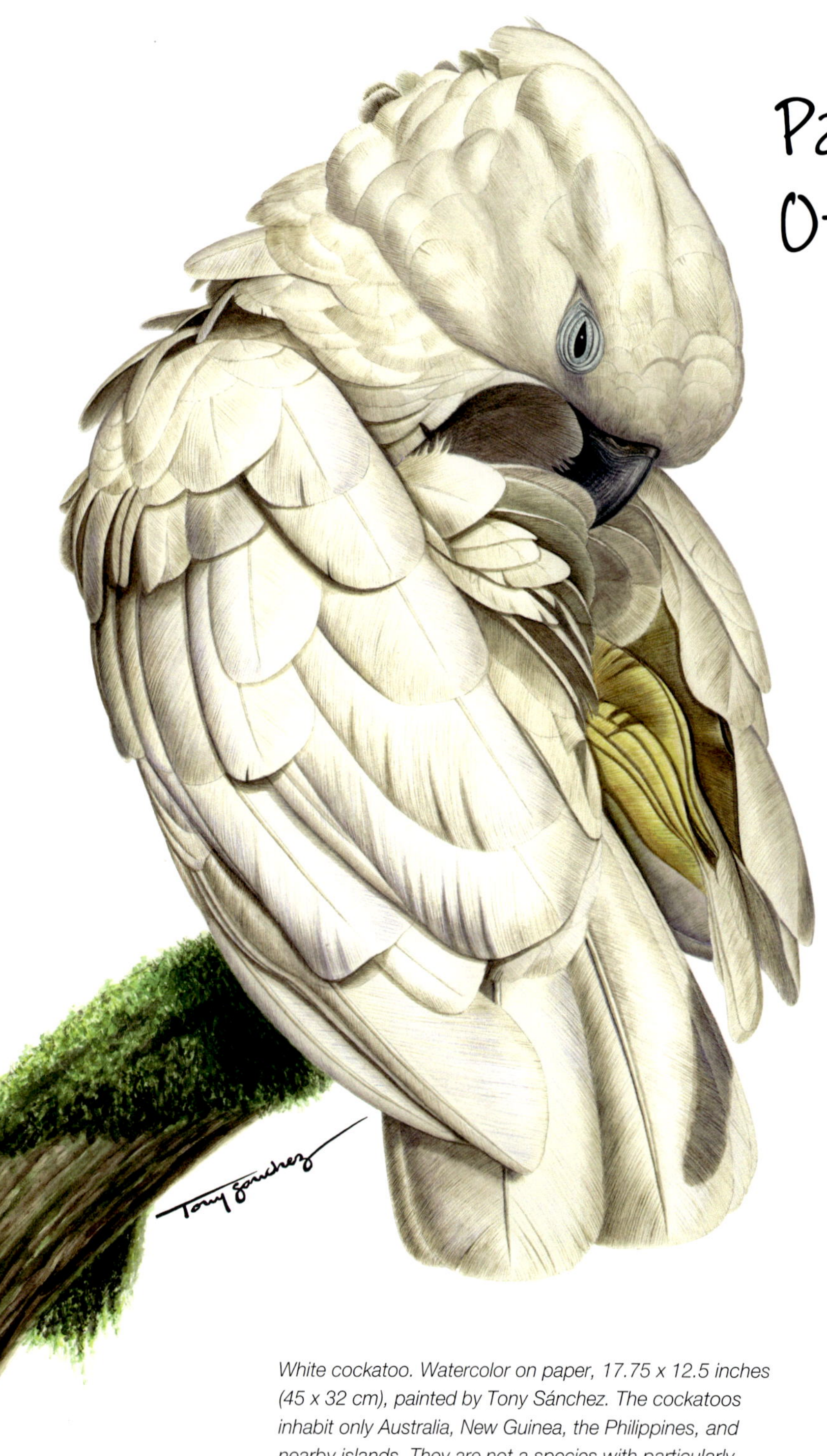

Parrots and Other Families

The psittaciformes—the scientific name of parrots, cockatoos, and parakeets—are a large family that is mainly distributed among tropical and subtropical climates, from Central America to Oceania. In Europe, they are considered to be pets, but there are actually healthy populations of birds that have escaped and returned to the wild, principally monk parakeets and rose-ringed parakeets. These boisterous bands occupy urban parks, where they construct immense colonies of nests in the highest trees. This family of birds is very popular with humans, because of their coloring and ability to imitate speech, which has encouraged illegal commerce to the point that some species are now in danger of extinction.

STRIKING COLORS

One of the challenges of drawing parrots is reproducing the iridescence of their plumage, which is composed of green, blue, and purple tones that are not produced by natural pigments, but by the structure of the feathers and the way they reflect light. Parrots and the rest of their relatives, however, are the only birds that produce a special red pigment. In most of the species of these families, there are practically no differences in the plumage of both sexes. Other details that the artist should keep in mind are the shapes of the toes, two opposing pairs, and the articulation that connects the upper jaw to the skull, which helps them apply a great amount of force when biting.

White cockatoo. Watercolor on paper, 17.75 x 12.5 inches (45 x 32 cm), painted by Tony Sánchez. The cockatoos inhabit only Australia, New Guinea, the Philippines, and nearby islands. They are not a species with particularly striking colors. Most of them are white, black, or gray, with an occasional red or yellow streak. Some species have vertical crests of feathers.

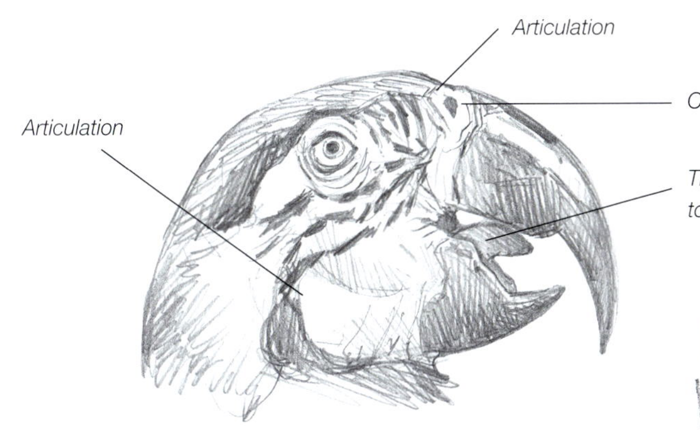

Opposable toes

Blue-crowned parakeet (Aratinga acuticaudata). All the psittaciformes have two pairs of opposable toes, which gives them a better grip for performing their acrobatics and manipulating their food. In this head of a macaw, you can see the most outstanding features.

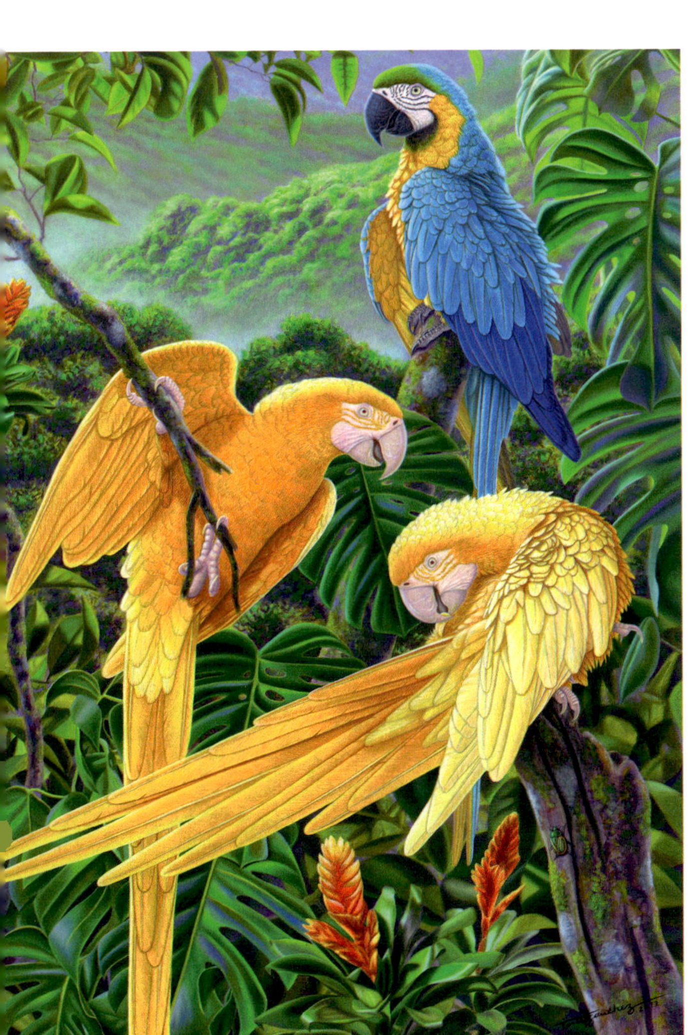

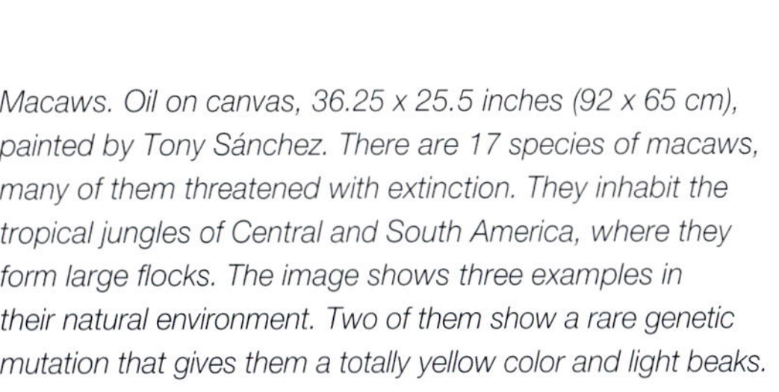

Macaws. Oil on canvas, 36.25 x 25.5 inches (92 x 65 cm), painted by Tony Sánchez. There are 17 species of macaws, many of them threatened with extinction. They inhabit the tropical jungles of Central and South America, where they form large flocks. The image shows three examples in their natural environment. Two of them show a rare genetic mutation that gives them a totally yellow color and light beaks.

Getting Close to Birds

TIM WOOTTON
SEDGE WARBLER
WATERCOLOR, 19.5 x 15.75 INCHES (50 x 40 CM)

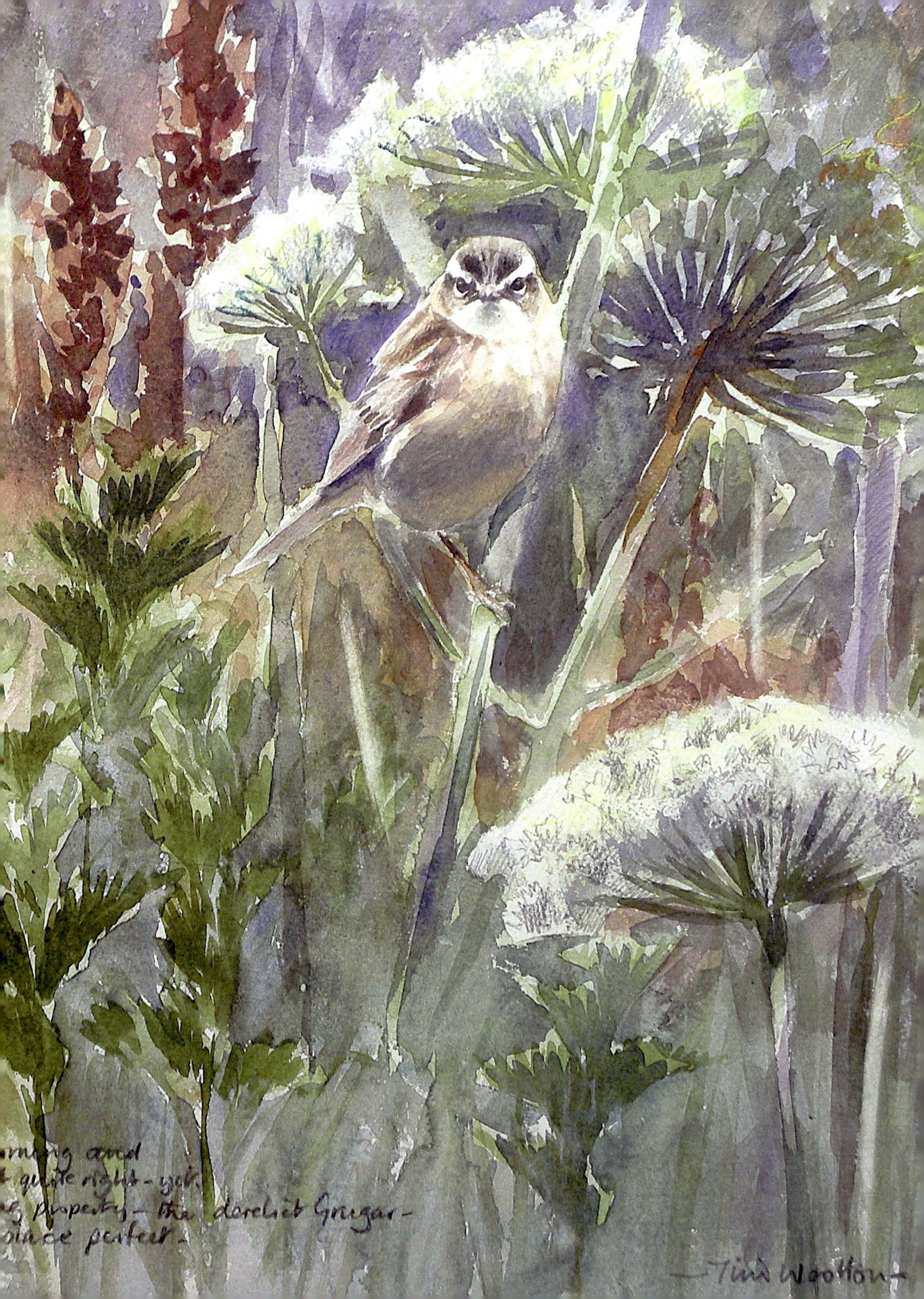
and
quite right - yet.
property - the derelict Grugar -
perfect -
Tim Wootton

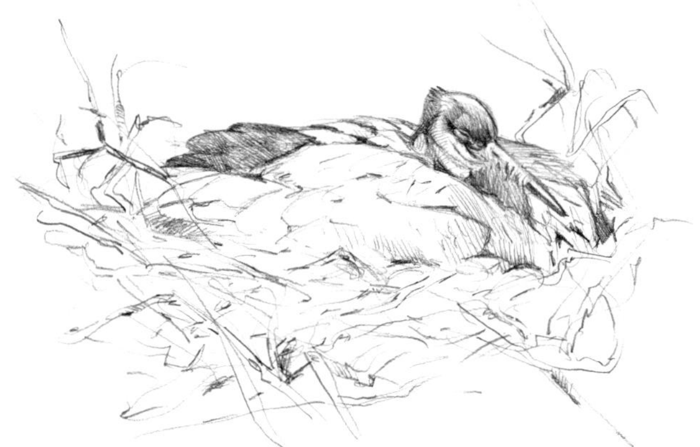

Working from Life
Understanding Birds

In the previous pages, we have included a large number of images to illustrate everything that is explained in the text. But these images also have another function, which is to supply examples and clear references for artists, in both poses and proportions.

In quite a few cases, the illustrations show intermediate states rather than finished work. This will help the reader understand the drawing process and even the application of color in a much more immediate way than a long explanation. Working from life is the best way to understand the movements and anatomy of birds, or any animal. Therefore, the work done in the studio as described until now should have prepared the artist for the moment in which he or she will come face to face with a figure in motion, sometimes visible for only a few seconds.

JUAN VARELA
CAMPO FLICKER (*COLAPTES CAMPESTRIS*)
WATERCOLOR, 10.5 x 14.5 INCHES (27 x 37 CM)

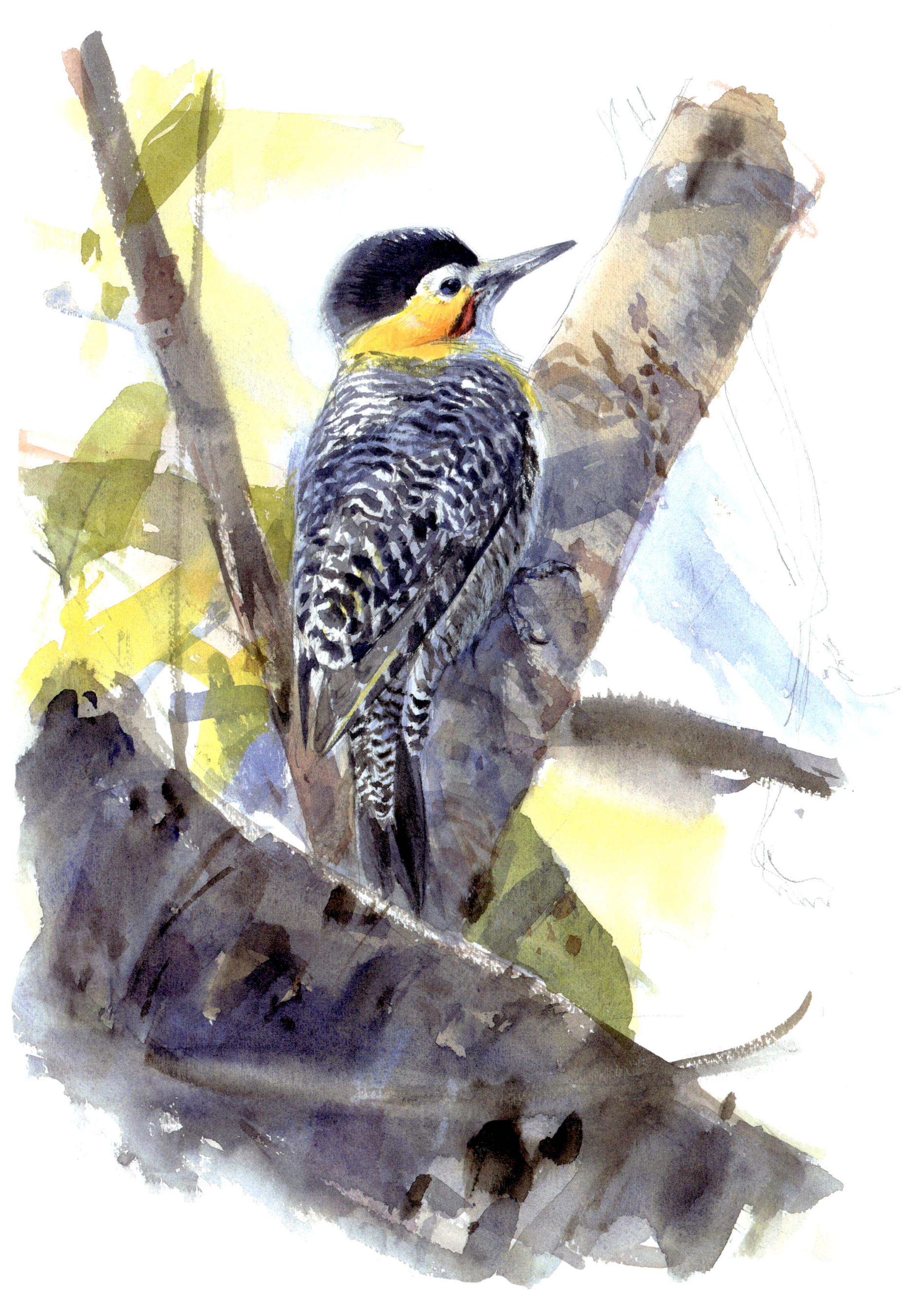

Observing Without Disturbing

Most birds do not allow anyone to get near them, unless they are accustomed to the presence of humans, like sparrows and pigeons in the city. Generally, it is necessary to use some type of optics, binoculars or telescopes, or a blind for viewers to hide behind. Many parks and nature reserves have observatories where viewers can comfortably sit and draw without bothering the birds. But, even from these places, it is nearly always necessary to use some kind of optics to get a better view of the details. Amateur artists usually start off with pair of 8 x 30 or 10 x 40 binoculars, and, in time, change to a telescope with a tripod that will leave their hands free to draw while they observe. When buying this equipment, it is best to go to a specialized shop and also to get some help from some association for the preservation of birds and nature, because its members will be very familiar with this type of equipment.

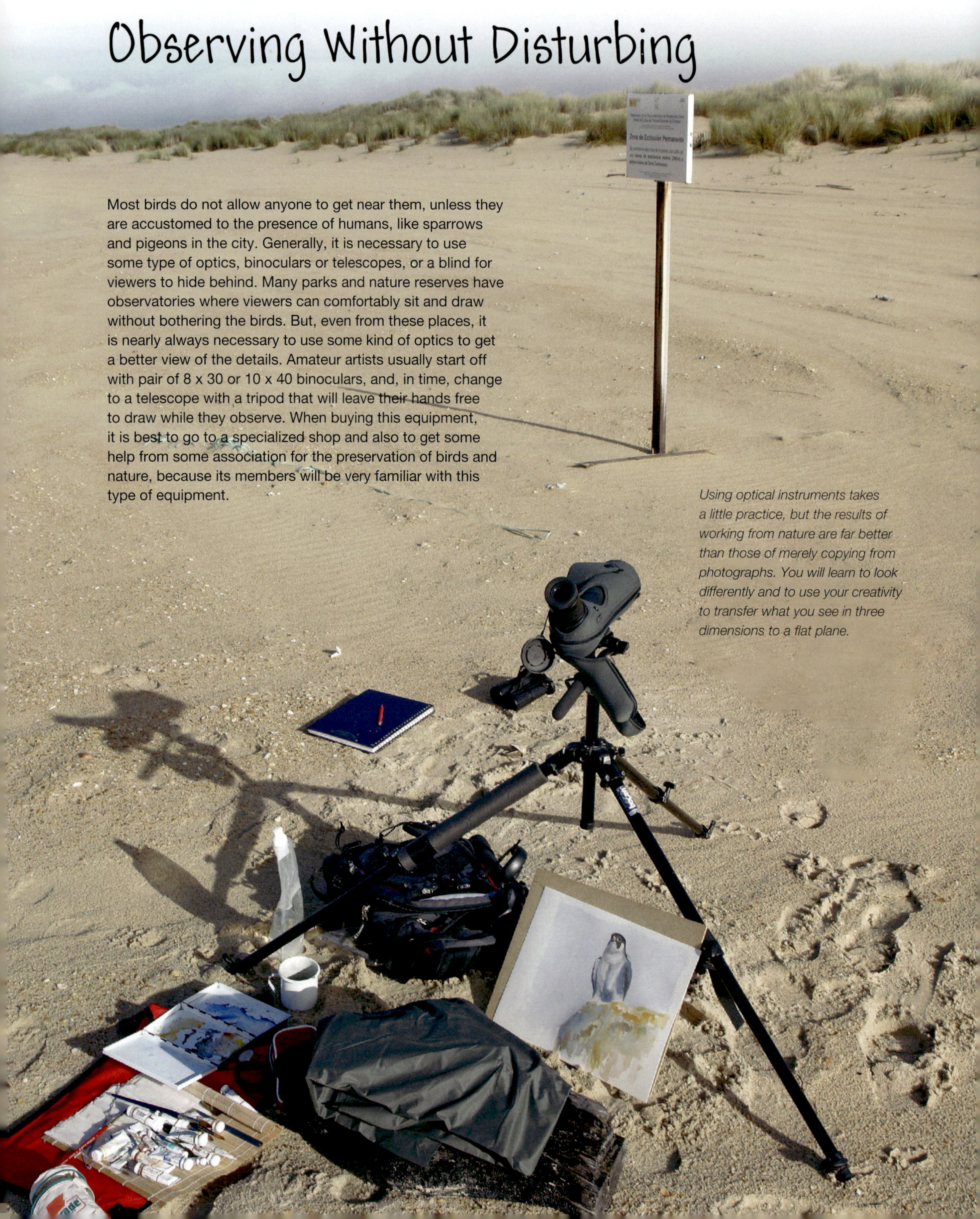

Using optical instruments takes a little practice, but the results of working from nature are far better than those of merely copying from photographs. You will learn to look differently and to use your creativity to transfer what you see in three dimensions to a flat plane.

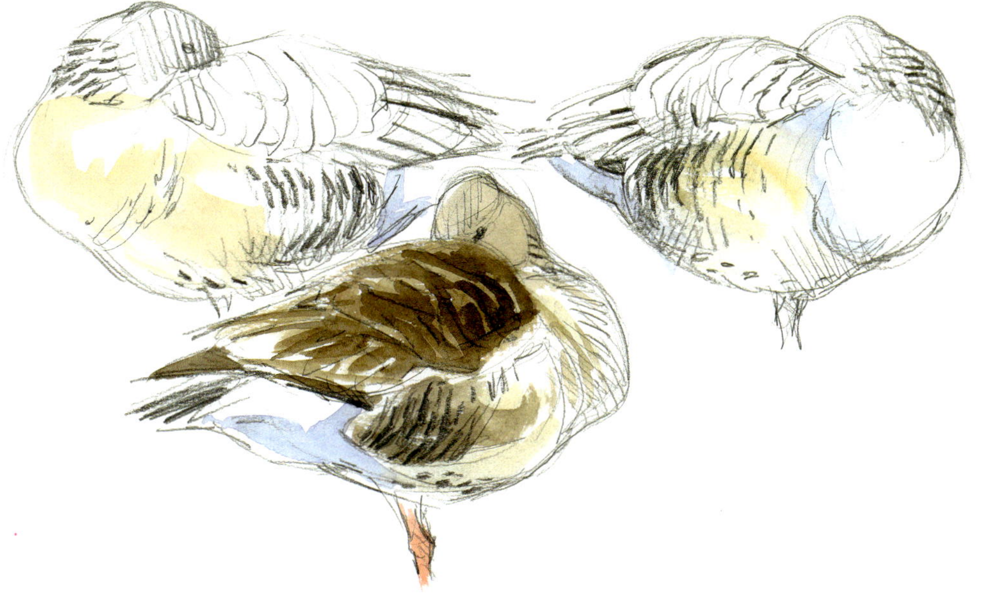

Graylag geese resting. A sketch, even unfinished, is more valuable to the artist for learning than several hours looking at books or nature videos on television. Frequently, small notes of color are enough to establish the essential light and tones.

FIELD SKETCHBOOK

In the chapter dedicated to materials and how to use them, we went into detail about the best and most convenient equipment for working in the field. A field sketchbook is used for collecting ideas, impressions, sketches, and written notes of interest. It is a training ground where you can draw without worrying about mistakes and without worrying about ruining promising work. It helps train your hand to work while guided by your eyes. In addition, when drawing, the proportions, postures, and shapes are imprinted in your memory and you will later remember them much more easily in the studio.

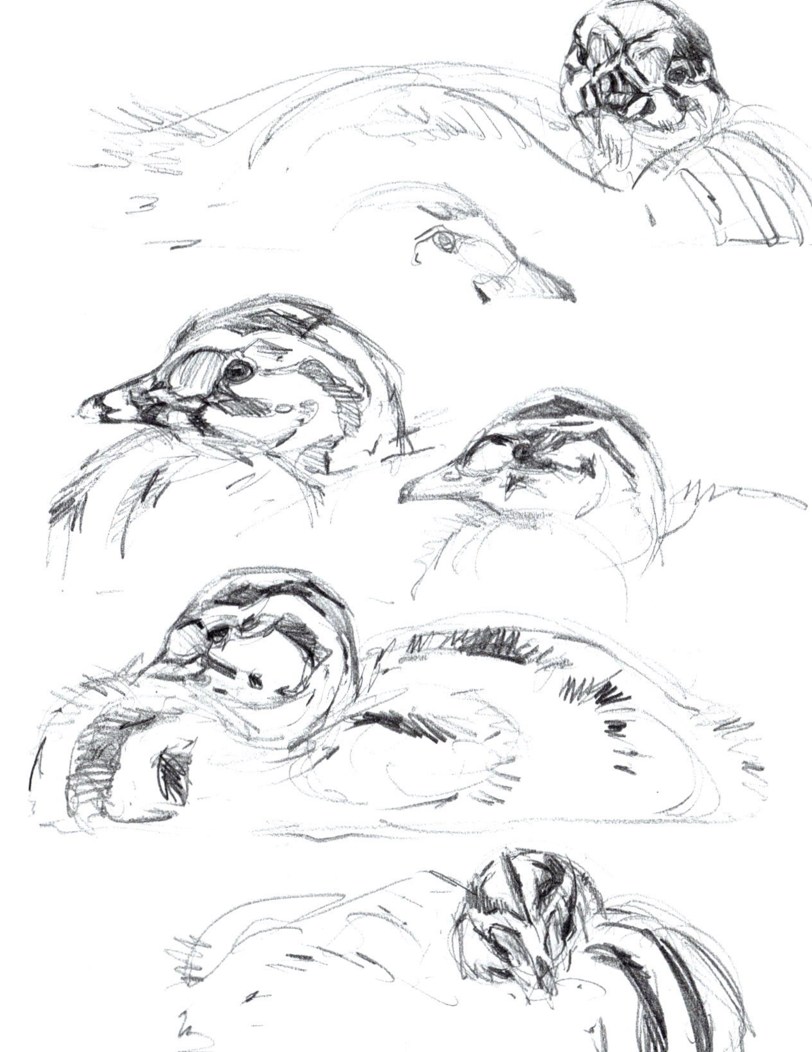

Great crested grebe chicks. It is a good idea to take advantage of the willingness of a model to fill pages of sketches. The need to draw correctly forces you to look carefully until you have a good understanding of its anatomy and movements. This creates a habit in the artist and increases his or her skill.

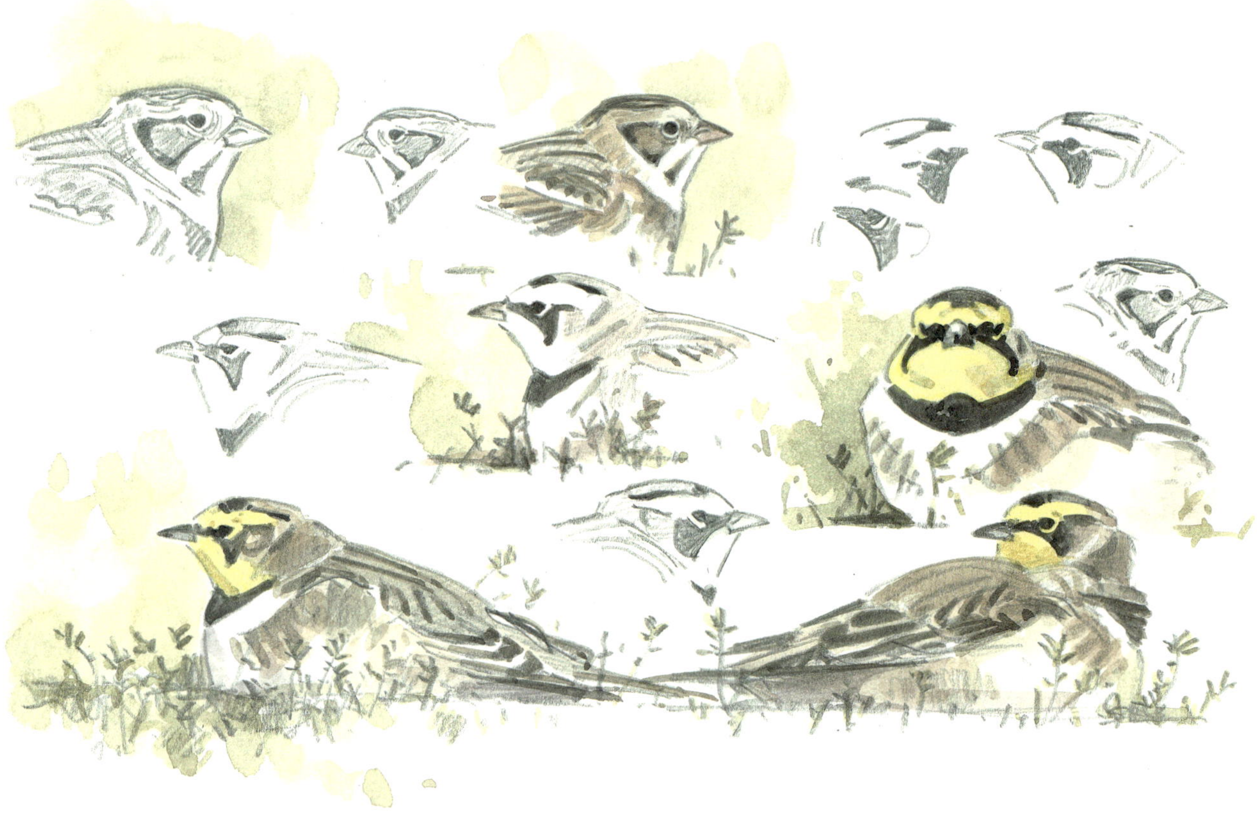

Capturing Movement

Sky larks and Lapland longspurs. Watercolor and pencil, 9 x 12 inches (23 x 30 cm), painted by Barry Van Dusen. A mixed group of birds allowed the artist to make a varied study of heads and the distribution of winter coloring in two species that frequent the United States during that season of the year. These notes are very useful in the studio, and they also reinforce the artist's memory of the session.

Drawing from nature does not mean drawing with a lot of detail. Large-format work and complex compositions are generally left for the studio. When working with moving models, you must avoid paying attention to details that are not essential for capturing the model. Studying details is a luxury that the artist can only afford when the figure is very still or when he or she finds a dead bird. But, most often, birds will flee when they see you, barely giving you time to draw a few lines.

MEMORY EXERCISES

The visual memory can be exercised, and, in fact, painters of birds have a great ability to remember the details of things they observe while they are drawing. The artist and writer Betty Edwards, whose work is included in the bibliography, proposes several exercises for developing the visual memory. Any type of exercise, however, becomes more useful as it is repeated to the point of becoming a habit.

FEAR OF EMPTINESS

A blank piece of paper usually demands respect, and the fear of making a mistake is sometimes so great that the lines become shaky and the model disappears before the artist can even finish blocking in the basic proportions. It is important to break the ice and begin drawing lines decisively, even if they are not correct. Begin warming up the hand, filling sheets, and letting the mind enter into a state of relaxation. With this as a goal, it is best to use inexpensive sketchbooks that do not cause such fear.

The images that you see in books were created in warm and comfortable studios, and their purpose is to illustrate the text that they accompany. They have little to do with the images that are collected in field sketchbooks of most good artists.

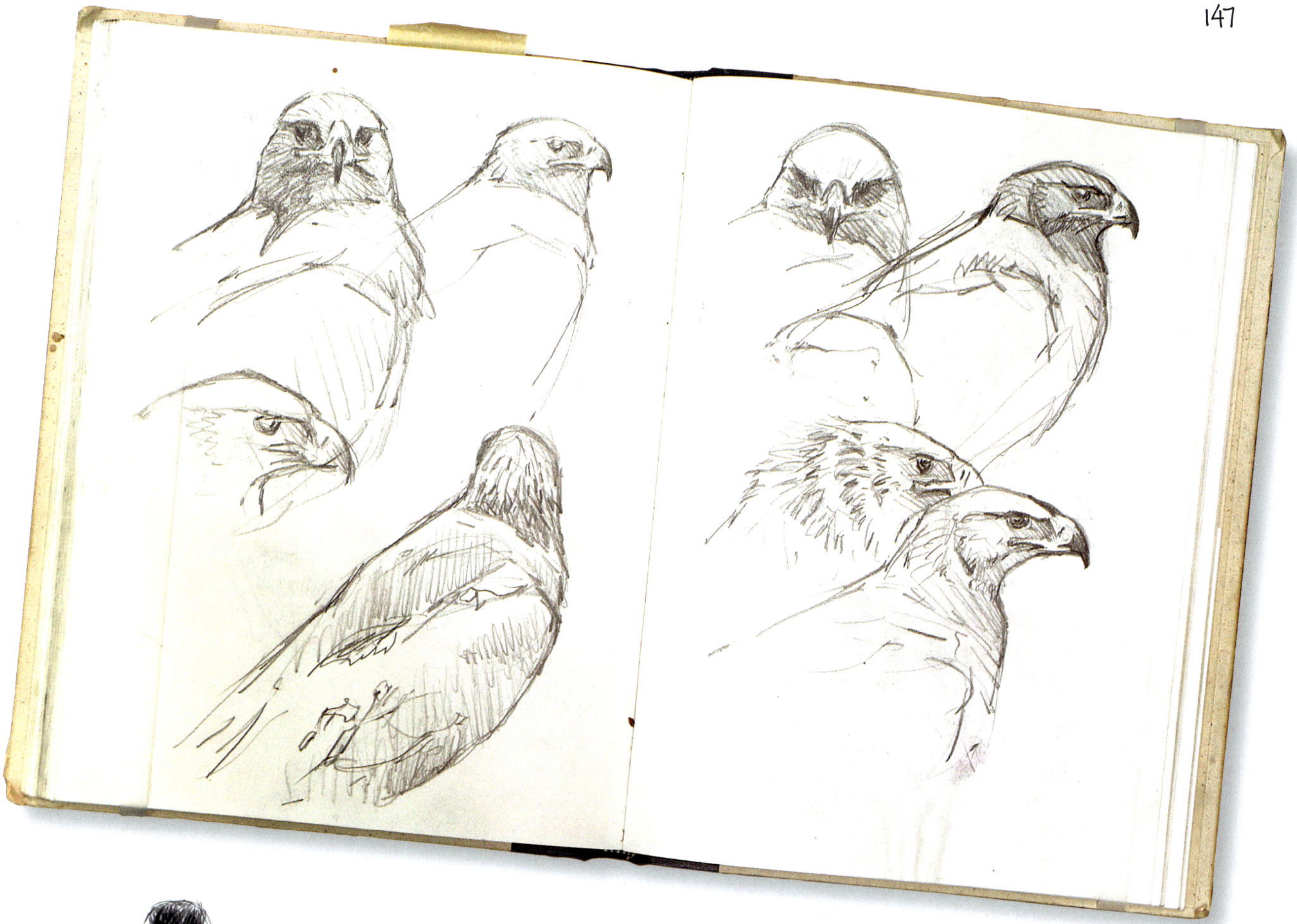

This sketchbook has drawings of a golden eagle. A notebook with inexpensive paper can contain a great amount of notations. The possibility of observing a bird for an extended period allows you to make studies of the different postures and views. This can be very useful for practice and for later use.

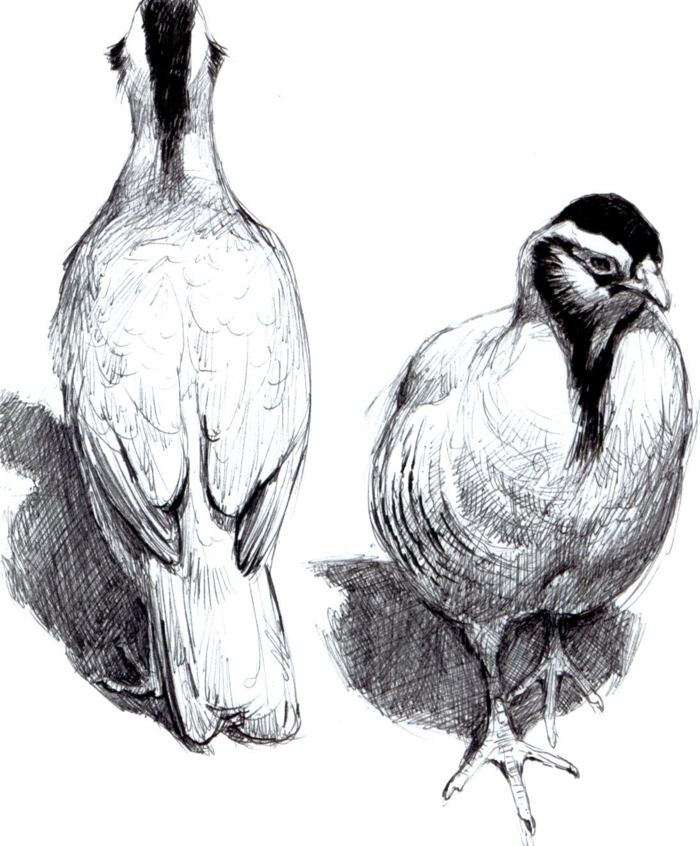

Arabian partridges. Bic pen on paper, 8 x 10.5 inches (20 x 27 cm), drawn by Paschalis Dougalis, 2001. This artist frequently works in the zoo in Berlin, where he can calmly observe the birds, which are accustomed to a human presence. He can add details little by little, even while the birds are moving. This way, he is able to capture their movement with a great level of detail.

The Gestural Drawing

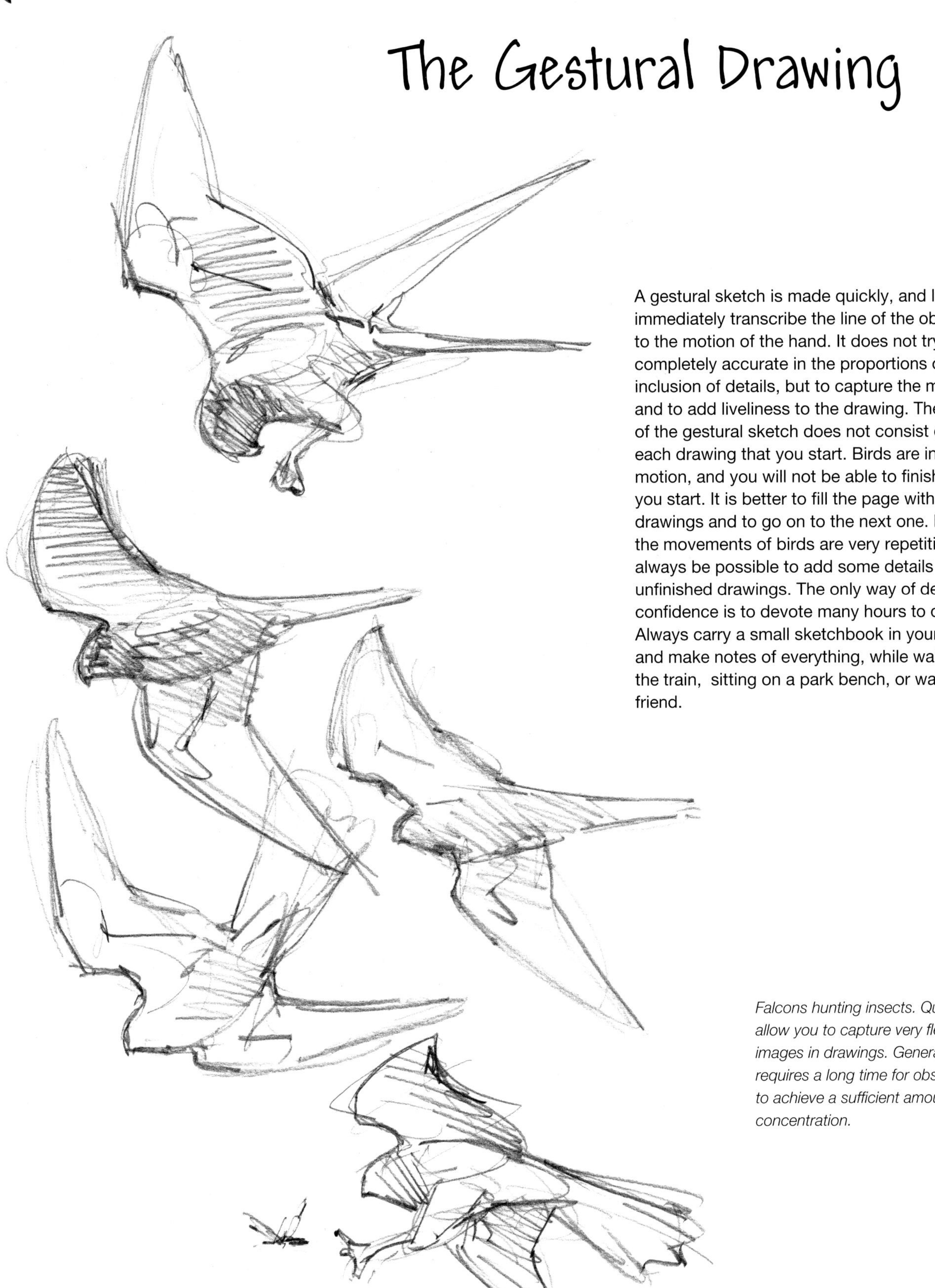

A gestural sketch is made quickly, and lets you immediately transcribe the line of the object to the motion of the hand. It does not try to be completely accurate in the proportions or in the inclusion of details, but to capture the movement and to add liveliness to the drawing. The process of the gestural sketch does not consist of finishing each drawing that you start. Birds are in constant motion, and you will not be able to finish what you start. It is better to fill the page with quick drawings and to go on to the next one. Because the movements of birds are very repetitive, it will always be possible to add some details to the unfinished drawings. The only way of developing confidence is to devote many hours to drawing. Always carry a small sketchbook in your pocket and make notes of everything, while waiting for the train, sitting on a park bench, or waiting for a friend.

Falcons hunting insects. Quick strokes allow you to capture very fleeting images in drawings. Generally, this requires a long time for observation to achieve a sufficient amount of concentration.

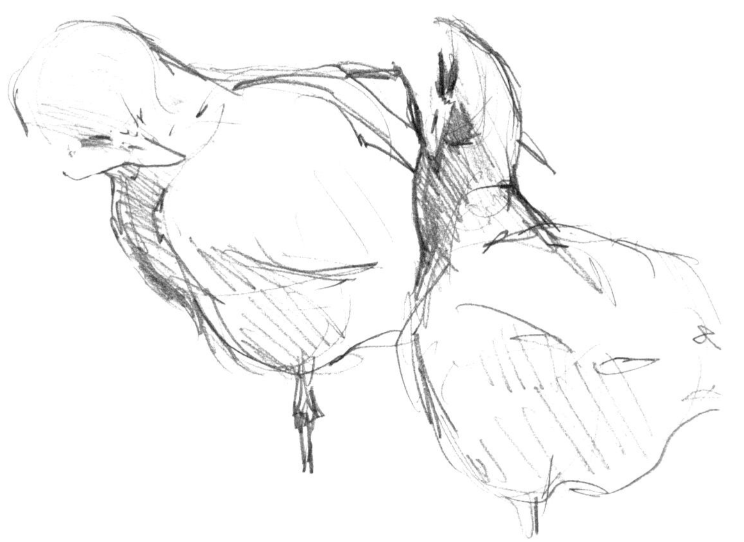

Eurasian coots. In this sketch, there was not a bit of time for drawing details. Preening birds move quickly, and this is the impression that the drawing is trying to give. Volume is indicated by adding a few lines of shading.

THE DETAIL

When you have drawn a species often and know it well, it is possible that what interests you are specific aspects of the plumage or capturing a particular pose. In that moment, all of your attention will focus on the shape of the beak, or extending an individual line. Thus, the field sketchbook will start becoming what it was meant to be: a source of information and a place for experimentation, not an object to show your friends, although you will certainly end up showing them a beautiful sketch that you are proud of.

Northern lapwings in their winter plumage. Parque Nacional de Doñana.

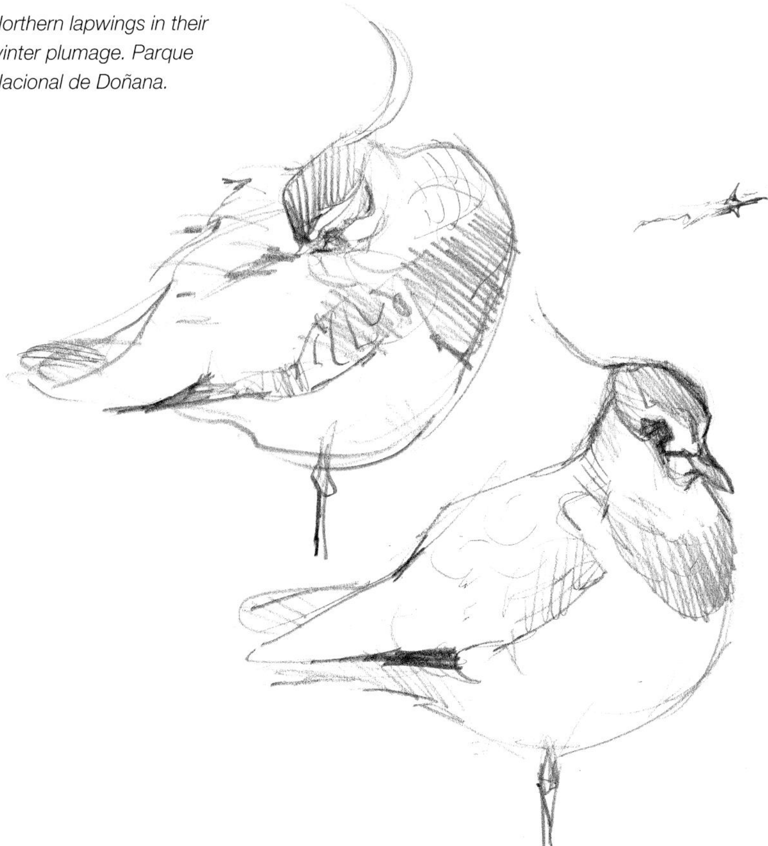

Red-footed falcon at Prespa Lake, Greece, 2006. Pencil drawing, 10.25 x 12 inches (26 x 30 cm), drawn by Paschalis Dougalis. Sometimes, birds give you the gift of remaining still, and you can focus on capturing details, poses, and proportions with accuracy.

In sketches made in the field, the notes on color can go as far as you want or as the time and circumstances allow. Color can be added to the base drawing, or, as some experienced artists do it, painted directly with a brush. When working with watercolors, the latter method requires a very confident stroke, as well as the ability to establish the tones and block in the composition quite accurately.

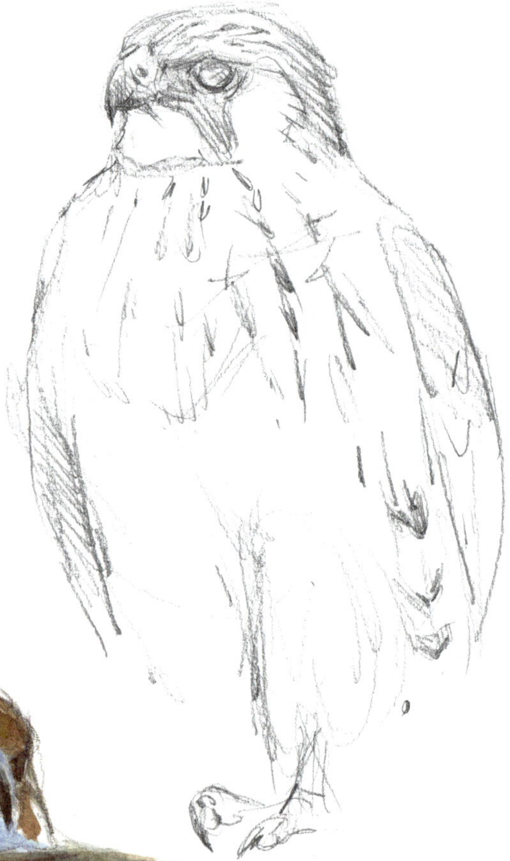

Including Color

COLOR CHOSEN IN THE FIELD OR IN THE STUDIO

Adding color to a drawing in the field is not the same as doing it in the studio. In the second case, the work responds to certain thought out criteria and personal styles of the artist; but, when working in the field, you will be more reactive, filtering the visual information and trying to incorporate complementary information that allows you to record the maximum amount of detail for later, when you are in the studio and under its artificial lights. The bird as an individual can show some interesting characteristics—for example, seasonal stages of plumage and curious alterations—but, above all, its colors will depend on the light at that moment. Therefore, it can be helpful to note on the drawing, or separately, the hour of the day and the atmospheric conditions, so that they will help you later understand the play of light and shadow reflected in the drawing.

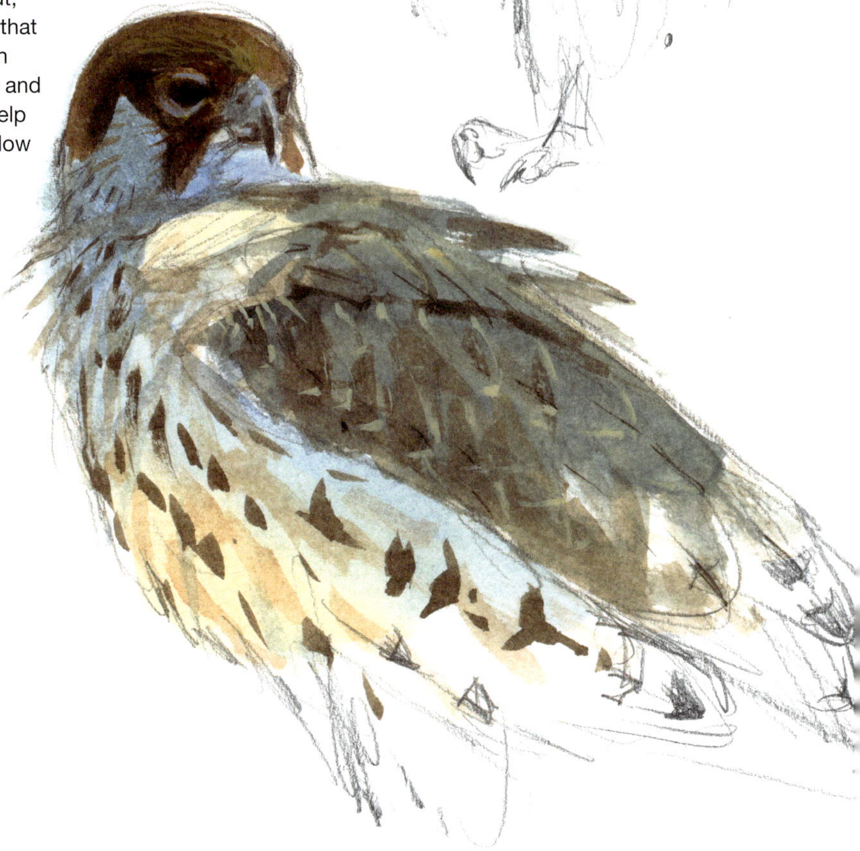

Young peregrine falcon. Watercolor and pencil, 8.25 x 12 inches (21 x 30 cm). The plumage, the color of the cere of the beak, and other details define the age of this young falcon drawn in the field. The artist also indicated the kind of light that existed at that moment through the strong contrast of shadows and illuminated areas.

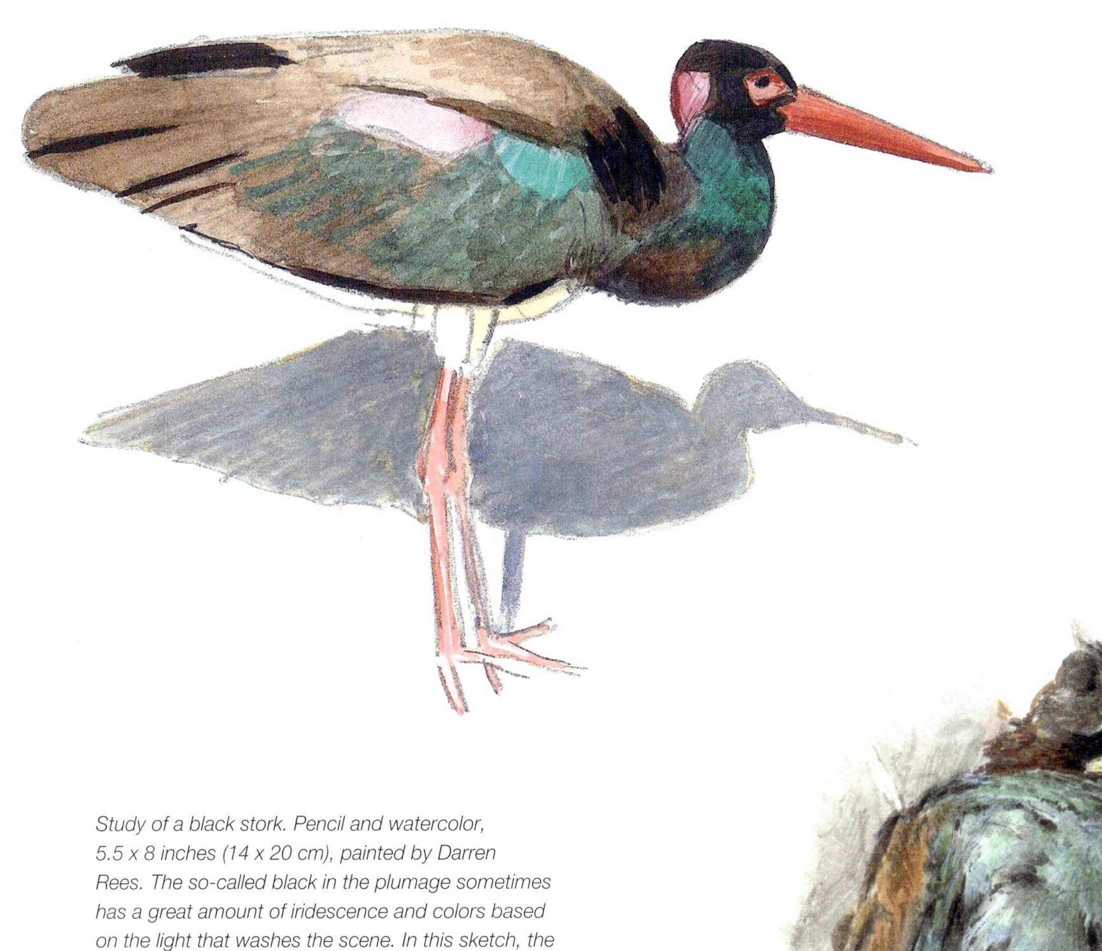

Study of a black stork. Pencil and watercolor, 5.5 x 8 inches (14 x 20 cm), painted by Darren Rees. The so-called black in the plumage sometimes has a great amount of iridescence and colors based on the light that washes the scene. In this sketch, the colors were emphasized and the pencil notes remind the artist of the impressions of the moment and the effect of the strong light, which is evidenced by the long shadow projected by the bird.

European bee-eater. Ballpoint pen and Copic markers, 9.5 x 13 inches (24 x 33 cm), drawn by Paschalis Dougalis. The casual discovery of the remains of a bird allowed him to make very detailed postmortem studies of its colors and proportions. Science museums and biology departments keep interesting collections of preserved birds and their skeletons, which are very useful for artists, especially from an anatomical point of view, but that also help refine the subject as a painting. The study of such details complements observation done in the field.

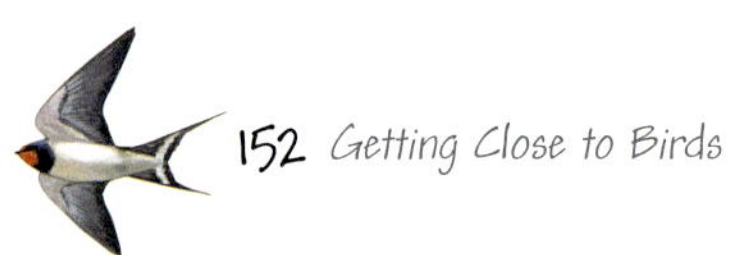

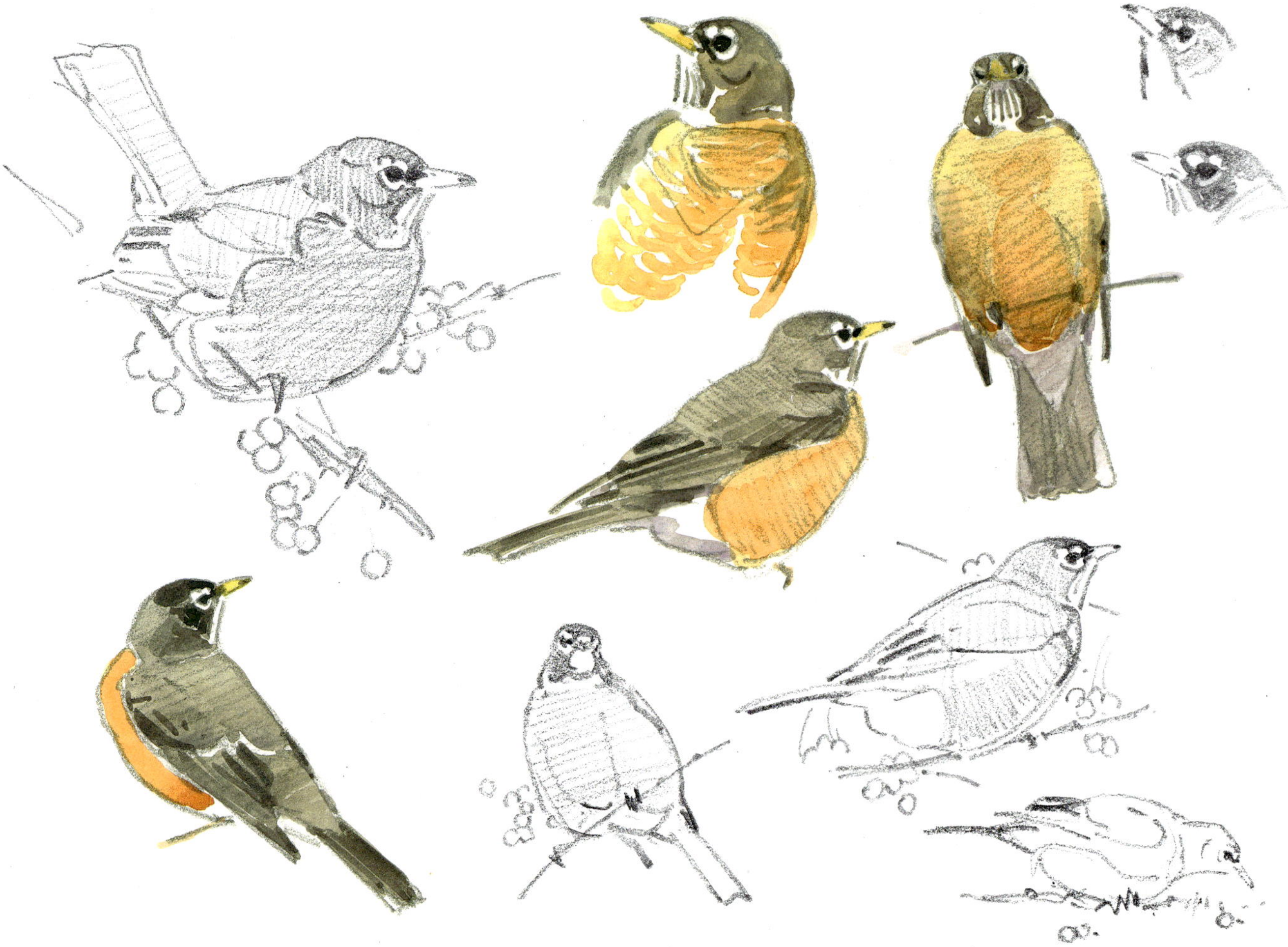

American robin and wild apples. Pencil and watercolor, 12 x 9 inches (30 x 23 cm), drawn by Barry Van Dusen. Some quick pencil sketches and simple touches of color are enough to collect the postures and play of light on a group of robins that are eating among the branches of an apple tree.

Applying Color to the Drawing from Nature

Starting to paint in the field is not only one more step in the collection of information, it is also a way to lose your fear of color and get used to using a medium that is somewhat more advanced than a pencil sketch. Painters that specialize in birds do not usually take complicated materials into the field. Oils, for example, are left in the studio, and often acrylics as well. If the objective is to limit oneself to making simple sketches, then watercolors, graphite pencils, and perhaps a small set of color pencils will be the ideal tools for working in nature. Six colors can be more than sufficient: ultramarine blue, crimson, medium cadmium yellow, burnt Sienna or Indian red, yellow ochre, and sap green, but the range can be enlarged with cobalt blue and raw umber. A small tube of zinc white or titanium white can be useful for adding a highlight or drawing the edge of a feather. Black is not necessary, because you can create a very dark tone by mixing other colors. Another good option is sepia.

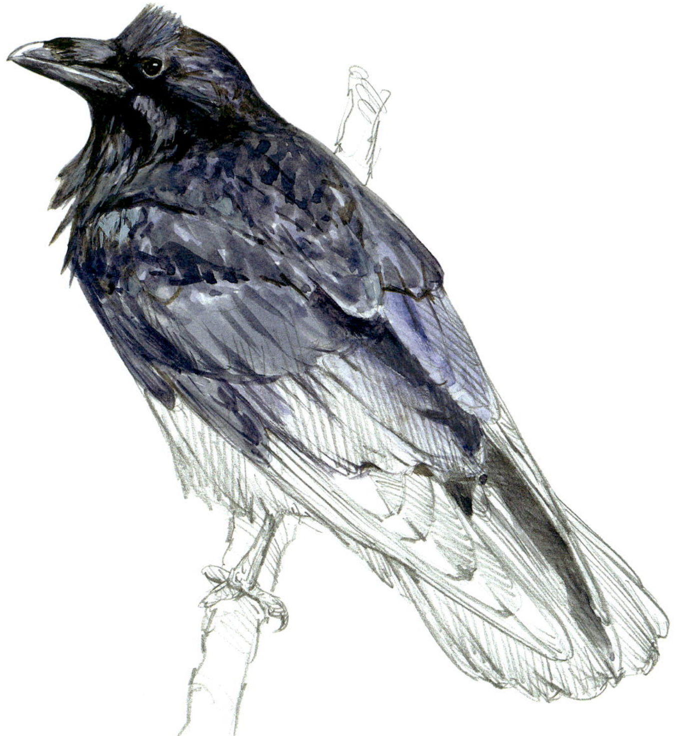

In this illustration of a crow, you can see the entire sketch-making process, from the tail to the head. The base drawing in pencil incorporates lines that suggest the direction and texture of the feathers. After the pencil, in a second step, the layer of watercolor dissolves the lines somewhat, but you can still see them showing through. Over the base of light tones, visible near the middle of the body, darker brushstrokes were applied following the direction of the growth of the plumage. The areas of base color that are left unpainted in this final process look like reflected light in the plumage.

When painting, there is always the challenge of the color of white areas of the subject. Many species have feathers in the ventral zone and even on large parts of their bodies that are without pigmentation. This gives the plumage a certain transparency and luminosity, and that lack of its own color implies that the tones that you see vary greatly according to the time of day and the local light. A large part of the shadow colors that can be seen on these surfaces can be made with combinations of cobalt blue, ultramarine blue, yellow ochre, and raw umber.

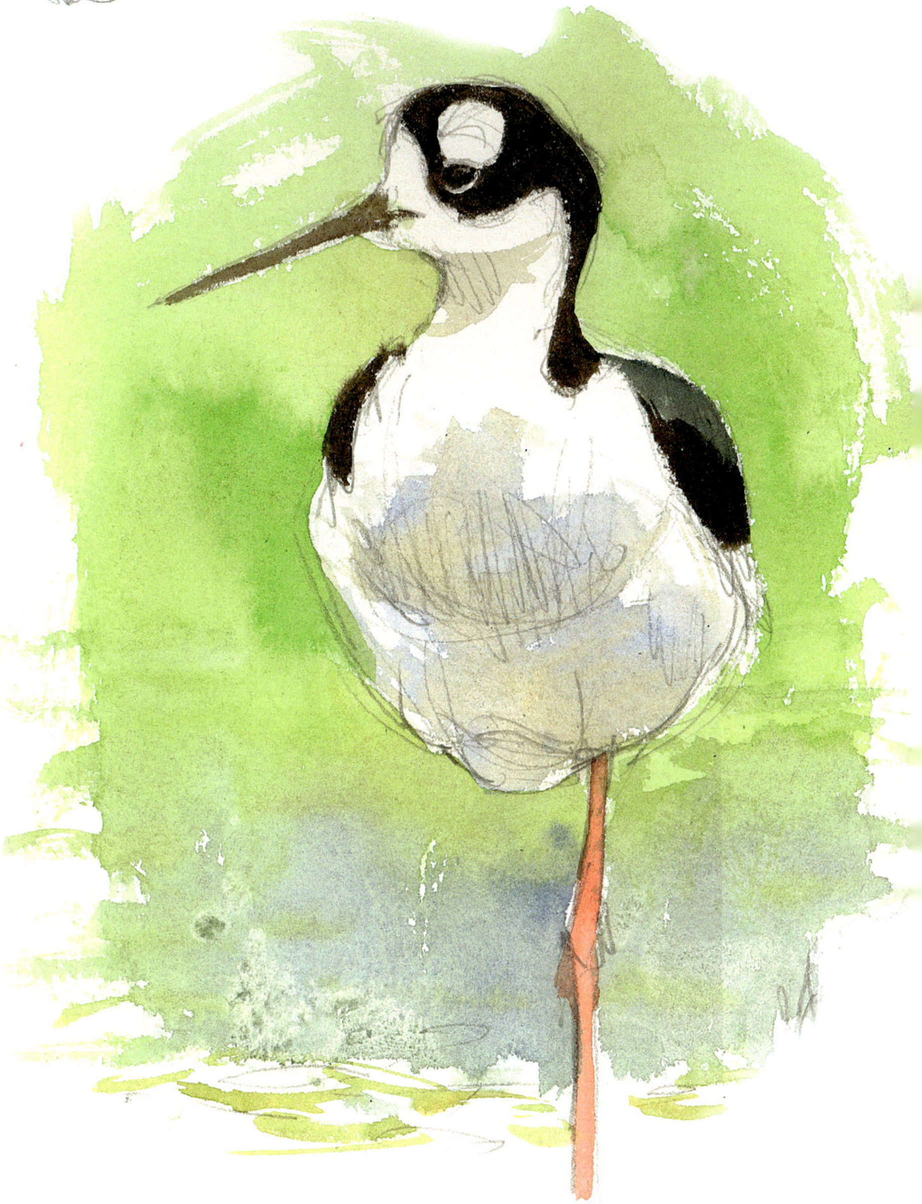

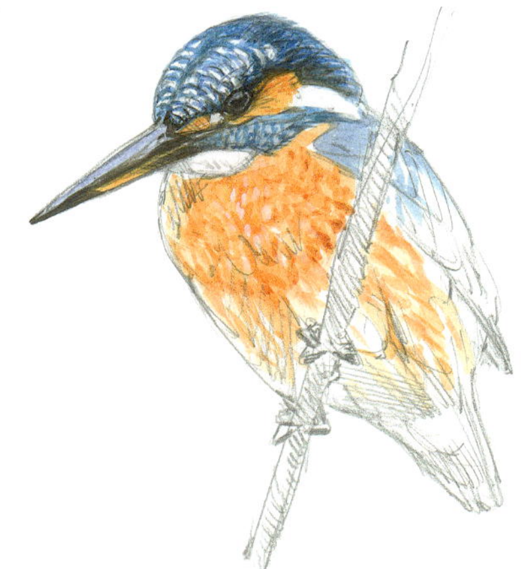

Birds in Their Habitats
Details and References

The first phase when working in the field is centered on the lines, in capturing gestures and movements. When you go one step farther and introduce a bit of color into the drawing, the level of difficulty increases, and the work becomes even more complicated if you decide to depict the bird in its habitat, catching the peculiarities of the light at that moment, the shadows cast by nearby elements in the scene, and the variety of colors. Although this is a sketch made in the field, and therefore exempt from the complexities related to making a painting in the studio, the drawing can incorporate useful details and reliable references.

However, you must not go too far. It is common to see works where the artist got carried away with the details and ended up with a bird that looks like it was cut out and pasted into a space where it does not belong.

JUAN VARELA
BLACK WOODPECKER (*DRYOCOPUS MARTIUS*)
WATERCOLOR, 10.25 x 14 INCHES (26 x 36 CM)

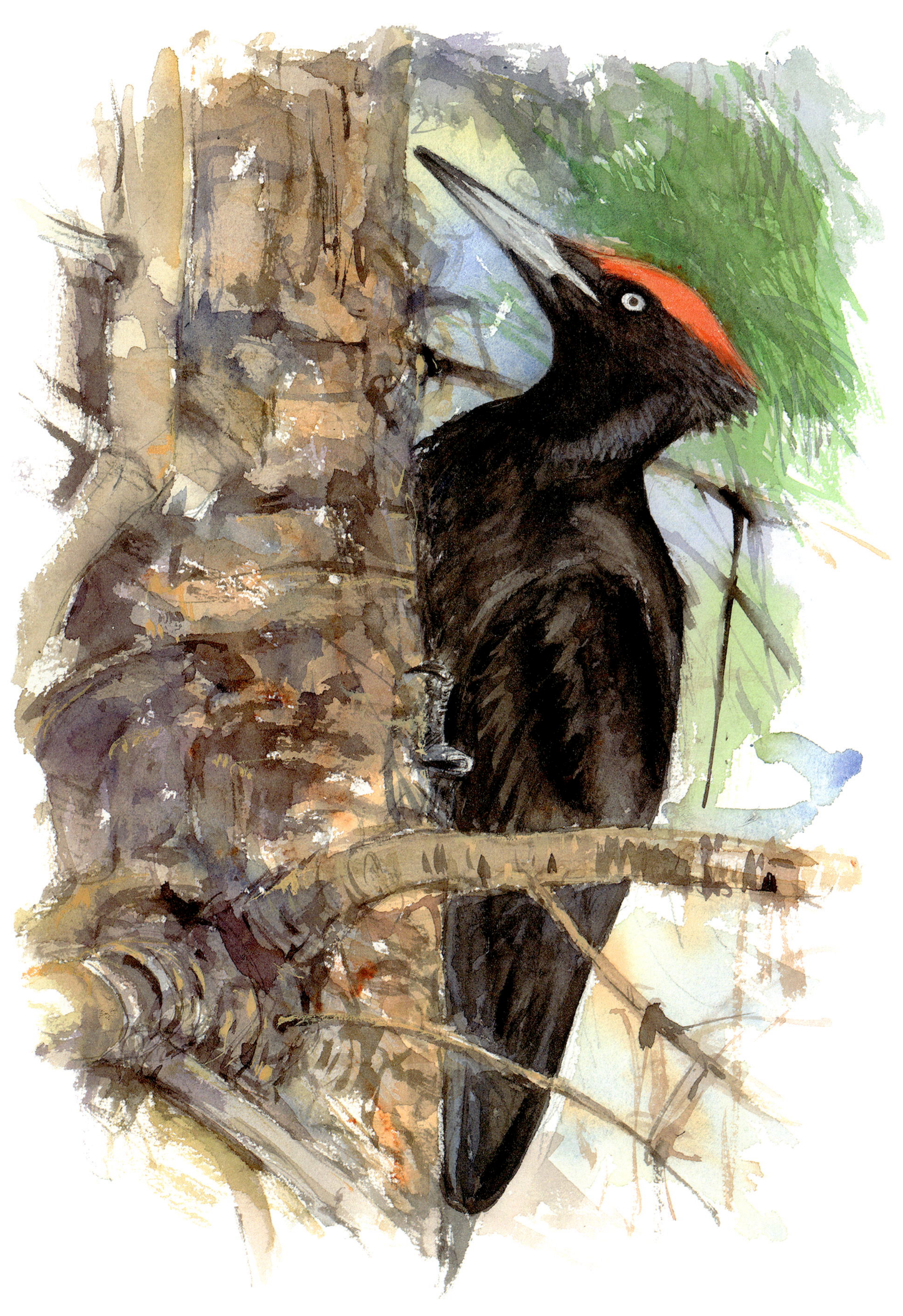

Light and the Environment

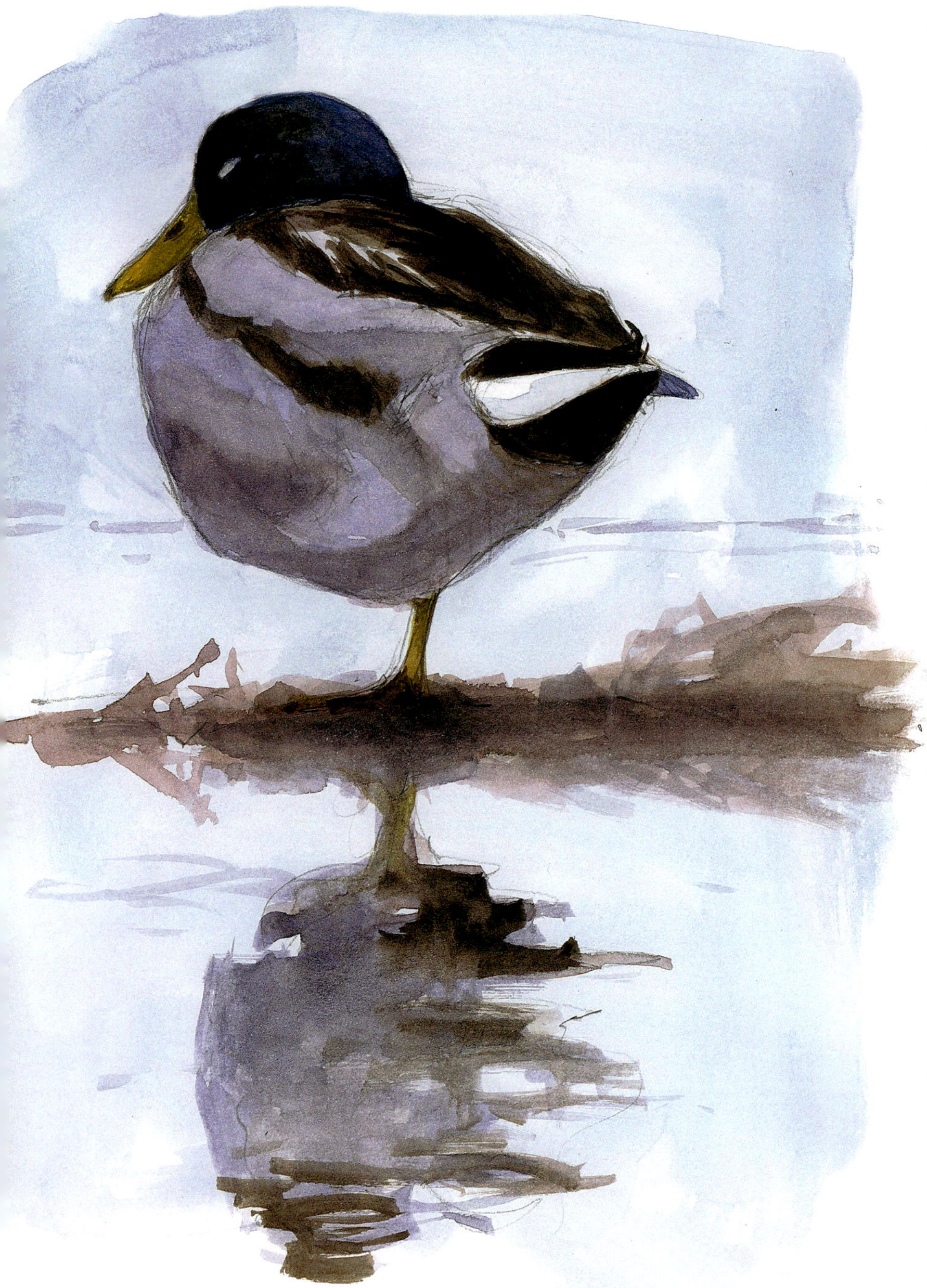

The simple illustrations in guides for identifying birds do not include more light and shadow than is necessary to create a sense of volume. When a bird is observed in its natural environment, the image that is perceived is modified by the direction and angle of the light that falls on it and the harshness of the shadows, so that the colors of the plumage and the bird's outline can be different from what they normally are.

It is not enough to make a small tonal sketch with a limited palette to show volume and a more or less accurate sense of colors. Artists want to include their impressions in their drawings in the field and to maintain those impressions when they resume working on their sketches in the studio.

COLOR IN CONTEXT

Colors only exist because of light, an object that reflects it, and an eye that sees it; therefore, the variations in tone that you see in the colors of a bird are a response to a situation in a specific context. It is very important to make simple sketches focused on understanding the chromatic and tonal structures. Many artists use very limited ranges of color—for example ultramarine blue, light red, and cadmium yellow—which is a good idea because it helps unify the coloration of the sketch. Having a personal archive and a large repertoire of schemes in your memory, like colors at dusk, backlighting, strong midday shadows, and so on, will help you resolve many of the problems that come up in studio work.

Mallard at dusk. All the properties of color are affected by environmental light. Even the brightest colors, like yellow, acquire a dull greenish tone in this image at dusk.

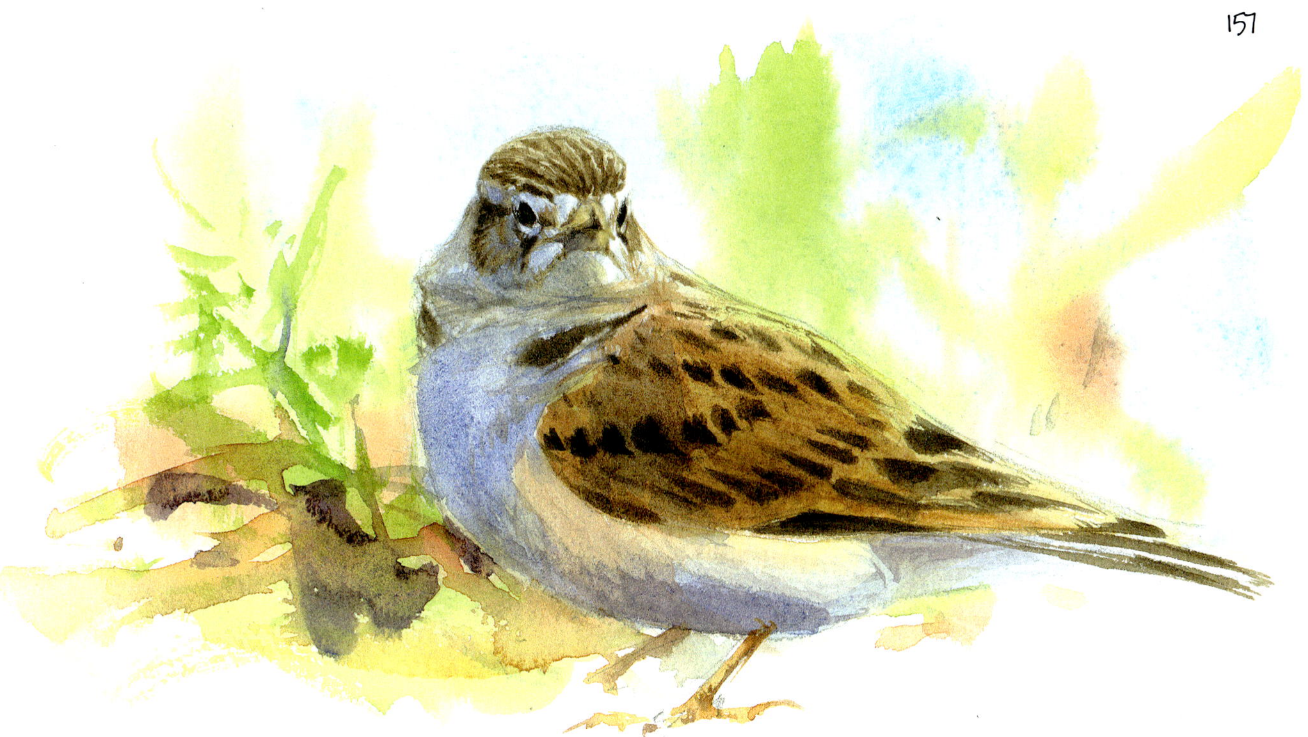

Greater short-toed lark. The bright light emphasizes the orange tones on the bird's back as well as the contrast with the shadows. The shadows are luminous, however, where the cobalt blue plays an important role. The yellow colors in the background help strengthen the environmental light.

Little tern hatching eggs. Watercolor, 8.25 x 12 inches (21 x 30 cm). In this field sketch, little attention has been paid to the details of the plumage and the structure of the plants. It was more interesting to make note of the environmental light and the play of shadows cast by the stalks onto the bird that is dozing on its nest.

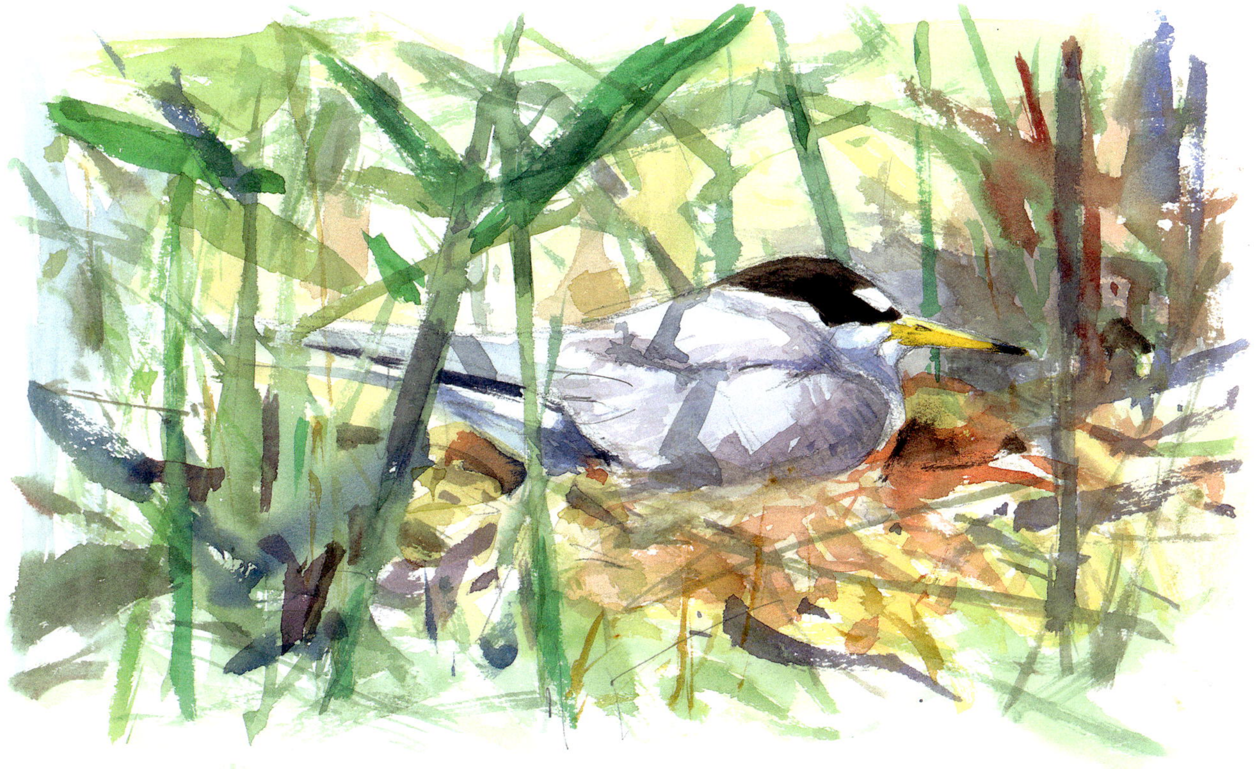

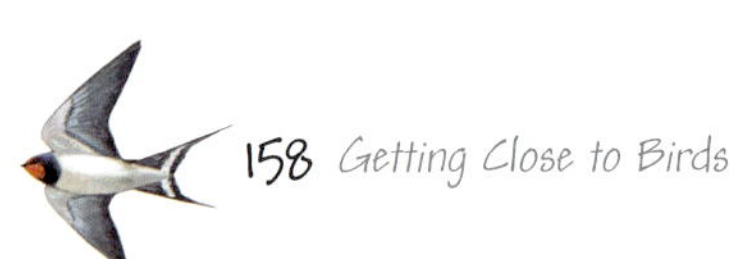

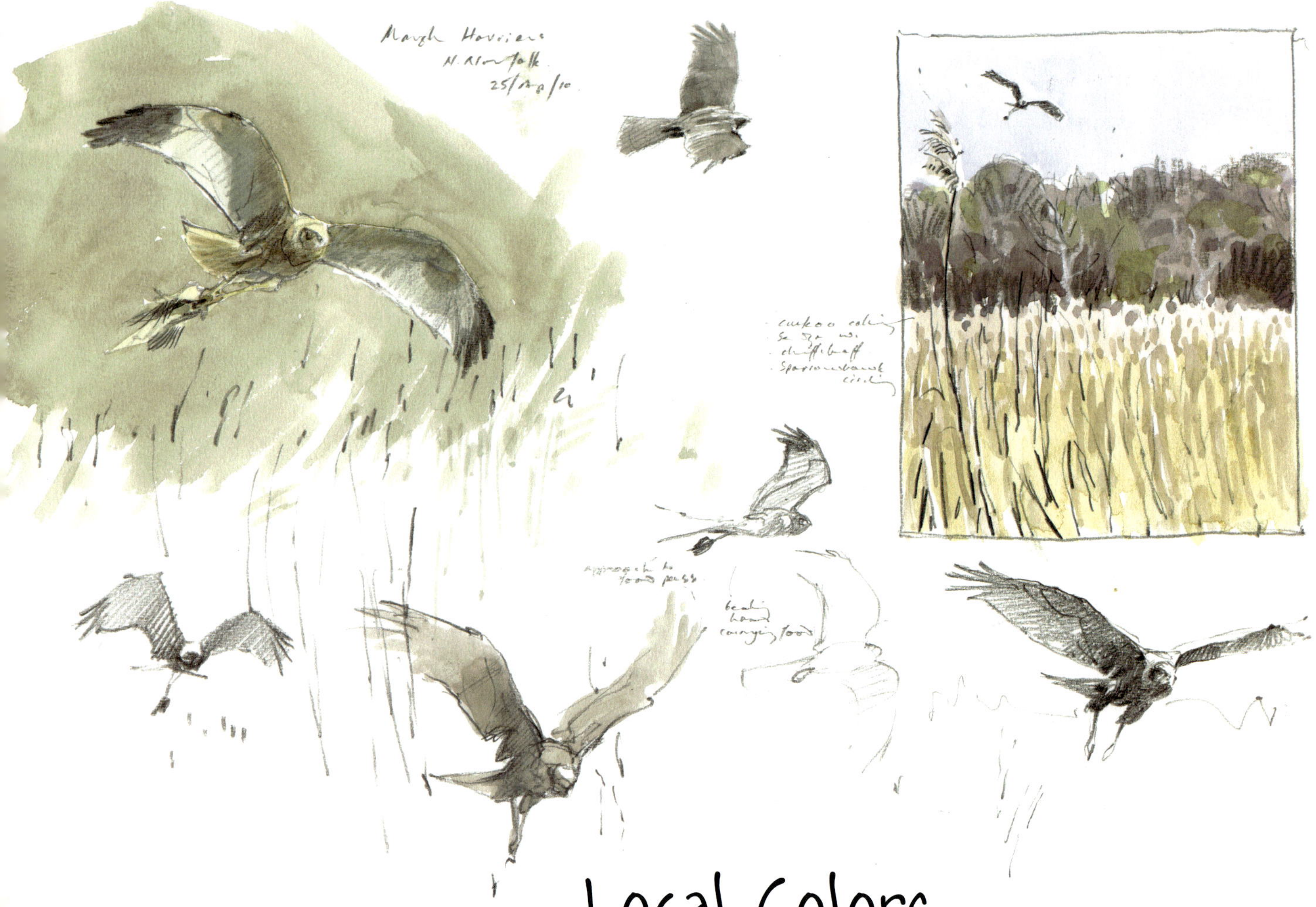

Local Colors

Study of a Western marsh harrier. Pencil and watercolor by Bruce Pearson. Sketches made from nature can provide a lot of information if you pay attention to the details. Here the artist not only made pencil drawings to capture different postures of flight, but he also included small compositional and habitat color sketches and written notations as reminders of his impressions when he was on-site.

A day's work in the field will inspire many ideas that would not spontaneously appear when you are locked in your studio or looking at photographs. In the field, the artist learns to look in a new way, to eliminate what is superfluous in the composition and to appreciate its distinctive elements and their placement in the image. The quality of the light is determined by several factors, among them the time of day and the season of the year, and also by the location. The filtered light of a forest is very different from the direct light that floods a field or a beach. Planning the play of warm and cool colors beforehand is the key to a good painting.

For all of these reasons, a bird seen in the field could never have the same color as it would in technical illustrations or in museum displays, because its colors would be in accordance with its surroundings.

The quality of field observations is reflected in the results of the work in the studio. All of the experience accumulated up until that time comes out surprisingly quickly during the creative process.

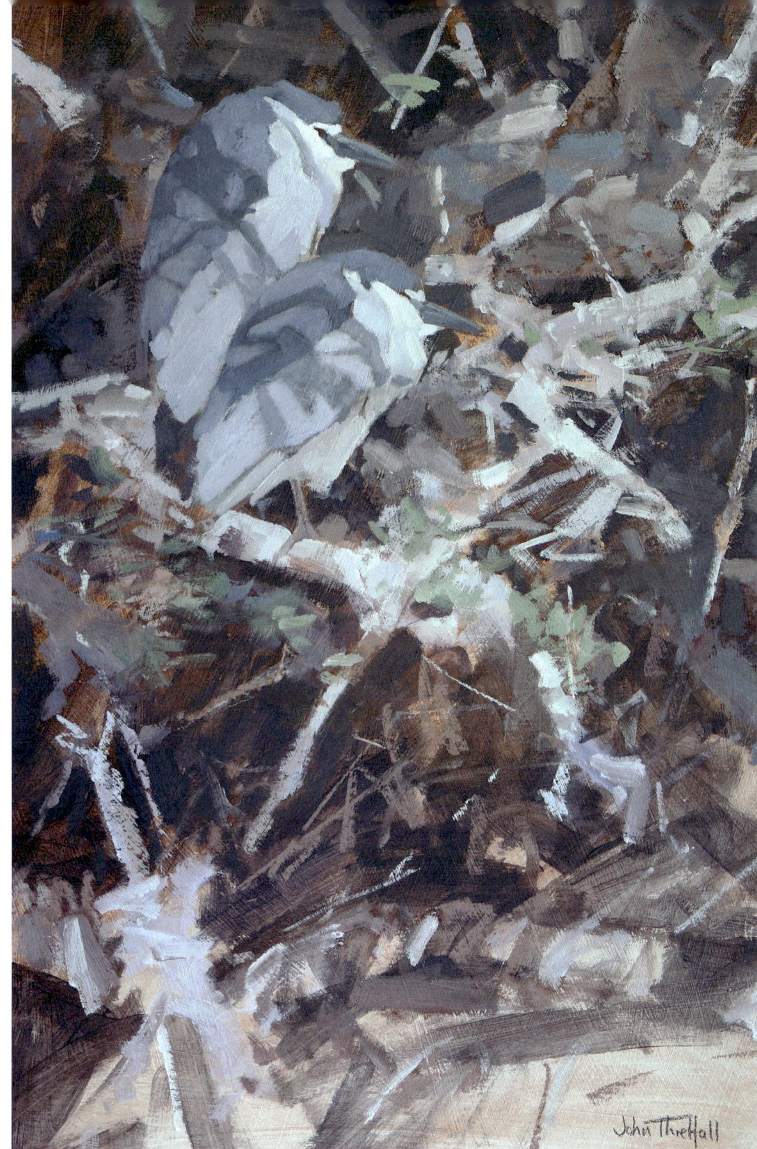

Night herons. Oil on board, 17.5 x 12.5 inches (44 x 32 cm), painted by John Threlfall. This work is completely unified in both the treatment of the forms of the birds and of their environment, which is painted with adjacent colors, in which you can see subtle touches of warm colors added into the cool color range. The shadows cast by the branches on the two birds perfectly integrate them into the scene.

Wood grouse. Winter colors and cool highlights make up this gouache sketch made in the field. More important than the details on the bird or the trees is the feeling of uncertain light from a particular time of year and a particular hour of the morning.

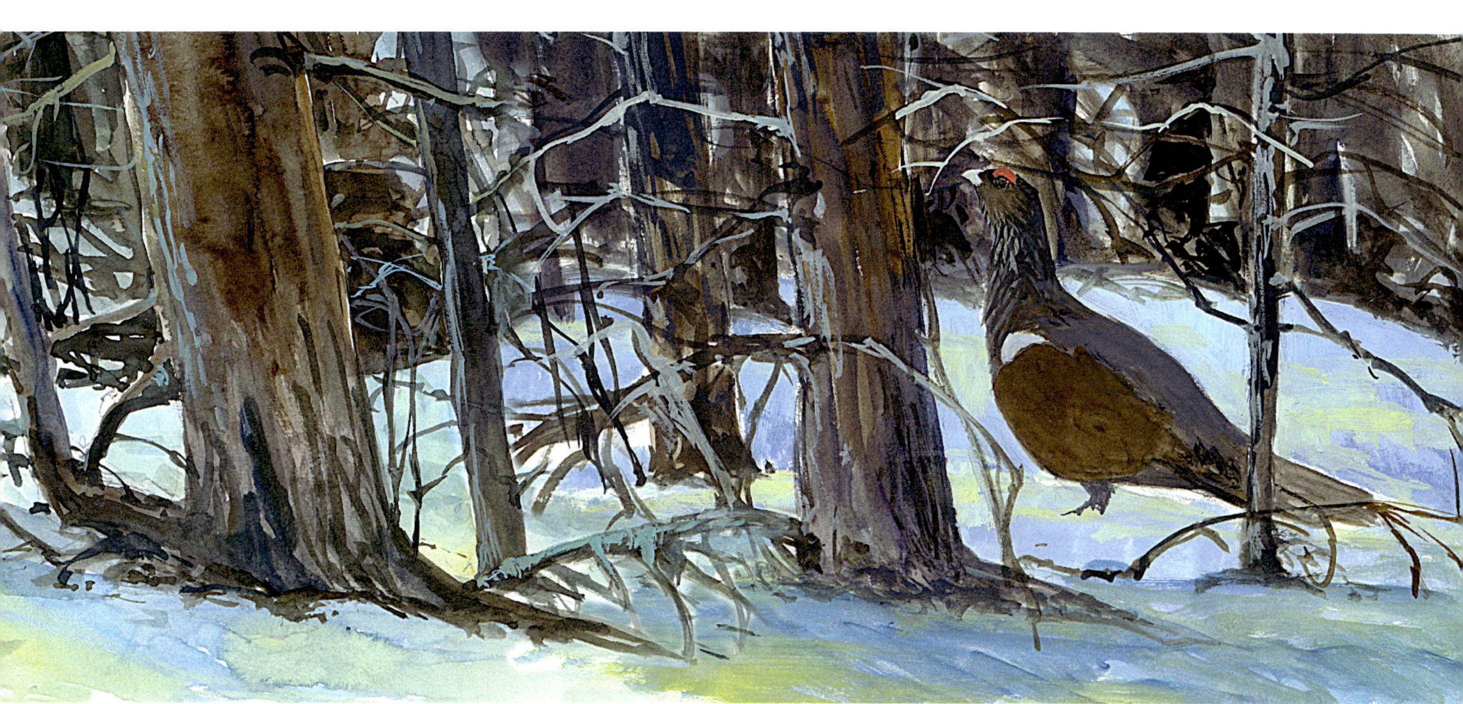

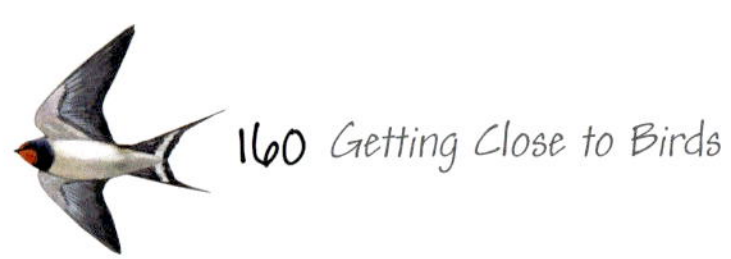

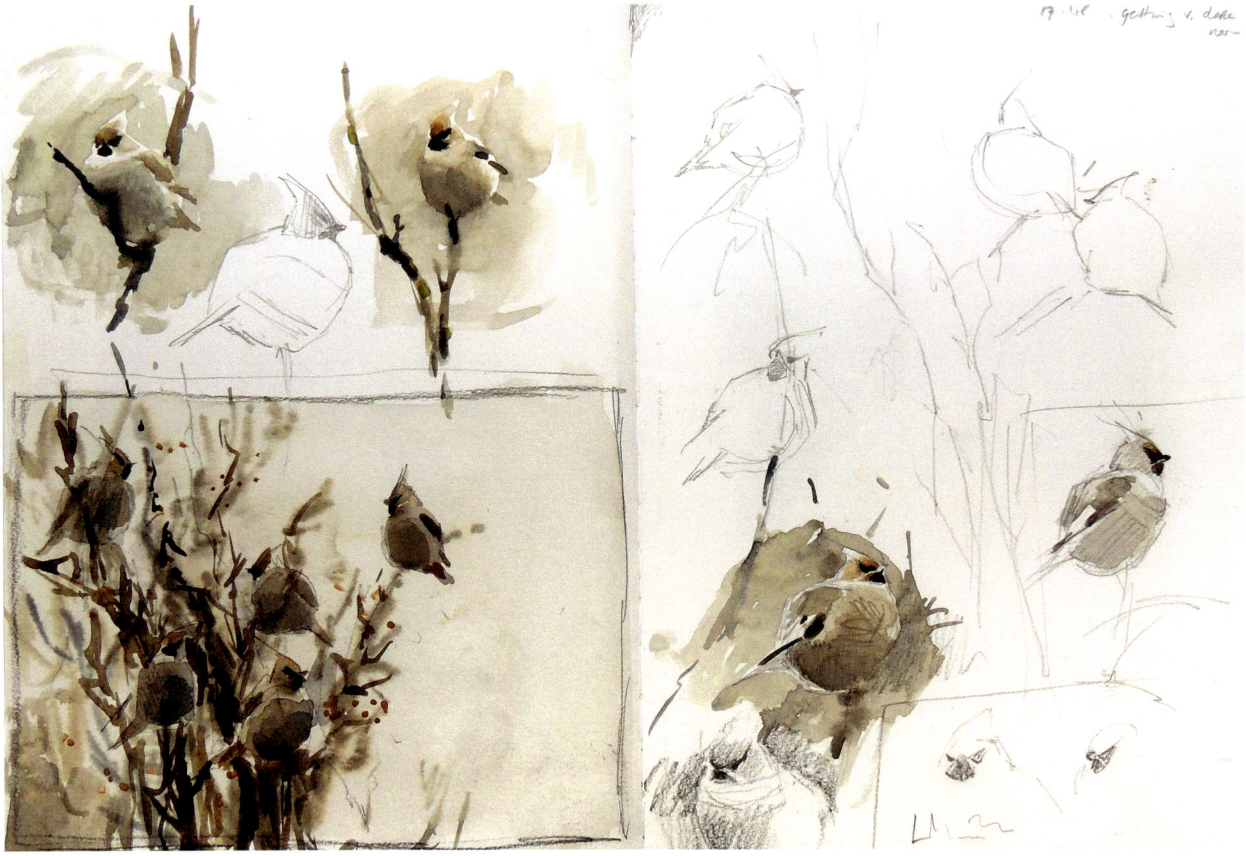

Compositional Studies

Study of the bohemian waxwing. Pencil and watercolor on paper, painted by Tim Wootton. The artist filled several pages with small compositional schemes, which will allow him to evaluate the different possible formats for the work and the postures of the birds that will be in the composition.

The possible variations of compositions are infinite, and the artist rarely has an exact idea of the work he or she is going to paint. There is a project, perhaps an idea of the structure and general tones of color, but the work will be constructed starting from simple pencil sketches, in which the artist attempts to summarize the atmospheric light, the poses, and the relationships among different elements. The sketches are probably the freest part of the artistic work. When you are making them, you should take on all the risks that you have to.

THE PATH OF THE EYE

The norms related to composition that rule in other types of painting are applicable here. The elements look different according to the format and proportions of the work, and they will be organized differently in each one. The arrangement of the figures causes your eye to follow a specific path that, in the case of a nature painting, is especially important, because it symbolizes the movement of the observer through the represented space, the feeling of being there. When watching birds with binoculars or a telescope, you tend to focus on the image and ignore the surroundings. However, to understand the context, it is important to alternate the use of optic aids with your own vision, because the telescope, especially when you are focusing on great distances, distorts the perspective and the relative size of the objects in the background.

Northern Wings. Oil on canvas, 30 x 30.75 inches (76 x 78 cm), also by Tim Wootton. The finished painting contains many of the elements that were conceived while working on the studies, but also new ones that came up during the painting process.

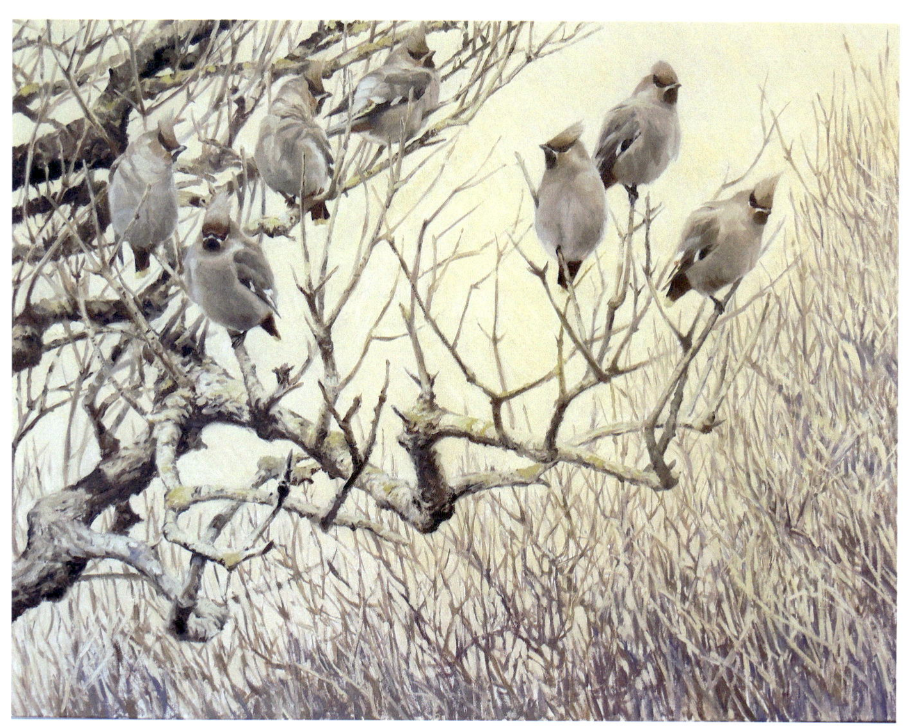

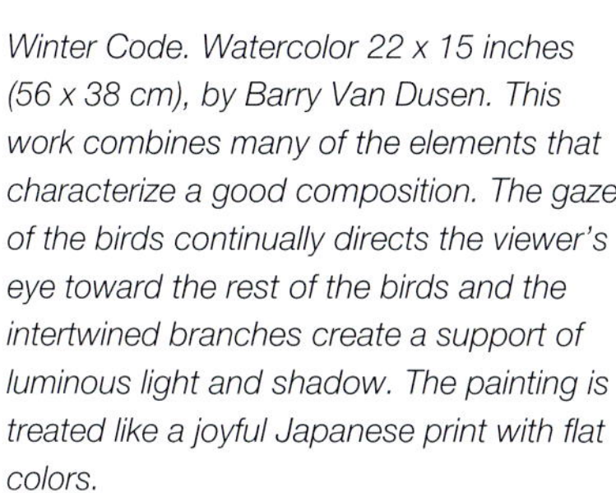

Winter Code. Watercolor 22 x 15 inches (56 x 38 cm), by Barry Van Dusen. This work combines many of the elements that characterize a good composition. The gaze of the birds continually directs the viewer's eye toward the rest of the birds and the intertwined branches create a support of luminous light and shadow. The painting is treated like a joyful Japanese print with flat colors.

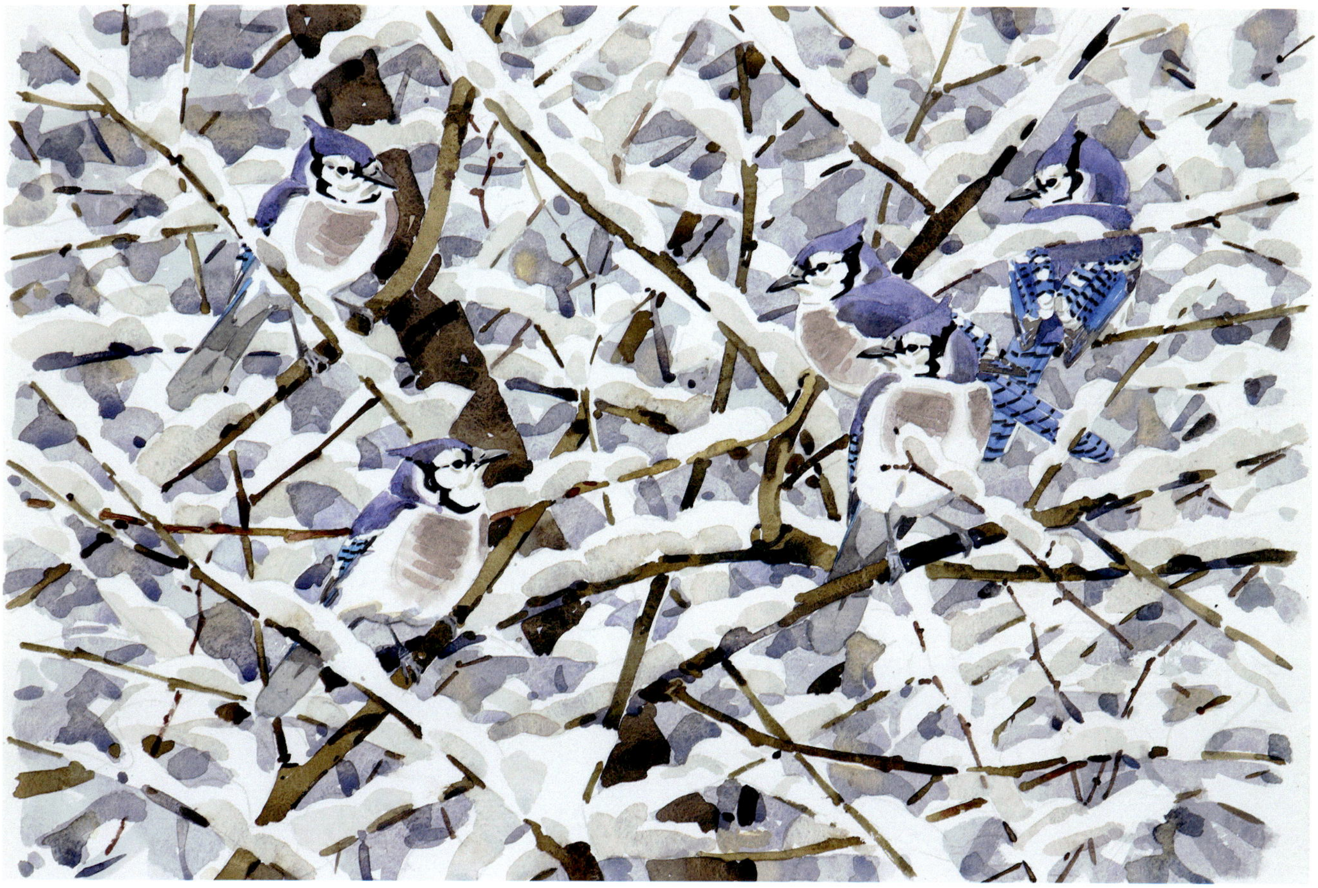

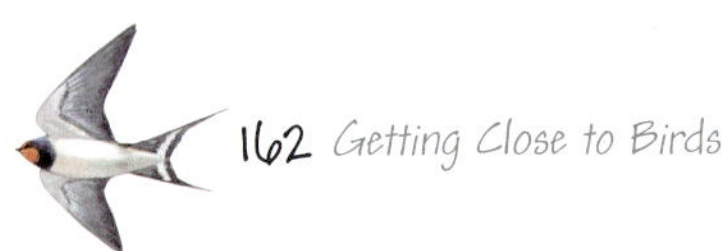

THE ENCLOSED IMAGE

Birds and the landscape are seen without frames, but they are enclosed by the edges of the paper when they are drawn. This means that the bird, or the birds, will occupy a specific position in respect to the margins and the other elements of the composition. The format of the work is the first choice that the artist makes: square, rectangular, vertical, or horizontal, each one has a meaning and its limitations. If it will be a portrait, the bird should be located in the foreground and occupy an important part of the space, but the reality is that birds appear before us unexpectedly and it is much more natural to depict them less prominently and more integrated into the landscape. The elements that accompany the main subject are as important as it is. The sky, the trees, and the rocks direct the eye; they have "weight" in the composition and should suggest a continuity outside the scene of the painting. In an enclosed image, the illusion created by the artist is communicated by the placement of the elements as well as the negative shapes created by them in the surrounding space. These shapes direct the eye of the viewer as much as the elements themselves. Something that the artist sometimes forgets is to place some reliable reference of the size of the bird in the environment. This leads to beautiful studio paintings that unfortunately show a poor indication of relative sizes, especially when there are several species of birds in the work.

Northern harrier. Acrylic on paper, 27.5 x 19.5 inches (70 x 50 cm), painted by Nick Derry. A Northern harrier in juvenile plumage flies past us as it hunts. The bright colors and the brushstrokes add tremendous liveliness and movement to the composition, which also creates a unity that perfectly integrates the bird with its surroundings by conserving the aerial space and the weightless feeling of flight.

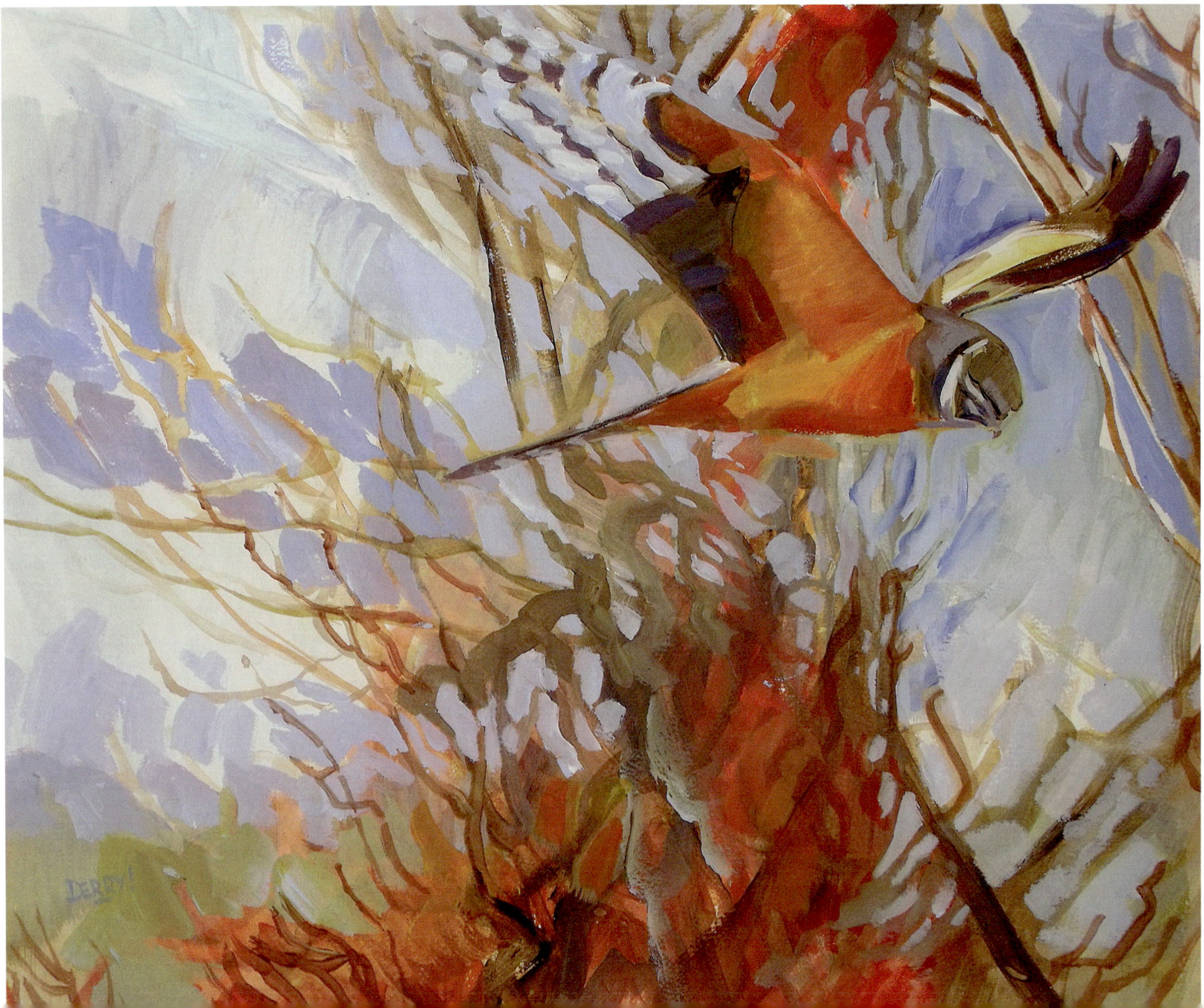

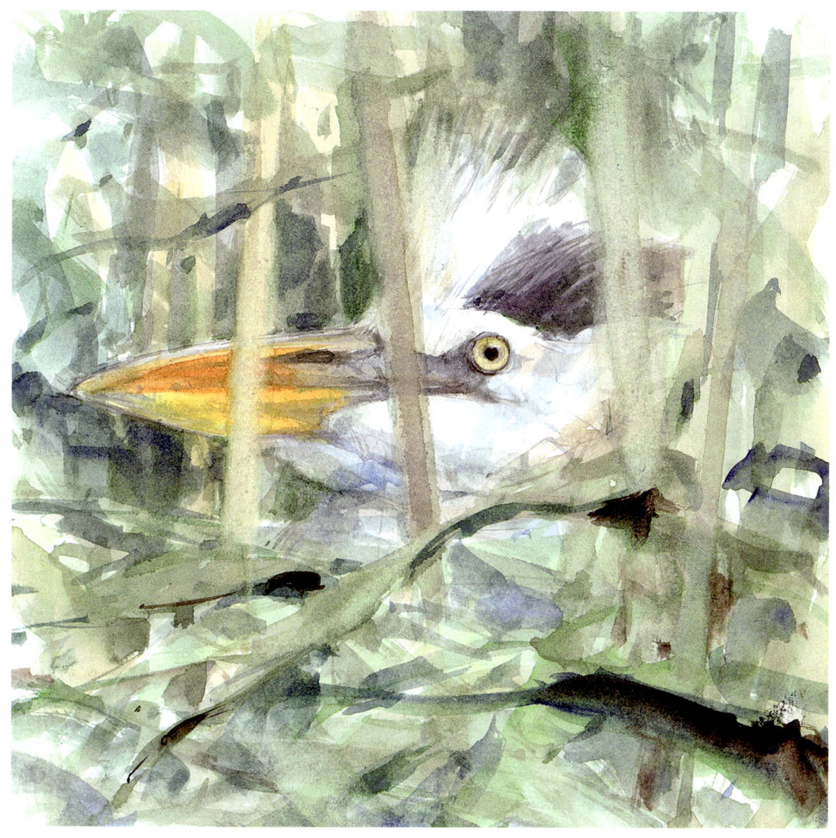

Heron's Gaze. In this watercolor painted in the field, the artist's attention was focused on a single fragment of the bird that appears from among the reeds. The gaze of a heron that can barely be seen in its hiding place is the main theme of the painting.

Owl in its Olive Tree. Watercolor, 19.5 x 27.5 inches (50 x 70 cm), painted by Juan Varela. When they are in their natural habitat, birds do not openly expose themselves, so sometimes the most accurate painting is one that shows them half-hidden, and causes the viewer to be surprised as he or she begins seeing them little by little. In this work, the owl is located near a place that artist's refer to as the golden mean—that is, the point where the viewer's eye goes to instinctively. Furthermore, however, the two branches of the olive tree cradle the figure and direct the eye toward it.

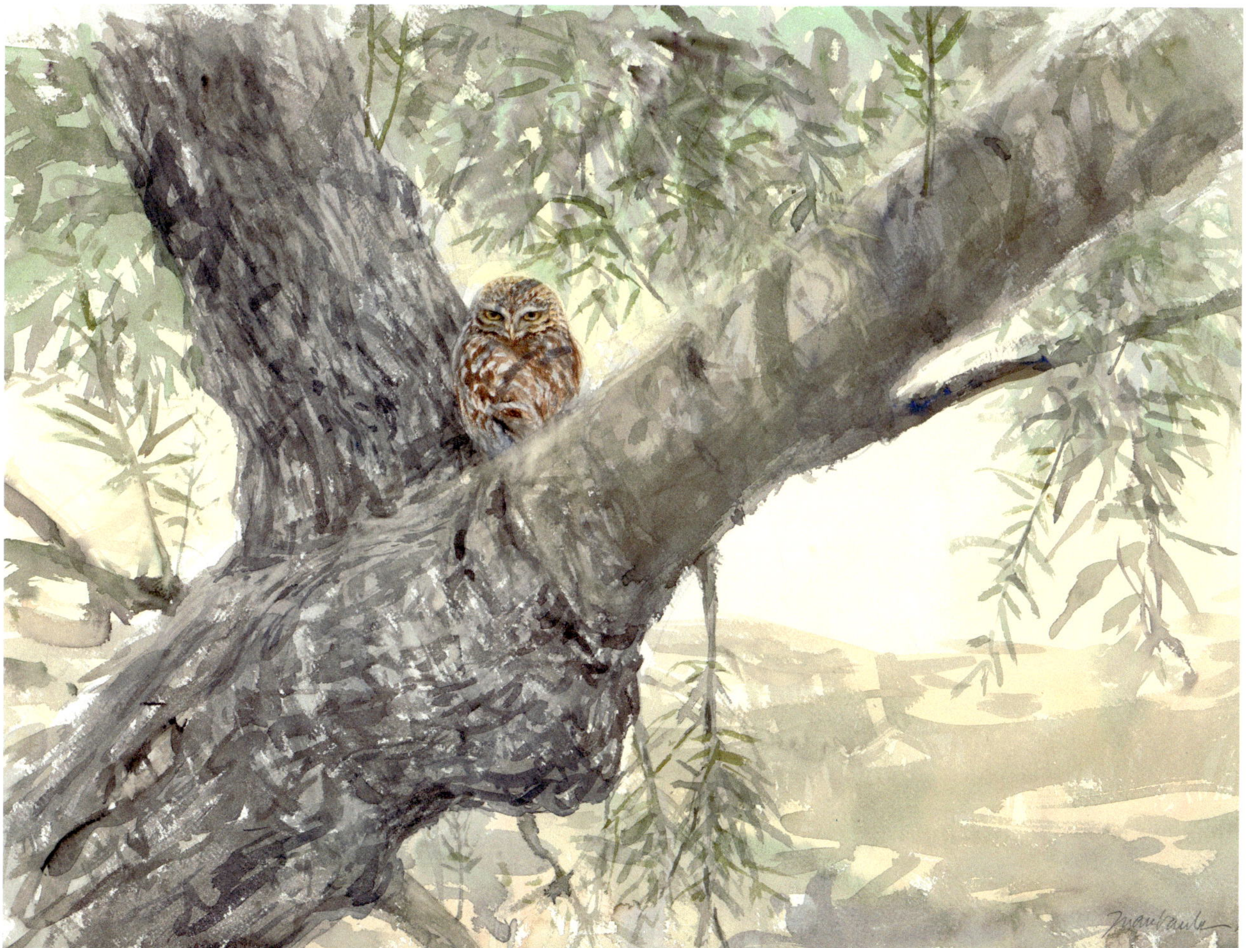

Birds in Groups

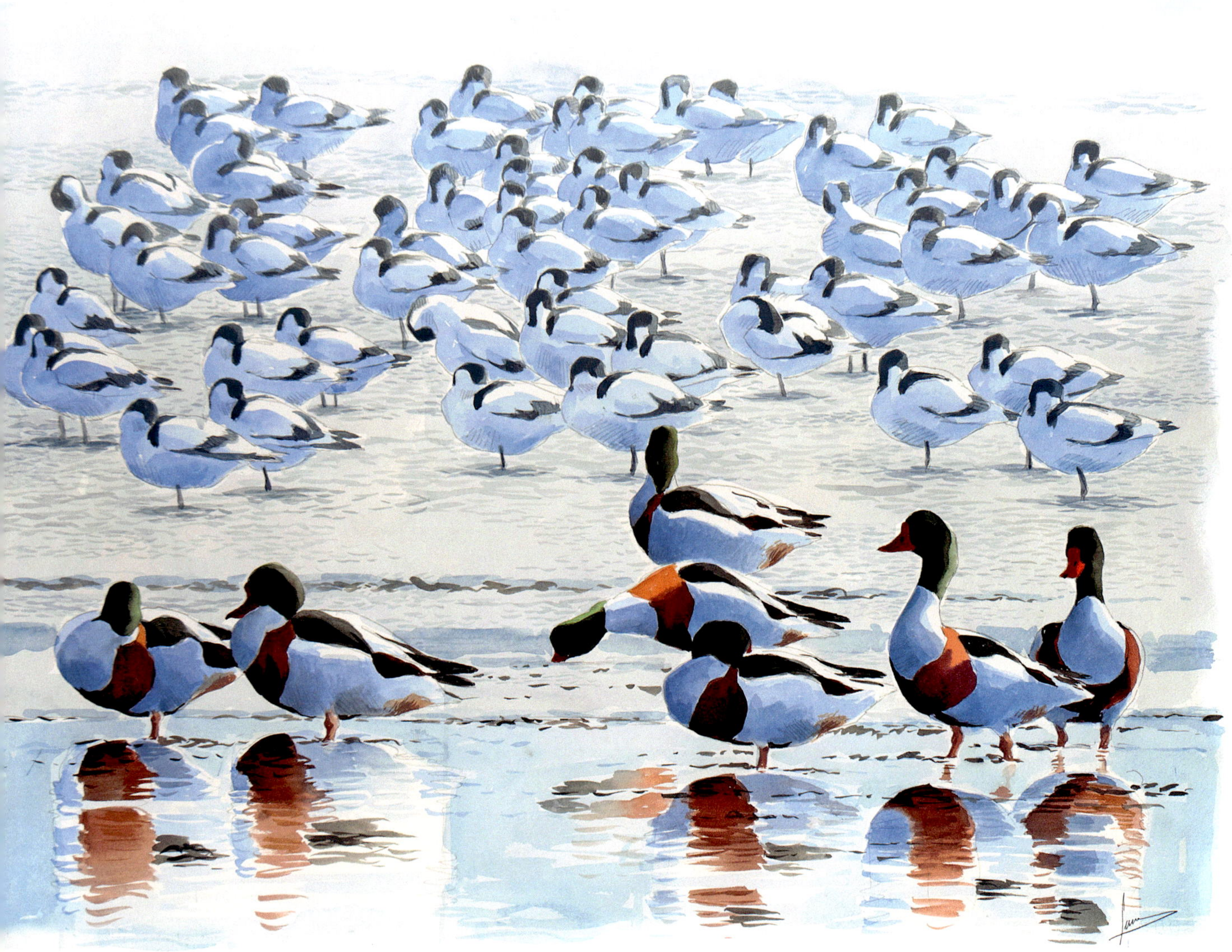

Pied Avocets and Common Shelducks. Watercolor, 29.5 x 21.5 inches (75 x 55 cm), by José Antonio Sencianes. The composition plays with a repeated module with slight variations that blend perfectly with the light and the time of day. The avocets in the background, in a careful study of random grouping, constitute a backdrop that becomes progressively indistinct in accordance with the laws of atmospheric perspective. It is interesting to see how the artist painted the reflections of the birds in the water with studied detail.

Compositions with many elements require making careful studies. In the natural state, groups of birds gather in different ways according to the time of year. In winter they tend to stay close together; but, during breeding season, they stay farther apart and compete more among themselves. The overall composition should respect these biological realities, but also risk playing with the elements of the composition, establishing relationships among them, creating lines of tension, searching for focal centers and all the theoretical guidelines that the artist is aware of. Birds in groups are not isolated individuals placed any which way onto the paper; the distribution must have a logic and a relation to the framing of the composition.

REFERENCES FROM NATURE

It is always helpful to make simple sketches of groups of birds in the wild, whether they are in flight, on the ground, or perched in trees. Even brief pencil lines or splotches of color can turn out to be useful for remembering the distribution or the structure of a group. A few photographs, even of poor quality, of a flock of swimming ducks, birds of prey in flight, or seagulls on the beach will allow you to study the spatial distribution and the relationships between the birds, including the shadows that they cast on each other.

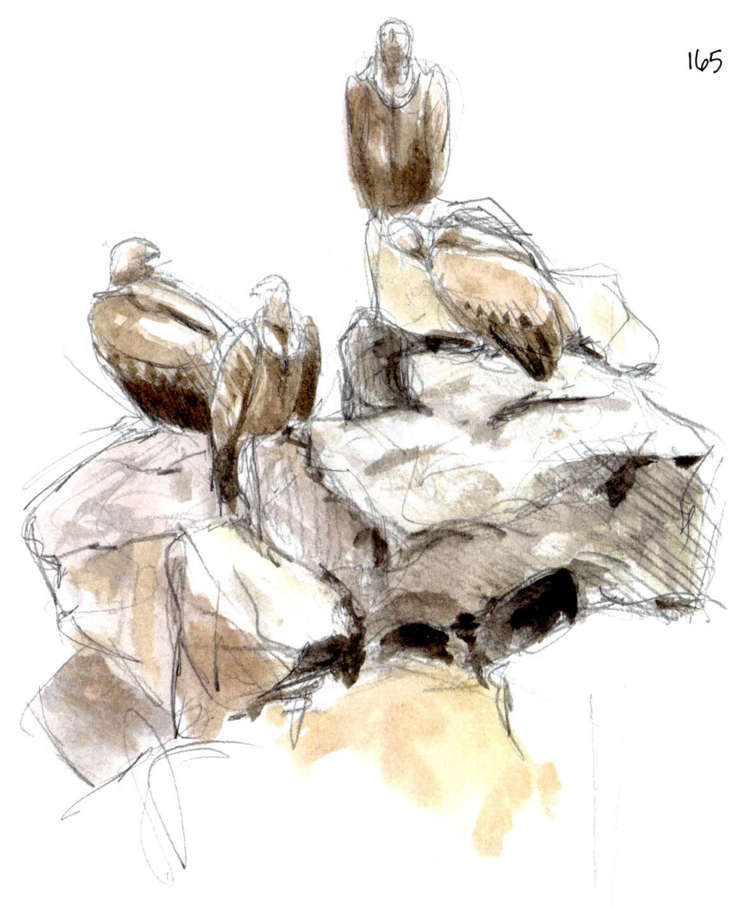

Griffon vultures. You must not miss the chance to make simple compositional sketches from nature. Sometimes, birds spontaneously form elegant geometries, and, with a few lines and some dabs of color, you can immortalize them in your sketchbook.

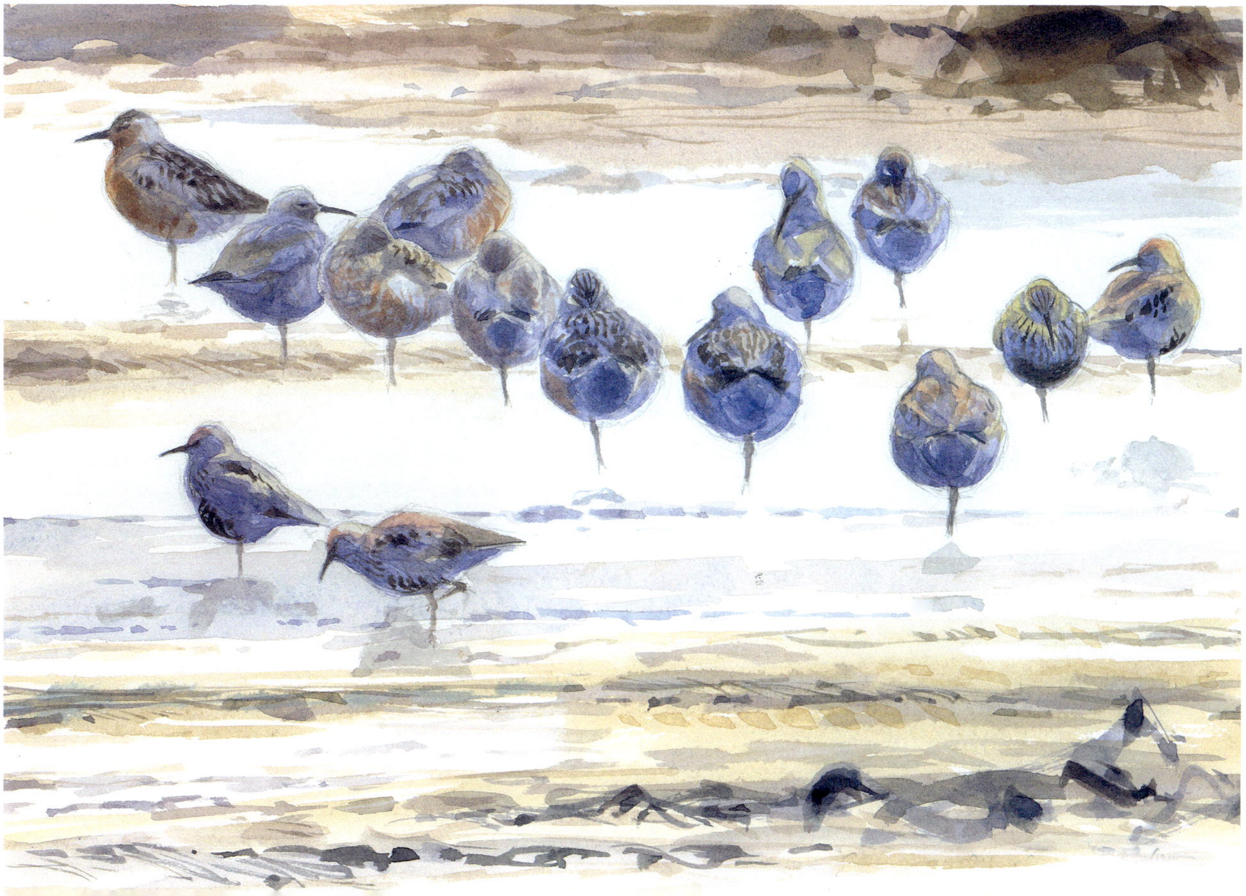

A Flock of Sandpipers in the Odiel River. Watercolor. At dusk, aquatic birds gather in groups to rest. The atmospheric light plays an important role and unifies the composition in which the two species of birds are arranged in a seemingly random way. The angled line, however, directs the eye and breaks the horizontal plane by adding a bit of movement. The light hitting the water gives it such a bright whiteness that the birds do not have any reflection at all.

In the Studio

JUAN VARELA
NAP AT DUSK
NORTHERN SHOVELER AND EURASIAN TEAL
OIL ON LINEN, 39 x 25.5 INCHES (100 x 65 CM)

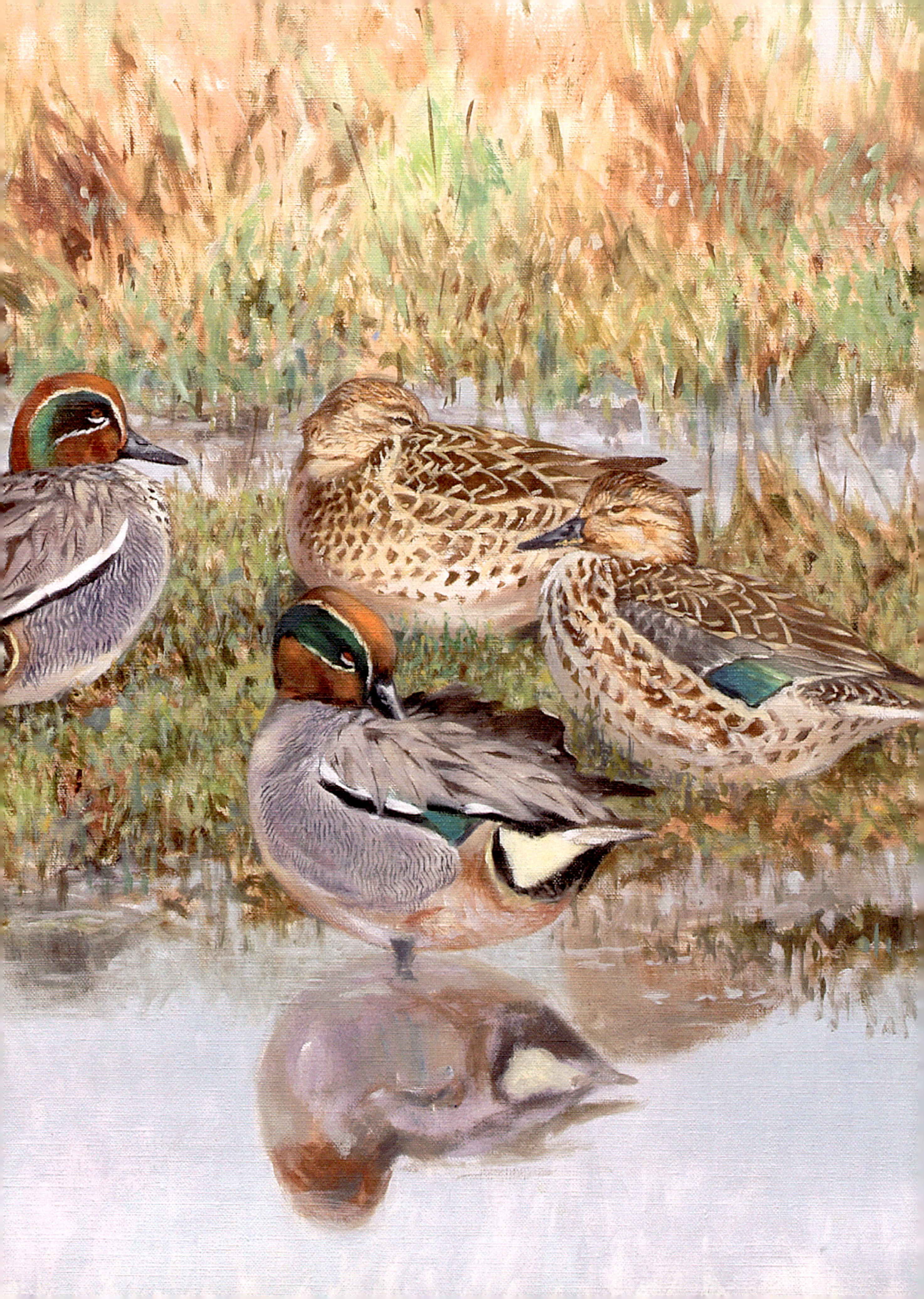

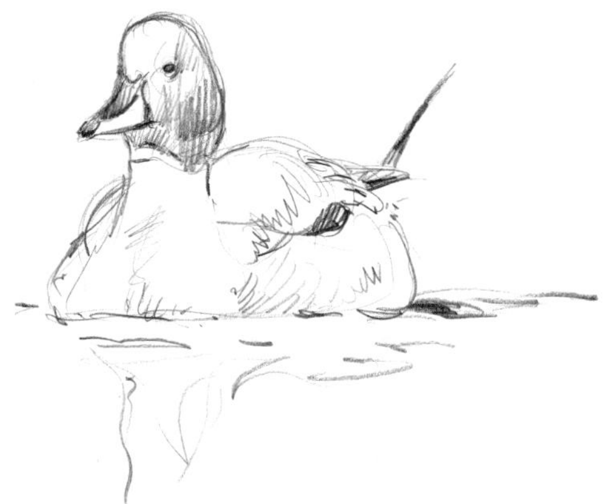

Think Big
Another Working Speed

Most of the work done in the field is done in small formats and mainly on paper. The use of oils and canvas is not common in this type of painting. Watercolor is a more immediate medium, easy to carry and quick drying, although acrylics have many fans for the same reason and because they can be quite opaque.

When you go into the studio things change. A watercolor that is calmly planned out can be painted on large-format paper, and oils, because they are slow drying, allow you to reconsider ideas and resume working on quick sketches made in the field from another perspective. In the studio, the spontaneity of field work translates into a project that progresses at a slower pace and lets you learn from the process.

DARREN REES
LITTLE AUKS, GREAT SKUA, AND PINK SNOW
ACRYLIC ON CANVAS, 39 X 47.25 INCHES (100 X 120 CM)

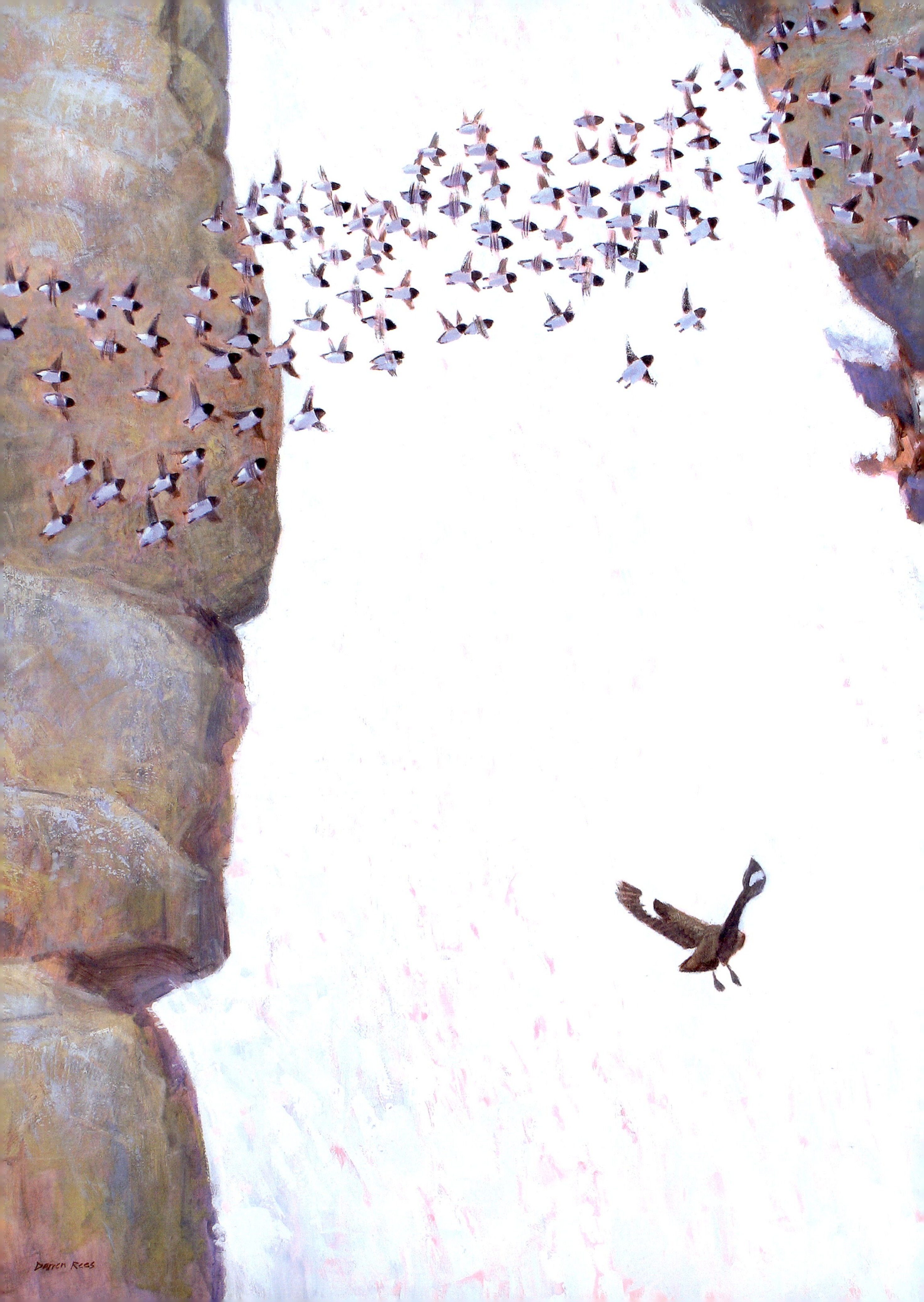
Darren Rees

Creative Work

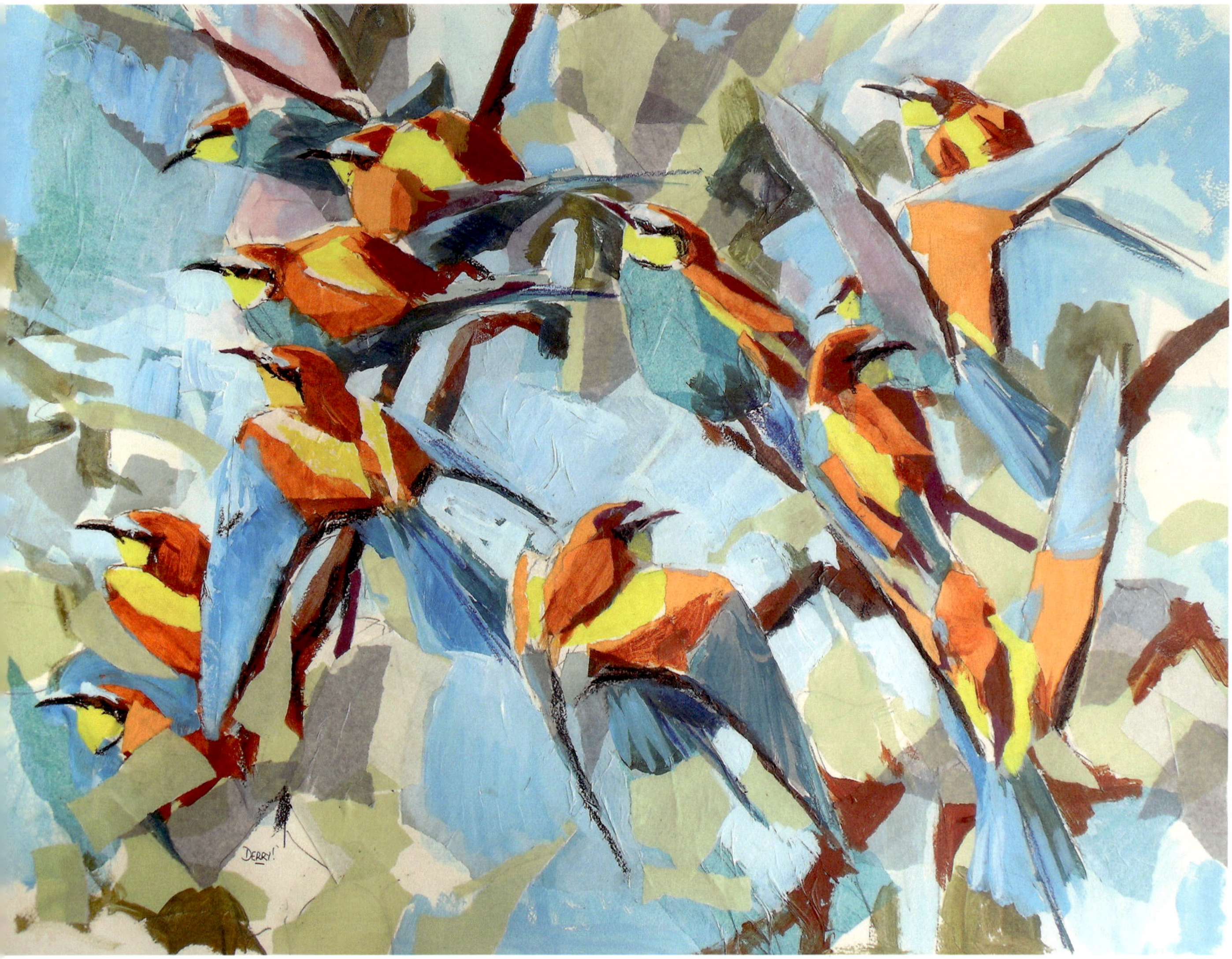

European Bee-eaters. Mixed media, 30 x 24 inches (76 x 60 cm), painted by Nick Derry. Everything is motion in this painting. At first glance, the eye is attracted to the rhythm of the color and the darkest lines. More careful observation begins to reveal the luminous details of the birds and their connection across the space. If the heads were eliminated, the work would be pure abstraction. The entire painting is somewhat reminiscent of Art Nouveau stained glass windows.

Having a large space to work in is not all that frequent. Many good artists work in their own homes, in the kitchen or in a corner of the living room, and they have to pick up their things when the space is needed for domestic use. In spaces like this, however, you can create excellent work in small and medium formats, and studies for larger work can be painted in temporary rented spaces or space shared by other artists. Talent is not at odds with any shortage or lack of means. The work of artist Darren Rees that precedes this page does not simply flow out of his imagination; it requires experience in the field and a series of preliminary studies that can easily be made in a small space.

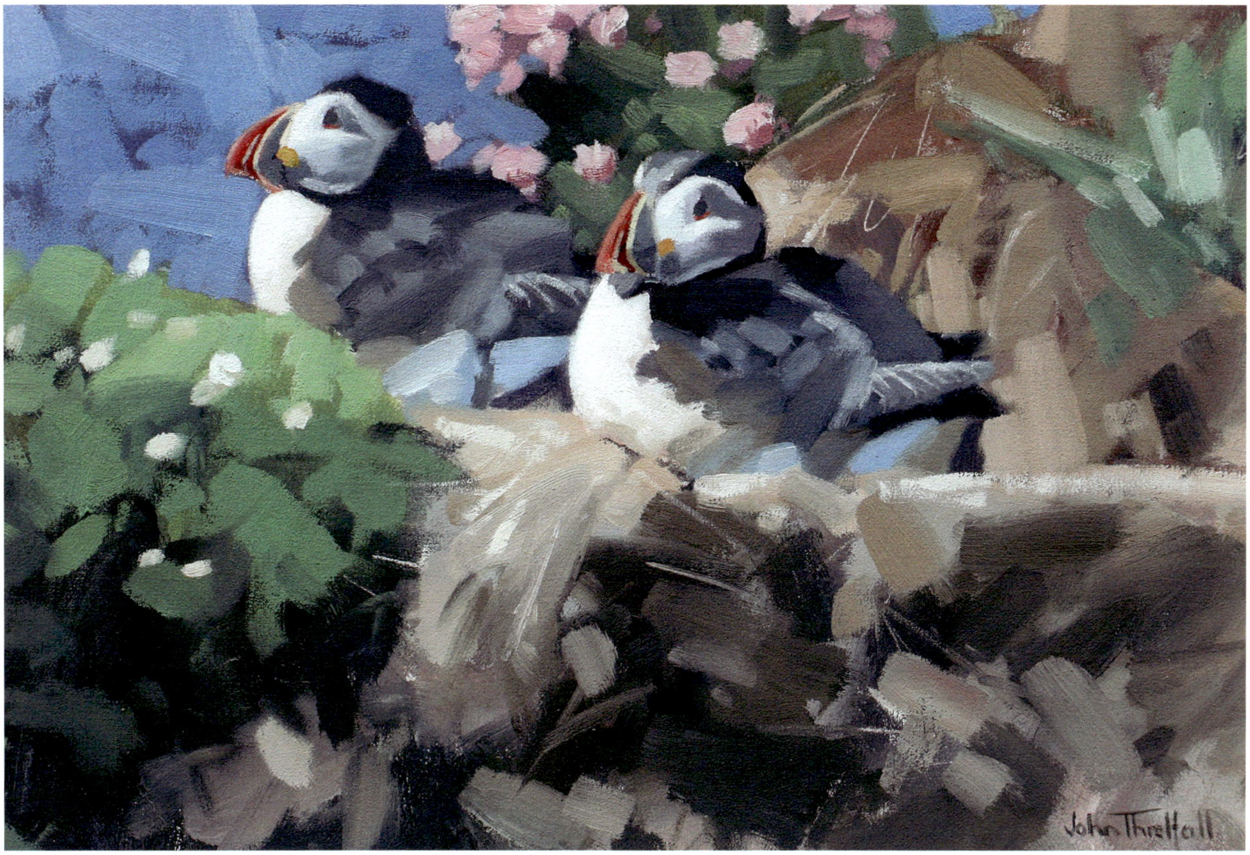

Loafing Around. Oil on paper, 9.5 x 15.75 inches (24 x 40 cm), painted by John Threlfall. The light is the essential element in this composition, and it is applied with wide brushstrokes. This painting demonstrates two things: that it is not necessary to have a large studio to enjoy painting birds and that painting birds does not consist of filling meticulous drawings with color.

STYLES OF WORK

Many times, painting birds is identified with photorealism, as if it were a possible technique. If you rule out illustration work, which is determined by the client, you can have total creative freedom. Birds are as interesting a subject as any other for exciting the imagination, and there is a wide range of expressive possibilities that can be explored. Some artists prefer to accurately define the bird and landscape, while others work in a more impressionistic and spontaneous manner, even playing with the forms of birds, distorting them and mixing them with the surroundings.

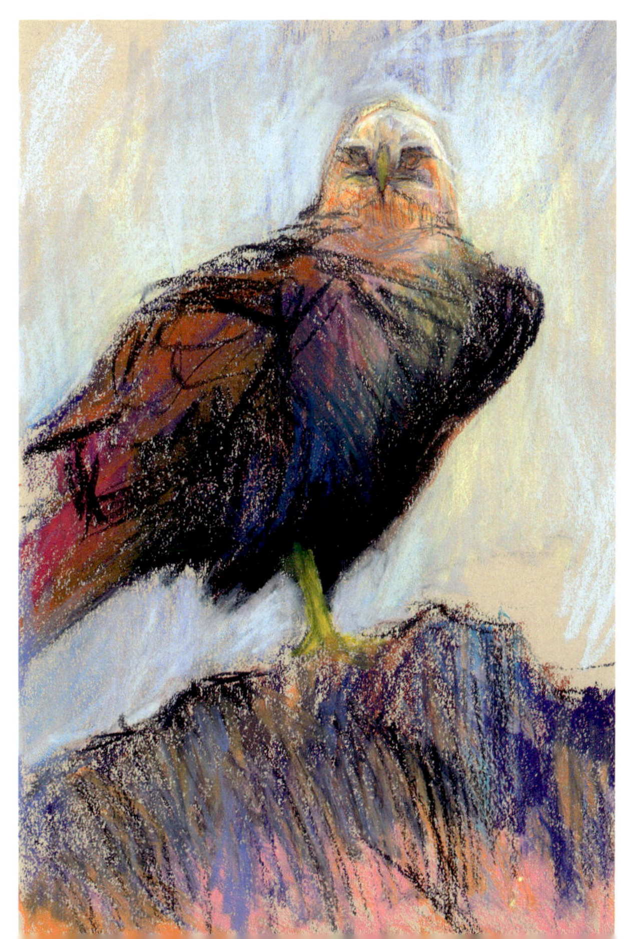

Bald Eagle. Oil pastels on gray paper, 8.25 x 12 inches (21 x 30 cm), by Juan Varela. This drawing plays with the possibilities of colors, starting with a subject that is, for the most part, black in color.

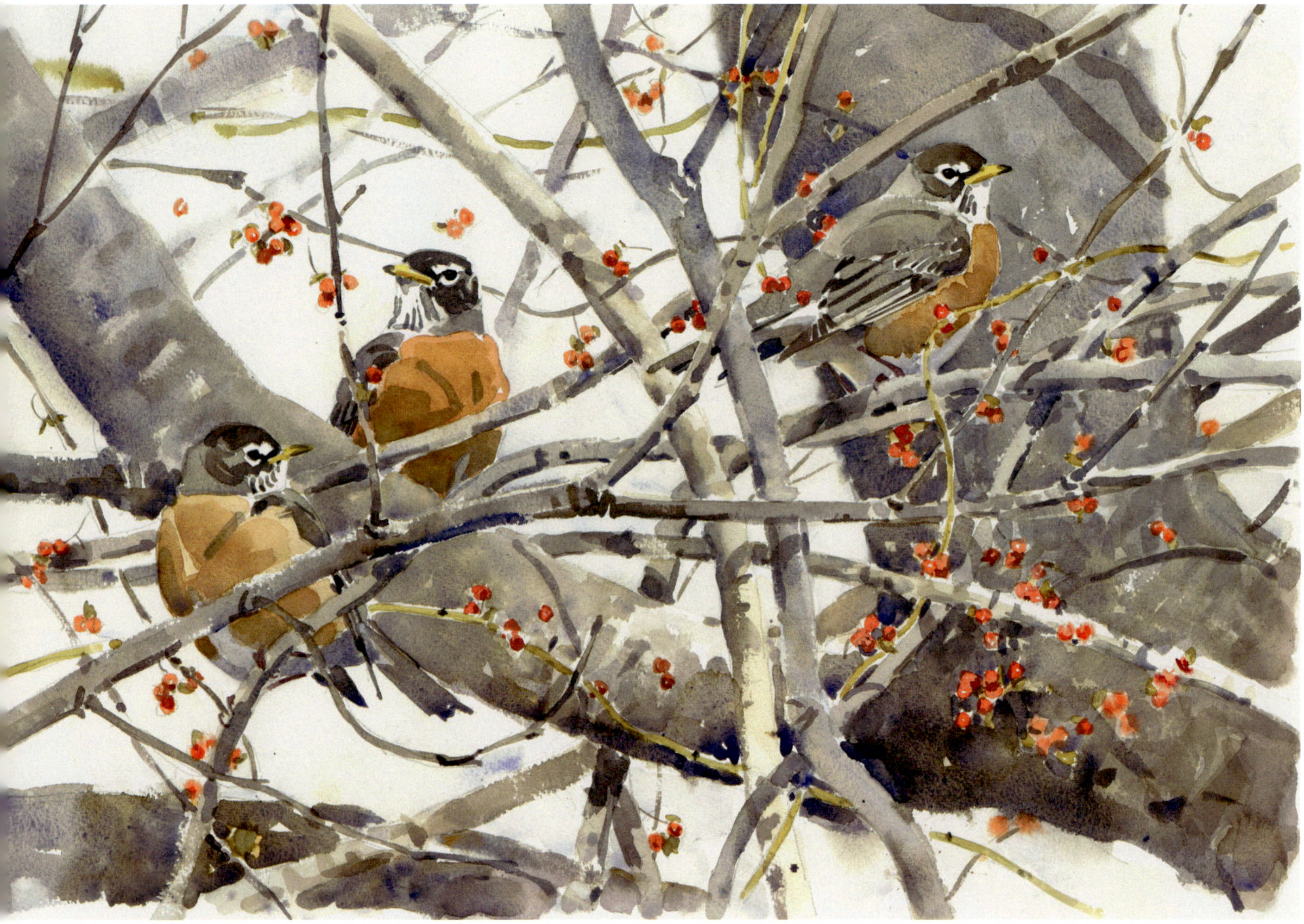

Robins and Nightshade. Watercolor, 15 x 22 inches (38 x 56 cm), by Barry Van Dusen. The artist used his observations in the field and his sketches, like the one on page 152, to create compositions in which birds play a role of equal importance to that of the environment that they inhabit. This work shows great economy of line, using only those that are needed.

Using Your Own Sketches

As was previously pointed out, sketches from nature are not only for collecting ideas for making paintings in the studio later. The main goal should be to internalize images in motion, saving the memory of shapes, of volumes, and of postures so that later they will come to mind when your hand is working on the paper. Paging through your own sketchbooks and remembering moments and circumstances helps to rekindle the imagination and returns you to specific times and places.

A sketch from nature should be considered a first step in the work of investigating the subject. You must carefully study the bird's anatomy, its conduct, and its relation to the environment. All of this provides material for working in the studio, when the subject is no longer in front of you to clear up any doubts that might come up.

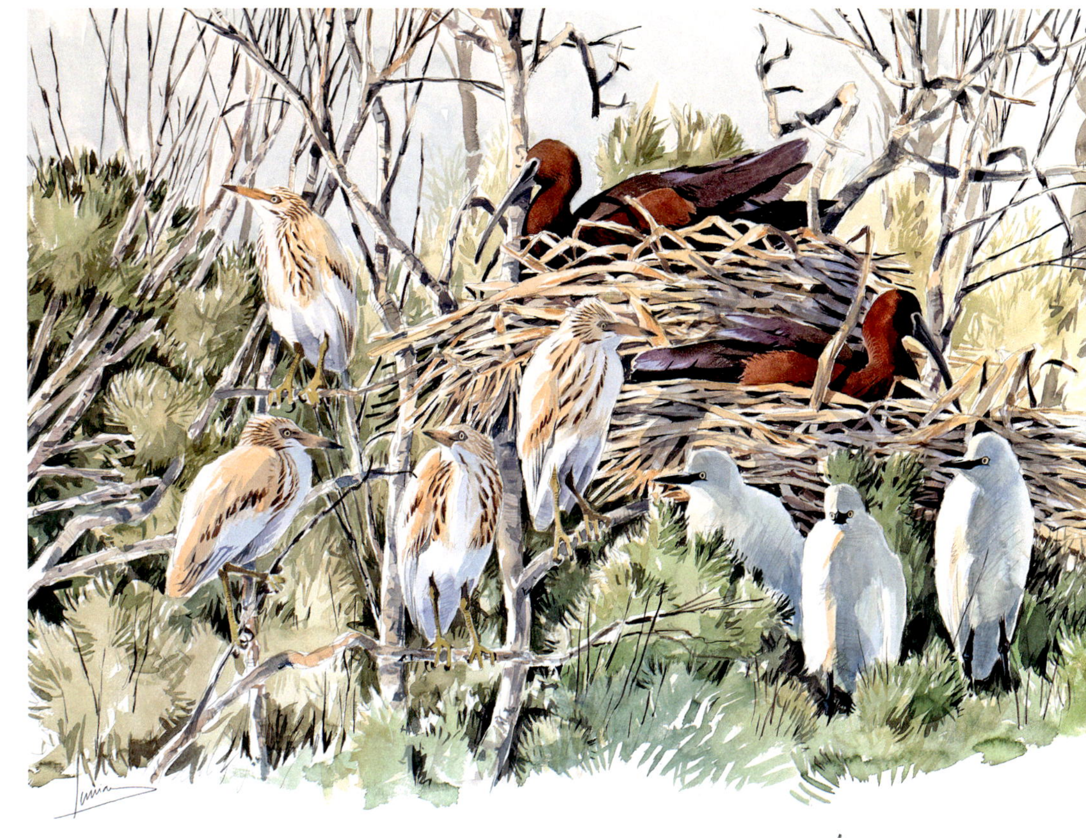

Squacco Herons and Glossy Ibis. Watercolor, 30.25 x 22.5 inches (77 x 57 cm), by José Antonio Sencianes. This very complex composition juggles several elements. The light is one of the most important ones, and it washes the entire scene and casts shadows in a believable manner. The arrangement of the herons is handled carefully to avoid becoming monotonous and to add movement, in contrast to the static attitude of the nesting ibis.

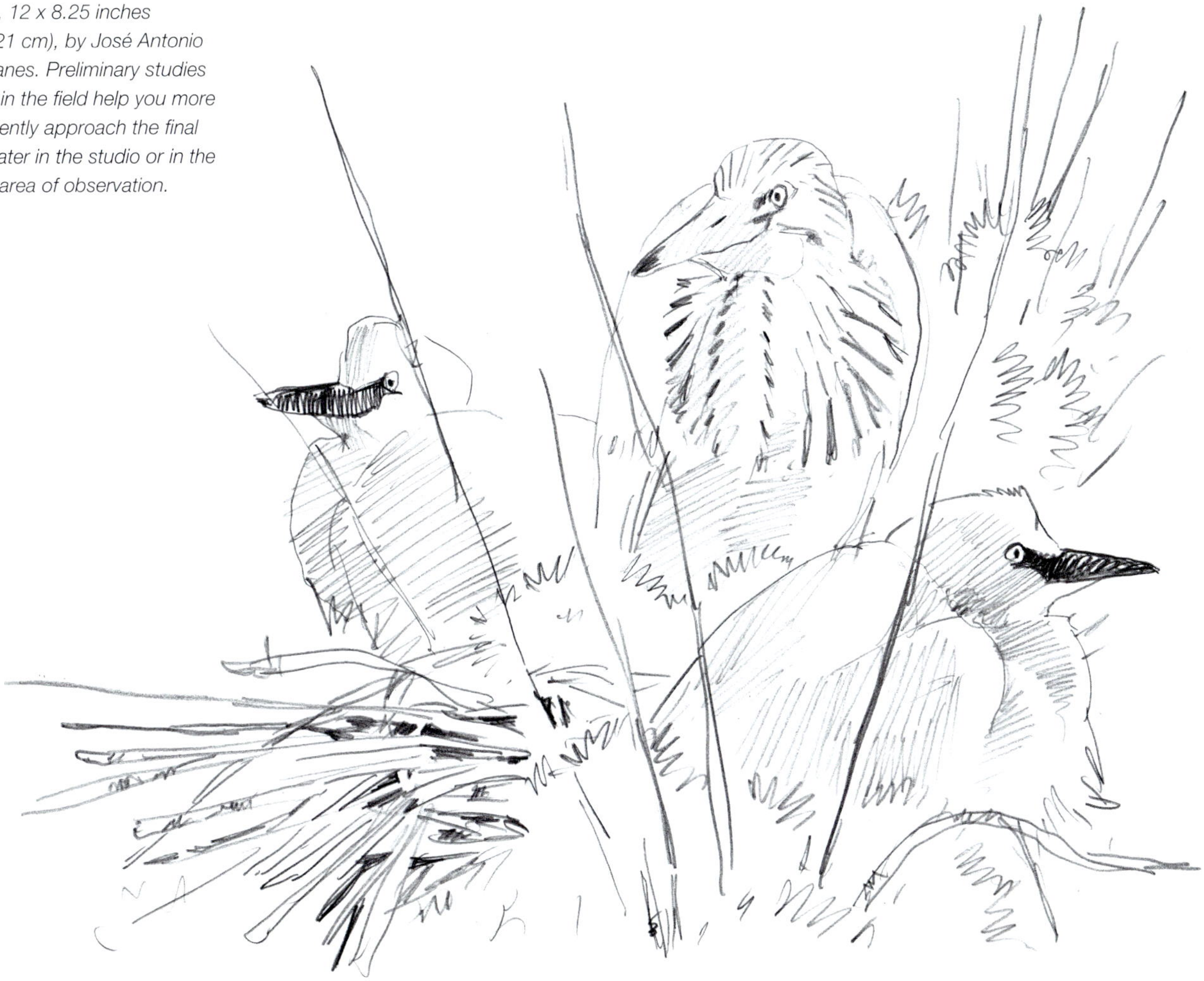

Squacco Herons. Pencil, 12 x 8.25 inches (30 x 21 cm), by José Antonio Sencianes. Preliminary studies made in the field help you more confidently approach the final work later in the studio or in the same area of observation.

Studies of Pelicans. Israel. Pencil and watercolor. Having a good personal archive is an inexhaustible source of references. The hours spent making sketches in nature are not, by any means, wasted time. Flocks of birds resting, like these pelicans, offer innumerable poses and angles. When returning to the subject in the studio, your memories of what you learned and experienced in the field will be reactivated.

A MATTER OF DIALOGUE

Working in the studio is like having a conversation with the painting in progress. This conversation might begin in the field when an observation and some notes on paper produced an idea and the urgency to go further in developing it. The conversation can also come up when going over your own sketches, having just a vague idea for a project. In any case, it is a conversation with the work in which the previously collected notes and sketches play an important part. It is not a good idea to work with a specific and unchanging idea without "listening" to the work itself. The sketch points the work in one direction; the work in process is a medium for learning and directing the artist in one of many possible directions.

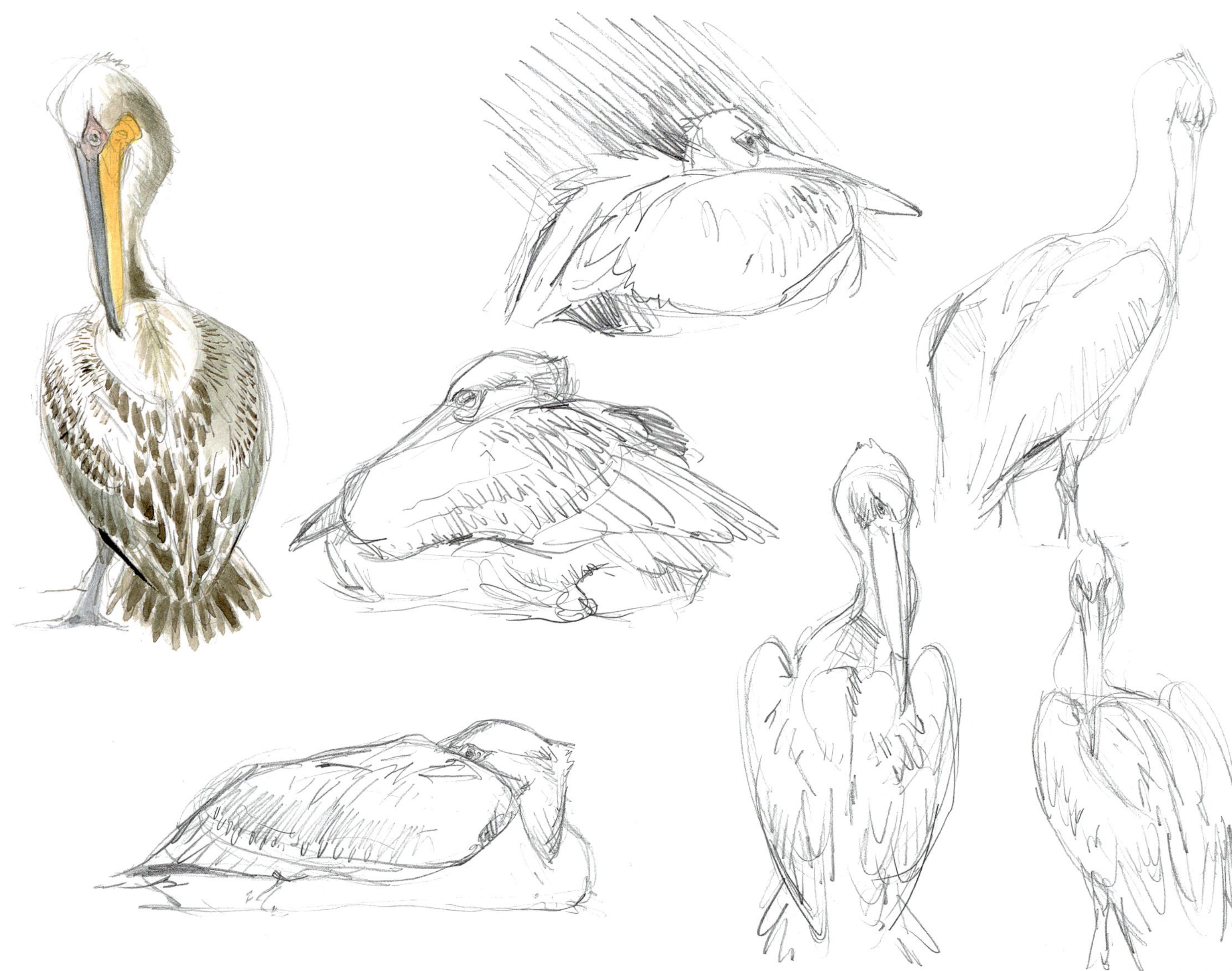

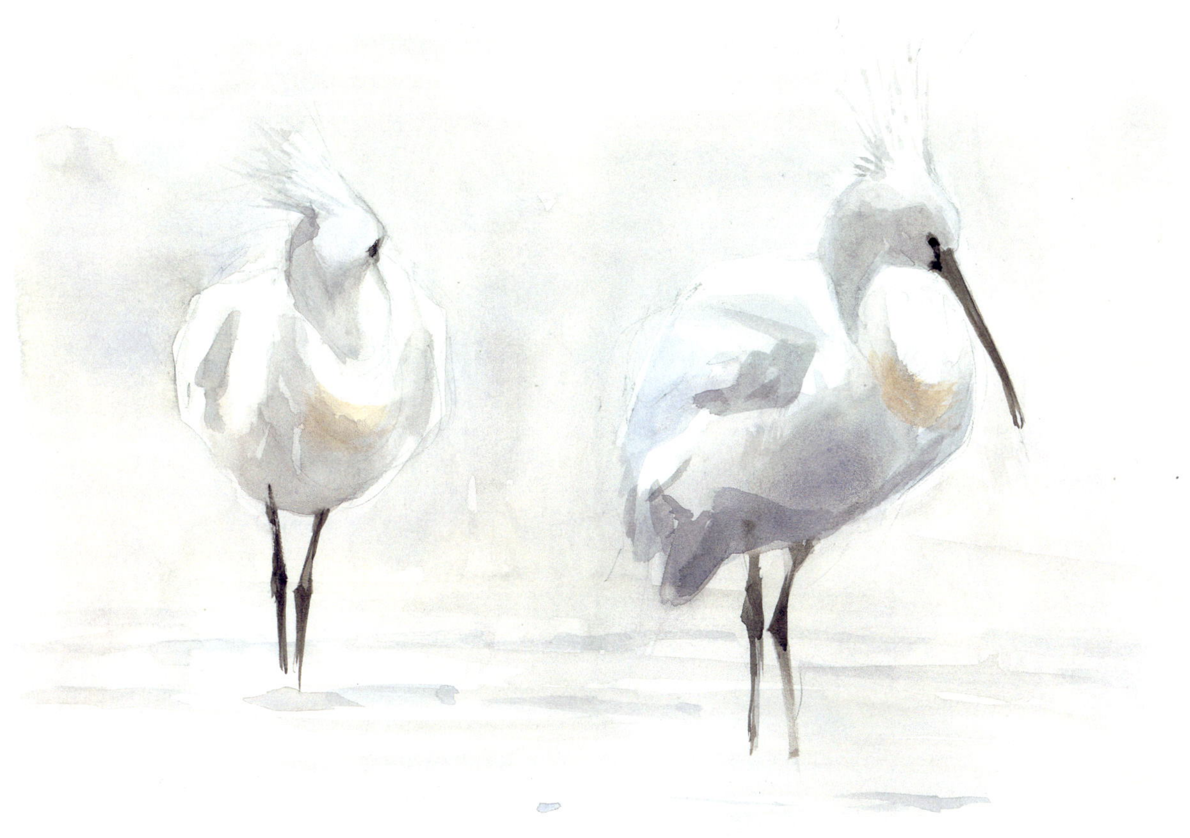

Two European Spoonbills. Watercolor, 10.5 x 14.5 inches (27 x 37 cm). Sketch from nature in the swamp at the Parque Nacional de Doñana, Spain.

Morning Breeze. Oil on linen, 36.5 x 25.5 inches (93 x 65 cm), by Juan Varela. This work from the studio exactly reflects the impression taken from nature, but the sketch is often only a reference for a whole series of options. In this case, the original idea was maintained—the general cool and misty feeling and the absence of other subjects apart from the two birds—but their postures have been changed.

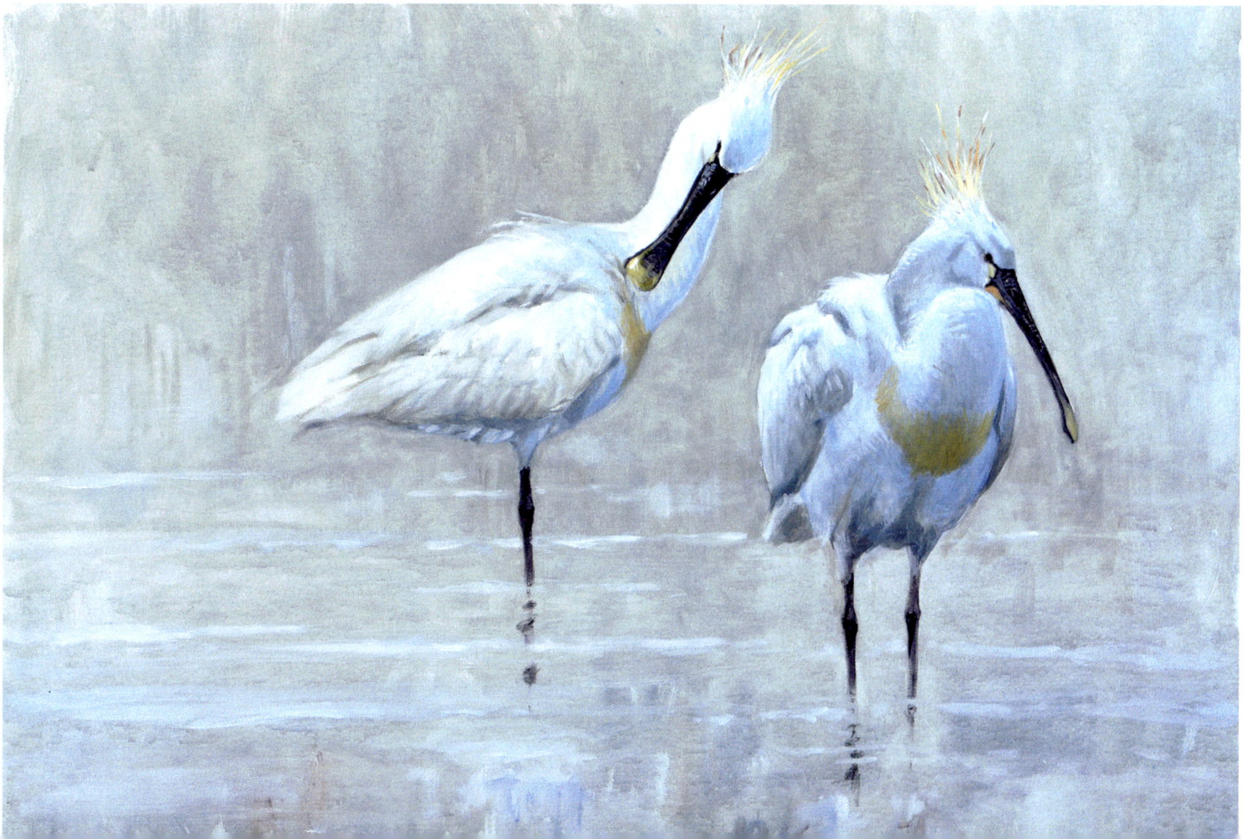

The Artist's Resources

The main source of information for a painter of birds should be his or her own observations in the field; however, these can also be supplemented by other resources, like photographs, videos, and specimens in collections. When we mention photographs, we are not referring just to pictures of birds taken by the artist or found in books or on the Internet; they can also be photos of landscapes and vegetation. Sometimes, it is necessary to have a good reference of how a wave breaks, what color the water is in the summer at sunset, and how a swimming bird is reflected in it. This does not mean that you are going to copy a landscape and then later paste a drawing of a bird on it; this almost never works and the results are not very believable.

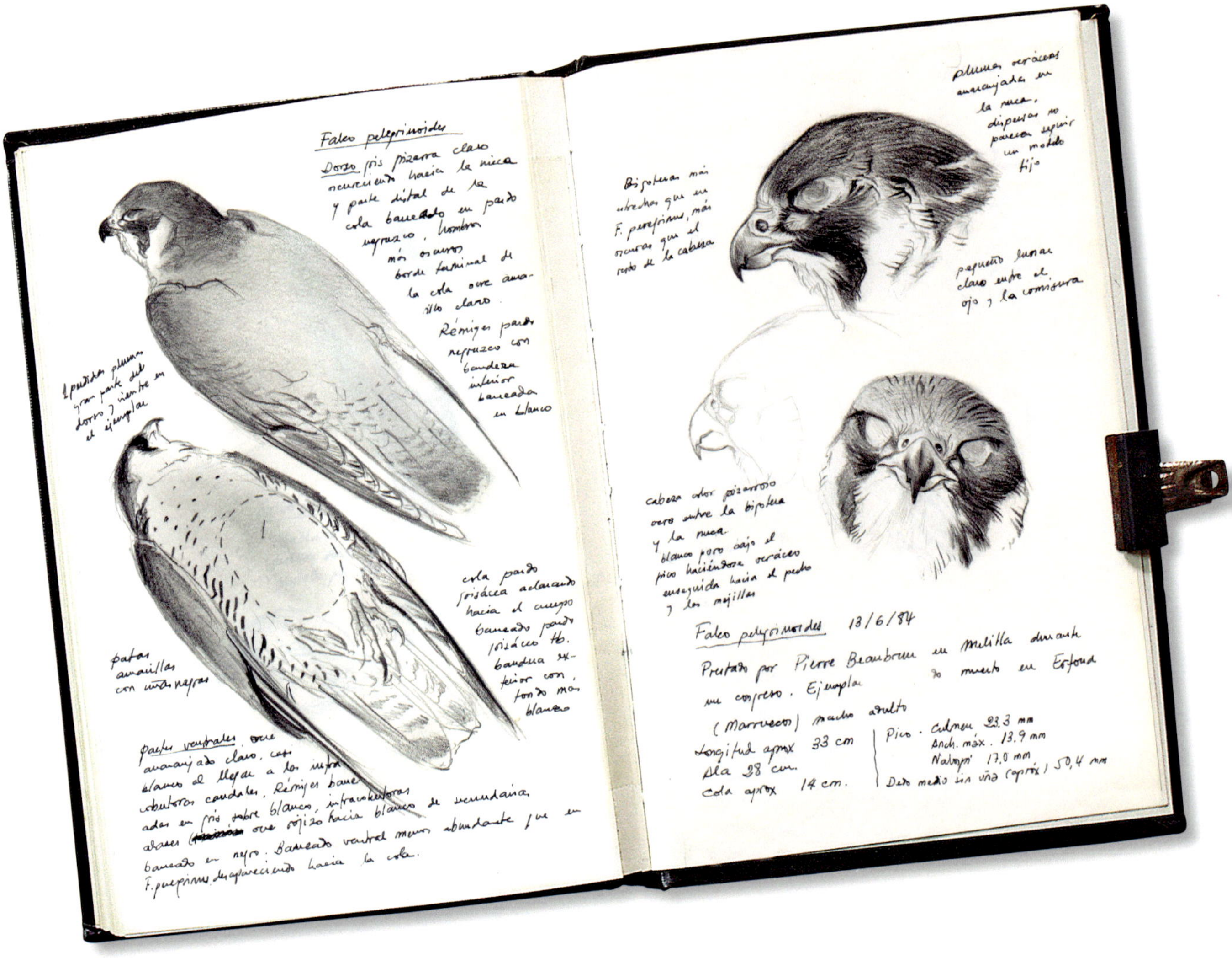

Postmortem study of a Barbary falcon in Morocco. The highways, unfortunately, and especially the secondary ones and those near forests and fields, annually supply many remains of birds for making postmortem studies. It is also possible to find the remains of birds in the field that were wounded by hunters or abandoned by predators. Finally, natural history museums collect numerous examples of preserved birds and carefully mounted skeletons.

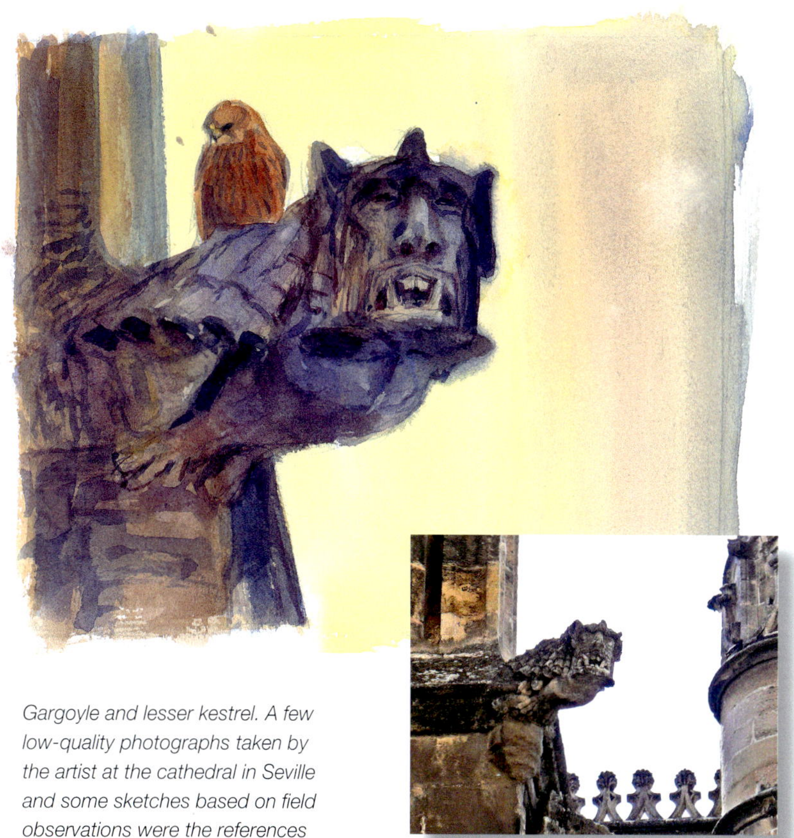

Gargoyle and lesser kestrel. A few low-quality photographs taken by the artist at the cathedral in Seville and some sketches based on field observations were the references for this oil painting.

PHOTOGRAPH

The painter can always carry a small camera when going into the field to take reference pictures. The photos do not have to be of great quality. Later, they will be useful for study, and they can also be printed and cut out to evaluate possible framing and compositions. It should never be forgotten that the eye captures the information in three dimensions and a photograph only in two. Therefore, what is seen in person is always more faithful than a photograph.

Montagu's harrier and a storm. This pastel sketch captures the quality of the light that falls on a wheat field before being "swallowed up" by a storm.

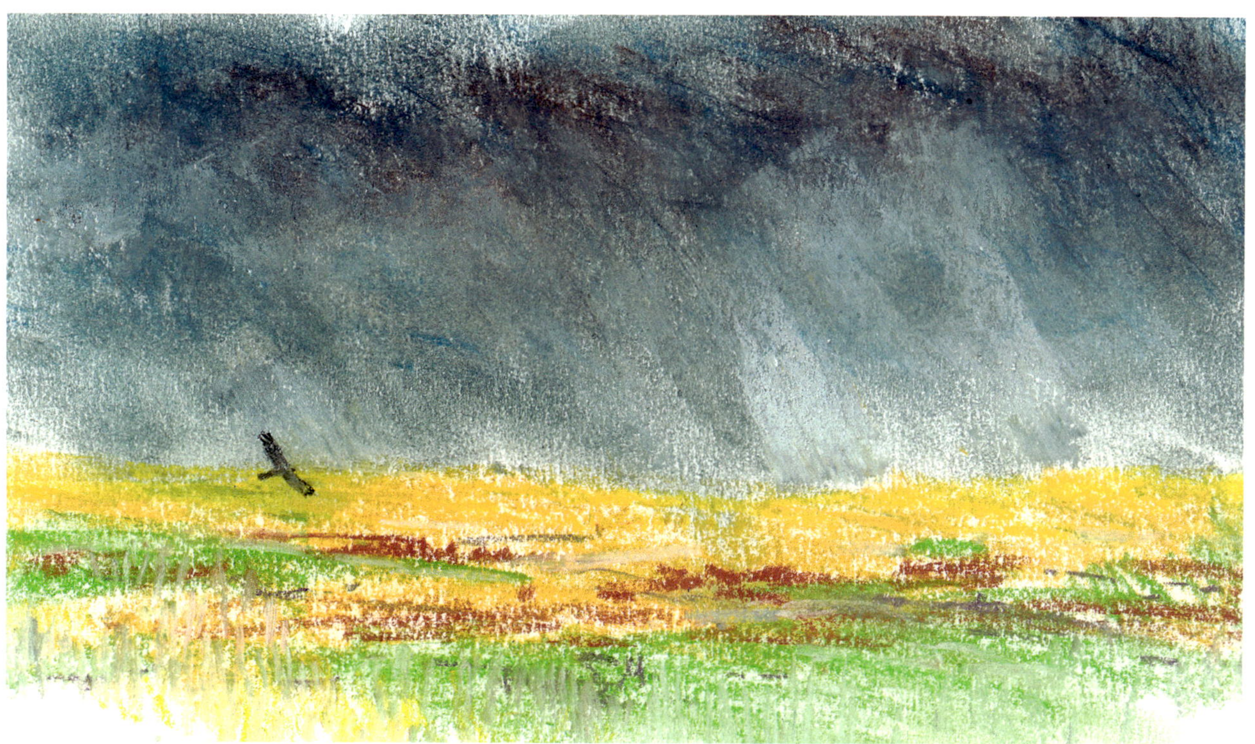

Other Views

Birds are a classic painting subject that has existed for many centuries. In the modern era, they have inspired paintings by well-known artists like Picasso and Monet, to name just a couple. Bird paintings have become their own artistic genre and are referred to as wildlife art. Nowadays, there are many associations of artists dedicated to wildlife art, and many museums and galleries that specialize in this kind of work, as well as many publications about the subject.

Painting birds, and nature in general, does not have to be limited to the classic techniques like oils and watercolor. It is the artist who should match the form to the content and choose the most appropriate media for what he or she wishes to illustrate. Even the most realistic art is a mere symbol or metaphor of reality. Opting for hyper-realistic formats should be a freely made decision of the artist, not an imposition by the market or the tradition of scientific painting.

Eurasian Wryneck. Collage and acrylic, 25.5 x 20 inches (65 x 50 cm), by Nick Derry. Glued color papers and opaque paint produced this unique work in which the flat colors and black lines remind us of printmaking techniques. Today, many artists are using the monotype technique or serigraphy to make their artwork.

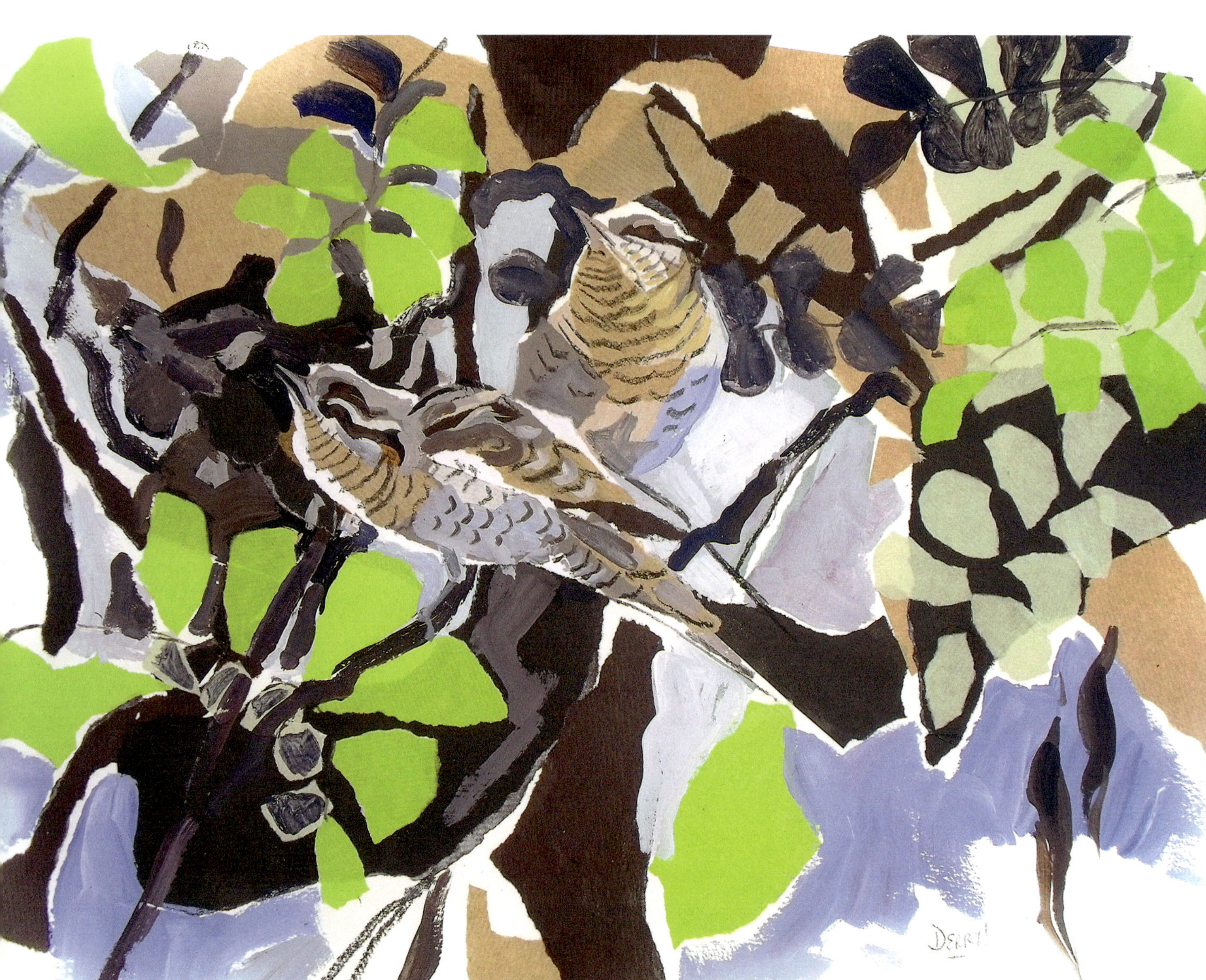

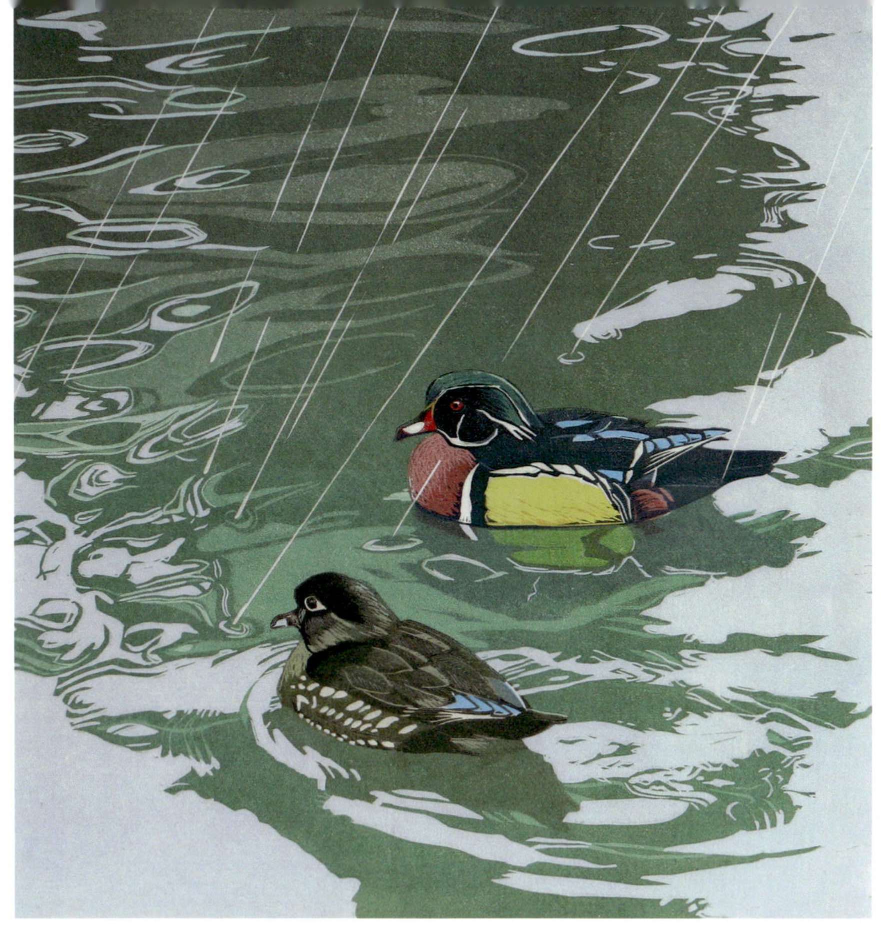

Shower With a Friend. Linoprint on Awagami Kozo paper, 15 x 15 inches (38 x 38 cm), by Sherri York. This humorous title about saving water is applied to ducks in the rain. This artist usually works with woodcuts and linocuts, which require a good knowledge of drawing techniques and the use of color, and she generally uses a limited color palette. Artists that work from nature find it very useful to work with just a few colors. Otherwise, they tend to lose the tonal relationships in the sketch.

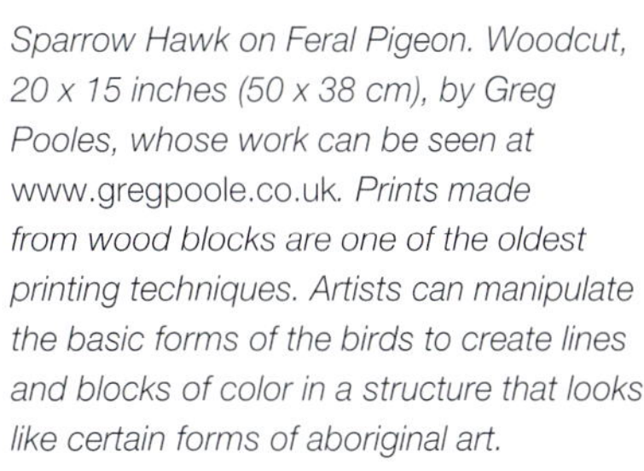

Sparrow Hawk on Feral Pigeon. Woodcut, 20 x 15 inches (50 x 38 cm), by Greg Pooles, whose work can be seen at www.gregpoole.co.uk. *Prints made from wood blocks are one of the oldest printing techniques. Artists can manipulate the basic forms of the birds to create lines and blocks of color in a structure that looks like certain forms of aboriginal art.*

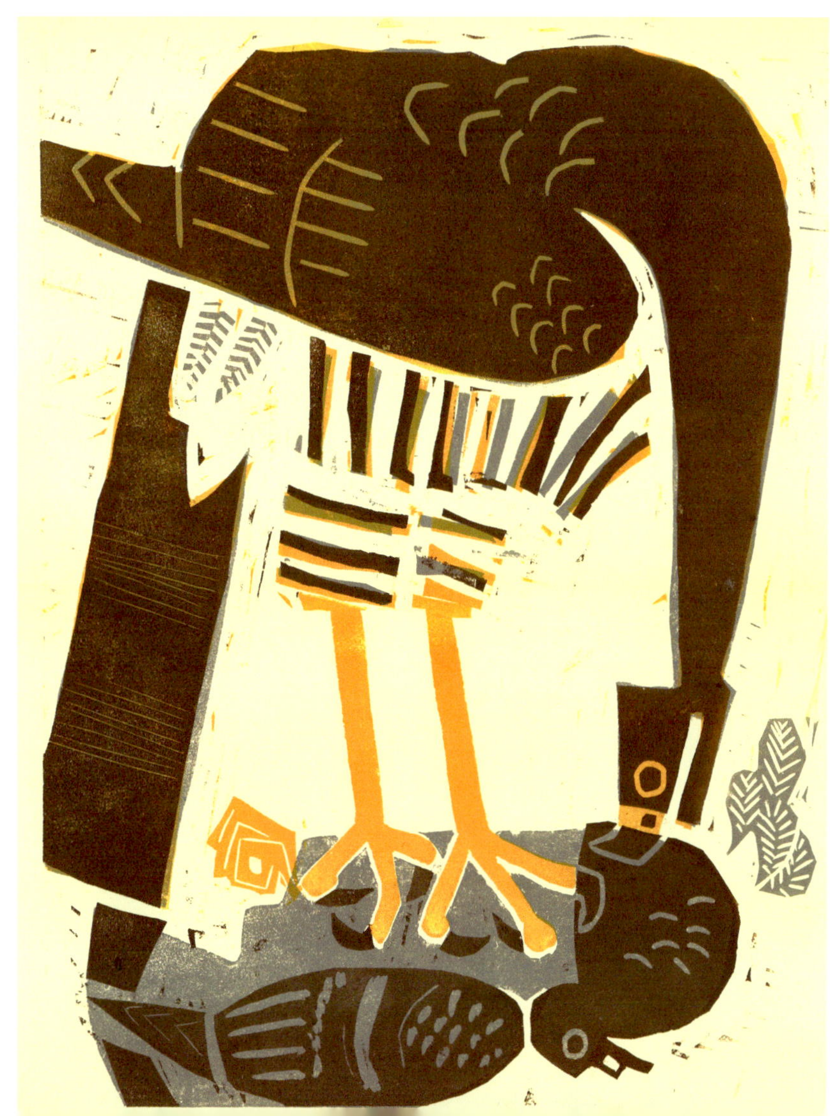

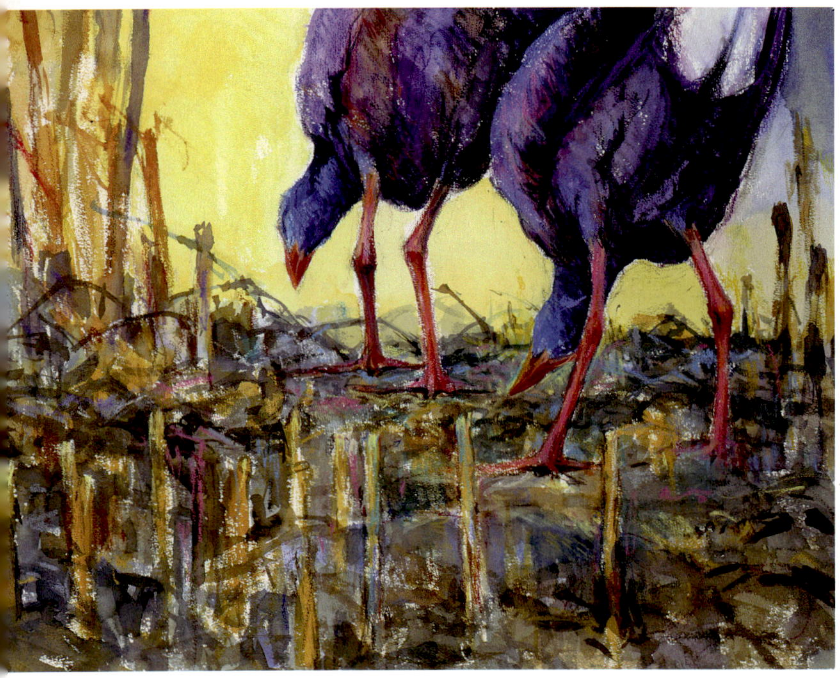

OTHER INNOVATIVE TECHNIQUES

Experimentation is part of making art, and therefore of painting birds. Mixing media and supports is a good way to achieve many very different effects. There are many artists that work with printing techniques like serigraphy, woodcut, monotype, linocut, dry point, and lithography, among others. Nor is it uncommon to find works that have incorporated oil and water-base media and collage techniques.

Birds are a very attractive subject for artists and direct observation of them sharpens your ingenuity and creativity.

Return to the Fields. Purple Swamphens. Mixed media on paper, 20 x 27.5 inches (50 x 70 cm), by Juan Varela. The combination of watercolor, gouache, and oil pastel sticks on paper with a rough surface, creating some very interesting effects.

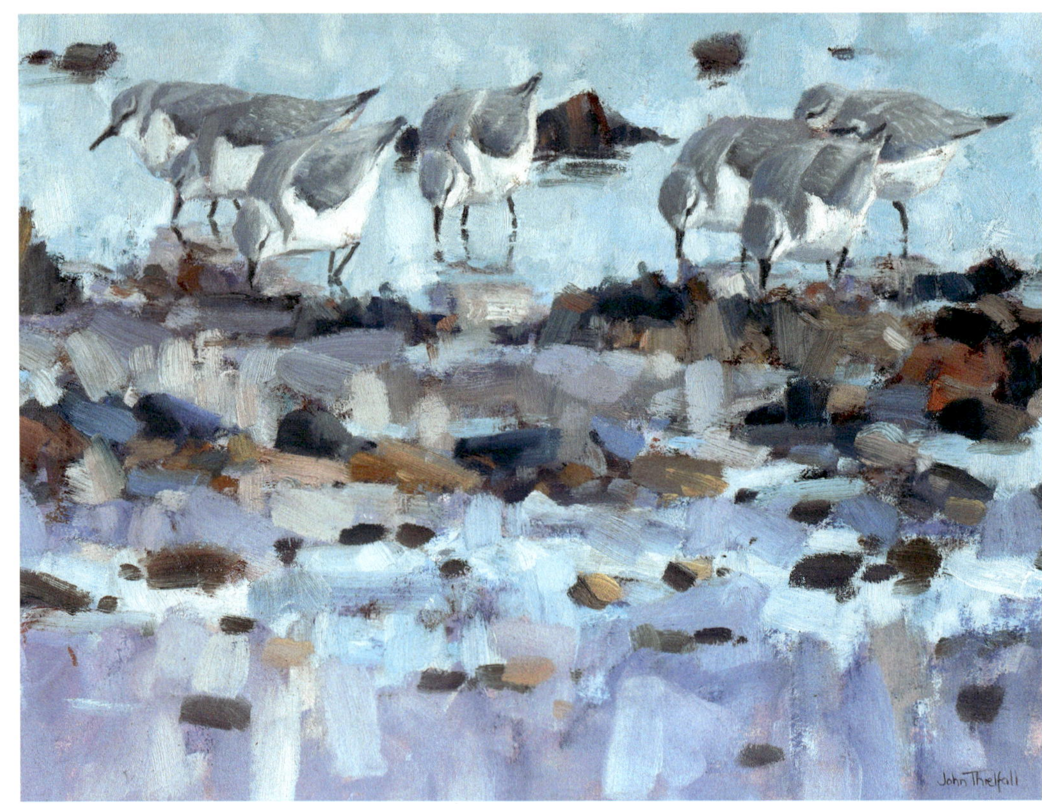

Sandpipers Eating. Oil on paper, 11 x 20.5 inches (28 x 52 cm), by John Threlfall. The birds and the landscape are indicated with thick strokes, with a careful balance of warm and cool tones. The lower part of the work is very loose and looks like Abstract Expressionism.

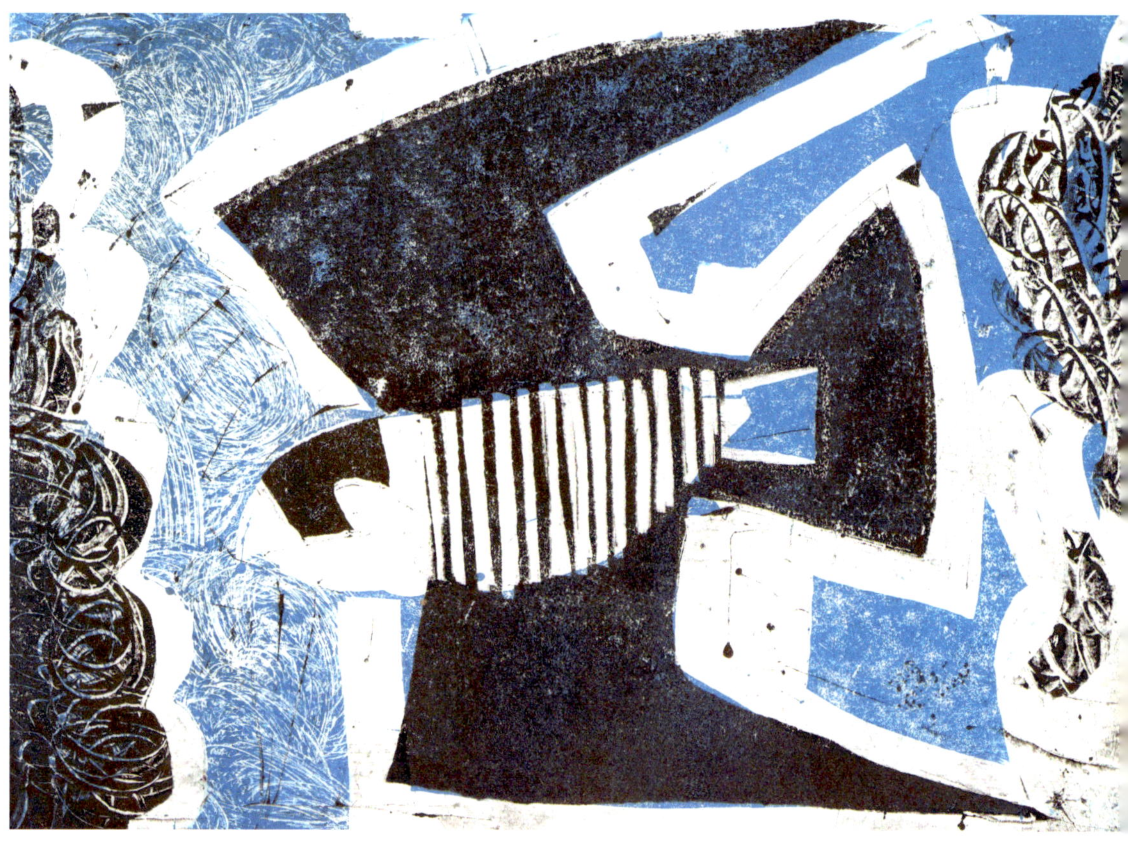

Peregrine, Avon Gorge. Monotype, 9.5 x 14 inches (24 x 36 cm), by Greg Poole (see other works at www.gregpoole.co.uk). Monotype is a printing technique that only produces a single print on paper. The result can be left as is or be used as a base for a mixed-media piece.

Peregrine falcon. Studies from nature, by Greg Poole. No matter what the technique or the personal style of the artist; what differentiates bird artists from artists who occasionally are inspired by them is that the former get their references and inspiration from direct observation in nature.

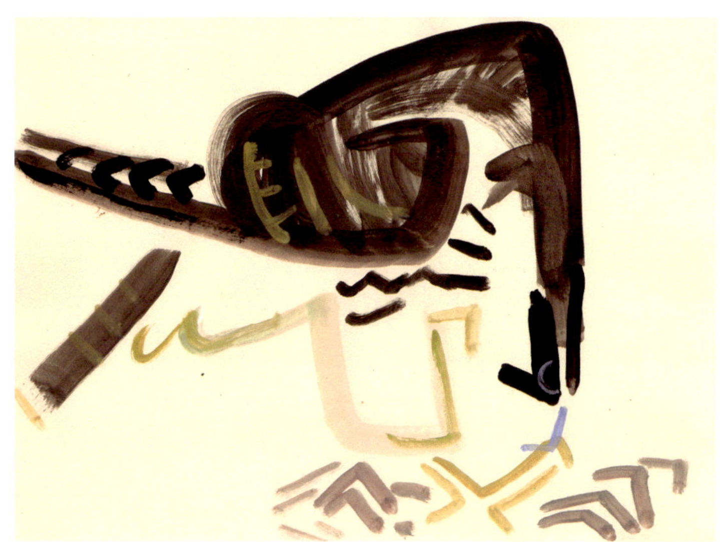

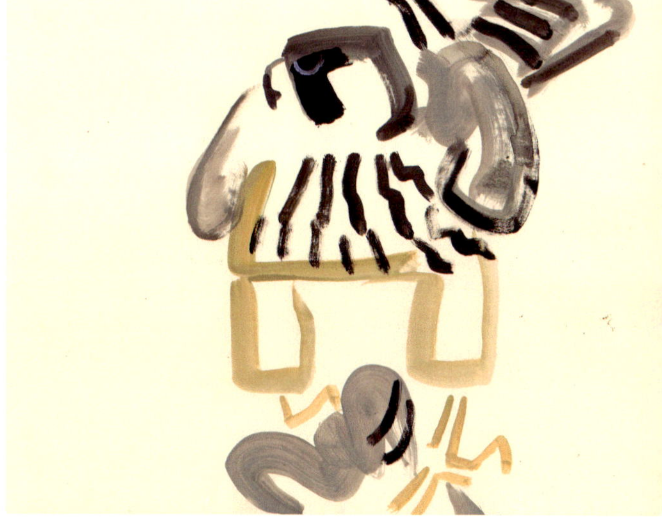

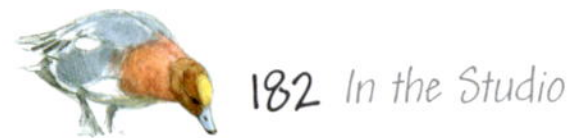

Scientific Illustration

Part of the work that bird painters do is made up of commissions: illustrations for books, magazines, and other kinds of scientific or educational publications. This work is required to be quite realistic, because the main goal of the publication, if not the only one, is the correct identification of the bird.

NEW USES AND NEW TECHNIQUES

Illustrations are planned from the beginning to be reproduced on a specific support, whether physical, like paper, or virtual, like a computer screen. For this reason, they should adhere to a series of conditions when created, such as techniques, format, and composition. Sometimes, an isolated portrait is required, with nothing to detract from the subject, while others include landscapes with many elements.

For the most part, illustrations of birds are painted in watercolor, gouache, or acrylics; but, more and more computer programs that emulate brushstrokes and drawing are being used. With this new method, you can directly create a virtual image that does not have to be digitized by scanning. The advantage here is that an artist who creates his or her work on paper can sell the original for framing, while the virtual image, even when printed on paper, is not considered a unique work of art, but rather a print.

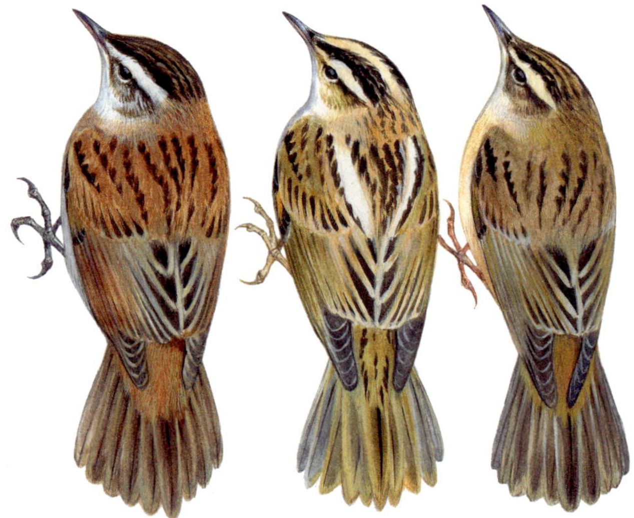

Three Warblers. Watercolor and gouache, 8.25 x 12 inches (21 x 30 cm), by Juan Varela. This typical example of a scientific illustration is an image of three similar species of warblers. Its purpose is to show how to distinguish them from each other by clearly showing the details. For this reason, the birds were not placed in natural poses or habitats, rather they were put on a white background to remove distractions and to clearly show the silhouette of each subject.

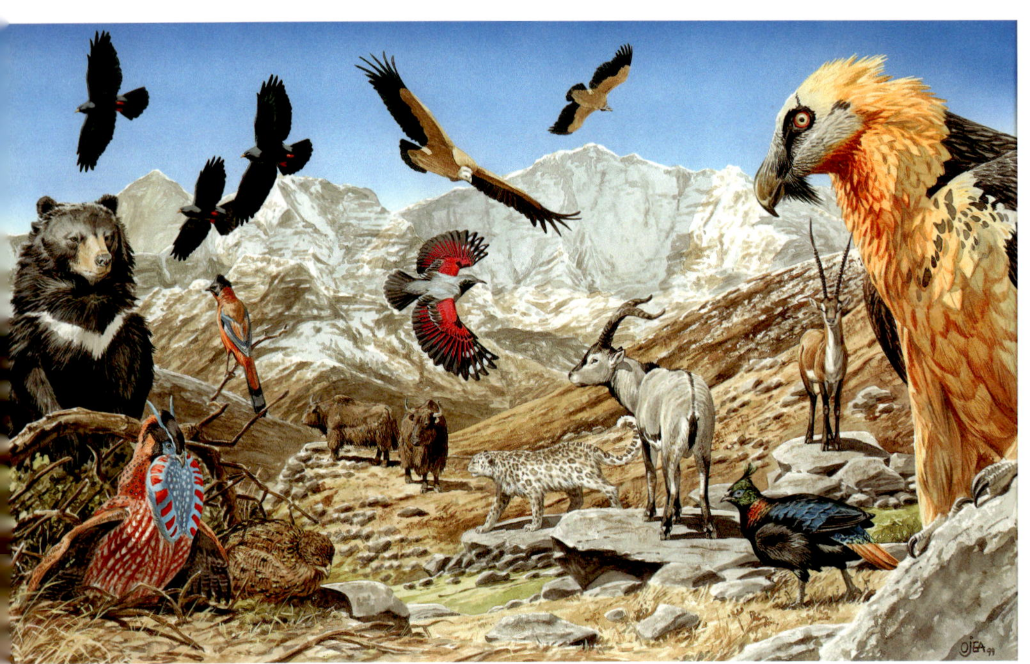

Asiatic Mountains. Watercolor on paper, 17.5 x 10.25 inches (44 x 26 cm), painted by Antonio Ojea. Paintings of this type are frequently requested by publishers, because they show communities of flora and fauna of a specific region in a very educational format. Two of this type of painting's challenges are maintaining the relationships of sizes and achieving a sense of depth without making the birds (and other animals) look crammed together, as if they were posing for a photograph.

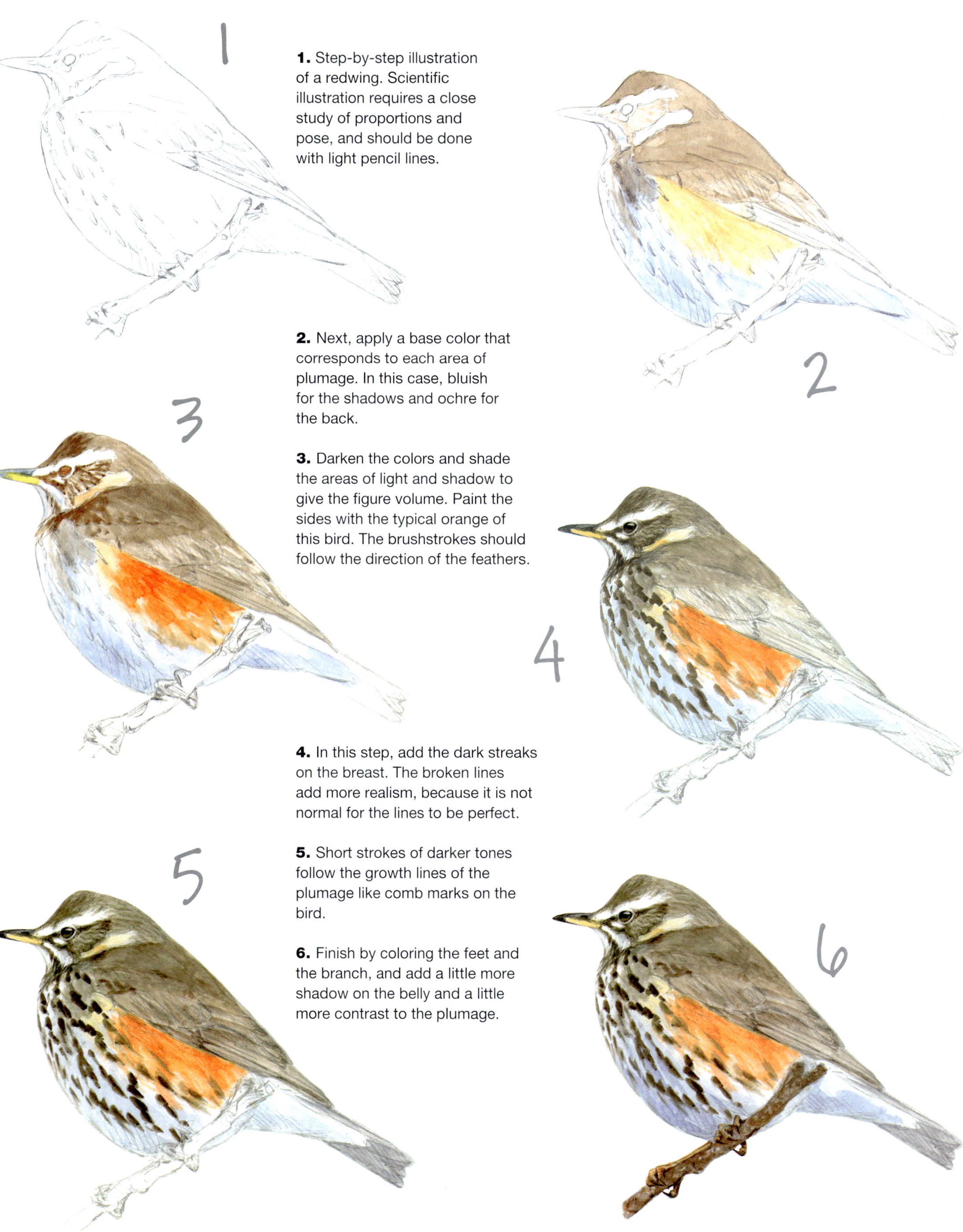

1. Step-by-step illustration of a redwing. Scientific illustration requires a close study of proportions and pose, and should be done with light pencil lines.

2. Next, apply a base color that corresponds to each area of plumage. In this case, bluish for the shadows and ochre for the back.

3. Darken the colors and shade the areas of light and shadow to give the figure volume. Paint the sides with the typical orange of this bird. The brushstrokes should follow the direction of the feathers.

4. In this step, add the dark streaks on the breast. The broken lines add more realism, because it is not normal for the lines to be perfect.

5. Short strokes of darker tones follow the growth lines of the plumage like comb marks on the bird.

6. Finish by coloring the feet and the branch, and add a little more shadow on the belly and a little more contrast to the plumage.

THE CLIENT'S NEEDS

Scientific illustration has helped spread knowledge for centuries, and you should not forget the magnificent drawings of Pisanello, Leonardo, and Durer. Despite the invention and popularity of photography, the services of illustrators have continued to be necessary, because of their ability to summarize.

The illustrator must understand the client's needs in detail, including the reproduction techniques and the size that will be printed. With this information, he or she can work at the required size, which frequently is one-and-a-half-times what it will be in the publication to avoid excessive reduction and the running together of lines.

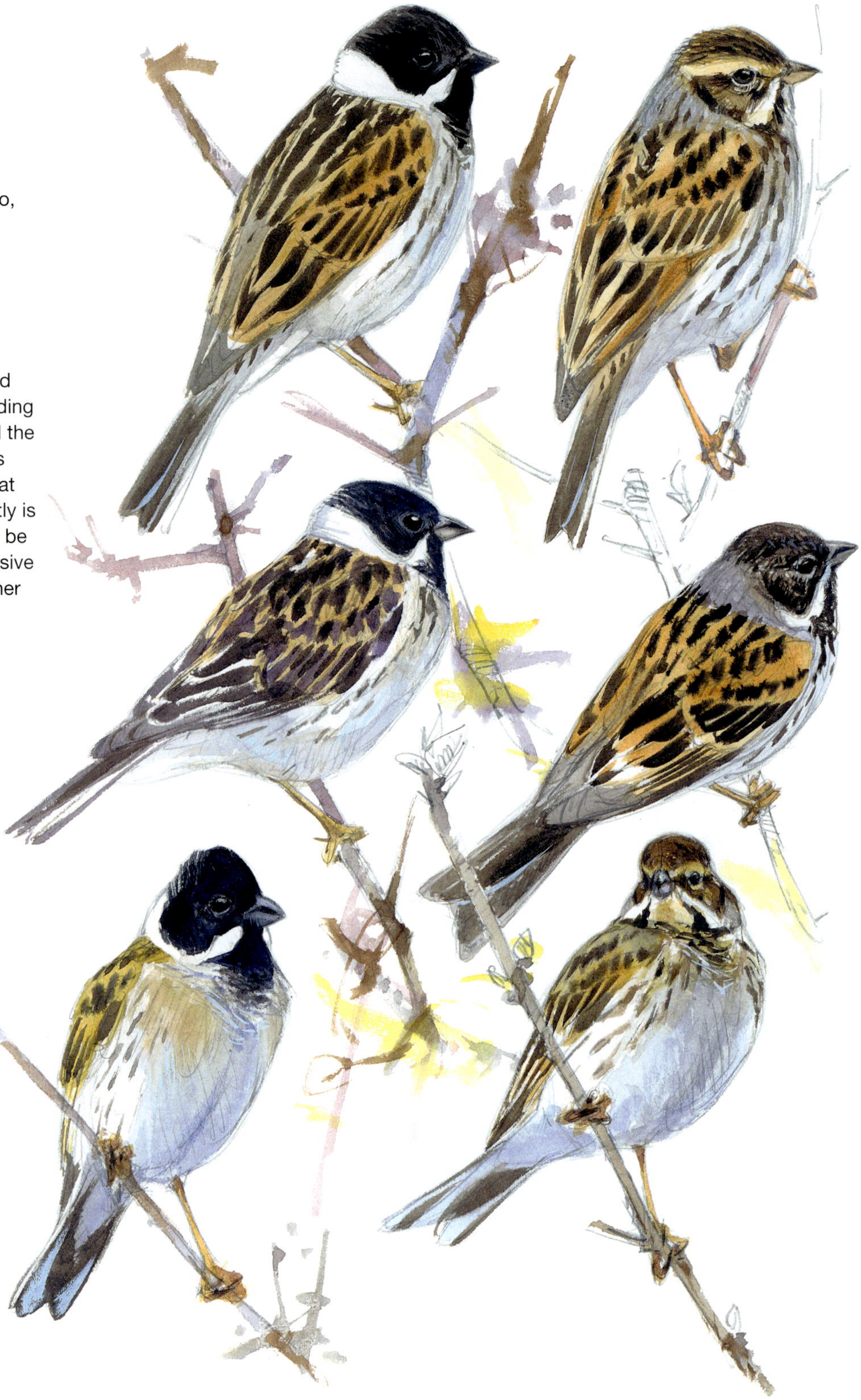

Subspecies of the common reed bunting. Watercolor on paper, 10.5 x 14.5 inches (27 x 37 cm), by Juan Varela. Most identification guides (not just those for birds) use illustrations instead of photographs, because a specialized illustrator can create compositions with similar species and emphasize the details that he or she feels are important. In this image, the differences between males and females are illustrated.

DIGITAL ILLUSTRATION

Nowadays, it is possible to send digitized images to a client; but, to do so, the illustrator must have a good flat scanner or a high resolution camera and a computer monitor that is correctly calibrated. Photo editing programs like PhotoShop allow you to change the tones and tints of a digital image and clean up the background, and you can even create a completely digital illustration. It is a good idea to remember that drum scanners have a maximum size limit for originals on a flexible support. If the artist sends an original that is too large or on a rigid support, like cardboard or stretched canvas, photographic means will have to be used to reproduce the image, and that will increase the client's costs.

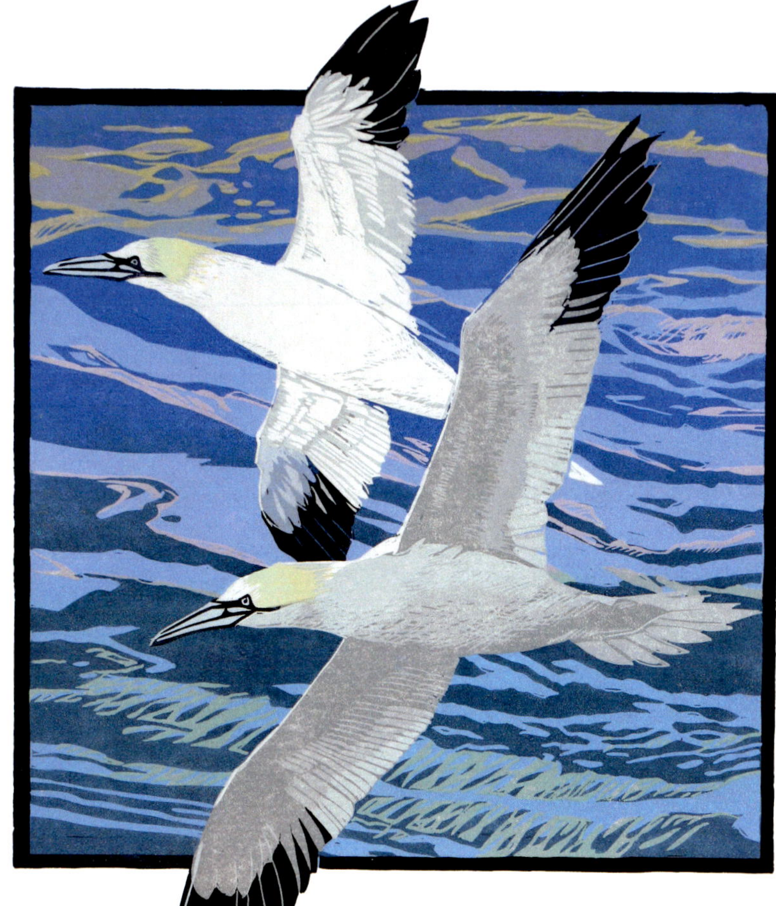

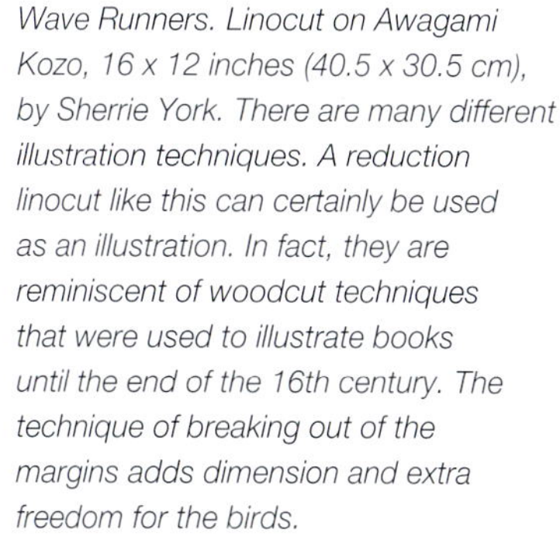

Wave Runners. Linocut on Awagami Kozo, 16 x 12 inches (40.5 x 30.5 cm), by Sherrie York. There are many different illustration techniques. A reduction linocut like this can certainly be used as an illustration. In fact, they are reminiscent of woodcut techniques that were used to illustrate books until the end of the 16th century. The technique of breaking out of the margins adds dimension and extra freedom for the birds.

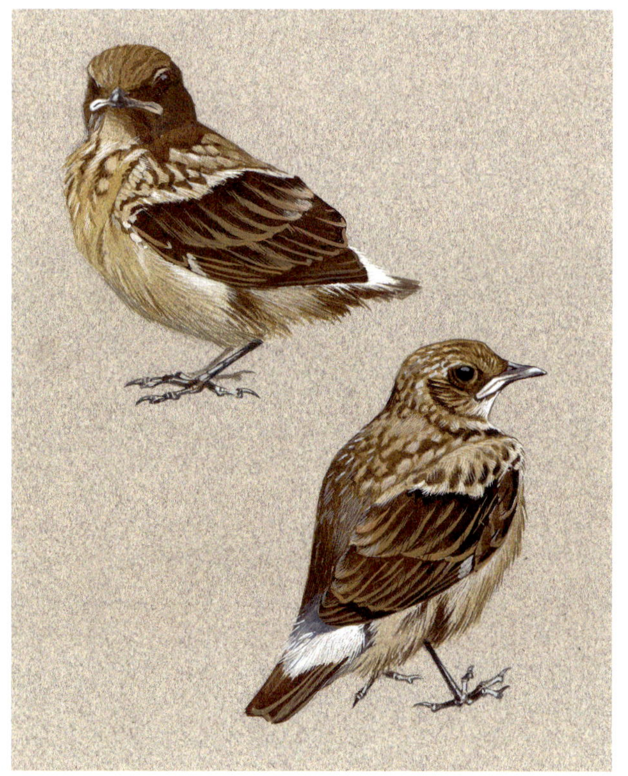

Northern wheatear chicks. Gouache on Canson paper. The use of color paper should be agreed to by the client, because it can cause some problems with the accuracy of the color or with fitting it into the text. A white background always lets you silhouette the image if necessary.

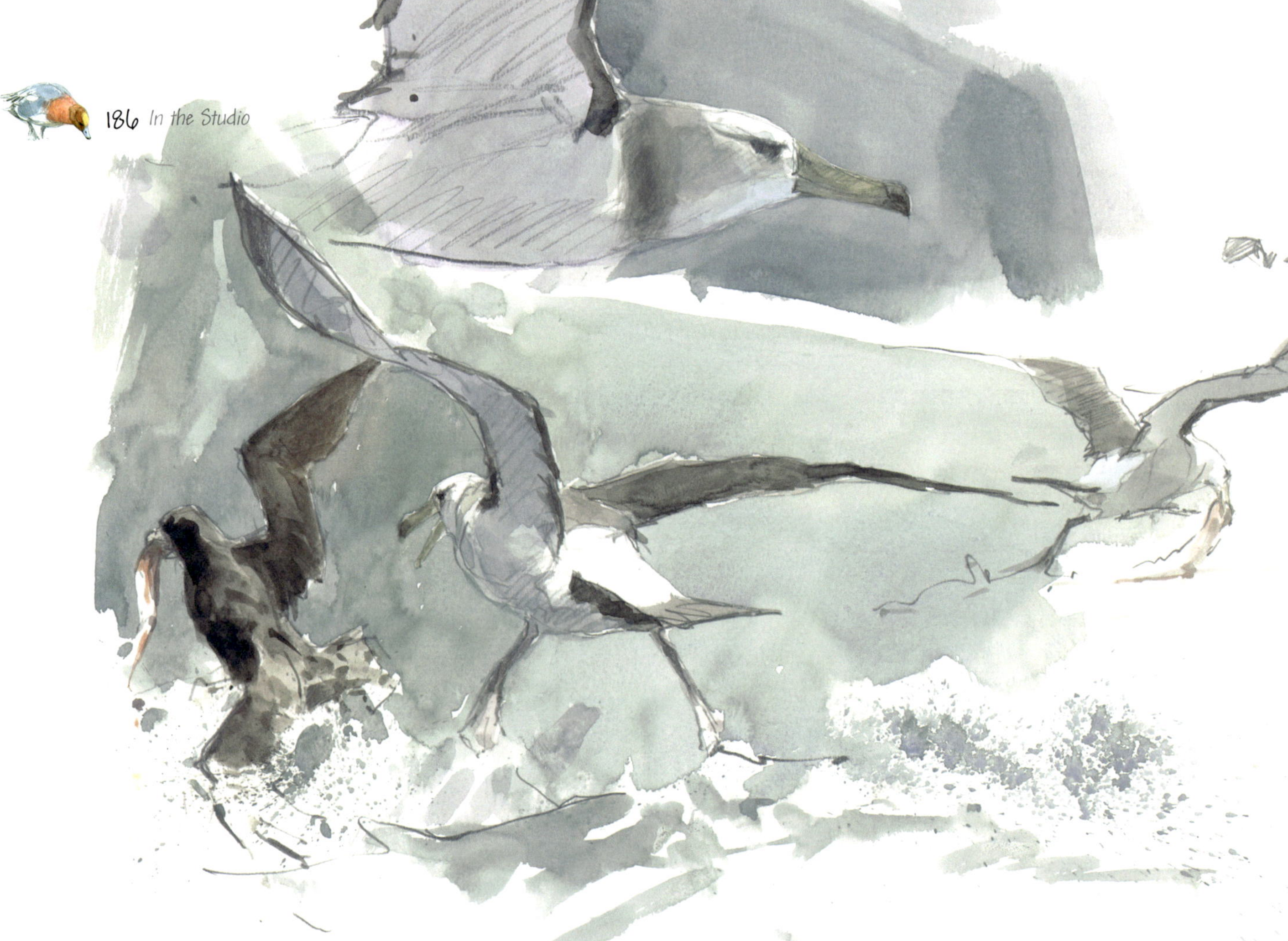

The Traveling Artist

Studies of albatroses. Watercolor by Bruce Pearson. This British artist is an indefatigable traveler. On his trips to the South Seas, as well as other regions of the world, he has made numerous sketches from nature, full of real strength and color. In his work, especially landscapes with birds, he combines pencil, watercolor, and oil pastel lines.

Birds are nearly everywhere, in the streets of the cities, in the gardens and parks, and in rural areas. But the greatest variety exist in those places that have been least touched by human beings. People who love bird-watching are by definition travelers, and painters of birds are, to a large extent, bird-watchers, and they are not content to sit in the living room and draw birds from the television.

WHERE TO SEE BIRDS

For watching and drawing birds in comfort, the best place is an observatory in a natural park; generally, these are located near swamps and lagoons; and, of course, there you will mainly see species that live in those environments. Observing birds in mountains or forested regions requires somewhat more preparation and experience, and, above all, patience and good optical equipment, like binoculars or a quality terrestrial telescope. Nature conservation associations and some ecological tourism companies organize bird-watching excursions guided by experts. Through them, you can become familiar with places and useful observation techniques without causing harm to birds or the natural environment.

Steller's Jay. Pencil and watercolor, 10.5 x 14.5 inches (27 x 37 cm), by Juan Varela. Studies of a species that is relatively common in the mountain forests on the West coast of North America. This sketch was done at the northernmost point of their distribution, in Alaska. When drawing the bird, the artist took notice of the slight differences in plumage between the individuals from this population and those that inhabit the southern zone.

USEFUL ADVICE

Traveling artists must keep in mind that it is not always possible to find an art supply store in the jungle and that losing a brush or running out of paper is an irreparable problem. When you pay a lot of money to take a trip, trying to save on paper and watercolors does not make sense. It is better to take fewer shirts and wash them daily than run out of cobalt blue or sketchbooks, because there wasn't room in the suitcase. A well-thought-out list and careful planning will prevent these problems.

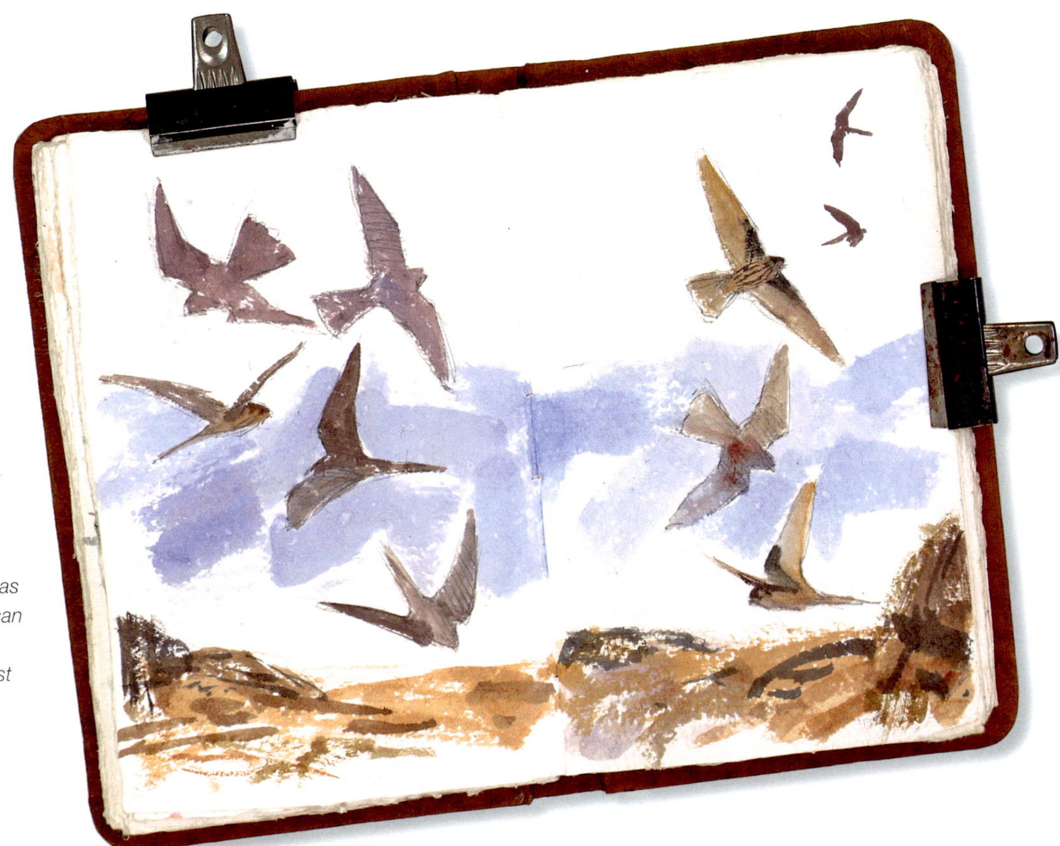

Eleonora's Falcons. Watercolor, 9.5 x 6 inches (24 x 15 cm), by Juan Varela. During trips, your mind is free to appreciate landscapes, and colors and ideas flow easily, although they also can become blurry over time. Your sketchbook should be your most faithful companion at all times.

Glossary

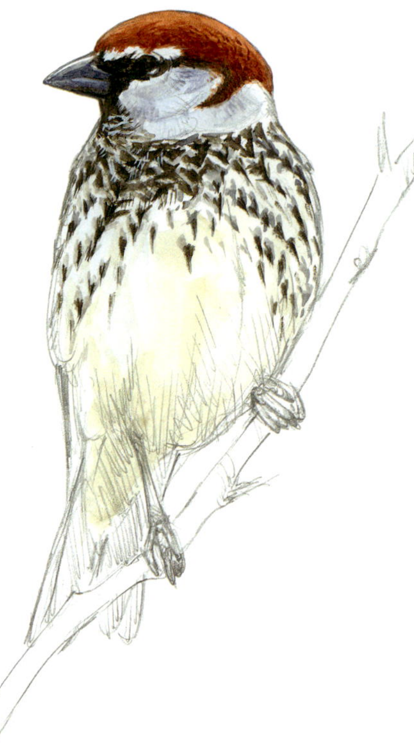

A

Acrylic. A type of paint whose pigments are suspended in an emulsion of acrylic polymers. It is water-soluble and fast drying, but it becomes water resistant when dry.

Alkyd. A type of oil paint whose binders are alkyd resins mixed with oils. Its main characteristic is a very fast drying time, less than a day.

C

Collage. An art technique that consists of sticking papers of different colors and textures and other objects onto a support.

E

Egg tempera. Tempera is a painting medium that uses water as a solvent and egg yolk as a binding medium. It is the oldest known painting technique, and was gradually replaced by oil paints after their invention at the end of the 14th century.

G

Golden Mean. The desirable relationship between two segments. It is a constant number found in many mediums from Greek architecture to music, and even in human anatomy. In a work of art, it highlights specific points that instinctively attract the viewer's eye.

Gouache. A water-soluble opaque paint made of pigments and binders similar to watercolors, but with an added white pigment. The name derives from the Italian *guazzo*.

L

Linocut Printing. A printmaking technique where a design is cut with gouges in linoleum sheets and inked to make color prints on paper. Xylography is a similar technique that uses wood instead of linoleum.

Lithography. A printing technique based on the immiscibility of oil and water that uses limestone as a matrix for making designs that are later printed.

M

Monotype. A print transferred onto a sheet of paper from an image painted on a nonabsorbent surface like glass.

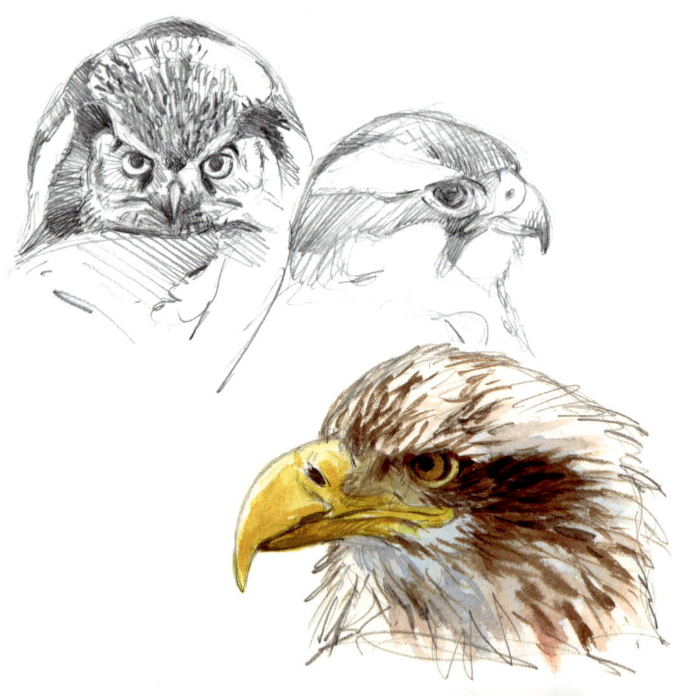

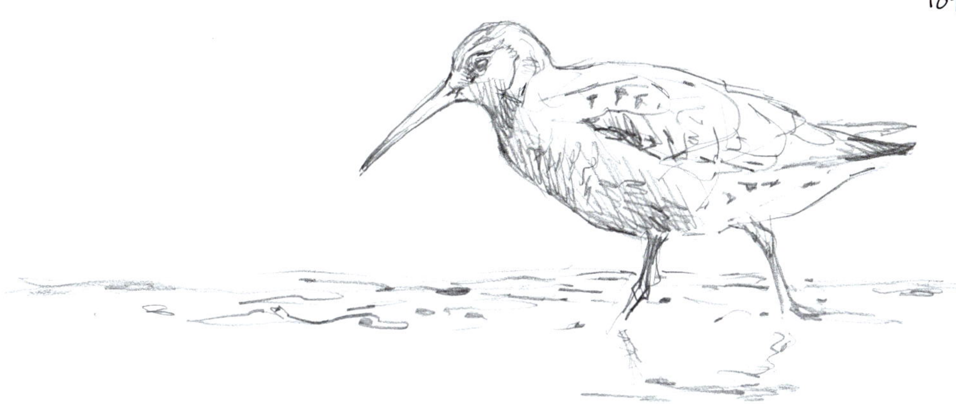

P

Pans. Small plastic or metal containers originally used for pressed powder make up, later adapted to hold watercolors.

Pastels. An art medium in the shape of a stick made of a mixture of pigments, binders, and sometimes chalk that is applied to, and mixed directly on, paper.

Pigments. Ground minerals or organic materials combined with binders to create paints.

Primer. A process used to prepare surfaces for painting. The most common primer is gesso, a mixture of animal glue binder and chalk that is applied on canvas or paper. The primer protects the support, improves adherence, and decreases absorbency.

Printmaking (Intaglio). All the techniques using a copper or other metal plate that is etched with acids or engraving tools. The base is inked and the image is transferred onto paper with a press.

R

Ramphotheca. The outer surface of a bird's beak that grows and wears out from use.

Remiges. The large feathers located on the posterior side of the bird's wing, which is the surface that creates lift.

S

Scanner. An electronic device equipped with an optic reader capable of capturing a color image, among other things, and converting it to digital information.

Scapula. Area of the back located close to the shoulder blade, or scapula. Set of feathers covering this area.

Shading. A study of the distribution of light, shade, and color.

Stylograph. Fountain pen for technical drawing with an ink cartridge, ending in a tube of varying thickness, developed to create lines of consistent thickness.

Sumi-e. A monochromatic ink drawing technique introduced in Japan in the mid-14th century by Zen Buddhist monks.

Support. A base for drawing and painting—for example, paper or canvas.

T

Tonal Values. The distribution of light, shade, and color executed in shades of gray.

W

Wash. Painting technique consisting of spreading a mixture of water and paint on paper to create areas of color and gradations. It is normally done with brushes and watercolor or India ink. Its practice dates back to the Middle Ages, and it was already mentioned by Cennino Cennini in 1437 in his treaties about painting.

Weight. Weight of the paper per unit of surface, generally expressed in pounds in North America and grams per square meter in Europe.

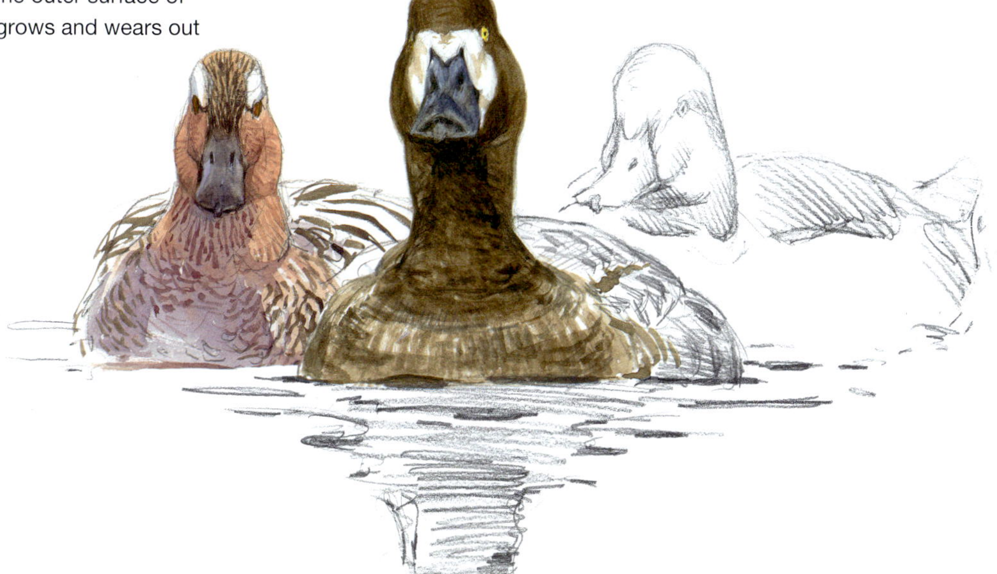

Birds Represented in This Book

COMMOM NAME	LATIN NAME	GEOGRAPHICAL REGION	PAGES
American Robin	*Turdus migratorius*	North America and Mexico	173
Aplomado Falcon	*Falco femoralis*	Mexico and Central and South America	29, 133
Aquatic Warbler	*Acrocephalus paludicola*	Africa, Asia, and Europe	90, 182
Arabian Partridge	*Alectoris melanocephala*	North Africa and Europe	147
Arctic Tern	*Sterna paradisaea*	Artic regions of America, Europe, and Asia and Antarctica	41
Bald Eagle	*Haliaeetus leucocephalus*	North America	8, 9, 71, 133, 171, 176
Bar-Tailed Godwit	*Limosa lapponica*	Europe, Asia, Alaska, and Oceana	25, 30, 124
Barbary Falcon	*Falco peregrinoides*	North Africa and Central Asia	175
Barn Owl	*Tyto alba*	All over the world except deserts and other hot zones	41
Barn Swallow	*Hirundo rustica*	Africa, America, Asia, and Europe	45
Bee-Eaters	*Merops apiaster*	North Africa, Asia, and southern Europe	24, 36, 151, 170
Berthelot's Pipit	*Anthus berthelotii*	Europe	84
Black Stork	*Ciconia nigra*	Central America, south Asia, Australia, Europe, and Oceana	142, 185
Black Vulture	*Coragyps atratus*	South America	46
Black Woodpecker	*Dryocopus martius*	North Africa, Asia, and Europe	154
Black-chested Buzzard-Eagle	*Geranoaetus melanoleucus*	South America	135
Black-crowned Night Heron	*Nycticorax nycticorax*	Tropical zones throughout the world except Australia	30, 159
Black-legged Kittiwake	*Rissa tridactyla*	North America, Asia, and northern Europe	107
Black-necked Stilt	*Himantopus mexicanus*	North, south, and central America	153
Black-winged Stilt	*Himantopus himantopus*	All over the world	54, 125
Blue Chaffinch	*Fringilla teydea*	Canary Islands	76
Blue-crowned Parakeet	*Aratinga acuticaudata*	South America	139
Bluethroat	*Luscinia svecica*	Europe and Africa	27
Bohemian Waxwing	*Bombycilla garrulus*	North, Central, and South America and Europe	160
Booted Eagle	*Aquila pennata*	North Africa, Asia, and southern Europe	31
Brambling	*Fringilla montifringilla*	Europe	110
Calidrid	*Calidris*	All over the world	19, 35, 165
Campo Flicker	*Colaptes campestris*	South America	142
Canary Island Stonechat	*Saxycola dacotiae*	Canary Islands	72, 77
Cetti's Warbler	*Cettia cetti*	Asia and Europe	77
Cinereous Vulture	*Aegypius monachus*	Asia and Europe	66
Common Buzzard	*Buteo buteo*	Africa, Asia, and Europe	102, 103, 134
Common Crane	*Grus grus*	Asia and northern Europe	54, 67
Common Eider	*Somateria mollissima*	North America, east Asia, and Europe	118, 119
Common Firecrest	*Regulus ignicapilla*	Asia and Europe	47, 77
Common Greenshank	*Tringa nebularia*	Africa, Asia, and Europe	124
Common Kingfisher	*Alcedo atthis*	Africa, Asia, and Europe	154
Common Pochard	*Aythya ferina*	North Africa, Asia, and Europe	51, 118
Common Raven	*Corvus corax*	Africa, Asia, North America, and Europe	153
Common Reed Bunting	*Emberiza schoeniclus*	Northern Asia and Europe	77, 184
Common Ringed Plover	*Charadrius hiaticula*	All over the world	77
Common Shelduck	*Tadorna tadorna*	North Africa, Asia, and Europe	164
Common Tern	*Sterna hirundo*	North, Central, and South America, Asia, and Europe	127
Cory's Shearwater	*Calonectris diomedea*	Atlantic, Pacific, and Mediterranean coasts	41
Curlew Sandpiper	*Calidris ferruginea*	Africa, Asia, and Oceana	123
Dartford Warbler	*Sylvia undata*	North Africa, Asia, and Europe	136, 137
Dunlin	*Calidris alpina*	North America, Greenland, and northern Europe	35, 52, 109, 122, 123, 180
Egyptian Vulture	*Neophron percnopterus*	North Africa, Asia, and southern Europe	55
Eleonora's Falcon	*Falco eleonora*	North Africa, Asia, and southern Europe	186
Eurasian Bittern	*Botaurus stellaris*	North Africa, southern Asia, and southern Europe	76
Eurasian Bullfinch	*Pyrrhula pyrrhula*	Asia and Europe	77, 136
Eurasian Coot	*Fulica atra*	North Africa, Asia, and Europe	6, 17, 149
Eurasian Curlew	*Numenius arquata*	Europe	32
Eurasian Eagle-Owl	*Bubo bubo*	North Africa, Asia, and Europe	38
Eurasian Nuthatch	*Sitta europea*	North Africa, Asia, and Europe	87
Eurasian Penduline Tit	*Remiz pendulinus*	Europe	105
Eurasian Reed Warbler	*Acrocephalus scirpaceus*	Asia and southern Europe	91
Eurasian Skylark	*Alauda arvensis*	Europe and Asia except for Arctic zones	146
Eurasian Sparrowhawk	*Accipiter nisus*	North Africa, Asia, and Europe	41, 179
Eurasian Spoonbill	*Platalea leucorodia*	North Africa, Asia, and Europe	175
Eurasian Stone-Curlew	*Burhinus oedicnemus*	Africa, Asia, and Europe	104
Eurasian Wigeon	*Anas penelope*	Asia and northern Europe	53, 115
Eurasian Wryneck	*Jynx torquilla*	Africa, Asia, and Europe	178
European Crested Tit	*Lophophanes cristatus*	Europe	14, 77
European Green Woodpecker	*Picus Viridis*	Asia and Europe	66
European Greenfinch	*Chloris chloris*	Europe	50, 77
European Robin	*Erithacus rubecula*	North Africa and Europe	56
European Serin	*Serinus serinus*	Europe, North Africa, and the Mediterranean	59
European Stonechat	*Saxicola rubicola*	North Africa, Asia, and southern Europe	80
Fieldfare	*Turdus pilaris*	Northern Europe	77
Gadwall	*Anas strepera*	Asia and Europe	116
Glossy Ibis	*Plegadis falcinellus*	Africa, North America, Asia, Europe, and Australia	172
Golden Eagle	*Aquila chrysaetos*	North Africa, North America, Europe, and Asia	28, 52, 63, 65, 102, 106, 133, 147
Goose	*Anser sp*	Africa, North America, Asia, and Europe	34, 98, 118
Grass Warbler	*Locustella*	Africa, Asia, and Europe	74
Great Black-backed Gull	*Larus marinus*	North Atlantic coasts	107
Great Cormorant	*Phalacrocorax carbo*	Africa, North America, Asia, Europe, and Australia	53, 126
Great Crested Grebe	*Podiceps cristatus*	Africa, Asia, Australia, and Europe	4, 5, 57, 145
Great Egret	*Ardea alba*	Africa, North, Central, and South America, Europe, and Asia	21
Great Grey Owl	*Strix nebulosa*	North America, Asia, and Europe	76
Great Reed Warbler	*Acrocephalus arundinaceus*	Africa, Asia, and Europe	93
Great Skua	*Stercorarius skua*	North, Central, and South America and Europe	169
Great White Pelican	*Pelecanus onocrotalus*	Africa, Asia, and Europe	67, 174
Greater Flamingo	*Phoenicpterus roseus*	Temperate zones of North Africa, Asia, and Europe	17, 50, 53, 121

COMMOM NAME	LATIN NAME	GEOGRAPHICAL REGION	PAGES
Greater Short-toed Lark	*Calandrella brachydactyla*	North Africa, Asia, and southern Europe	157
Greater White-footed Goose	*Anser albifrons*	Arctic zones of Asia, Europe, and North America	88
Grey Heron	*Ardea cinerea*	Africa, Asia, and Europe	163
Grey Wagtail	*Motacilla cinerea*	North Africa, Asia, and Europe	98
Greylag Goose	*Anser anser*	Asia and northern Europe	99, 145
Griffon Vulture	*Gyps fulvus*	Africa, Asia, and Europe	66, 130, 133, 165
Guacamayo	*Ara sp*	Central and South America	35, 139
Gyrfalcon	*Falco rusticolus*	North, Central, and South America, Asia, and Europe	113
Harlequin Duck	*Histrionicus histrionicus*	North America, Greenland, and Russia	31
Hawfinch	*Coccothraustes coccothraustes*	North Africa, Asia, and Europe	52
Hen Harrier	*Circus cyaneus*	Asia and Europe	102, 168
Hoopoe	*Upupa epops*	North Africa, Asia, southern Europe	38
Humboldt Penguin	*Spheniscus humbolti*	South America, Antarctica, south Australia, New Zealand, and South Africa	83
Jack Snipe	*Lymnocryptes minimus*	North Africa, Asia, and northern Europe	122
Kentish Plover	*Charadrius alexandrinus*	North Africa, Asia, and southern Europe	124
Lapland Longspur	*Calcarius lapponicus*	Northern Europe	146
Lesser Black-backed Gull	*Larus fuscus*	Northern Europe	127
Lesser Kestrel	*Falco naumanni*	North Africa, Asia, and Europe	175, 177
Little Auk	*Alle alle*	Arctic coasts	169
Little Bunting	*Emberiza pusilla*	East Asia and northern Europe	47, 79
Little Egret	*Garzetta garzetta*	Africa, southern Asia, and Australia	49
Little Grebe	*Tachybaptus ruficollis*	Africa, Asia, and Europe	78
Little Owl	*Athene noctua*	North Africa, Asia, and Europe	35, 163
Little Tern	*Sternula albifrons*	All over the world except the Americas	2, 3, 129, 156
Long-legged Buzzard	*Buteo rufinus*	Africa and southern Asia	130
Long-tailed Tit	*Aegithalos caudatus*	Europe except for Scandanavia	44
Mallard	*Anas platyrhynchos*	Africa, North America, Asia, and Europe	74, 108, 114, 117, 119, 156, 168
Merlin	*Falco colombarius*	North America and northern Europe	11
Montagu's Harrier	*Circus pygargus*	Central Africa, Asia, and Europe	102, 176
Moustached Warbler	*Acrocephalus melanopogon*	North Africa, Asia, and southern Europe	97
Northern Gannet	*Morus bassanus*	North Atlantic and Mediterranean coasts	185
Northern Hawk Owl	Various species	All over the world except deserts	133
Northern Lapwing	*Vanellus vanellus*	Africa, eastern Asia, and northern Europe	48, 149
Northern Pintail	*Anas acuta*	Africa, North and Central America, Asia, and northern Europe	119, 168
Northern Shoveler	*Anas clypeata*	North, Central, and South America, Asia, and northern Europe	116
Northern Wheatear	*Oenanthe oenanthe*	Africa and Arctic zones of North America, Asia, and Europe	185
Pallid Swift	*Apus pallidus*	North Africa, Asia, and Europe	40
Peregrine Falcon	*Falco peregrinus*	All over the world except Antarctica	32, 62, 64, 133, 148, 150, 181
Pied Avocet	*Recurvirostra avosetta*	East Africa, Asia, and Europe	164
Plain Swift	*Apus unicolor*	Canary Islands and Madeira	53
Purple Swamphen	*Porphyrio porphyrio*	Africa, south Asia, Australia, and New Zealand	180
Red Crossbill	*Loxia curvirostra*	North America, Asia, and Europe	76
Red Knot	*Calidris canutus*	Africa, North, Central, and South America, Asia, and Europe	98
Red-breasted Merganser	*Mergus serrator*	North America, Asia, and Europe	7, 118
Red-footed Falcon	*Falco vespertinus*	Africa, Asia, and Europe	149
Red-necked Phalarope	*Phalaropus lobatus*	Europe and Arctic zones of North America and Asia	111
Redwing	*Turdus iliacus*	Northern Europe	62, 63
Ring-necked Duck	*Aythya collaris*	North and Central America	116
Ring-necked Pheasant	*Phasianus colchicus*	South Asia, North America, Europe, and Oceana	45
Rock Dove	*Columba livia*	All over the world	34, 51, 57, 179
Rose-ringed Parakeet	*Psittacula krameri*	South America and tropical zones of Africa and Asia	36
Ruby-throated Hummingbird	*Archilochus colubris*	North and Central America	64
Ruff	*Philomachus pugnax*	Africa, Asia, and Europe	191
Rufous-tailed Scrub Robin	*Cercotrichas galactotes*	Africa, Asia, and southern Europe	44
Rustic Bunting	*Emberiza rustica*	East Asia and northern Europe	74, 75, 87
Saker Falcon	*Falco cherrug*	Central Asia and Europe	132
Sanderling	*Calidris alba*	Arctic zones of North America, Asia, and Europe	18, 89
Scops Owl	*Otus scops*	Africa, Asia, and Europe	59
Short-eared Owl	*Asio flammeus*	Africa, Asia, North, Central, and South America, and Europe	12, 13
Short-toed Snake Eagle	*Circaetus gallicus*	Europe, Central Asia, and India	41
Sooty Shearwater	*Puffinus griseus*	Coasts in the southern hemisphere	63, 186
Spanish Imperial Eagle	*Aquila adalberti*	Spain and Portugal	22, 23, 61
Spanish Sparrow	*Passer hispaniolensis*	Mediterranean lands	108
Squacco Heron	*Ardeola ralloides*	Africa and south Asia	67, 121, 172
Steller's Jay	*Cyanocitta stelleri*	North America	187
Stone-Curlew	*Burhinus oedicnemus*	Asia and Europe	83
Streaked Fantail Warbler	*Cisticola juncidis*	Africa, Asia, Europe, and Oceana	39
Tawny Owl	*Strix aluco*	Asia and Europe	31
Teal	Various species	Africa, Asia, Central, North, and South America, and Europe	166
Water Pipit	*Anthus spinoletta*	Europe	43
Western Marsh Harrier	*Circus aeruginosus*	Africa, Asia, Australia, and Europe	111, 158
Whimbrel	*Numenius phaeopus*	North, Central, and South America, Africa, Asia, and Europe	123
White Cockatoo	*Cacatua alba*	Oceana	138
White Stork	*Ciconia ciconia*	Southern Africa, Asia, and Europe	82, 88
White Wagtail	*Motacilla alba*	North America, Asia, and Europe	109
White-winged Snowfinch	*Montifringilla nivalis*	All over the world in alpine and subalpine zones	99
Wood Duck	*Aix sponsa*	North America	179
Wood Grouse	*Tetrao urogallus*	Europe and mountainous zones in the southern hemisphere	159
Woodchat Shrike	*Lanius senator*	Africa, Mediterranean lands, and Europe	30
Woodlark	*Lullula arborea*	Europe	76
Yellow-browed Warbler	*Phylloscopus inornatus*	Asia	87
Yellow-rumped Warbler	*Dendroica coronata*	Asia and Europe	28
Yellowhammer	*Emberiza citrinella*	Northern Europe	39

Bibliography

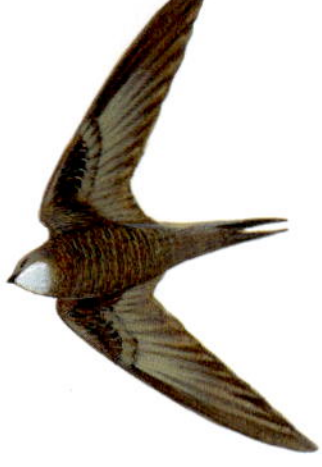

- Busby, John. *Drawing Birds*. Cristopher Helm, 2004.
- Doerner, M. *The Materials of the Artist and Their Use in Painting*. Mariner Books, 1949.
- Edwards, Betty. *Color*. Penguin Group (USA) Inc., 2004.
- Edwards, Betty. *Drawing on the Right Side of the Brain*. Penguin Group (USA) Inc., 2012.
- Micklewright, Keith. *Drawing*. Laurence King Publishing Ltd., 2005.
- Muir Laws, John. *The Laws' Guide to Drawing Birds*. Heyday Books, 2012.
- Parramón. *Learning to Paint in Watercolor*. Barron's Educational Series, 1997.
- Pearson, Bruce. *Troubled Waters. Trailing the Albatross, and Artist's Journey*. Langford Press, 2013.
- Threlfall, John. *Drawn to the Edge*. Langford Press, 2013.
- Walker Leslie, Clare. *Nature Drawing: a Tool for Learning*. Kendall Hunt, 1995.
- Walker Leslie, Clare. *The Art of Field Sketching*. Kendall Hunt, 1995.
- Walker Leslie, Clare and Roth, C.E. *Nature Journaling*. Storey Books, 1998.
- Wootton, Tim. *Drawing and Painting Birds*. The Crowood Press, 2010.

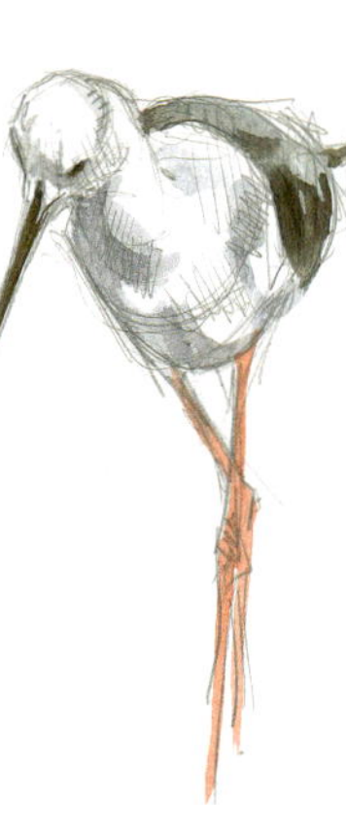

Web Sites of Interest:

Artists for Nature Foundation (ANF)
www.artistsfornature.com
International organization devoted to the conservation of nature through the arts.

SEO/BirdLife
www.seo.org
The only Spanish organization devoted to the study and conservation of birds.

Asociación Española de Artistas de la Naturaleza (AEAN)
artistasnaturaleza.blogspot.com.es
An organization of Spanish artists who specialize in this genre.

Leigh Yawkey Woodson Art Museum
www.lywam.org
Organizes the annual *Birds in Art* exhibit, the best-known exhibit about birds in the arts.

Society of Wildlife Artists (SWLA)
www.swla.co.uk
British organization of nature artists.

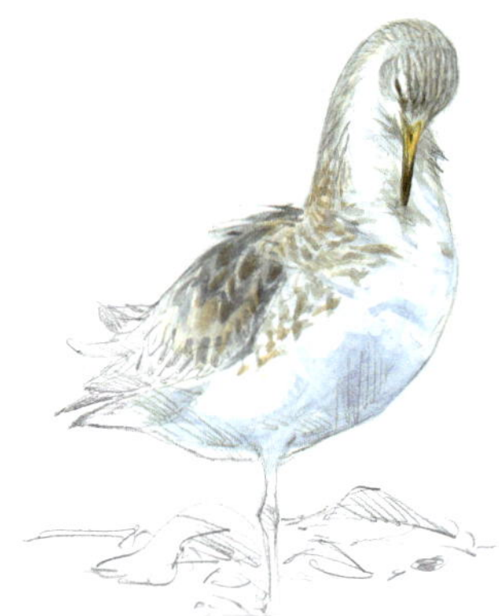

Acknowledgments

We would like to express our heartfelt gratitude to the following artists whose work has embellished these pages for their selfless contribution. All of them enjoy long professional careers and have showed their work in many exhibits and publications.

Antonio Ojea. *Candeleda, Spain. Illustrator and painter. Author of several publications and frequent contributor to WWF Spain. He is a member of the Spanish Association of Nature Artists (AEAN).*

Barry Van Dusen. *Massachussets. Contributor to the Artists for Nature Foundation (ANF) and to the Massachussets Audubon Society. Named Master Artist by Leigh Yawkey Woodson Art Museum.*

Bruce Pearson. *Cambridge, England. Author of numerous books and television documentaries. A member of the Society of Wildlife Artists (SWLA) and contributor to many art projects and nature conservancy.*

Darren Rees. *Hampshire, England. A winner of the Natural World and RSPB Fine Art Awards. Member of the SWLA and contributor to the ANF.*

Greg Poole. *Bristol, England. Member of the SWLA and frequent contributor of ANF. Specializes in printmaking techniques.*

John Threlfall. *Dumfries and Galloway, Scotland. Award winner of several editions of the National Exhibition of Wildlife Art and a member of the SWLA.*

José Antonio Sencianes. *Sevilla, Spain. Graphic designer and painter. Member of the AEAN. Works for the Board of Scientific Investigation of Doñana, Spain.*

Nick Derry. *Wolverhampton, England, residing in France. Member of the SWLA and winner of the Birdwatch Artist of the Year award, among others.*

Paschalis Dougalis. *Kozani, Greece, established in Germany. Author of numerous publications about birds and nature and a contributor to ANF.*

Sherrie York. *Colorado. Artist and illustrator, specializing in linocuts. A frequent contributor to ANF.*

Tony Sánchez. *Gran Canaria, Spain. Painter and illustrator with a renowned professional specialty in the painting of psittaciformes.*

Tim Wootton. *South Yorkshire, England. Winner of numerous awards, such as the Wildlife Artist of the Year in 2010. Contributor to ANF.*

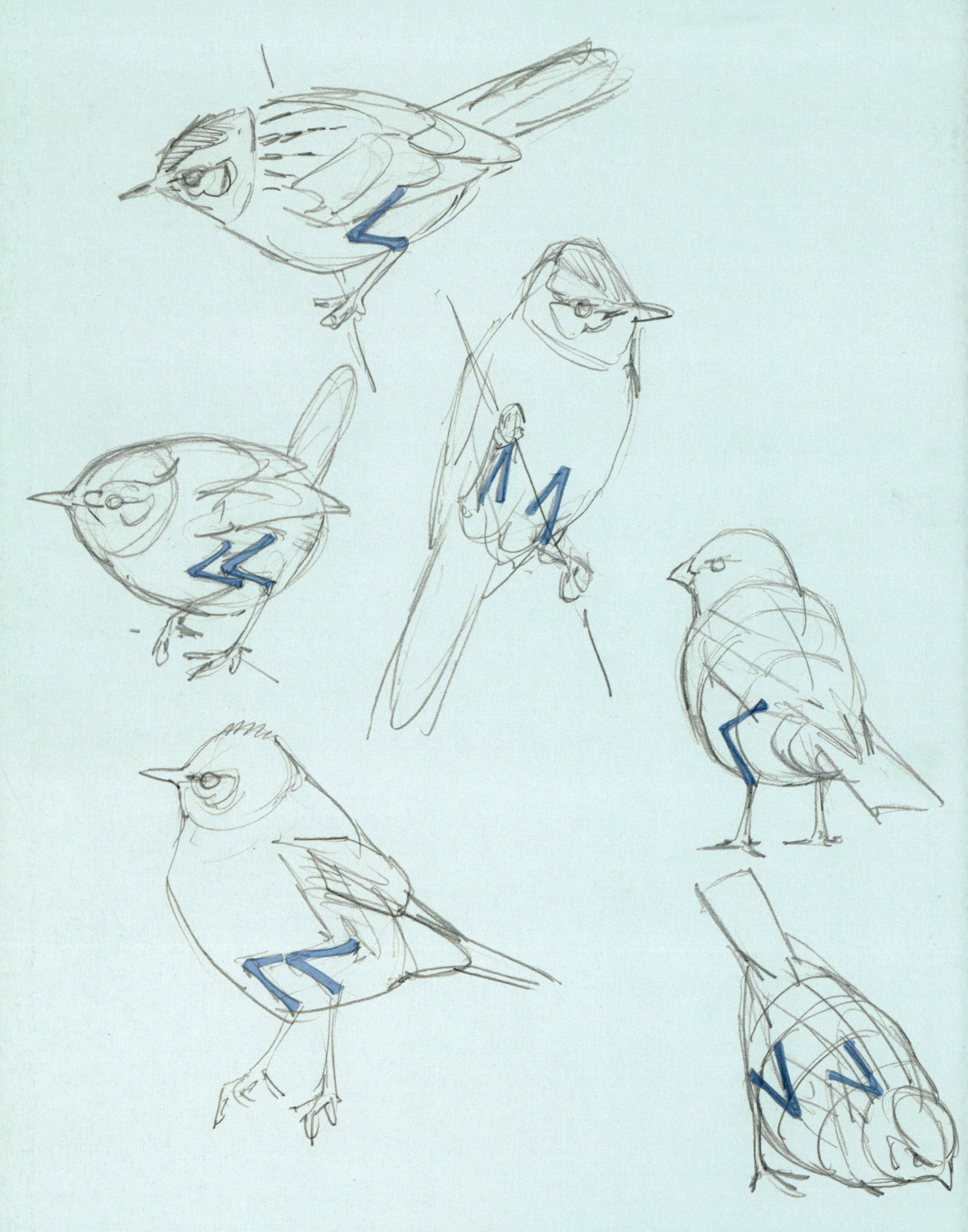